Fighting Words and Feuding Words

Anger and the Homeric Poems

Thomas R. Walsh

LEXINGTON BOOKS

A Division of
ROWMAN & LITTLEFIELD PUBLISHERS, INC.
Lanham • Boulder • New York • Toronto • Oxford

Greek Studies: Interdisciplinary Approaches

On the front cover: A calendar frieze representing the Athenian months, reused in the Byzantine Church of the Little Metropolis in Athens. The cross is superimposed, obliterating Taurus of the Zodiac. The choice of this frieze for books in *Greek Studies: Interdisciplinary Approaches* reflects this series' emphasis on the blending of the diverse heritages—Near Eastern, Classical, and Christian—in the Greek tradition. Drawing by Laurie Kain Hart, based on a photograph. Recent titles in the series are:

Dionysism and Comedy
by Xavier Riu
Contextualizing Classics: Ideology, Performance, Dialogue
Edited by Thomas M. Falkner, Nancy Felson, and David Konstan
The Pity of Achilles: Oral Style and the Unity of the Iliad
by Jinyo Kim
Between Magic and Religion: Interdisciplinary Studies in Ancient Mediterranean Religion and Society
Edited by Sulochana Asirvatham, Corinne Ondine Pache, and John Waltrous
Iambic Ideas: Essays on a Poetic Tradition from Archaic Greece to the Late Roman Empire
Edited by Antonio Aloni, Alessandro Barchiesi, Alberto Cavarzere
The Ritual Lament in Greek Tradition, Second Edition
by Margaret Alexiou
revised by Dimitrios Yatromanolakis and Panagiotis Roilos
Homeric Variations on a Lament by Briseis
by Casey Dué
Imagining Illegitimacy in Classical Greek Literature
by Mary Ebbott
Tragedy and Athenian Religion
by Christiane Sourvinou-Inwood
The Usable Past: Greek Metahistories
Edited by K. S. Brown and Yannis Hamilakis
The Other Self: Selfhood and Society in Modern Greek Fiction
by Dimitris Tziovas
The Poetry of Homer: New Edition, Edited with an Introduction by Bruce Heiden
by Samuel Eliot Bassett
A Penelopean Poetics: Reweaving the Feminine in Homer's Odyssey
by Barbara Clayton
Homeric Megathemes: War-Homilia-Homecoming
by D. N. Maronitis
The Visual Poetics of Power: Warriors, Youths, and Tripods in Early Greece
by Nassos Papalexandrou
Fighting Words and Feuding Words: Anger and the Homeric Poems
by Thomas R. Walsh
Diachronic Dialogues: Authority and Continuity in Homer and the Homeric Tradition
by Ahuvia Kahane

Fighting Words and Feuding Words

LEXINGTON BOOKS

A division of Rowman & Littlefield Publishers, Inc.
A wholly owned subsidiary of The Rowman & Littlefield Publishing Group, Inc.
4501 Forbes Boulevard, Suite 200
Lanham, MD 20706

PO Box 317
Oxford
OX2 9RU, UK

British Library Cataloguing in Publication Information Available
Library of Congress Cataloging-in-Publication Data

Walsh, Thomas R.
Fighting words and feuding words : anger and the Homeric poems / Thomas R. Walsh.
p. cm.—Greek Studies: Interdisciplinary Approaches
Includes bibliographical references (p.) and index.
ISBN 978-0-7391-1264-9
1. Homer—Criticism and interpretation. 2. Homer—Language. 3. Epic poetry, Greek—History and criticism. 4. Achilles (Greek mythology) in literature. 5. Odysseus (Greek mythology) in literature. 6. Trojan War—Literature and the war. 7. Mythology, Greek, in literature. 8. Greek language—Semantics. 9. Anger in literature. I. Title. II. Series.
PA4037 .W28 2002
883/.01—dc21 2001057857

Printed in the United States of America

Do mo bhean chéile agus do m'iníon

7

i gcuimhne m'athair léannta

fil súil nglais
fégbas Érinn dar a hais;
noco n-aceba íarmo-thá
firu Érenn nách a mná
–"Colum Cille"
(*EIL* 29)

Contents

Foreword

Greek Studies: Interdisciplinary Approaches

Building on the foundations of scholarship within the disciplines of philology, philosophy, history, and archaeology, this series spans the continuum of Greek traditions extending from the second millennium BCE to the present, not just the Archaic and Classical periods. The aim is to enhance perspectives by applying various disciplines to problems that have in the past been treated as the exclusive concern of a single given discipline. Besides the crossing-over of the older disciplines, as in the case of historical and literary studies, the series encourages the application of such newer ones as linguistics, sociology, anthropology, and comparative literature. It also encourages encounters with current trends in methodology, especially in the realm of literary theory.

Feuding Words and Fighting Words: Anger and the Homeric Poems, by Thomas R. Walsh, is a monumental contribution to Homeric studies. This book, in combination with the earlier book of Leonard Muellner, *The Anger of Achilles: Mênis in Early Greek Epic* (Cornell University Press, 1996), provides Classicists with a definitive account of the semantics—and the poetics—of three central words for "anger" in the Homeric tradition. Muellner's work concerned *mênis*, while Walsh's now concentrates on *kótos* and *khólos*. Perhaps the most important aspect of Walsh's acute readings is his remarkable discovery of a working definition of these two Homeric words, as formulated within the epic by the epic itself. At *Iliad* 1.74–83, the seer Calchas is quoted in the Homeric narrative, and his mantic words, as quoted by epic, reveal the basic convergences and divergences in the meanings of all three words for "anger," *mênis* and *kótos* and *khólos*. This Homeric "folk definition" of those three words, each of which inherits its own poetics despite the fact that they are partial synonyms, amounts to a *tour de force* in the art of epic poetry. That art, as Walsh shows, is linked to the art of the seer: the mantic vision of Calchas translates into the poetic vision of Homer. The vision of the seer, further, can translate into the vision of Homer's interpreters. Walsh's book has illuminated this vision.

Gregory Nagy

Acknowledgments

At the end of this project I encountered an image showing *ira* besting *patientia* (Rosenwein 1998, 15). On seeing that image, I could only think of those I need to acknowledge here. Certainly *patientia* showed a white flag long ago, though my study of anger continued the battle. My debt is made the greater by my amazement at those who have waited so long without losing faith for me to be done with this project. With the hope that the understanding of our Homeric texts is enhanced through this study of the *Iliad*'s central emotion, I hereby acknowledge those who have encouraged this work to its completion.

As I begin to recall those names, the list grows to become unmanageable. At the beginning stands my teacher, Michael Nagler, whose work gave a crucial boost to what is outstanding in Homeric studies in the last quarter of the twentieth century. Also at the beginning of my study was the Berkeley Homer group, especially Gary Holland, Mary McGarry, and Dan Petegorsky, a vital intellectual collectivity that grew to include Carole Newlands, Maud Gleason, Joan Burton, and others, who, I hope, will excuse this summary catalog. The central idea of this book began in that group's robust reading of Homer, however lonely its working out came to be.

The series editor, Gregory Nagy, a beacon shining steady and bright on the ideas developed here, supported my style of scholarship in ways that mean more to me than I can say: I acknowledge his faithful tolerance for a slow scholar's work. (Those experienced in the academic world know how rare is such a heart and the trust that dwells within it.)

As a comparatist, I approach Homer with a range of disciplines and texts, so that I have incurred a tremendous debt that can never be fully repaid to my teachers in fields outside Homeric studies. Hoping not to implicate them in any misstatements I may have made, I deeply thank these scholars and teachers: G. Holland (for all things Indo-European), D. Melia (for Celtic languages and literatures), R. Stefanini (for Hittite and Luvian), B. A. van Nooten (for Sanskrit), and M. Schwartz (for Old Iranian). In addition, I am fortunate to have learned friends, family, and colleagues who have at different moments read my work and encouraged the many revised versions of this book: E. J. W. Barber, R. B. Branham, R. Holway, B. Louden, C. S. Littleton, H. Sarf (†), T. D. Walsh (†), and L. Watkins.

I thank those who helped me deal with the maddening details that accompany book production, L. Gibbs (for initial help preparing an index), as well as Maura Giles (for an important and revealing copy-editing job early-on). At the end of the project, Paul Psoinos gave professional and timely copy-editing assistance that drove me to finish the work with an eye to his high standards. The index was given rigorous professional guidance as to its shape and substance by Marla Wilson of Printed Page Productions. Included here must be Steven Siebert, without whom this manuscript could not have appeared; his intimate knowledge of Nota Bene's features and his scholarly attention brought into line a complicated manuscript. The virtues of this book have been magnified by the elegant copy finally produced under all these professionals' wise guidance. They have contributed to a task whose shortcomings must only be laid at my door

As a teacher, I thank my colleagues at Occidental College in the Comparative Literature Department (now in the Department of English and Comparative Literary Studies) for their encouragement and support throughout my writing, especially M. Ronk, M. Near, W. Montag, and J. Wyatt. The classical studies support faculty helped me remember that even a small college without a classics department can encourage the study of Homer. (I single out here E. J. W. Barber, E. Frank, M. Homiak, M. Horowitz, K. King, C. S. Littleton, and, most especially, M. Near.) Finally, the Dean of Faculty's office made available financial support for publication from the Brown Fund of Occidental College, which together with generous support from the Center of Hellenic Studies, brought this project to a conclusion.

To those many others whose names would swell the catalog beyond the limits of the genre, please accept my thanks in this summary fashion. Greater debts of affection and trust are signaled at my dedicatory page—Laura and Sarah can still know where the dedicatory signs point. My final thanks will be for those who come to read this text and find it in their spirits to add what I missed, to emphasize what I failed to highlight, and to correct my errors, all with the high purpose of steering me and others away from false leads and towards truer conceptions of the Homeric tradition.

Abbreviations

AALM	*Atti dell'Accademia Nazionale dei Lincei*
AAntH	*Acta Antiqua Academiae Scientiarum Hungaricae*
AC	*Acta Classica*
AJP	*American Journal of Philology*
AnnCagl	*Annali della Facoltà di Lettere e Filosofia dell'Università di Cagliari*
BLS	*Proceedings of the Berkeley Linguistics Society*
BSL	*Bulletin de la Société de Linguistique de Paris*
CA	*Classical Antiquity*
CJ	*Classical Journal*
CP	*Classical Philology*
CQ	*Classical Quarterly*
CW	*Classical World*
DELG	P. Chantraine, *Dictionnaire étymologique de la langue grecque* (Paris: Klincksieck, 1968–80)
DLL	E. Laroche, Dictionnaire de la langue louvite (Paris: Maissonneuve, 1959)
EC	*Études Celtiques*
EIL	G. Murphy, ed.,3 *Early Irish Lyrics: Eighth to Twelfth Century* (Oxford: The Clarendon Press, 1956)
GB	*Gräzer Beiträge*
Gl	*Glotta*
GRBS	*Greek, Roman and Byzantine Studies*
HSCP	*Harvard Studies in Classical Philology*
IEW	J. Pokorny, *Indogermanisches etymologisches Wörterbuch* (Bern: Francke, 1959)
IF	*Indogermanische Forschungen*
JHS	*Journal of Hellenic Studies*

JIES	*Journal of Indo-European Studies*
KZ	*Zeitschrift für vergleichende Sprachforschung auf dem Gebiete der indogermanischen Sprachen*
LAC	*L'Antiquité Classique*
LCM	*Liverpool Classical Monthly*
LEC	*Les Études Classiques*
LfgrE	B. Snell and H. Erbse, eds., *Lexikon des frühgriechischen Epos*. (Göttingen: Vandenhoek & Ruprecht, 1955–)
LSJ	H. Liddell R. Scott and H. S. Jones, *A Greek English Lexicon*, 9th ed. (Oxford: Oxford University Press, 1940)
MSS	*Münchener Studien zur Sprachwissenschaft*
PBA	*Publications of the British Academy*
PCPhS	*Proceedings of the Cambridge Philological Society*
PMLA	*Publications of the Modern Language Association*
REG	*Revue des Études Grecques*
RHA	*Revue Hittite et Asianique*
RhM	*Rheinisches Museum für Philologie*
TAPA	*Transactions of the American Philological Association*
TPS	*Transactions of the Philological Society*
UCPCP	*University of California Publications in Classical Philology*
WJA	*Würzburger Jahrbücher für die Altertumswissenschaft*
YCS	*Yale Classical Studies*
ZCP	*Zeitschrift für celtische Philologie*

Introduction

Homeric Anger

Across the landscape of Homeric studies there are monuments that demonstrate how central anger is to whatever the early Greeks—audience and performers alike—imagined the Homeric narratives to be about. By our own various references to the powerful concept of anger, we seem to wave it as a magic wand for conjuring meaning. The titles of some of the most insightful works in Homeric studies at times seem to me part of an inscription recording a magician's incantation, set up in the agora of Homeric studies:

The Wrath of Athena
The Wrath of Paris
"Der Zorn des Paris"
Götterzorn bei Homer
"The Wrath of the Gods"
"The Anger of Poseidon"
Homers Zorn des Achilleus und den Homeriden Ilias
"The Wrath of Thetis"

This list can easily be expanded to include the analysts' attempts to find the *Ur-Ilias* by styling it the *mênis*- ("anger-") poem.[1] So too the literary critic will confidently locate the subject of the Homeric *Iliad* in this central concept; for example, according to C. Whitman, "the Wrath of Achilles had probably been an epic subject for generations when Homer found it."[2]

Such conversations about anger have continued from antiquity to the present day, with the first scholium telling us that the variety of Homeric terms for anger are just so many synonyms:

> ὥσπερ ἐπὶ συκῆς πρῶτον μέν ἐστιν ὄλυνθος, εἶτα φήληξ σῦκον ἰσχάς, οὕτω πρῶτον ὀργή, θυμὸς χόλος κότος μῆνις. ὅμως ὁ ποιητὴς ὡς συνωνύμοις ὀνόμασιν ἐπὶ Ἀχιλλέως χρῆται· "ἠὲ χόλον παύσειεν ἐρητύσειέ τε θυμόν" (A 192)· "οὐδ' ὄθομαι κοτέοντος" (A 181)· "αὐτὰρ ὁ μήνιε νηυσὶ παρήμενος" (A 488).
>
> (Erbse 1969–77, vol. 1, 4: Schol. A ad *Il.* 1.1)
>
> Just as for the fig-tree, there is first the *ólunthos*, then the *phḗlēks*, the *sûkon*, the *iskhás*, so too there is first *orgḗ*, [then] *thumós, khólos, kótos, mênis*. Nonetheless the performer uses these words as synonyms in respect to Achilles: "He would stop his *khólos* and restrain his *thumós*" (A 192). "Nor would I care for you in your *kótos*" (A 181); "and he raged [*mḗnie*] sitting by the ships" (A 488).

This ancient observation—pointing out that anger has as vigorous a cohort of synonyms as the fig—provides a background question for this study. Do the words for anger in Homeric texts present us with mere synonyms, so that the scholiast's careful conspectus of terms for Achilles' anger in *Iliad* 1 may be accurately called synonymous? Or should we look more carefully? Should we examine anger more closely than we do figs?[3]

Indeed, we have at least thirteen words for anger in Homer,[4] and one of them has special status as the subject of the *Iliad*, as is made clear by the rigorous poetics of Homeric prooemial style.[5] An epic whose characters cross the Trojan plain to slaughter one another depends upon the very emotion that drives them to pursue the war. We can join critics, ancient and modern, in acknowledging that an understanding of anger is crucial to any reading of the Homeric texts.

One question remains: How surely do we know that to which we have so readily agreed? For all our certainty about Homeric anger, our studies have produced only a few substantial works devoted to analyzing this important concept. Indeed, the semantics of the entire range of anger terms in Homer remains obscure, despite a number of promising excursions into this area of study. In 1879, J. H. H. Schmidt discussed the Greek synonyms for anger in *Synonymik der griechischen Sprache*. Table 1 groups the Homeric words as they are cited by Schmidt.

Table 1. Schmidt's list of anger terms

Category 1.	μένος, μενεαίνειν; θυμός; χόλος, χολοῦσθαι
Category 2.	σκύζεσθαι; χαλεπαίνειν, χαλεπός; ὀδύσσεσθαι; χώεσθαι
Category 3.	κότος, κοτεῖν; μῆνις, μηνίειν, μηνιθμός, μήνιμα

From a commonsense point of view, Schmidt's categories are quite reasonable. The first category shows what we might call natural anger,[6] while the items in the last category are selected on the basis of anger's temporal duration. In itself, longevity indicates a kind of grudge or ill will.[7] The second category is a kind of catchall, where anger can lead to various points on the emotional spectrum, from anxiety to hate.[8]

Schmidt's categories are to some degree in harmony with mine; after all, I am about to suggest that *kótos* is characterized by "duration," and we can all recognize that *mênis*, Homeric anger par excellence, is extensive in a similar fashion. Nevertheless, Schmidt's list sometimes separates terms that are, when viewed through Homeric poetic practice, linked by ring-composition. Indeed, no categorization that neglects poetics could tell us that *khṓesthai* and *khólos* need to be grouped together, but Homeric poetry does in fact link them as coordinated elements in ring-composition.[9] Clearly, to go beyond lexical completeness, we need to take Homeric poetics into account.

In 1950, J. Irmscher published *Götterzorn bei Homer*, his 1947 Berlin dissertation directed by W. Schadewaldt. As the title indicates, his treatise is primarily concerned with divine anger. In his first chapter, Irmscher ambitiously sets out to cover thirteen words for anger.[10] He isolates the violation of *timḗ* as the central motive for anger in the *Iliad* and goes on to argue that in the *Odyssey* it is human *húbris* that motivates Zeus's wrath; Irmscher, however, falls short of producing a definitive treatise on the semantics of Homeric anger. Indeed, Irmscher exhibits some problems of method, especially in his neglect of the oral-poetic character of Homeric diction. Thus, although he acknowledges the traditional nature of Homeric poetry, we do not see the necessary attention to issues of context and diction in traditional poetics. To proceed in his manner, admittedly, makes the lexicographical work more straightforward, as a variety of Homeric words can be readily cataloged and then included in a single analysis.[11]

Nonetheless, this laudable impulse to lexical inclusiveness itself presents a problem. Do all the words that Irmscher cites really belong together?[12] For example, in the analysis of Zeus Xenios, the terms *kótos*, *mênis*, and *khólos* seem interchangeable.[13] At the very least, we need an analysis of the context and diction in which these terms are found if we are to judge them synonyms. Indeed, we cannot grasp the relationship of these words, one to another, without a close study of Homeric traditional usage, as revealed through a detailed review of Homeric poetics as it relates to each term. To proceed otherwise neglects our most important resource in the understanding of Homeric poetry, the traditional use of context and diction through its customary practice in these poems.[14] Indeed, we will see that *khólos* and *kótos* are rigorously kept separate, with very few waverings, throughout Homeric poetry.

Comparable in scope to Irmscher's work, P. Considine (1969) produced a study of "divine wrath" in the Near East and Greece, assembling many important parallels that abound in Homeric, Mesopotamian, Canaanite, and Hittite texts. As with many other studies on anger, Considine's method here does not focus on the poetic usage of particular words for anger. Thus, we are left without a clear notion of the boundaries that mark the territory covered by different lexical items. That Homeric narrative is intimately bound up with a complex poetics must simply never be ignored. For example, in discussing Hera's "disarming address" to Aphrodite, where Hera alludes to Aphrodite's *kótos* against the Trojans as a possible impediment to her helping Hera in the *Diòs Apatḗ*, Considine seriously underestimates what is being said when he translates *Il.* 14.191–92: "Will you *be cross* [*kotessaménē*] and refuse me, because I am on the Danaans' side and you are on the side of the Trojans?"[15] Now the divinity's reference to *kótos* here is far from an attempt to minimize their conflict. Rather, it is an attempt to remove the most powerful hindrance to Hera's request for Aphrodite's help, namely, the *kótos* of Zeus. In his work on the lexicon for anger in Greek (1966, 1985, 1986), Considine carefully considers the lexical variety of Homeric diction, especially in opening and exploring the semantic field, all the while capably demonstrating that adequate analysis requires a detailed study of context. One needs to add, however, that in Homeric poetry, context is more than a paraphrase of the immediate narrative moment in which the term occurs. The richness of the language requires us to study each passage's form and place it in the wider diction of the poems in addition to the narrative context in which the lexical item occurs.[16]

One of the most frequently cited articles on the terminology for aggressive impulses in Homer is A. W. H. Adkins's "Threatening, Abusing and Feeling Angry in the Homeric Poems" (1969). The author is concerned with five words: *neikeíein* "to quarrel," *apeileîn* "to threaten," *okhtheîn* "to be troubled," *khṓesthai* "to be angry," *meneaínein* "to rage."[17] Adkins discusses two distinct words for anger (*khṓesthai, meneaínein*), even while attending to the relationship between *khṓesthai* and *okhtheîn*, where he concludes that the subject has a more positive attitude toward action if he is in a situation where *khṓesthai* is appropriate than he has when *okhtheîn* is appropriate. As was the problem with the studies by Irmscher and Considine, Adkins makes no attempt in his brief article to set out systematically the meaning of *khṓesthai* within the formal poetic context of Homeric poetry. Instead, one passage is juxtaposed with another in a manner that depends on the associative skills of the researcher. Adkins's distinction that *okhtheîn* signifies "a psychological response of frustration, distress and anger"[18] and that *khṓesthai* means "confusedly grief and anger at once" is neither systematic nor satisfying.[19]

What remains to be done is to make clear the syntagmatic relationship between anger terms and their immediate context and the paradigmatic relationships they have with one another; without such study, the relationship that obtains between, for example, *khólos* and *khṓomai* remains invisible; without a commitment to the system in which these terms have their function, it is difficult to arrive at the hypothesis that drives *Feuding Words and Fighting Words*, that *khólos* and *kótos* are distinct from one another.

Before addressing my own method, I want to suggest that as difficult as the problem of studying a large lexical field is for the Homerist, it is even more so for the cultural historian who tries to sort out from the galaxy of Homeric vocabulary the notions that best characterize Homeric anger in order to establish large-scale cultural trends of great importance. A cultural historian may, with understandable dismay, balk at the suggestion that a full-scale formulaic analysis is in order before anyone may venture into the terrain of Homeric narrative.

Yet it is precisely this problem that will be encountered by those who, trying to put the Greeks in context, take the words for granted in the interest of a seemingly more important enterprise. For example, E. Voegelin makes a problematic claim about Homeric *khólos*:

> It will have become clear . . . that in Homeric society a lordly wrath is not a private state of emotions. A *cholos*, a wrath, is a legal institution comparable to a Roman *inimicitia* or a medieval feud. . . . Hence, in the compact Homeric *cholos* one must distinguish between the emotional, wrathful reaction against damage inflicted on a man's status and the customs that regulate the course of the emotion.[20]

Here Voegelin is justified to say that there is an anger that as a legal institution parallels cultural structures such as can be observed in the Roman institution of *inimicitia*/*amicitia*. But *that* anger is not *khólos*—it is *kótos*. For *kótos* is directly related to the incipient vocabulary of Greek legal institutions (including *díkē* "judgment," "justice"; *húbris* "outrage"; and the like), especially as the terms relate to the traditional institutions of reciprocity. And, as I will demonstrate, *khólos* bears little resemblance to a "legal institution." The only way to sort out *khólos* from *kótos*, however, is to study systematically the semantics of anger that makes clear such a distinction. Indeed, without such work, it is hard to imagine how a cultural historian can distinguish which word describes "a lordly wrath" and which "a private state of emotions."

My emphasis on Homeric matters steers the discussion away from later Greek material. Indeed, the reader will notice that missing from this book is an extended analysis of the literature on anger in the ancient world after the early Greek period. Fortunately, as this book went to press an important book on ancient anger appeared, one that provides just such an extended analsysis. W. V. Harris's *Restraining Rage* (2001), focusing on the restraint of anger, exhaustively covers a vast panorama of Greek and Roman thinking about anger, with a central aim of examining Greco-Roman antiquity's yearnings for the repression of anger. The importance of this project goes without saying, especially given the philosophical tradition's tenacious speculation on this topic (Harris 2001, 84–128).

In contrast, I focus my discussion of anger on Homer in order to fill what seems to me a lacuna. As can be surmised from my comments above, the study of anger in antiquity has often taken Homeric anger for granted or at least as worthy only of being confined to a review-chapter serving as background for the rest of antiquity. Despite this drawback, the studies of anger in the later literature have been admirably vigorous (as now with Harris and with even more recent work [Braund and Most 2003]); we Homerists should emulate that vigor.

Yet, to study anger in Homer is not the same as to account for anger in the whole of Greek and Roman antiquity. It is, I must say, quite different. For the Homeric texts present problems of poetics and of form that simply cannot be sped over in the interest of getting to later philosophical texts and historical data. If philology is the art of slow reading, the study of Homer is the art of slow and steady reading: for to deal with poetics is not merely to correlate lexical glosses with immediate context. One must view the lexical data within the traditional matrix that is its life's blood. The task of the Homeric scholar, now, is to treat Homer not merely as an antecedent to "the polis" (Harris 2001, 27), but as a poetic intervention into profound cultural issues, an intervention that deserves a full and robust intellectual engagement. Such a vigorous Homeric poetics is a humane way to make more meaningful the dialogue between Homerists and other readers of the ancient world.[21]

At the heart of a systematic poetics of Homeric narrative are the traditional meanings together with the traditional forms that produce those meanings within the practices of oral poetry. In the words of L. Muellner: "Obviously semantic analysis cannot be effective without an awareness of such considerations of technique."[22] This kind of complexity of Homeric poetic semantics can be enriched by looking at how the highly developed anger systems of other cultures such as the Ifaluk are deployed within their traditional forms of discourse. By turning to the anthropological literature on emotions, where anger is conceived of as a social phenomenon, I hope to give the Homeric material a comparative context. The following examples can begin to show how an anthropologically informed approach might begin to work.[23]

For example, C. Lutz, in *Unnatural Emotions*, her ethnography of the Ifaluk in the Southwest Pacific, gives an account of their emotional life as it relates to the way the Ifaluk organize their cultural perception of anger:

> The Ifaluk speak about many types of anger. There is the irritability that often accompanies sickness (*tipmochmoch*), the anger that builds up slowly in the face of a succession of minor but unwanted events (*lingeringer*), the annoyance that occurs when relatives have failed to live up to their obligations (*nguch*), and, finally, there is the frustrated anger that occurs in the face of personal misfortunes and slights which one is helpless to redress (*tang*). But each of these emotions is sharply distinguished from the anger which is a righteous indignation, or justifiable anger (*song*), and it is only this anger which is morally approved.[24]

Lutz establishes the way words for emotions are charged with meanings that are conceptual, political, moral, and, more generally, cultural. In short, such a study implies that through the consideration of emotional vocabulary, it is possible to come to terms with critically important conceptual features of a given culture.

Similarly, M. Rosaldo in her *Knowledge and Passion* (1980) describes the dynamics of emotion as manifested among the Ilongot in Northern Luzon in the Philippines.[25] Rosaldo's discussion is worth quoting at length for her account of how the terms that define the Ilongot cultural understanding of anger are to be taken:

> My grasp of Ilongot ideas of the dynamics of emotion grew through a series of interviews in which I addressed myself to questions about the use of *liget*, *bea*, and related words. I knew that the importance of heart and feelings in Ilongot accounts of action had more to do with general notions of vitality, conflict, and cooperation than with a "psychologistic" sense of persons, but had little understanding of how Ilongots thought emotions worked. The net of senses associated with emotion words was my introduction. By asking informants . . . I found, first, that of words characterizing the heart, *liget* was by far the richest in its associations; and in exploring ways that words like "difference" (*'apir*), "strength" (*'eret*), and "quick" (*awet*) resemble *liget*, I began to see in a term that I had understood initially to mean no more than "anger" a set of principles and connections with elaborate ramifications for Ilongot social life. . . . And so, building from families of terms and contexts, I developed a grasp of certain Ilongot metaphors, and of the loose conceptual scheme that underlies them and describes the principles working "energy, anger, passion" in their world.[26]

The Homerist should emerge from an anthropologist's analysis of anger with renewed expectations that semantic work can move beyond the well-tended groves of lexical classification and into the wilder forests of words and things. If, as M. Rosaldo describes them, metaphors for anger might be based on a "loose conceptual scheme that underlies them," it may be that philological rigor will not have the flexibility to unearth loose schemes as well as it does the tightly constructed ones.[27]

What will be the link between an analysis of Homeric anger words and an analysis that draws from work outside classical studies? The links will be various, but a secure way for the reader of Homeric poetry to begin is, at the outset, to lay the foundation for the work by close attention to and analysis of early Greek diction. R. Sacks suggests that this approach to "the problem of recovering tradition" involves two steps.[28] The first step is to collect all the attestations of a traditional phrase; and the second step is to search out "those patterns which, with all their complexities, are actually displayed by Homeric phrases."[29] Sacks reminds us how far we are from an adequate description of Homeric practice.

The approach to "searching out" needs to be determined from the outset, since the meanings we find, as hermeneutics has taught us, are intimately bound up with the meanings that we search for. Do we have any control over our first steps, or are we bound to choose our objects of study at random? I return to Sacks's observations for direction: "Studying Homer is not like studying an existing language. If we want to focus on the theoretical in our analyses of the

English language, we may take some comfort in being native speakers and thus experts in the language's synchronic 'traditions.' No such expert can ever again exist for Homer. . . ."[30] The problem of the nonliving tradition confronts us immediately. On whom could we rely to be as fluent in Homeric diction as the singer and audience once were? However, certain revelations in the narrative can bring us closer to that expert understanding. These revelations can occur in the form of the folk definition. I will return to this term later in this Introduction, but for now I note that within the text there survive statements about terms such as *mênis*, *khólos*, and *kótos* that go beyond exemplifying the meaning of the term. As we will see, once a native explanation of a term is found, the meaning of that term can be tested alongside that definition. We will also see that this process can guide and ground our study more firmly than even the best of our own intuitions as a nonnative audience.

In the give-and-take of an anthropological field situation, researcher and informant, ideally, find ways to communicate the principles that underlie their statements. I have, of course, no informants to interview. Nonetheless, though we can interact with neither poet nor audience, we may take heart that the Homeric poems show human actors both involved in and commenting upon their social structure, in what will be a variety of ways.[31] Indeed, that these texts are epics in form makes possible moments such as that of Calchas's definition (described below). One aspect of epic, its expansiveness, makes it a good place to look for an informed definition of a term denoting anger.[32] Once that definition is given, if it is confronted by an inquiry that both illuminates rigorous connections and exploits loose conceptual schemes, it may yield insight, to use M. Rosaldo's words, into Homeric culture's "set of principles and connections [that have] elaborate ramifications for [its] social life."[33]

The student of Homeric poetry is left with a struggle if not a dilemma: to use the methods of linguistics, anthropology, and the other intellectual disciplines for studying human culture and at the same time maintain sharp focus on the poetry, a task the social scientist sees as secondary. Thus, the student of Homeric poetry must keep in mind the poetic object in question, all the while avoiding the siren-song of the applied methodology. This act balances the real and the fictional, and it is indeed difficult to draw documentary evidence about a culture from its creative narrative art.

Because I have suggested that this study will turn to anthropological and linguistic cultural inquiries in order to understand the poetry of the *Iliad* and the *Odyssey*, and because it will be evident that this process will be engaged after we have addressed formal issues, it is wise to ask whether social or literary perspectives have priority in my work. The methodological distinction between a social study and a textual one demands more theoretical rigor than I intend to apply here. But it will become evident that I am not trying primarily to reconstruct archaic or bronze-age social structures by combing through the evidence of the Homeric texts. Since I begin my analysis with close readings of words, passages, and texts, my focus is primarily on those texts, the aim being to draw out of the cultural categories examined, such as the notion of "feud" or "aggression," a conceptual field that will be of value to students of the *Iliad* and the *Odyssey*. Thus, even if an archaic Greek cultural practice is found out by sheer hard work, it is placed immediately into the service of the text. In sum, this is a work of poetic analysis using the tools at our disposal—which include social theory—to organize evidence and give shape to conclusions. But those conclusions remain, unflinchingly, about the text.

In pursuing the usefulness of bringing to bear anthropological insights onto the study of literature, in trying to understand the way that structural analysis of texts illuminates those texts, I have found compelling the insight of Marshall Sahlins as he, from the anthropologist's perspective, confronts the way structural analysis interacts with history. For Sahlins, "a set of historical relationships . . . at once reproduce the traditional cultural categories and give them new values out of the pragmatic context," so that to analyze the "structure" of a cultural system is not to deny its historicity, nor can a study of history be innocent of the structural system that, for a given culture, provides meaning for the events undergone by the human actors within that culture.[34] Sahlins thus sees structure and history as inextricably related. My use of this observation is to apply it to the experience of a text, so that the structure that we labor to bring forth is set beside the text itself. Although this is not the place to establish securely the analogy on which my use of this idea depends (text : poetics :: history : social structure), let me again assert that the observations on Homeric poetics in this book are made not only in order to understand the system that lies behind the texts but also in order to deal directly with and illuminate the *Iliad* and the *Odyssey*.[35]

I return to M. Rosaldo for a clue to our opening enigma: Why does anger, important as it is for Homer, still need to be explored at the most basic levels? Rosaldo's research provides us with a theoretical basis from which to understand why the central concept of the *Iliad* is not yet clearly grasped. She suggests that the distinction between symbolic and ordinary language has led students of culture to underrate the complexity, and the cultural specificity, of ordinary words. It might be thought, she suggests, that

> in contrast to the "symbol" . . . are the more ordinary, strictly referential terms of daily language—words perhaps like "anger," "red," or "blossom," the understanding of which requires little more than an ability to recognize the discrete emotional states, plants, or colors that their names conventionally denote.[36]

But then:

> Having distinguished what appear to be symbolic terms from the transparent common sense on which to found translation, such analysts prove incapable of appreciating the ways in which apparently foreign and peculiar deeds may by

> themselves have common sense interpretations. And at the same time, their approach ignores the fact that common sense in other cultures is ultimately as demanding of interpretation as is apparently obscure "symbolic" form.[37]

Anger is so much a common part of the way of life for a Homeric warrior that we have come to set aside the terms for the concept of anger as an item of inquiry. This mistake is even harder for us to observe since in our own lives the term "anger" is also part of day-to-day existence; in other words, we think we already know what it is. In fact, our referral of *mênis* to English wrath is itself an attempt to claim a transparent meaning for this term. Surely, we think, this anger is just like the wrath of the Old Testament Yahweh, an exalted anger.[38] I mean to say that anger, for Homer, has been taken by readers as a "strictly referential term," the meaning of which we recognize immediately. Further, the lexica do not indicate the systematic nature of the distinction between *khólos* and *kótos* to be elucidated in this study.[39] The dictionaries acknowledge a difference in intensity between the two, but crucial contextual features have yet to be examined for their rich elaboration of the semantic force of these terms. Such terms are "demanding of interpretation" in M. Rosaldo's words, just as much as terms of great social significance—such as, for example, "justice."

The importance of anger has been acknowledged in Homeric studies primarily for *mênis* but not for the dozen or so other Homeric terms for anger. A word like *khólos* seems less likely to draw our attention precisely because it is the mere unmarked term for anger.[40] M. Rosaldo's observation that studies of other cultures tend to gravitate to what is considered a priori the symbolically laden material might account for our neglect of the other words for anger, including *khólos*.[41]

Thus, Homerists still need to address systematically, even if belatedly, the central concept of the field. Perhaps, we can show, as M. Rosaldo shows for the Ilongot, that the emotion of anger is part of a system, a net of senses intricately related to Homeric social life. Such a result should not surprise us, since the most recent anthropological and linguistic studies of the emotions have indicated the central importance of anger to cultural studies.[42]

Before we proceed, I note that Homerists are not alone in coming late to these issues. Awareness of the importance of anger is a recent development even in the social sciences. Sociological and psychological studies of aggression, some researchers complain, pay too little attention to anger. Favoring behavioral, and hence measurable and quantifiable models, our own culture's tendency has been to exclude the emotions from analyses of aggression. Consider the summary given by R. Novaco:[43]

> Until recently, the concept of anger has taken a backseat to that of aggression. The extensive research conducted on human aggression in psychological laboratories in the 1960s and 1970s virtually excluded anger except as a

> precondition induced to facilitate aggressive behavior. Behavioristic traditions favored the study of observable action over subjective experience. Consequently, anger received little attention. However, this neglect of anger as subject matter also occurred in the psychoanalytic literature. . . . In fact, one rarely, if ever, finds the word "anger" in the subject index of psychoanalytic books prior to the last decade.[44]

We are thus presented with a remarkable series of facts. First, the proem to the *Iliad* signals to us that anger is central to the epic's analysis of the forces that lead human beings to destroy each other. Second, we fall short of coming to terms with the complex Homeric diction relating to anger. Third, and finally, the social sciences, even as they pursue the ethnography and psychology of primary cultures, have also until recently neglected to observe that human aggression may be rooted psycho-emotionally and culturally in anger.[45]

In terms of method, then, we need three approaches. First, we must focus on anger itself as a semantic field in Homeric poetry. Second, we need to study closely the specific diction for anger in the medium of Homeric verse. And third, we need to set this research within the context of anthropological and social research into the formation and expression of emotions in human groups. The main methodological focus of this book depends upon the first two approaches, especially as they relate to the system of anger displayed in the two words *kótos* and *khólos*, in the course of which the third approach is drawn into service for a thorough study of the linguistic and poetic evidence. But how then should we approach that poetic evidence?

A good overview of the approach to diction taken here is presented by R. Sacks in the introduction to *The Traditional Phrase in Homer* (1987). Sacks's emphasis, along with that of those he cites in the field (including Frame, Lowenstam, Muellner, Nagy, Shannon, Sinos, Slatkin, Watkins, and others), is to discover the "depth" of traditional phraseology through "the method of collecting all attestations and looking for a pattern or patterns, contextual and otherwise."[46] I find it comfortable to link the present endeavor to Sacks's declaration in his work that "the central assumption . . . is . . . that we should still be searching out those patterns that, with all their complexities, are actually displayed by Homeric phrases."[47] I add only that by using poetic analysis coupled with a look at the comparative material displayed through anthropology, historical linguistics, and other approaches beyond the purview of ordinary Greek language study, we have acquired a powerful tool for the analysis and interpretation of the Greek text.

Where has that kind of work been done with respect to anger in Homer? It should not surprise us that the most rigorous examination of anger has been produced in the study of *mênis*, especially since that word initiates Homeric discourse. I introduce the material on *mênis* here because in the study of this important word, method has made all the difference for our coming to terms with anger in Homer.

That such approaches can have powerful results is clear from the work of Leonard Muellner and Calvert Watkins,[48] who have both shown that *mênis* can be illuminated by the rigorous study of Homeric diction. Indeed these studies demonstrate that *mênis* is a taboo word, never used by speakers in reference to their own anger.[49] *Mênis* is part of a systematic cultural taboo whose roots can be found in the violations that lead to it.[50] That *mênis* has as its source the productive root *men-* is certain, although the process of formation has posed problems, reviewed in detail by Muellner (1992 and 1996, with Watkins 1977a). I am encouraged by Muellner's success in establishing the taboo meaning of *mênis* through a rigorous approach to Homeric diction. Among Muellner's findings (Muellner 1996), I single out as relevant to my work in this book the following conclusions about *mênis* as a word for anger in Homeric narrative: first, *mênis* is avoided in contexts when one speaks of one's own anger; second, in the *Iliad* the noun *mênis* refers exclusively among mortals to Achilles; and third, there is a complex sociolinguistic structure that houses this term.[51]

Given the success of this method as applied to *mênis*, the other words in the lexicon of Homeric anger should receive the same rigorous attention that has been given to the first word of the *Iliad*. In *Feuding Words and Fighting Words*, then, I focus on two of those words for the following two reasons: first, in order to expand our understanding of the range of anger terminology in early Greek epic; and second, because a specific passage in Book 1 of the *Iliad* singles these two words out for special consideration.

In this book, my approach, then, is to gather and discuss all the examples of two terms (*khólos* and *kótos*), in order to examine them with reference to Homeric diction. In the process of doing this, the anthropological, linguistic, and social topics that arise are to be treated insofar as they are helpful toward understanding Homeric narrative. Note that even as I adhere to the principle of collecting all the examples, the collection is ultimately grounded in an observation from within the culture. Rather than producing an abundance of linguistic data that would be true to lexical completeness while capsizing the central goal of coming to terms with the productive use of anger in this poetry, I ground my arguments in the words of the prophet Calchas in Book 1 of the *Iliad*. I emphasize that the group of words selected for study is not arbitrary but can be said to stem *as a group* from an interpretation in the text.

Now it is time to introduce the passage that will be often in the foreground and always in the background of this book. In this Introduction, the passage highlights the intricacy of Homeric diction for anger. The final four verses of this passage provide the original stimulus for this book.

Near the opening of the *Iliad*, the Achaean prophet, Calchas, requests that Achilles protect him from Agamemnon's wrath once the source of the plague is revealed:

ὦ Ἀχιλεῦ, κέλεαί με, Διὶ φίλε, μυθήσασθαι
μῆνιν Ἀπόλλωνος ἑκατηβελέταο ἄνακτος.

τοιγὰρ ἐγὼν ἐρέω· σὺ δὲ σύνθεο καί μοι ὄμοσσον
ἦ μέν μοι πρόφρων ἔπεσιν καὶ χερσὶν ἀρήξειν·
ἦ γὰρ ὀίομαι ἄνδρα χολωσέμεν, ὃς μέγα πάντων
Ἀργείων κρατέει καί οἱ πείθονται Ἀχαιοί.
κρείσσων γὰρ βασιλεὺς, ὅτε χώσεται ἀνδρὶ χέρηι·
εἴ περ γάρ τε χόλον γε καὶ αὐτῆμαρ καταπέψῃ,
ἀλλά τε καὶ μετόπισθεν ἔχει κότον, ὄφρα τελέσσῃ,
ἐν στήθεσσιν ἑοῖσι· σὺ δὲ φράσαι εἴ με σαώσεις.
(*Il.* 1.74–83)

O Achilles, beloved of Zeus, you order me to speak the anger of Apollo, king, far-shooter. So, I will tell you, but promise me and swear that, yes, you will truly help me in word and deed. Now, I think I will enrage a man who has mighty rule over all the Argives, and the Achaeans obey him. For a king is stronger when he comes to be angry with a lesser man; for, if in fact he can swallow his *khólos* down on the very same day, he can later keep *kótos* in his heart until he brings it to its *télos*. You must take thought of protecting me.

In line 75 the text shows that *mênis* signifies the anger of Apollo represented by the plague that ravages the Achaean camp. Quite rightly, Calchas worries that his revelation of the source of Apollo's anger will lead to a mortal's anger (*ándra kholōsémen, Il.* 1.78). This observation may be true of anyone, but Calchas is concerned about the political power *this* man wields: *hòs méga pántōn / Argeíōn kratéei kaí hoi peíthontai Akhaioí* "Who has mighty rule over all the Argives, and the Achaeans obey him," *Il.* 1.78–79. Next, Calchas introduces yet another word for anger (*khṓsetai*).

Finally, Calchas opposes one kind of anger to another in a systematic fashion, that is, in a way that implies some regular difference between the two: *khólos* is immediate (*autêmar* "on this very day," *Il.* 1.81) and is related metaphorically with the physiological process of digestion (*katapépsēi* "swallows down, digests," *Il.* 1.81). In addition, *khólos* is surpassed in its consequences by the last kind of anger here cataloged, *kótos*; for *kótos* has consequences that reach out far beyond the present (*metópisthen* "in the future," *Il.* 1.82), and *kótos* may, in the course of things, reach some end to which it by nature tends (*óphra teléssēi* "until he brings it to pass," *Il.* 1.82).

Calchas's own words indicate that there is an opposition between *khólos* and *kótos*. Grammatically, K. Ameis and C. Hentze point to the chiastic pairing of *khólos* and *kótos*, helped by the placement of the particle *ge* after *khólo*n in *Il.* 1.81.[52] The arrangement formed by Calchas clearly plays on a set of oppositions between *khólos* and *kótos* in a way that needs clarification. First, how can we say that *khólos* may last only the day, while *kótos* has a teleology of its own? How active is the metaphor in *katapépsēi*? How consistent is any of these propositions with the rest of Homeric language?

Moreover, what about their formal features? Of all the words for anger these are the two that are closest in form to one another. They both begin with a velar and belong to the same noun-paradigm; each has two syllables and could take part in similar alliteration and assonance patterns.[53] Thus, on purely formal grounds, these two words for anger may be studied together as part of the sensitive workings of Homeric formular diction. Yet only three times in the manuscript tradition do these two words serve as variants for each other (*Il.* 14.111, *Il.* 24.584, and *Od.* 13.342).

I will be looking closely at the issues that arise from my selecting these two words for anger as exemplary of Homeric culture's construction of anger. To close this Introduction, however, let us consider a feature of Calchas's speech that might independently indicate to us the speaker's value for the study of Homeric language: Calchas presents us with a folk definition of anger terms.

This latter point is important enough to elaborate further, at least briefly. In reference to the theoretical value of such kinds of folk speech, consider the following two statements by a folklorist as he considers the force of folk definitions:

> Naive native speakers' definitions represent a basic source of such [empirical] data. Their value lies in the fact that folk definitions express not merely the meanings of individual lexical items but also underlying semantic relationships between the defined term and the defining term(s).[54]

And again:

> To understand the significance of folk definitions for the study of semantics it is necessary to recognize two fundamental facts about defining. First, definitions are not in any way an artifact of linguistic analysis or of formal lexicography. It seems likely . . . that "defining is a cultural universal." . . . Second, all definitions reflect one basic law of natural language: a natural language serves as its own metalanguage. . . . Folk definitions, then, offer more than just recurrent patterns in the definitions of individual terms which may point to possible semantic components. They are expressions of significant relationships among lexical items which form the basis for native speakers' understandings of the meanings of those items.[55]

Seen in the light of Manes's observations, Calchas's statements constitute a folk definition of two Homeric terms for anger.[56] Thus, let this study in the semantics of anger begin with the definition of *khólos* and *kótos* provided us by Calchas, the prophet of the Achaeans. Indeed, we can prepare for our encounter with the basic Homeric concept by quoting Odysseus's fillip to his friends:

> τλῆτε, φίλοι, καὶ μείνατ' ἐπὶ χρόνον, ὄφρα δαῶμεν
> ἢ ἐτεὸν Κάλχας μαντεύεται ἦε καὶ οὐκί.
> (*Il.* 2.299–300)

> Take heart, comrades, and wait awhile, until we determine whether Calchas prophesies the truth, or not.

Notes

1. The titles in the list refer respectively to: Clay 1983; Collins 1987; Heitsch 1967; Irmscher 1950; Woodhouse 1930, Chapter 4; Lidov 1977; Petersen 1920; and Slatkin 1986. And see now *The Anger of Achilles* (Muellner 1996). For a typical analytic statement, see Leaf 1886, I.xxiii: "The original poem, the work of 'Homer' himself was the Μῆνις Ἀχιλλέως. . . ."

2. Whitman 1958, 182.

3. On synonyms in Homer see Paraskevaides 1984 and Martin 1989, 14 ("When we do pay attention to context, synonymity recedes"). For the question of functional synonymity and the formula, see Bakker and van den Houten 1992.

4. Using Irmscher's list, see note 11.

5. For the significance of the opening word in prooemial style see van Groningen 1946, 284–87 and Kahane 1992 and 1994 (for *mênis*, see 52–58).

6. "Zorn als Ausfluss des natürlichen Wesens des Menschen bezeichnen, als eine starke Regung oder Offenbarung des Gemütes oder der Seele" (Schmidt 1879, 551).

7. "Den Kern der dritten Gruppe machen zwei Substantive und zwei Verben aus, welche den dauernd in der Seele wonenden *Groll* bezeichnen" (Schmidt 1879, 551).

8. Schmidt 1879, 551.

9. See, for example, *Od.* 8.227 with *Od.* 8.238. So, too, Calchas refers to *khólos* just after using the phrase *basileùs . . . khṓsetai* (*Il.* 1.80–81) "A king . . . will be angry."

10. *mênis*, *khólos*, *khōomai*, *kótos*, *odússomai*, *ménos*, *ékhthos*, *miséō*, *alastéō*, *skúzomai*, *ágamai*, *némesis*, and *khalepaínō*.

11. For further problems with Irmscher's work (especially its lack of statistical information), see Considine 1966, 15–16. Considine acknowledges that both *mênis* and *khólos* receive "rather unsatisfactory treatment" in Irmscher.

12. Most disturbing is the absence of analysis of poetic context. Without contextual analysis firmly rooted in the study of traditional diction, it would be nearly impossible to uncover the relationship of, say, *khólos* to *khṓomai*.

13. Irmscher 1950, 81–86. On the relation of Zeus Xenios to anger see Watkins 1987b, 298–99, Muellner 1992, 130–31 and 1996, 37.

14. Again, see Martin 1989, 12–14, for articulation of this method.

15. Considine 1969, 139–40.

16. Considine's recent work on *mênis* has helped advance a more rigorous study of this term (Considine 1985, 1986). Cf. Muellner 1992 and now Muellner 1996, 177–89.

17. Adkins 1969, 7–20.

18. Adkins 1969, 15.

19. Adkins 1969, 17.

20. Voegelin 1956, 89.

21. In addition to Harris 2001, see also an excellent brief review of the state of this research in Laurenti and Indelli 1988, 1–8; for the relationship of the philosophical to the literary implications of anger see Anderson 1964, especially 149–73, with Galinsky 1988 for the later literature. As this book went to press, appeared Braund and Most 2003.

22. Muellner 1976, 15.

23. For a brief introduction to the anthropology of anger see Tavris 1989, 48–69; see also, especially for a review of the debate between the physicalists and social constructivists, Myers 1988; Hochschild (1983, 201–22) succinctly reviews the study of

emotion "from Darwin to Goffman"; a collection of classic essays on the topic of the emotions can be found in Calhoun and Solomon 1984. In the social sciences, a valuable reference for research on the emotions is the collection of Lewis and Haviland (1993; on anger, especially 537–46). The classic study in the social sciences is that of Averill (1982, 1983). Lutz (1988) reviews the anthropology of emotions in general.

24. Lutz 1988, 157.

25. For the Ilongot, see also M. Rosaldo 1984, and her discussion of the relationship between feuding, raiding, and beheading.

26. M. Rosaldo 1980, 45.

27. As informed by anthropology, classical studies have blossomed of late, but the field of anthropology is too vast for me merely to cite it passing. Yet some works provide methodological perspectives that have informed this book: besides the important works of Detienne (see especially 1981, Chapter 6, for an analysis of the interaction of 20th century anthropology and the Greeks), Vernant, and Burkert, let me cite works that consciously take on the relationship between the literary text and anthropology: Kurke 1991, 7–12 and 88–96; Nagy 1979, 1990a and b, 1992; and Martin 1989. As to social life and anthropological modeling for the ancient world see D. Cohen 1991, where he applies a model derived from Mediterranean anthropology to the moral life of Athens (see Chapters 1 and 2 for the theory and method); see too Humphreys 1978 and Zeitlin's overview of Vernant's work (in Vernant 1991b, 3–24).

28. Sacks 1987, Introduction, 1–30.

29. Sacks 1987, 17.

30. Sacks 1987, 23.

31. Sacks 1987, 19. For problems related specifically to the relationship of field worker to informant see Clifford 1988, 48–50 and 72–75. Though we should not romanticize the "informant" as a source, to have access to no living informed member of a culture threatens the success of any anthropological inquiry. Just such a situation imperils a project on Homeric discourse, since we deal without the perspective provided by dialogue with a competent member of the culture. Yet the limitations thus imposed on work in early Greece parallel the problems newly discovered with respect to the dialogue between an outsider anthropologist and an insider informant. Anthropology's maturation—its realization that its very hallmark, the relationship between outsider and insider, is loaded with difficulties—emboldens those of us who work in pre-ethnographic cultures to attempt to reconstruct, even if imperfectly, the relationship that mirrors that of the dialogue between an informant and a researcher. For anthropology's cognizance of the pitfalls faced by the researcher in approaching any culture, the "crisis in ethnographic authority," see Clifford 1988 and the collection of essays in Clifford and Marcus 1986. Cf. Finley 1986, 118.

32. For the importance of the expansion aesthetic see Martin 1989, 206–30.

33. See again M. Rosaldo 1980, 45.

34. M. Sahlins 1985, 125. See Dougherty and Kurke 1993, 5–6, for an application of Sahlins' work to cultural poetics.

35. Besides Sahlins 1985, see also Sahlins 1976, 1981.

36. M. Rosaldo 1980, 21.

37. M. Rosaldo 1980, 22.

38. On this kind of anger, see Considine 1969.

39. E.g., Cunliffe 1963, *LSJ*, *LfrGE*, s.vv.

40. There have been exceptions to this general neglect, as for example in the study of *éris* ("strife") by Hogan 1981, and Nagler 1988 and 1992; see also Dumézil 1980 on *ménos* ("anger") and *lússa* ("rage").

41. That *khólos* should be neglected *because* it is common fits in nicely with M. Rosaldo's remarks. For *khólos* as the unmarked term for anger, see Considine 1985, 162 n. 2, "In Homer the unmarked word for anger is *khólos*, in Classical Greek *orgḗ* and in later and Modern Greek *thumós*"; cf. Considine 1986, 53. See also Turpin 1988, 258 ("dénomination non-marquée de la colère"). Curiously Considine 1986 omits *kótos* in his review of Homeric anger terms.

42. See, for example, Lakoff and Kövecses 1987 and Lutz (in Holland and Quinn 1987), who covers the ethnographic importance of anger and its role in a community's organization of its social life. See also M. Rosaldo 1980, and R. Rosaldo 1984; on the meaning of emotions as part of a culture's semiotic practice, see Myers 1988 and 1991. A variety of critical work continues to be produced in this area (see, e.g., Heider 1991). Anthropological work in the area of emotion and aggression needs to be attended to by the Homerist, who can also make a contribution to ethnographic projects from the evidence provided by our archaic Greek texts.

43. In Novaco 1986, 3.

44. Add here Tavris's complaints (1989, 39). For more on the slighting of emotion in the sociological literature, see Hochschild 1983, 201–4. The literature on aggression has begun to include extensive study on anger's role as a social problem; see Geen 1990, 115–25. In the context of world mythology, note that Aho 1981 does not single out anger as a specific cause of violence in the sacral mythology of war. See also Lemerise and Dodge 1993, 537.

45. Two psychoanalytically informed studies of Homer consider the psychological questions relating to Achilles, while leaving aside the question of anger (MacCary 1982 and Holway 1989). For psychoanalysis and anger, see Novaco 1986, 2–6.

46. Sacks 1987, 17. See also 1–3.

47. Sacks 1987, 13.

48. Muellner 1992, 1996; Watkins 1977a.

49. Muellner's book on *mênis* (1996) is a watershed in the study of anger in Homer, both for providing rigorous method with sophisticated readings of crucial passages, and for engaging the necessary comparative material. A major thrust of this work is to apply a social and linguistic category (taboo) in the course of analyzing the traditional diction that is Homeric usage. Important questions regarding the nature of such a taboo are raised in Turpin 1988; see also Muellner 1992; Muellner's work details the nature of this constraint (1996, 191–94). See also Nagy 1979, 74 and Nagy 1990a, 227 and 238.

50. Watkins 1977a; Muellner 1992. For more on *mênis* and *khólos* see chapters 2 and 3. Also see Considine 1966, 16–22; as well as 1985 and 1986; Nagy 1979, 15–18; 1990, 227, 238, and 263; Turpin 1988. Janko 1992, 106 questions the hypothesis that *mênis* refers to divine wrath; see also Kahane 1994, 50–58. While providing the definitive study of *mênis*, Muellner (1996) analyzes the way the taboo mechanism functions in the Homeric poems.

51. Schwyzer 1931, rejected in Schwyzer 1939, 260; see now Muellner 1996, 186–89, where the appendix ("The Etymology of *Mênis*," 177–94) reviews the comparative evidence and comes to the conclusion that "Watkins's revival of Schwyzer's etymology appears to be the most consistent with the word's meaning and usage" (194).

52. Ameis and Hentze 1894 at *Il.* 1.81 for a succinct and telling note on the style of this passage.

53. On sound-patterns in Homer see Shewan 1925, and on word-play in Homer see Louden 1995; note that Louden (30) catches a pun involving *khólos* (with *khōlós* "lame") at *Od.* 8.304–8.

54. Manes 1980, 122.

55. Manes 1980, 123.

56. Compare Nestor's definition of *mêtis* "cunning intelligence" (*Il.* 23.313–18), as discussed by Detienne and Vernant 1974, 11–23; also Frame 1978, 85; and note the contrast with *nóos* at line 590. See too Menelaus's observations on *kóros* "satiety" in *Il.* 13.636–39. Such passages can profitably be approached with Manes's notion of the folk definition.

Part I

Feuding Words

Chapter One

The Prophet Defines

Within the first hundred lines of the *Iliad*, the Achaean prophet, Calchas, presents a definition of anger (*Il.* 1.74–83). The immediate context is that Achilles has just called an assembly in response to the suffering of the Achaeans. So great is their suffering that, Achilles suggests, they are on the brink of entirely abandoning their efforts on the Trojan plain (*Il.* 1.59–67). In response to Achilles' suggestion that the anger of Apollo is at issue (*Il.* 1.64), Calchas comes to ask for his protection, for the prophet will reveal that the cause of the suffering is the action of none other than Agamemnon. After Calchas solicits Achilles' help (*Il.* 1.76–77), he proceeds to identify the source of his misgiving by sharpening the distinction between two kinds of anger, *kótos* and *khólos*:[1]

> ἦ γὰρ ὀίομαι ἄνδρα χολωσέμεν, ὃς μέγα πάντων
> Ἀργείων κρατέει καί οἱ πείθονται Ἀχαιοί·
> κρείσσων γὰρ βασιλεὺς, ὅτε χώσεται ἀνδρὶ χέρηι·
> εἴ περ γάρ τε χόλον γε καὶ αὐτῆμαρ καταπέψῃ,
> ἀλλά τε καὶ μετόπισθεν ἔχει κότον, ὄφρα τελέσσῃ
> ἐν στήθεσσιν ἑοῖσι· σὺ δὲ φράσαι εἴ με σαώσεις.
> (*Il.* 1.78–83)

> Now, I think I will enrage a man who has mighty rule over all the Argives, and the Achaeans obey him. For a king is stronger when he comes to be angry with a lesser man; for, if in fact he can swallow his *khólos* down on the very same day, he can later keep *kótos* in his heart until he brings it to its *télos*. You must take thought of protecting me.

To paraphrase Calchas, he needs protection because his revelation will anger someone;[2] in addition there are two kinds of anger.[3] One is *khólos*, which can be dealt with immediately. To indicate this feature of *khólos*, Calchas uses the metaphor of digestion (*katapépsēi*, *Il.* 1.81). The second kind of anger is *kótos*, which will not be brought to an end until the angered party has in some sense completed it (*óphra telésséi*, *Il.* 1.82), a point that Calchas emphasizes by claiming that *kótos* will last into the future (*kaì metópisthen*, *Il.* 1.82).

Furthermore, the social status of the angered party is relevant. Calchas is particularly concerned with arousing the anger of a superior, specifically a *basileús* (*kreíssōn gàr basileùs hóte khṓsetai andrì khérēi* "For a king will be stronger, when he comes to be angry with a lesser man," *Il.* 1.80).[4] Thus, at issue here are questions of time, social class, and bodily experience:

> Time: *autêmar*, *kaì metópisthen*, *óphra telésséi*
> Social class: *basileús, andrì khérēi*
> The body: *katapépsēi, en stḗthessin.*

In Table 1.1, I show how these terms can be aligned with *khólos* and *kótos*, in order to highlight the specific terms of Calchas's definition.[5]

Table 1.1. The terms of Calchas's definition

Category	***Khólos***	***Kótos***
Time	*autêmar*	*kaì metópisthen,* *óphra telésséi*
Class	*andrì khérēi*	*basileús*
Body	*katapépsēi*	*en stḗthessin*

Kótos seems connected with the social status of the *basileús.*[6] The phrase *andrì khérēi* certainly contrasts with *basileús*, in a way that says something about its relationship to *khólos*. I suggest that the person of lower class (*andrì khérēi*) and his superiors are capable of having *khólos*, while *kótos* belongs primarily (within the context of this definition) to a *basileús.*[7] Indeed, Calchas fears not just anyone's anger but that of a king.[8]

As for the category of time, Calchas emphasizes the longevity of *kótos* in comparison with *khólos*. He claims that *kótos* has its own *télos* that must be reached before the *kótos* can come to an end. The implication is that *khólos* is more malleable, more subject to modification than is *kótos. Autêmar* ("in a day's time") does not limit *khólos* in its duration. Rather, it indicates that there is no intrinsic *télos* ("end") to *khólos*.

As to the the third category in Table 1.1, that of the body, the metaphor of digestion in *katepépsēi* is associated with *khólos*.[9] One implication of this association is that *khólos* has a special relation to corporeal experience. G. Kirk suggests that the notion of "ripening" or "cooking" or "digestion" is specifically related to Homer's Achilles. I agree, but need to add that this passage and Calchas's description indicates that *khólos* has relevance to the body beyond the thematics of the anger of Achilles.[10] In Chapter 11 of this book, I will suggest that the use of digestion can be motivated, as Calchas indicates, by a consideration of the etymology of *khólos*. For the present purpose of analyzing *kótos*, I note only that the metaphor of digestion exclusively calls to mind the anger that Calchas styles *khólos*.

Calchas has introduced these terms in such a way that *kótos* is a marked term in contrast to *khólos*, the unmarked term.[11] That is to say, Calchas presents us with an opposition that points to an asymmetric relationship between the two terms. The questions we have to pose ourselves are these: When we take Calchas as our informant, does the Homeric text allow us to say that this opposition is consistently asymmetric in a way that is productive for the poetic system? Is *khólos* unmarked with respect to the marked term *kótos*?

The notion of an asymmetrical contrast—a marked/unmarked opposition—between *khólos* and *kótos* directs us to the Homeric semantics of anger so that we can approach that topic with a specific goal in mind. Just how do these terms contrast, and how does Calchas's formulation fit with the contrasts that we unearth? For *kótos*, Calchas suggests that we regard this term as an especially delimited semantic unit, one whose major features include issues of class, the body, and time. As for *khólos*, in Part II I will attempt both to sketch its role as the unmarked term for anger—the most generic item in the rich epic vocabulary of anger—and to argue that the features of *khólos* have particular and dramatic importance for the Homeric poems.

One of the asymmetric features distinguishing the opposition between marked and unmarked forms is frequency of distribution: "The one of the two entities that is consistently more widely distributed . . . is called unmarked."[12] This observation is relevant to the study of these two terms for anger, since in the case of Calchas's definition we see that *khólos* and *kótos* differ in frequency of use, with *khólos* and its related forms occurring 138 times, while *kótos* and related forms show 27 instances throughout the two Homeric epics.

Having accepted Calchas as our informant and having interrogated his statement, I now seek independent support of his definition for each term. To justify taking this approach, to accept Calchas's lead, I briefly turn to a few passages that emphasize the distinctive nature of *kótos* and *khólos*.

To suggest that *kótos* is as important as Calchas indicates, I ask if there is any other similar characterization of *kótos*, perhaps one that also flags key terms such as *télos* in order to point to longevity as a feature of *kótos*. We see these features in *Iliad* 4, when Pandarus, spurred on by Athena, shoots and wounds Menelaus. At the sight of Menelaus's wound, Agamemnon launches into a chilling speech that refers to the anger of Zeus against the Trojans, especially because the oath that marked the duel in Book 3 has been violated:

<u>ἔσσεται ἦμαρ</u>, ὅτ' ἄν ποτ' ὀλώλῃ Ἴλιος ἱρὴ
καὶ Πρίαμος καὶ λαὸς ἐυμμελίω Πριάμοιο,
Ζεὺς δέ σφιν Κρονίδης ὑψίζυγος, αἰθέρι ναίων,
αὐτὸς ἐπισσείῃσιν ἐρεμνὴν αἰγίδα πᾶσι
<u>τῆσδ' ἀπάτης κοτέων· τὰ μὲν ἔσσεται οὐκ ἀτέλεστα</u>.
(*Il.* 4.164–68)

<u>There will come a day</u> when holy Ilium will perish and Priam and the people of spear-skilled Priam, and Zeus, the son of Kronos, ruler-on-high, dweller in the sky, he himself will shake the dark aegis over them, all of them, <u>having *kótos* over this deception; now these things will be accomplished</u>.

This is the only place in the *Iliad* where Zeus is explicitly said to have *kótos* against the Trojans, although we will also see a simile that continues the theme in the *Patrocleia.*[13] It is worth elucidating what the *kótos* of the chief god means here.[14]

The duel between Paris and Menelaus alludes to the beginning of the war.[15] Without doubt, the meaning of this duel is deepened because of the allusion to the ingrained enmity between Paris and Menelaus. The profound taboo against violating oaths is made all the worse by the *apátē*, the deceit, that has come to mirror the original crime. Homer's allusion to the abduction of Helen appears the more prominent through the use of this highly charged word for anger. *Kótos*, even as it focuses the allusion to a past event, also points to the anger that will be fulfilled *in the future*, as marked by the repeated word *éssetai* ("it will be"). Behind this scene, at this moment, is the violation of the oath and what that violation mirrors, the anger of Zeus Xeinios at the Trojans for Helen's abduction. The passage itself is a five-line unit ringed by the future *éssetai* and closed by a word whose root reminds us of what Calchas had earlier highlighted as a characteristic of *kótos: a-tél-esta*. Agamemnon's formulation is in Homeric grand style, with Zeus at the center of a ring bounded by characteristic features of *kótos*, the whole structure showing that *kótos* is rooted in past events and that its future is projected onto a chain of recorded human events.

The issue of *télos* and its relation to Agamemnon's speech shows its character even more clearly when we consider D. Lohmann's analysis,[16] which links *Il.* 14.166–68 with *Il.* 14.160–61 through ring-composition. The following lines emerge with striking force:

εἴ περ γάρ τε καὶ <u>αὐτίκ'</u> Ὀλύμπιος οὐκ <u>ἐτέλεσσεν</u>,
ἔκ τε καὶ ὀψὲ <u>τελεῖ</u>, σύν τε μεγάλῳ ἀπέτισαν,
σὺν σφῇσιν κεφαλῇσι γυναιξί τε καὶ τεκέεσσιν.
(*Il.* 4.160–62)

If in fact the Olympian <u>has not immediately accomplished this</u>, he will <u>finish</u> it though later, and they will make great restitution, with their own lives, their wives, and their children.

In these words, Agamemnon is presenting an eschatology of the Trojan conflict; as Menelaus lies wounded, his brother wonders at the outcome of it all, and his conclusion is that the violation of the oath guarantees Olympian favor so as to link the result with the *kótos* of Zeus.

Having looked at Agamemnon's speech and affirmed that Calchas, as informant, has alerted us to a feature of Homeric anger that is worth pursuing, let us again look to the same speech, where Agamemnon uses the word *khólos*, and see if it too supports our informant's data. Near the end of his speech after the wounding of Menelaus, Agamemnon, with a continued focus on *télos*, shifts attention to his own situation—what will his *kléos* look like if the boast (*eukhōlḗn, Il.* 4.173) is given to the Trojans? Indeed, he imagines quite the opposite of his confident assertion about Zeus's *kótos*; he calls to mind a vision of mocking Trojans dancing on Menelaus's grave:

> καί κέ τις ὧδ' ἐρέει Τρώων ὑπερηνορεόντων
> τύμβῳ ἐπιθρώσκων Μενελάου κυδαλίμοιο·
> "αἴθ' οὕτως ἐπὶ πᾶσι χόλον τελέσει' Ἀγαμέμνων,
> ὡς καὶ νῦν ἅλιον στρατὸν ἤγαγεν ἐνθάδ' Ἀχαιῶν,
> καὶ δὴ ἔβη οἶκόνδε φίλην ἐς πατρίδα γαῖαν
> σὺν κεινῇσιν νηυσί, λιπὼν ἀγαθὸν Μενέλαον."
> (*Il.* 4.176–81)

And one of the haughty Trojans thus would say, dancing on the grave of glorious Menelaus: "Would that Agamemnon thus accomplish his *khólos* against all, even as he has now vainly led the Achaean army here, and indeed he has left for home to his own fatherland with empty ships, having lost good Menelaus."

An observer might well want to interrogate the narrative here by asking a pointed question: Isn't *kótos* the anger related to *télos*? Why does Agamemnon imagine Trojans styling the anger of the leader of the expedition as a *khólos* that is to be brought to an end by Agamemnon? To follow Calchas's definition in this regard, I begin by contrasting the first part of Agamemnon's speech with the second.[17] In the first part, the major emphases are on oaths, deceit, and Zeus's exercise of retributive power. In the second part, the emphasis shifts to the boast of the victor (*eukhōlḗn, Il.* 4.173) and to the death of individual warriors (*túmbōi . . . Meneláou, Il.* 4.177); further, in the first part, Zeus keeps oaths from being made in vain (*hálion, Il.* 4.158), but later the text turns to the vanity of the siege itself (*hōs kaì nûn hálion stratòn ḗgagen, Il.* 4.179). With this structure in mind, we are invited to see the anger of the king, in the words of his disgruntled army, not as the high *kótos* of the king but rather as the mundane *khólos* of an enraged leader, so ineffectual that he steers his wrath to only a feeble end frustrating the entire endeavor and costing his brother's life.[18]

The interpretation of the anger terms in Agamemnon's speech depends on an understanding of the cultural oppositions as presented by Calchas still earlier in the text. Calchas's earnest speech is highly programmatic: the system of Homeric anger terms that he presents is not to be taken lightly. For, the *Iliad* is centered on *mênis*, and the meaning of anger terms not only is highlighted at the outset of the narrative but has also been contrasted during the momentous duel of Menelaus and Paris.

The meaning of *kótos* in our next passage seems in harmony with the meaning gleaned from the passages already discussed. In fact, echoes of Agamemnon's words reverberate in Book 5, when Aeneas tries to reassure Pandarus and inspire him to fire at Diomedes, who has only just begun his *aristeía*. Not only does this scene contain *kótos*, but it also brings *kótos* and *mênis* into close proximity:

> ἀλλ᾽ ἄγε τῷδ᾽ ἔφες ἀνδρὶ βέλος, Διὶ χεῖρας ἀνασχών,
> ὅς τις ὅδε κρατέει καὶ δὴ κακὰ πολλὰ ἔοργε
> Τρῶας, ἐπεὶ πολλῶν τε καὶ ἐσθλῶν γούνατ᾽ ἔλυσεν·
> εἰ μή τις θεός ἐστι <u>κοτεσσάμενος</u> Τρώεσσιν
> ἱρῶν <u>μηνίσας</u>· χαλεπὴ δὲ θεοῦ ἔπι <u>μῆνις</u>.
> (*Il.* 5.174–78)

> But come, and with your hands outstretched to Zeus, shoot your arrow at the man who has control and is doing many evils against the Trojans, because he has loosed the limbs of many and good [warriors]; unless he is some god with <u>*kótos*</u> against the Trojans, with <u>*mênis*</u> over holy things; difficult is the <u>*mênis*</u> of a god.

In encouraging Pandarus to take a shot at the leader of the Achaeans, Aeneas mounts the only possible counterargument against Pandarus's skill as a bowman, namely, that if Diomedes is a god with *kótos*, then a bowshot is useless. To paraphrase Calchas, a god in *kótos* will be so until the *télos* is reached. Ironically, Aeneas assures Pandarus that he should take a shot at the Achaeans' leader, not only on the grounds that Pandarus is a superior archer (*Il.* 5.171–73) but also because no god's *kótos* is at issue at Troy. For Aeneas, a god's *kótos* seems a remote possibility, and he does not conceive of Diomedes in his battle-fury as a god with either *kótos* or *mênis.* While he may be correct to think that *kótos* is remote, there is a narrative gesture toward the destruction of Troy, which in the view of the *Iliad*'s narrator involves the *kótos* of a god.[19]

To return to the issue of the future and *kótos*, a particular focus of Calchas's definition, I note that at least two other passages explicitly refer to the longevity of *kótos*. The first example is from the *Odyssey*:

> οὕτω νῦν ἀπόπεμπε, Διὸς δ᾽ ἐποπίζεο μῆνιν,
> μή πώς τοι <u>μετόπισθε κοτεσσάμενος</u> χαλεπήνῃ.
> (*Od.* 5.146–47)

> Thus now give him escort, and shrink from incurring the *mênis* of Zeus, lest he come <u>in the future to have *kótos*</u> and become enraged against you.

Here, when Hermes warns Calypso, three other anger terms (*mênis, khalepaínō,* and more elusively, *ópis*) are also drawn into the semantic mix,[20] but the future occasion of anger is based on the concept of *kótos*. Thus, Hermes validates Calchas's special fear of *kótos* with the aorist participle *kotessámenos* having a causal force: "because he has come to have anger (*kótos*), beware lest he take it ill in the future" (the subjunctive *khalepḗnēi* pointing toward the future). Hermes appears to counsel Calypso not to engage in a grudging or feuding relationship with Zeus.[21] In this case, *metópisthe,* along with the future orientation of the subjunctive, takes over the duties belonging to the notion of *télos*.

Kótos also refers to a future potential anger in the only passage where the anger of Achilles is called *kótos*. Agamemnon claims extravagantly that he is not frightened of Achilles' *kótos*; he imagines an extreme case in which the wrath of the Phthian king can be dismissed with a wave of the hand:

> οἴκαδ' ἰὼν σὺν νηυσί τε σῇς καὶ σοῖς ἑτάροισι
> Μυρμιδόνεσσιν <u>ἄνασσε</u>, σέθεν δ' ἐγὼ οὐκ ἀλεγίζω,
> <u>οὐδ' ὄθομαι κοτέοντος</u>.
> (*Il.* 1.179–81)

> Go home with your ships and your companions, and <u>rule</u> over the Myrmidons, but I won't care about you, <u>nor do I have concern for your *kótos*</u>.

The power of Agamemnon's insult here stands out when set beside Calchas's definition, where *kótos* is styled both as the anger of a *basileús* and as the wrath that can be serious trouble in the future. The wrath of a king can involve the entire social body (e.g., the Myrmidons, *Il.* 1.180), and as *his* particular anger it can cross space and time to exact its vengeance. Furthermore, the notion of the length of time implies both that *kótos* endures, and, more important, that it may have as its source something outside the immediate narrative context, projected either back into the distant past or forward into the distant future; here, for example, Agamemnon dismisses a possible *kótos* from Achilles so as to present an extreme and limiting case, where the anger of grudge, extensive over time, might make the situation extremely volatile so as to be worthy of the worry that Calchas assigned to *kótos* in *Iliad* 1.

I am developing a sense of *kótos* that locates it in a world beyond the immediate narrative context. Agamemnon, for example, styles Zeus's wrath over the Trojans, the wrath that will mean the death of all Trojans, as *kótos*, and Aeneas has linked *kótos* with *mênis*; finally, Agamemnon imagines Achilles' *kótos* in Phthia. To conclude my preliminary observations about *kótos*, I suggest that this word typically draws attention to something that the narrative thematizes as significant on a large scale, such as the end of the Trojan war, the anger of

Achilles as king, or the like. This suggestion can be strikingly supported from the next passage, *Il.* 13.516–17 (quoted below).

By presenting *kótos* in a battle context, this passage poses a problem with regard to Calchas's assertion that *kótos* is opposed to *khólos*. For this opposition depends in large part on the longevity of *kótos* and its source outside the events of the primary narrative context. In contrast, *khólos* can signify battle-fury in particular, so that it need last only the length of a battle or of a war, or for the duration of the emotional state of a warrior subject to *khólos*. Furthermore, *khólos* can come as a response to an attack, or conversely it can initiate an attack. Finally, this kind of anger can be kindled by taunts or other speech acts that can lead directly to the violence of battle.

Thus the use of *kótos* in a battle context should give us pause. For contextual reasons scholars have been tempted to interpret *kótos* in *Il.* 13.517 as if it were synonymous with *khólos*; nevertheless, the passage also gives us the formula *emmenès aieí* that corroborates the notion that *kótos* is distinguished by its duration over time. Were *kótos* indeed so close in meaning to *khólos*, then the distinction that Calchas drew in *Iliad* 1 would seem rather less definitive than we thought.[22]

In this passage, Aeneas and Idomeneus are attacking one another; Aeneas launches his spear at Idomeneus, and Idomeneus avoids it (*Il.* 13.503). Idomeneus in turn hits Oenomaus (*Il.* 13.506) and kills him, after which he retrieves his spear but is not able to remove the armor of Oenomaus. Then Deiphobus, while Idomeneus barely holds his own in his gradual retreat, takes a shot at him:

> τοῦ δὲ βάδην ἀπιόντος ἀκόντισε δουρὶ φαεινῷ
> Δηίφοβος· <u>δὴ γάρ οἱ ἔχεν κότον ἐμμενὲς αἰεί</u>.
> (*Il.* 13.516–17)

> With glistening spear Deiphobus took a shot at [Idomeneus] as he gradually stepped back; <u>for, yes, he held *kótos* against him, steadfast, unending</u>.

The first point of note is that *khólos* never occurs with the phrase *emmenès aieí*. Second, most scholars have interpreted this passage so that *kótos* is provoked by the death, earlier in the book, of other warriors, especially that of Asius at *Il.* 13.387–416. Although it is possible to relate a warrior's fury to an earlier death in the same book, another interpretation, one rather more compatible with Calchas's definition and with the sense of *emmenès aieí*, is readily available. Indeed, *kótos* occurs in an explanatory *gár* clause referring to an old legend, one cited later in the scholia. At lines 516–17, the scholiast comments on *kótos*:

> {τοῦ δὲ βάδην ἀπιόντος} ἀκόντισε {δουρὶ φαεινῷ/} Δηΐφοβος· {δὴ γάρ οἱ ἔχεν κότον ἐμμενὲς αἰεί}: <u>ὡς ἀντεραστὴς Ἑλένης</u>, ὡς μαρτυρεῖ Ἴβυκος καὶ Σιμωνίδης.
> (Schol. T Hom. *Il.* 13.516–517)

> "Deiphobus {as he gradually stepped back} shot at him {with his shining spear}," because he was a rival for Helen's love, as Ibycus notes, and Simonides.

Here the source for anger is the rivalry of Helen's suitors, an interpretation also cited by Eustathius:

> Ἕτεροι δὲ ἀκολουθοῦντες τῇ Σιμωνίδου καὶ Ἰβύκου ἱστωρίᾳ φασίν, ὡς ἀληθῶς ἀεὶ ἐνεκότει τῷ Ἰδομενεῖ Δηΐφοβος ὡς ἀντεραστῇ. ἤρα γάρ, φασί, καὶ αὐτὸς τῆς Ἑλένης.
>
> (Eustathius 944.43)

> But others, following the account of Simonides and Ibycus, suggest that truly Deiphobus always had *kótos* against Idomeneus, because he was a rival in love. For, they suggest, he too loved Helen.

Unfortunately, our most ancient authority also suggests that those who propose that Helen loved Idomeneus must be wrong, since he was an old man. Eustathius evinces a more sophisticated sense of Helen's taste in men than does the scholiast. With Eustathius, I take *kótos* here as referring to this tradition. Thus, when Idomeneus and Deiphobus meet on the battlefield, an old rivalry can flare up, just as in *Iliad* 6 an old friendship can be rekindled between Glaucus and Diomedes.[23]

Kótos, then, refers to a long-term anger outside the immediate battle's context, an anger such as that spurred by the ancient rivalry for Helen as bride. Such an anger can be motivated by the strife over Helen, a central source for Iliadic *kótos*.

Having thus laid the groundwork for Part I by reviewing a few telling passages in the light of Calchas's definition, I now turn to the formal process of understanding *kótos*. Following the method I described earlier, I will group the examples in a way that begins with formal regularity at the level of the word and then moves toward larger units. To recapitulate briefly, by proceeding from formal to contextual matters we move from more simple to more complex units, thereby pointing to regularities in form prior to establishing oral-literary features. Thus, in Chapter 2, after a look at grammatical forms, I turn to phraseological patterning and other formal structures. The discussion will continue with a close reading of selected narrative contexts that emerge as significant from the formal observations. These narrative contexts will be chosen especially in order to explore the validity of Calchas's definition of *kótos*.

Notes

1. The entire speech topicalizes anger: *mênin Apóllōnos* (75; cf. 64: *ekhṓsato Phoîbos Apóllōn*); *khṓsetai* (80); with *kholōsémen* (78); *khólon* (81); *kóton* (82).

2. With *ándra* the object of the transitive *kholōsémen*, cf. Kirk 1985 at *Il.* 1.78 and see *Il.* 18.111, *Od.* 8.205, and *Od.* 18.20.

3. The notion of two kinds of anger is reminiscent of Hesiod's division of the kinds of *éris* (*Works and Days* 11–12), on which see Gagarin 1990, Nagler 1988 and 1992. On the notion of bipolarity in Greek culture, see Lloyd 1971, with Homeric applications relevant to this context at 183–90.

4. The status of Achilles and Agamemnon relative to *krátos* ("power") is at issue throughout the quarrel. See *Il.* 1.280, where Achilles' *krátos* is compared with Agamemnon's; and in the subsequent speech Agamemnon assures the Achaeans that Achilles' *krátos* is not powerful enough to persuade others.

5. Note that Calchas's definition uses more terms to define *kótos* than *khólos*. He is clearly at pains to describe the term for which he needs Achilles' protection.

6. Issues surrounding kingship are complex (cf. Morris 1986, 98–102, for example), but my argument only need accept a relative hierarchy between the *basileús* and a man ranked lower on the social scale.

7. That *khólos* is the unmarked term for anger (see note 10) indicates that it cuts across social class. Thus both the lesser man and the king are capable of *khólos*. The unmarked term need not be specified at every point in Calchas's definition. See note 11.

8. The issue of class, status, kingship, and the like is vexed; see Rihll 1986; Finley 1977; Donlan 1982; Morris 1986; Posner 1979, 33–35. The words of Calchas need imply only the most basic differentiation, the leaders and the led, the powerful and those deprived of power, or the like; still, Calchas's formulation may fit a more complex social formation. For our present purpose, we need to keep in mind that anger may be differentiated by the place on the social hierarchy that the angered party occupies. See Nagy 1990a,, 153–68, on this aspect of wealth and power in archaic Greece and note the special place of the *mántis* as "middle man" (163).

9. See above. The metaphorical nature of this term will be explored in Part II.

10. Kirk 1985, 4.513.

11. On the notion of markedness as useful to Homeric studies, see Nagy 1990a, 5–8; cf. Martin 1989, 29–30. For a valuable overview of markedness theory, see Moravcsik and Wirth 1986. On the importance of the Prague School for literary studies, see, for example, the collection by Garvin 1964.

12. Moravcsik and Wirth 1986, 3.

13. See the simile at *Il.* 16.384–93.

14. On the structure of this speech, see Lohmann 1970, 43–44.

15. Leaf 1886, 87.

16. Lohmann 1970, 43–44.

17. Cf. again Lohmann (1970, 43–47) who divides the speech into two parts (I: 155–70, "Klage um Menelaos und Rache für den Eidbruch"; and II: 171–82, "Klage über die eigene Schande").

18. Note that this passage contrasts an immediate possibility with a future fulfillment in diction close in form to Calchas's definition: *eí per gár te . . . kaì autē̂mar* in *Il.* 1.81 is directly comparable *eí per gár te . . . kaì autík'* in *Il.* 4.160, while (*Il.* 1.82)

allá te kaì metópisthen ekhei kóton, óphra telésseī is an expanded variation of *ék te kaì opsè teleî* (*Il.* 4.161).

19. See Muellner 1996, 48–49 for an example of divine *mênis* in this kind of context. On *kótos* and the destruction of a culture, see *Il.* 16.384–92.

20. See the preliminary discussion in Watkins 1977a and Muellner 1992; the definitive formulation is now in Muellner 1996, 18–19, 193.

21. On *kótos* and the notion of feud, see Chapter 5.

22. See Leaf 1886 ad loc., as discussed below. Janko 1992 at *Il.* 13.517, "As is shown by *emmenès aieí* (5x in Homer), a *kótos* is a grudge, more lasting than *khólos,* but its cause lies within the present battle."

23. As *kótos* is related to the notion of the feud, it is the negative counterpart to the positive concept of *xenía*, or "guest-friendship." Both negative and positive terms serve to make a society cohesive, as in the theory of Black-Michaud 1975. See also Seaford 1994 for considerations of the relationship between cycles of vengeance and those of reciprocity (for example, 204–5).

Chapter Two

Forms and Formulae

Kótos in Its Noun Forms

The formal details concerning the noun *kótos* are straightforward. The substantive *kótos* is attested six times in the *Iliad* and the *Odyssey*, each time in the accusative case.[1] Each of these instances occurs at the hephthemimeral caesura, in other words, always in the second hemistich of the verse and preceding the bucolic diaeresis. This particular placement of *kótos* is in accord with a well-known feature of formulaic style, namely that word end is typically found in this verse position.[2] These citations avoid the other positions in which a word shaped ˘˘ can be found.[3] I exclude from this set of instances the only other form of the noun found in our manuscripts of Homer, the dative singular at *Il.* 14.111:[4]

πείθεσθαι, καὶ μή τι κότῳ ἀγάσησθε ἕκαστος.

This line is anomalous with respect to Calchas's definition. Besides presenting the only place in Homer where a form of *kótos* other than the accusative occurs, this is also one of the few places where the manuscript tradition gives the editor a choice of readings between *khólos* and *kótos*. For now I note that for *Il.* 14.111, few editors concern themselves with the question of whether *khólōi* is to be preferred to *kótōi*. From the point of view of frequency of use, *kótōi* seems to be the *lectio difficilior*. But, as I will show, Calchas's definition provides a better solution for this textual problem. For, though *khólos* is often used to signify the particular kind of anger that is caused by offensive speech, *kótos* is never so used. The reading most consistent with Homeric style in the *Iliad* and the *Odyssey* is *khólōi*. Indeed, Eustathius reads *khólōi*, which suggests that he had a clear understanding of the difference between these two forms of anger.

There are significant grammatical and phraseological features to be observed with reference to the noun *kótos* in the accusative case. For ease of reference, I reproduce below the lines in which these forms appear (as presented in Appendix 1):

Group 1

Il. 8.449 ὀλλῦσαι Τρῶας, τοῖσιν κότον αἰνὸν ἔθεσθε
Il. 16.449 υἱέες ἀθανάτων, τοῖσιν κότον αἰνὸν ἐνήσεις
Od. 11.102 λήσειν ἐννοσίγαιον, ὅ τοι κότον ἔνθετο θυμῷ
Od. 13.342 πατροκασιγνήτῳ, ὅς τοι κότον ἔνθετο θυμῷ

Group 2

Il. 1.82 ἀλλά τε καὶ μετόπισθεν ἔχει κότον, ὄφρα τελέσσῃ
Il. 13.517 Δηίφοβος· δὴ γάρ οἱ ἔχεν κότον ἐμμενὲς αἰεί

From these lines emerge the following features relating to the verse syntax of *kótos*.

A. In Groups 1 and 2, the dative object of the verb governing *kótos* explicitly points to the object of anger (*toîsin*, *hoi*, *toi*), except in Calchas's definition (*Il.* 1.82), where tact or fear suppresses the implicit object (*moi*) of the *kótos* of the *basileús* ("king"). (See point *B* below.)

B. In each of the lines in both Groups 1 and 2, the figure who is either the subject or the object of anger is specifically named: *Trôas*, *huiées athanátōn*, *ennosígaion*, *patrokasignḗtōi*, *Dēíphobos*. Calchas's definition (*Il.* 1.80–84) emerges as the one exception to this formal tendency. So as to avoid mentioning his own role in the matter, Calchas has deliberately put his words in a general form and deletes his own name. In this case, as in point *A* above, the exception is motivated by the rhetorical context, a feature highlighted by the way that the poet fills out the line with particles and an adverb. The formulaic anomaly is thus a product of narrative rhetoric. This point is important, since modern readers are often inclined to see either Calchas or Achilles or both as deliberately provoking Agamemnon. In this passage, Calchas tries to avoid angering Agamemnon by suppressing the name of the subject and object of *kótos*.

C. In Group 1, a verb whose subject is the agent instigating the *kótos* (*éthesthe*, *enḗseis*, *éntheto*) occurs in the cadence of the verse. The common element in Group 2 is the verb *ékhō* introducing a phrase that highlights the extraordinary durative power of *kótos* (*óphra telésseī*). The verb *ékhō* expresses having *kótos* and thereby marks its stative force,[5] in which case the subject and object, when expressed, regularly occur in the segment of the line before *kótos*. The verbs used with *kótos*, then, are *ékhō*,[6] *títhēmi*, and *híēmi*.

D. Group 1 has a dative object placed immediately before *kóton*, the main verb occurring immediately thereafter.

E. Group 2 is subjective, because its focus is on the person who has *kótos*; and Group 1 is objective, because its focus is on the entity against whom *kótos* is directed.

F. Each line in Group 1 involves the *kótos* that a god is "placing on" (with forms of *títhēmi*) or "inspiring in" (cf. Cunliffe on *enhíēmi* with the dative) a mortal or mortals, while in Group 2 the *kótos* is that of mortal against mortal.

Discussion of Phrases Based on the Noun

In my consideration of the formulaic contexts for the substantive *kótos*, I continue to focus on the way in which the various examples support or fail to support the features that Calchas associates with *kótos* in *Il.* 1.74–83.

Κότος + αινός

The epithet *ainós* occurs with *kótos* twice (Group 1). *Ainós*, which may modify other nouns besides *kótos*,[7] such as *phúlopis* ("battle tumult") and *dēiotḗs* ("slaughter"), has a special function in the context of battle.[8]

Given the prevalence of *ainós* with these highly charged words relating to war, is there anything that can be said about the two occurrences of *kóton ainón*? In her discussion of *ákhos*, F. Mawet (1979, 316) says that "l'épithète caractéristique d'*ákhos* est *ainón*. . . . Cette adjectif confère aux substantifs qu'il qualifie un aspect d'épouvante et d'horreur." Can her observations cast light on the use of *ainós* with *kótos*? This question is in part methodological, so I turn to a point of method beyond the lexicography of single words:

> When a poet's units of expression are not single words but metrically fixed groups of words, and when these groups of words have existed before him in a tradition, any single word has maintained or acquired in time a sense which is more rigid, resonant, and intricate than it might be for a poet who lacks such a medium.
>
> (Muellner 1976, 15)

Since a method that studies groups of words may best account for the way that formulae behave, I look to the way that *ainós* and *kótos* interact. Moreover since the epithet *ainós* is shared by *khólos* and *kótos*,[9] its use further tests Calchas's clear distinction between these two anger terms. Is there a significant relationship between *kótos* and *ainós*?

In the first instance, Hera and Athena are being chided by Zeus for pursuing their violence against the Trojans, a violence rooted in *kótos*:

> τίφθ' οὕτω τετίησθον, Ἀθηναίη τε καὶ Ἥρη;
> οὐ μέν θην κάμετόν γε μάχῃ ἔνι κυδιανείρῃ
> ὀλλῦσαι Τρῶας, τοῖσιν <u>κότον αἰνὸν</u> ἔθεσθε.
>
> (*Il.* 8.447–49)

> Then why are you two so upset, Athena and Hera? It can't be that you were worn out in the man-glorying battle, destroying Trojans, against whom you have set a terrible *kótos*.

Hera throws this phrase back at Zeus in Book 16, when she compels him to abandon Sarpedon:

> πολλοὶ γὰρ περὶ ἄστυ μέγα Πριάμοιο μάχονται
> υἱέες ἀθανάτων, τοῖσιν κότον αἰνὸν ἐνήσεις.
> (*Il.* 16.448–49)

> Many are the sons of the immortals in battle about the great city of Priam, against whom you will incite terrible *kótos*.

In each of these passages, the speaker sets the *kótos* against the background of the actual fighting by referring to the battle itself (*mákhēi* in *Il.* 8.448 and *mákhontai* in *Il.* 16.448). And in each case *kótos* is used as a kind of argument that the battle itself is only the immediate environment within which the conflict is played out. *Kótos* is thus employed as Calchas used it in *Il.* 1.73–84, as a limiting term that puts the immediate context in perspective, a perspective that, in the light of Zeus's ironic criticism of Hera and Athena, refers to the origin of the war.[10]

Thus *kótos* is here related to the Trojan War not as effect to cause but as background to foreground. The war is the backdrop from which the rigors of *kótos* emerge. On the mortal level, Hera and Athena inspire a *kótos ainós* among the Trojans; and it is of further significance for Calchas's definition that Zeus alludes to the exhausting duration of the struggle: *ou mén thēn kámetón ge* (*Il.* 8.448). On the immortal level, Hera succeeds, in Book 16, in turning the tables on Zeus, when *kótos ainós* (*Il.* 16.449) comes to be a potential threat among the gods precisely because their sons fight in the Trojan War. But does grief motivate *kótos* here? No: *kótos* does not arise out of concern for death in battle. Indeed, Hera had already pointed out that Zeus's sentimental attachment to Sarpedon posed a serious threat to divine order:

> αἰνότατε Κρονίδη, ποῖον τὸν μῦθον ἔειπες.
> ἄνδρα θνητὸν ἐόντα, πάλαι πεπρωμένον αἴσῃ,
> ἂψ ἐθέλεις θανάτοιο δυσηχέος ἐξαναλῦσαι.
> (*Il.* 16.440–42)

> Most terrible [*ainótate*!] son of Kronos, what a word this is you speak! A man, being mortal, long since doomed by fate—that's whom you wish to save from thunderous death.

In speaking to Zeus, Hera most often addresses him with the vocative phrase *ainótate Kronídē* (6 times); only Hera uses this formula in speaking to Zeus.[11] In this case, given the threat that his concerns for Sarpedon have initiated, it is understandable that Zeus should be one possessed of *ainós* to the superlative degree. In Hera's assessment, the threat Zeus poses is to one of the basic aspects of fate: the time assigned for an individual's life, here indicated by an ancient formula (*pálai peprōménon aísēi*, *Il.* 16.441). In consequence, the gods, subject to fate as they are, would deeply resent Zeus's invoking of special privilege to save his darling.[12] I conclude that the association of *kótos* with *ainós* may suggest a formulaic linkage of the phrase's two elements (*kótos* and *ainós*) with matters that continue without interruption until they reach a *télos*. In other words, the formula *kóton ainón* is consistent with Calchas's definition.

I suggest, then, that we regard these two passages as supporting Calchas's definition. The long-lasting *kótos* presents us in Book 8 with a focal point for the long-standing conflict that is at the heart of the poem, namely the Trojan War. When Zeus contemplates saving Sarpedon, Hera's fear is that in so doing he will precipitate a feud among the gods.[13] *Ainós* points to the war itself through its formulaic connection with *phúlopis* and *dēiotḗs*, as well as with *ákhos*.[14] Later, it becomes clear that *kótos* bears directly on the central issues of the Trojan War.

Κότος + ἔχω

In Appendix 1, Group 2, *Il.* 1.82 and *Il.* 13.517 (also cited above) suggest, especially in the light of Calchas's definition, that *kótos* has characteristically an extended power of duration. This observation is consistent with the use of the verb *ékhō* indicating the persistence of the state of anger. That *ékhō* has this function with *kótos* can be supported by glancing at Group 6 (in Appendix 1), where we find the phrase that the formula *kekotēóti thumôi* occurs four times.

In one of these four occurrenes, *Od.* 19.71, the phrase *kekotēóti thumôi* occurs with the verb *ékhō:*

> δαιμονίη, τί μοι ὧδ' <u>ἐπέχεις κεκοτηότι θυμῷ</u>;
>
> Mistress, why do you persist thus with a heart filled with *kótos*?

Here the preverb *epí* strengthens the notion of duration already present in *ékh-kóton*.[15] Note too that *epí* is used as a prefix to *kótos* in later Greek.[16] Thus, the verb *epékhō* reinforces the sense of duration that I am suggesting is at the heart of the formula *kekotēóti thumôi*.[17]

The duration of *kótos* emerges as an issue in both lines cited as Group 2 (*Il.* 1.82 and 13.517). Both these lines indicate explicitly that duration is a characteristic of *kótos*. The first line (*Il.* 1.82) is from Calchas's speech, where Calchas seems particularly worried about this kind of anger especially because it cannot be finished in a day's time, as I demonstrated through a discussion of *metópisthe* and *télos* (see my Introduction and Chapter 1). Because the second example (*Il.*

13.517) seems puzzling, it needs special treatment here. For, although that line points to the length of *kótos* (through *emmenès aieí*), the cause of that anger remains ambiguous in its immediate narrative context. To address this problem, I will first look at other passages where duration is explicitly put forward as a mark of *kótos*, and then return to *Il.* 13.517 so as to provide a solution to the problems it seems to pose.

Note that other occurrences of *kótos* include explicit statements of duration. For example,

> *Od.* 5.147 μή πώς τοι μετόπισθε κοτεσσάμενος χαλεπήνῃ
>
> . . . lest in the future he bear it ill against you because of κότος

where *metópisthe* recalls for us Calchas's definition. See also

> *Il.* 4.168 τῆσδ' ἀπάτης κοτέων· τὰ μὲν ἔσσεται οὐκ ἀτέλεστα
>
> . . . with *kótos* over this deceit; these things will not be unfulfilled

where the root *tel-* makes evident the importance of the future accomplishment, as did *teléssēi* in Calchas's definition.[18] As discussed in Chapter 1, in *Od.* 5.147, Hermes admonishes Calypso to send Odysseus away lest, in the future, the *kótos* of Zeus assert itself (*Od.* 5.146-47):

> οὕτω νῦν ἀπόπεμπε, Διὸς δ' ἐποπίζεο μῆνιν,
> μή πώς τοι μετόπισθε κοτεσσάμενος χαλεπήνῃ.
>
> Thus send him off, and revere the *mênis* of Zeus, lest in the future he bear it ill against you because of *kótos*.

Here, in a passage remarkable for its complex anger terminology,[19] the future occasion of anger is stressed, a feature of *kótos* verifying Calchas's special fear of it. In sum, these passages suggest that the use of *ékhō* with *kótos* is significant because it points to the longevity of the persistent wrath that is *kótos*.

Κότος + θυμός

In the last section, we looked at the formula *kekotēóti thumôi* in *Od.* 19.71 (the other attestations of this phrase occurring at *Il.* 21.456, *Od.* 9.501, and *Od.* 22.477). A review of the passages cited above in Group 1 (Appendix 1) also indicates that *kótos* is linked with *thumós* in the phrase *kóton éntheto thumôi* (*Od.* 11.102 and *Od.* 3.342). Indeed, there are other formulaic contexts in which *kótos* and *thumós* are related. For example, *kótos* is semantically linked to *thumós* in a phrase like (*Il.* 14.191) *ēé ken arnḗsaio kotessaménē tó ge thumôi* ("or would you deny [me] out of *kótos* in your heart").

In my view, *thumós* is not so implicated in the meaning of *kótos* as are *ainós* and *ékhō* discussed above. *Thumós*, when it signifies the location of an emotion, is too generic to be definitive for the meaning of *kótos*. There are, as it turns out, 7 lines that show *kótos* in close relation to *thumós* and 16 lines that show *khólos* in a similar relation.[20] I conclude that *thumós* is as comfortable with *khólos* as with *kótos*.[21] Interestingly, one of the rare cases in which our manuscript tradition shows *khólon* as an alternative reading for *kóton* (*Od.* 11.102) occurs in the formula *kóton éntheto thumôi* (used also in *Od.* 13.342) to be contrasted with *Il.* 6.321 where we see *khólon tónd' éntheo thumôi*. Given the kind of flexibility emerging in the use of *thúmos* with both of these terms for anger, it may be, as I will argue in Chapter 5, that the meaning of *kótos* has less to do with the psychological nature of emotion than it has to do with the social structure of human conflict.

Syntax, Context, and Meaning

I conclude my examination of Groups 1 and 2 by reviewing syntactic features of these lines that indicate the formulaic coherence of phrases involving *kótos*. For all the examples in Group 1, the entire section of the line after the caesura (including the *kótos* phrase) is a complete clause. Furthermore, with the exception of Calchas's line (*Il.* 1.82), all the lines in Groups 1 and 2 can be schematized in a way to show a formular style supported by the syntax:

{TARGET of *kótos* } + *kóton* + {PREDICATION}

Here the details that fill in the structure distinguish among the culturally important differences between gods and men: gods actively dispense *kótos* (as shown by the verbs *títhēmi* and *híēmi*), while mortals only hold or maintain it, as can be seen schematically in Table 2.1.

Table 2.1. Distinctions between mortals and gods in regards to *kótos*

	VERBS	TIME
GODS	τίθημι ἵημι	[no marker]
MORTALS	ἔχω	μετόπισθε ἐμμενὲς αἰεί

There is a significant difference in the operation of *kótos* depending on whether mortals or immortals are involved. For gods, lengthy duration is merely assumed, so there is no need for an explicit reference to time. Thus, that Hera and Athena, in Zeus's eyes, should be pursuing a relentless anger against the Trojans over a long period of time is understood.[22] This longevity certainly applies as well to the *kótos* of Poseidon in the *Odyssey*, which according to Teiresias will dog Odysseus throughout his return (*Od.* 11.102); and according to Athena (*Od.* 13.342), Poseidon's *kótos* against her favorite has been of great concern to her throughout the return of Odysseus.[23] In contrast to the situation of the gods, who need no marker of duration, for mortals the duration of *kótos* needs to be specified through the use of *ékhō* and adverbs signifying duration (*metópisthe, emmenès aieí*).

This examination of the formal and semantic alignments of *kótos* in the accusative case at the hephthemimeral caesura points to noun phrases consistent with crucial features of Calchas's definition. A formal analysis shows that *kótos* occurs only in the accusative case and always at the bucolic diaeresis. It is twice accompanied by *ainós* ("dread"). The subjective grouping, where the focus is on the person who has *kótos* rather than on the cause of *kótos,* characterizes *kótos* as something one "has" (*ékhein*), whereas the verbs describing the instilling of *kótos* by a god are verbs that mean "place" or "send forth."[24]

A number of features of these lines are consistent with Calchas's definition. First, Teiresias at *Od.* 11.102 indicates the anger of a superior (a god) against an inferior (a mortal), just as Calchas took pains to segregate the king's anger from that of an inferior man. Duration of *kótos* is highlighted in *Il.* 13.517, in accord with Calchas's concern that the king's anger will last beyond a day's time. In fact, this example, by referring us to rivalries between Helen's suitors, shows us that *kótos* can refer to events even beyond the limits of the current narrative. We will see that the limits can be extended even further, such as when Agamemnon points to Achilles' *kótos* only to locate it in the never-never land of a *nóstos* for Achilles (*Il.* 1.181).[25]

Each of these examples falls into line with Calchas's definition. First, the formula *emmenès aieí* shows that *kótos* is of extensive duration. Second, it is clear that *kótos* relates to hierarchy in a way that affects how power is represented in the narrative. Indeed, a god can oppose a mortal, as a king can oppose a commoner. Thus, Calchas's definition is paradigmatically extended, as might be expected, to include conflict between god and mortal as well as between a *basileús* ("king") and a man of lesser rank.[26]

At this juncture I resume the discussion of *Il.* 13.517 in order to help summarize the case I have made thus far for Calchas's definition of *kótos*. I proposed in Chapter 1, that, although the battle context of this scene seems to pose a problem for Calchas's meaning of *kótos* (in opposition to *khólos*), the longevity of *kótos* is quite appropriate to sworn rivals for Helen. That the formula *emmenès aieí* underscores the notion of anger's longevity can be strongly supported by considering the other passages that use this formula.[27]

In the following simile, for example, Odysseus and Diomedes are seen to press on relentlessly against Dolon:

ὡς δ' ὅτε καρχαρόδοντε δύω κύνε, εἰδότε θήρης,
ἢ κεμάδ' ἠὲ λαγωὸν ἐπείγετον <u>ἐμμενὲς αἰεὶ</u>

χῶρον ἀν' ὑλήενθ', ὁ δέ τε προθέῃσι μεμηκώς,
ὥς τὸν Τυδείδης ἠδ' ὁ πτολίπορθος Ὀδυσσεὺς
λαοῦ ἀποτμήξαντε διώκετον ἐμμενὲς αἰεί.
(*Il.* 10.360–64)

As when two sharp-toothed dogs, at the sight of prey—either a deer or a hare—press on *emmenès aiei* through the forested space, and it rushes ahead shrieking, thus did those two, Diomedes and city-sacking Odysseus, cut him off from the host and pursue him *emmenès aiei*.

Here the phrase *emmenès aieí* forcefully presents the characteristic tenacity of the hunting dogs; indeed, the phrase *emmenès aieí* ("steadfastly without ceasing") is embedded in both parts of the simile. This simile, like an ecphrastic tableau, presents the generic pursuit of prey by predator in order to visualize the pursuit of Dolon by the Achaeans. There is, we might say, something basic being claimed for the running down of Dolon. It is not merely that *aieí* conveys the force of "always," but that "always" conveys the notion of an innately predisposed activity. Even though the actual event is merely a single instance of pursuit during a hunt, the scene is presented as continual.[28]

A similar concern drives the use of the phrase *emmenès aieí* in the Cyclops episode of the *Odyssey*. Odysseus and his companions are turning the stake in Polyphemus's eye, when, through a simile, the narrative pictures the turning and pushing motion:

ὀφθαλμῷ ἐνέρεισαν· ἐγὼ δ' ἐφύπερθεν ἀερθεὶς
δίνεον, ὡς ὅτε τις τρυπῷ δόρυ νήιον ἀνὴρ
τρυπάνῳ, οἱ δέ τ' ἔνερθεν ὑποσσείουσιν ἱμάντι
ἀψάμενοι ἑκάτερθε, τὸ δὲ τρέχει ἐμμενὲς αἰεί.
(*Od.* 9.383–86)

They pushed [the stake] in the eye; but I lifted from above and turned it, as when a man pierces with an auger the ship's timber, and from beneath they whirl it around with a strap, laying hold of it on each side, and it revolves *emmenès aieí*.

The turning of the stake is presented as *emmenès aieí*, as an event in process, one that is continual and relentless. In this last passage, the particular turning motion of the *trúpanon* ("auger") may apply to the immediate action of the shipwright in the simile. But the generic force of the phrase works well here just as it does in the Dolon episode. The force of *emmenès aieí* is generic and produces an image of the drill running deeply forever into the timber.

My third example for this meaning of the phrase *emmenès aieí* ("steadfastly without ceasing") is from the *Odyssey*, when Penelope addresses the suitors in the following manner:

κέκλυτέ μευ, μνηστῆρες ἀγήνορες, οἳ τόδε δῶμα
ἐχράετ' ἐσθιέμεν καὶ πινέμεν ἐμμενὲς αἰεί. . . .
(*Od.* 21.68–69)

Hear me, suitors, manly ones, who have become so eager to eat and drink this home *emmenès aieí*. . . .[29]

The phrase clearly emphasizes in a striking way that the suitors have been extraordinarily persistent in their rapacity over many years' time. It is not merely that they consume Odysseus's store on this particular evening, but also that they have been comporting themselves in this way throughout his long absence. They pursue his wealth as predators, instinctively and without ceasing, pursue prey. Indeed, the predation of the suitors has a thematic relation to the *Odyssey*: their activity, like the violation of Menelaus's *oîkos* by Paris, is the founding event of the *Odyssey*'s narrative. It is in this sense that the suitors "ever relentlessly" eat and drink.

Summary

The phrase *emmenès aieí* points to the long-lasting nature of the action being described. Penelope's use of this phrase emphasizes the long-standing and relentless exploitation of her *oîkos* by the suitors. So too the Achaeans' pursuit of Dolon is magnified by the simile in which predator hunts down its prey in a vision rooted in nature. These examples corroborate the conclusion I came to above in Chapter 1, namely, that the *kótos* in *Il.* 13.517 specifically refers to just such a context of extensive duration, where that anger term highlights the extraordinary duration of the conflict between the rivals for Helen.

Kótos in its Verbal Forms: The Boundaries of the Aorist

The denominative verb based on *kótos* is far more prevalent than the noun.[30] Moreover, the aorist participle middle exhibits a formal regularity as strict as we have seen in the substantive. The sigmatic aorist forms derived from *kótos* tend to be clustered after the main caesura. As with the noun *kótos*, the verbal forms in the aorist show—in almost all cases—a dative object: *ándressi*, *toi*, *Trō̃essin* (twice), *toîsin*, *huîi*. In one case, the object is not expressed (*Il.* 14.191).

This last variation is easily explained by reference to its context, in which Hera attempts to persuade Aphrodite to help in the seduction of Zeus. As we saw in *Il.* 1.82, the scene exhorts pressure of a rhetorical kind to avoid naming in direct speech the individuals who may have grounds for *kótos*.[31] In *Il.* 1.82, Calchas avoids naming Agamemnon; in a similar fashion, Hera frames her reference to *kótos* by suppressing the *moi* ("to me") that would otherwise be the explicit object of Aphrodite's *kótos*. Within the formal confines of Homeric discourse, this passage shows the power of Homeric verbal artistry when it comes to managing rhetorical force.[32]

In Groups 3 and 4 of Appendix 1, the *kótos* phrase occupies the second half of the verse from the trochaic caesura to the end of the line. The formulaic system at work here suggests that these lines belong to a family of phrases in which the essential idea involves *kótos*.[33] Indeed, new advances in the study of Homeric diction promote the use of the notion of nucleus and periphery, through which we can style the *kótos*-phrase as the nucleus around which there are peripheral elements, identifying the circumstantial aspects of the anger.[34]

Like the nouns *kótos* and *khólos*, the aorist middle participial forms derived from the substantive are metrically identical. There is, however, little overlap in Homer with regard to the usage of these forms. Thus *kotessámenos/-ē* always occurs in O'Neill's position 9 in the hexameter, while *kholōsámenos/-ē* in its 15 occurrences in the *Iliad* and the *Odyssey* occurs 13 times in position 3,[35] and only twice in position 9.[36]

This phrase-family highlights *kótos* (Group 4) with select words or phrases (in *Od.* 5.147 and *Od.* 19.83, *khalepaínō*; in *Il.* 14.191, *tó ge thumôi*; in *Il.* 18.367, *kakà rhápsai*); note also the use of a god's epithet (*obrimopátrē*) or epithet and name (*Phoîbos Apóllōn*). Research on such patterns indicates that variation in the first half of the line is to be expected, since fixity of phrase is especially characteristic of the end of the line and flexibility of phrase is characteristic at the beginning of the line.[37]

Discussion of phrases

Khalepós and derivatives

The adjective *khalepós* and its verbal derivative *khalepaínō* are used with a variety of anger terms in Homer.[38] Watkins notes that the verbal form can have as its angered party either a mortal or an immortal but that *khalepós* is the epithet, within the *Iliad*, of *mênis* alone, and in the *Odyssey* it only once qualifies *khólos*. I hasten to add to Watkins's observations that *khalepós* never qualifies *kótos*. There is a distinction, then, between derived and basic forms because *kotessámenos khalepḗnēi* is a competent Homeric collocation although Homeric diction never uses *khalepós* to modify *kótos*.[39]

Is there anything special, then, to say about the relationship of *khalepaínō* to *kótos*? We have seen that the verb *khalepaínō* can be used with *mênis*, *kótos*, and *khólos*.[40] In fact, *kótos* and *ópis*, via *khalepós*, are formally linked in *Il.* 16.386, where Zeus's *kótos* determines the sorry fate of a group of people who have violated *thémis*. All the lines in this section, then, use *khalepaínō* as an unmarked term meaning "to grow angry, to be angry." The function of *kotessámenos / -ē* in these lines is to define the exact *kind* of anger the subject has come to have, and in so doing continue a basic distinction among words for anger. The function of *kótos* as a marked form turns out to be critical to understanding how it is used.

The adjective *khalepós* and its verbal derivative can link *kótos* and *mênis* through the rhetorical figure of the "universalizing doublet." In this case, the doublet encompasses two types of anger in complementary distribution. For now we can say, with Watkins (1977, 193), that *mênis* is "une notion dangereuse, qu'il faut craindre; une notion sacrale, 'numineuse' (*theôn*)."[41] As for *kótos*, its purview is more earthly because of its associations with violations on the culture's secular rather than sacral level.

This picture of anger should be expanded to include *ópis* and its derivatives that Watkins neatly correlates with *mênis*.[42] *Kótos* also occurs with *ópis* (another word for anger):

> ὅτε δὴ ἄνδρεσσι <u>κοτεσσάμενος χαλεπήνῃ</u>
> οἳ βίῃ εἰν ἀγορῇ σκολιὰς κρίνωσι θέμιστας,
> ἐκ δὲ δίκην ἐλάσωσι, <u>θεῶν ὄπιν</u> οὐκ ἀλέγοντες.
> (*Il.* 16.386–88)

> Since he [Zeus] <u>had *kótos* and came to be enraged</u> against the mortals who had made judgments violently in the community, crooked judgments, and because they drove out justice, and did not revere the <u>*opis* of the gods</u>.

Kótos and *ópis* serve here to underscore the severity of Zeus's wrath, precisely because of their relationship to terms such as *dikē*.[43] Compare this with Hermes' warning to Calypso that she must send Odysseus home or face the anger of Zeus:

> οὕτω νῦν ἀπόπεμπε, Διὸς δ' <u>ἐποπίζεο μῆνιν</u>,
> μή πώς τοι <u>μετόπισθε κοτεσσάμενος χαλεπήνῃ</u>.
> (*Od.* 5.146–47)

> Thus dispatch [him] now, and <u>revere the wrath</u> of Zeus, lest <u>in the future, out of *kótos*, he come to be angry</u>.

This passage seems almost distilled so as to contain the most ominous of Homeric words for anger (especially *ópis, mênis,* and *kótos*).[44] Hermes might well muster the strongest possible warning, since Calypso is hardly eager to send off Odysseus; she even makes excuses (*Od.* 5.140–43) and resents being cheated of her mortal pet (*Od.* 5.119). Hence he alerts her in detail about Zeus's anger down to what is according to Calchas (*Il.* 1.82) a chief defining characteristic of *kótos*, the matter of time: *metópisthe*.

Both passages show how the concept of anger is refined to a specific meaning through the use of marked terms to focus the thematic value of more generic words such as *khalepaínō*. In each of these cases, Zeus's *kótos* is thematized as the motivation causing him to "bear it ill" (*khalepaínō*). The second passage also alludes to Zeus's power but in a context where *kótos* plays a prominent part, a feature I will be examine closely in my analysis of the phrase *kekotēóti thumōi.*

A Whole Line Formula: *hērṓōn, toîsín te kotéssetai obrimopátrē*

Obrimopátrē is used exclusively as an epithet of Athena, although never with her name.[45] In the Homeric texts, each instance of the epithet occurs with an explicit reference to anger. This epithet suggests Athena's role as an angry god. In the nominative, the term occurs only in this whole-line formula and only with the verb *kotéssetai*. The other two examples of the epithet *obrimopátrē* referring to Athena are in the genitive case, and they both point, once again, to Athena's anger, which is not represented as *kótos* but, in the first instance (*Od.* 3.135), as *mênis*, and in the other instance, as *khólos* (*Od.* 24.540). In analyzing the meaning of *kotéssetai* in these passages, we will need to compare and contrast Athena's relationship to all three terms, *khólos, kótos,* and *mênis*.

The repeated phrase *kotéssetai obrimopátrē* occurs in arming scenes where Athena has just taken up her spear, with the form *kotéssetai* focussing the description of her spear through a specification of its function.[46] After putting her helmet on and climbing into her chariot, Athena takes up her spear just before Hera grabs the reins to drive the two goddesses to Zeus in order to persuade him that Ares should be stopped:

> ἐς δ' ὄχεα φλόγεα ποσὶ βήσετο, λάζετο δ' ἔγχος
> βριθὺ μέγα στιβαρόν, τῷ δάμνησι στίχας ἀνδρῶν
> ἡρώων, οἷσίν τε κοτέσσεται ὀβριμοπάτρη.
> Ἥρη δὲ μάστιγι θοῶς ἐπεμαίετ' ἄρ' ἵππους·
> αὐτόμαται δὲ πύλαι μύκον οὐρανοῦ, ἃς ἔχον Ὧραι,
> τῇς ἐπιτέτραπται μέγας οὐρανὸς Οὔλυμπός τε,
> ἠμὲν ἀνακλῖναι πυκινὸν νέφος ἠδ' ἐπιθεῖναι.
> τῇ ῥα δι' αὐτάων κεντρηνεκέας ἔχον ἵππους.
> (*Il.* 5.745–52 = *Il.* 8.389–96)

She climbed on the blazing chariot, and she took up the spear, heavy, great, massive; with it she subdues the ranks of men, of heroes, those against whom she, whose father is powerful, has *kótos*. And Hera quickly struck the horses with the whip. And the sky's doors creaked on their own, those maintained by the Horai, to whom are entrusted the great sky and Olympus, to open up the thick cloud or to close it again. And right through there they drove their goaded horses.

These lines occur in a doublet[47] each pointing to the *kótos* of Athena, but in neither case is it clear why this particular kind of anger is highlighted when Athena takes up her speech. Can it be that *kótos* belongs to the generic force of Athena in epic, every bit as much as her spear or her helmet?[48]

Yes, as can be seen from a pair of lines that themselves seem to be a unit:

βριθὺ μέγα στιβαρόν, τῷ δάμνησι στίχας ἀνδρῶν
ἡρώων, οἷσίν τε κοτέσσεται ὀβριμοπάτρη.

These lines in their balance and verbal artistry help us to go further into the sense of *obrimopátrē*. Note the repetition of initial syllables **sti***barón* and **stí***khas*, and the framing of the couplet by the repetition of the initial syllable *bri-* of **bri***thú* in *o***bri***mopátrē*,[49] in each case the symmetry being reinforced by the sequence *-ī-/-i-*. In other words, the structure of this couplet draws on the traditional convention of ring-composition, with the asyndetic string of adjectives and the resonance of *brithú* with *obrimo-* at the beginning and end of the structure.[50] Do these two lines have the earmarks of a ritual or cultic collocation signifying Athena?[51] In each of these cases (*Il.* 5.746–47, *Il.* 8.390, and cf. *Od.* 1.100), Athena's role as tamer of the ranks of men is pointed to by a generic statement,[52] signaled by the subjunctive and the gnomic *te*.[53] Furthermore, in neither case does the *kótos* referred to have an immediate referent in the narrative's context: in *Iliad* 5 Athena and Hera are angry at Ares, not at the *stíkhas andrôn*; and *Iliad* 8 emphasizes the goddesses' anger at Zeus, not at the Trojan mortals. Finally, in the beginning of the *Odyssey*, Athena's attempt to help Telemachus does not motivate her *kótos* in any direct sense.

Obrimopátrē constitutes a possessive compound whose meaning relates the goddess to Zeus as "she of the powerful father." Connections are suggested to a family of words containing *bri-*, although the initial *o-* poses difficulties for positing a direct link as does the length of the vowel.[54] The thematic relation of *brim-* to contexts of anger is made in Hesychius's gloss: *brimós· mégas, khalepós*[55] and even more in the gloss *brimaínetai*: *thumaínetai, orgízetai*. It may be significant that in each of the passages showing *obrimopátrē,* explicit reference is made to her father: in Book 5 of the *Iliad* she and Hera approach Zeus in order to persuade Ares to give up fighting in the mortals' battle; in Book 8, once again Hera and Aphrodite seek Zeus's intervention; finally at the very end of Book 24 of the *Odyssey*, she institutes, with the aid of Zeus's thunderbolt, the truce that marks the end of Odysseus's *nóstos* ("return").

Further, it is noteworthy that no immediate context is given for Athena's anger in the passages containing *kotéssetai.* The passages with *kótos* in Group 5 of Appendix 1 are unlike *Od.* 3.135, where the wrath of Athena is directed against the Achaeans and is styled *mênis*, and those passages are also different from the scene at the very end of the *Odyssey*, where Athena is herself not angry but is trying to end the enmity of the Ithacans in order thereby to quell the *khólos* of Zeus (*Od.* 24.544). Indeed, in this stylized passage, *khólos* clearly has no intrinsic *télos*: mortals are being asked to control the *khólos* of Zeus through the action of stopping their quarrel (*Od.* 24.542–43).[56] Our brief look at the epithet *obrimopátrē* shows how Homeric language and poetics functions to preserve ancient themes in the very process of making a narrative.

Before leaving the wrath of Athena, look more closely at the way that her *kótos* can be said to correspond with Calchas's definition. The passages from the *Iliad* are doublets in which Hera and Athena prepare to assist the Greeks, who are being routed by the Trojans in fulfillment of the *Diòs boulḗ* ("the plan of Zeus"). In the first passage Hera outfits the chariot (*Il.* 5.729–32); then Athena arms (*Il.* 5.733–47); finally, the arming scene is completed by her assumption of her *énkhos* described in this traditional couplet.[57] But why are the *stíkhas andrôn hērṓōn* deserving of her violence? Perhaps the answer lies in the meaning of *kótos*, which functions as the term for a long-term anger. In this case the reference is to the war at large. That the two goddesses are motivated by such a general concern is clear in the words of Hera, spoken just before the arming and the preparation of the chariot:

> ὢ πόποι, αἰγιόχοιο Διὸς τέκος Ἀτρυτώνη,
> ἦ ῥ' ἅλιον τὸν μῦθον ὑπέστημεν Μενελάῳ,
> Ἴλιον ἐκπέρσαντ' εὐτείχεον ἀπονέεσθαι,
> εἰ οὕτω μαίνεσθαι ἐάσομεν οὖλον Ἄρηα.
> (*Il.* 5.714–17)

> O, Atrutone, child of aegis-bearing Zeus, vain was that profound promise we made to Menelaus, that having sacked well-built Ilium we would return, seeing that we now let deadly Ares rage.

The promise (*hupéstēmen*) alluded to here was made in the form of a *mûthos*, a term Richard Martin has clearly shown refers to an authoritative speech-act by one in power.[58] So this promise by Hera and Athena to Menelaus is a serious matter, even though it is outside the immediate context; indeed, the content of the promise is succinctly phrased: they are to sack Troy (*Ílion ekpérsant' euteíkheon*) and to return home (*aponéesthai*), the effective reference of the pair of phrases being the *Iliad* and the *Odyssey* themselves.[59]

In summary, the promise to Menelaus functions as a cause of the two major Homeric traditions that culminate in our *Iliad* and *Odyssey*, so that this passage refers to a point near the outbreak of the war and the allegiances and promises made at the war's inception. If the promise is to be fulfilled, it will be at a level appropriate to *kótos*, an anger that temporally and geographically goes beyond any individual's local concerns. The doublet at *Il.* 8.391 has a similar value, where *kótos* refers to Athena's generic propensity to subdue human beings, also manifest in *Od.* 1.101, when she is about to visit Ithaca. For the moment, remember that the two Iliadic examples of this formula allude to the hatred of Athena and Hera for the Trojans. Once again, *kótos* refers to the roots of the basic conflict of the poems, the feud-like aggression that we call the Trojan War.

Let me return to the epithet of Athena used with *kótos*. Note that the epithet itself, *obrimopátrē*, is used in two other places in the *Odyssey*, each having to do with anger. The anger of Athena occurs significantly in Nestor's account of the failed *nóstos* that he tried to provide Odysseus and the others.[60] One of the causes of the failure is the *mênis* of Athena:

> τῶ σφεων πολέες κακὸν οἶτον ἐπέσπον
> μήνιος ἐξ ὀλοῆς γλαυκώπιδος ὀβριμοπάτρης,
> ἥ τ' ἔριν Ἀτρεΐδησιν μετ' ἀμφοτέροισιν ἔθηκε.
> (*Od.* 3.134–36)

> Many of them reached a horrible end because of the deadly *mênis* of the grey-eyed one whose father is powerful (*obrimopátrēs*), and she made strife between the Atreids.

This *mênis* is aimed at Oilean Ajax for raping Cassandra in Athena's sacred domain, so her wrath ends up providing a source of strife among the Atreids. In the *Odyssey*, Athena is called *obrimopátrē* ("she whose father is powerful") immediately as Zeus's lightning bolt falls at the feet of the contenders, the members of the house of Odysseus and the surviving relatives of the suitors:

> καὶ τότε δὴ Κρονίδης ἀφίει ψολόεντα κεραυνόν,
> κὰδ δ' ἔπεσε πρόσθε γλαυκώπιδος ὀβριμοπάτρης.
> (*Od.* 24.539–40)

> And then the son of Kronos cast off a smoldering bolt, and it fell at the feet of the grey-eyed one, whose father is powerful.

Here Athena's role as the "daughter of the powerful father" (*obrimopátrēs*) is highlighted because she has just, on her own, tried to squelch the battle between the two rival groups (*Od.* 24.529–35), but it takes the lightning bolt of Zeus to get Odysseus to back off, at which point Athena discloses that the real issue is the anger of Zeus:

> διογενὲς Λαερτιάδη, πολυμήχαν' Ὀδυσσεῦ,
> ἴσχεο, παῦε δὲ νεῖκος ὁμοιίου πτολέμοιο,
> μή πώς τοι Κρονίδης κεχολώσεται εὐρύοπα Ζεύς.
> (*Od.* 24.542–44)

> Laertes' son, descended of gods, craft-ridden Odysseus, hold it! Stop the contention of balanced war, lest wide-browed Zeus, the son of Kronos, be in a state of *khólos*.

Thus Athena here prevents the *khólos* of her father against Odysseus, whom she is trying to protect. Indeed, this activity resembles those instances of *mênis* that are mentioned only as potential and "le but est toujours de ne pas la provoquer."[61]

Thus, we have the epithet *obrimopátrē* alongside three different forms of anger, *khólos*, *kótos*, and *mênis*, so it is worthwhile to summarize the connection between the epithet and its possible congeners. The first term of the possessive compound *obrimo-pátrē* points to the semantics of force. In particular, *o-brimo-* is to be set alongside forms like *brímē* (-*i*-), *bríthō* (-*i*-), if we accept the short -*i*- of *obrimopátrē* as coming in by analogy with adjectives in -*imos*, such as *álkimos*,[62] and if we accept the initial *o*-.[63] There are thematic reasons for making these moves as well. The following lines from Homeric Hymn 28 show Athena's power to quake Olympus, almost a gloss on the Homeric couplet under discussion:

> σείσασ᾽ ὀξὺν ἄκοντα· μέγας δ᾽ ἐλελίζετ᾽῞Ολυμπος
> δεινὸν ὑπὸ βρίμης γλαυκώπιδος. . . .
> (*Homeric Hymn* 28.9–10 [Allen 1936, 88])
>
> Shaking her sharp spear; and great Olympus was shaking terribly beneath her "the powerful grey-eyed one." . . .

The elements analogous to the Homeric lines include the suppression of the name Athena, the use of the epithet *glaukṓpidos* ("grey-eyed") together with a form based on *bri*-, indicating force, and the spear as a metonymic identification of her force. In addition, Zeus is mentioned at the end of this passage.[64] The power of Athena in such passages is related to anger, if we accept a connection between *obrimo*- and the anger sense of words like *brīmáomai*.[65] Finally, note that by comparing the instances of the epithet *obrimopátrē*, we see that *kótos* is contrasted with both *mênis* and *khólos*, because the latter two have specific reference within the immediate narrative context, whereas the form based on *kótos* is rooted in Athena's mythic relationship with mortals and the basic issues of the Trojan conflict. It is becoming, thus, increasingly clear that *kótos* is a marked term in Homeric diction, one that demands a reference point beyond the current conflicts of the narrative's action.

ꕥ

While it is possible for a Homeric figure to do or say something that inspires *khólos* in someone, in contrast, *kótos* must be present or arise from a social situation in the background of the immediate narrative context. Note that the aorist participle middle of *kotéō* (Groups 3 and 4 of Appendix 1) never occurs as part of a loquitur formula.[66] This distinguishes *kótos* sharply from *khólos*, precisely because *kótos* never arises as the description of a state leading to an angry speech whose cause is an immediate and local narrative context (a situation often connected with *khólos*). *Kótos* is regularly based on something external to the immediate narrative itself,[67] such as the origin of the dispute between Paris and Menelaus, the rivalry for Helen, the origin of the allegiances of particular gods to particular mortals, and the like. If *kótos* consistently refers to something as basic as the Trojan War, as we might have expected from Calchas's definition, it makes sense that it should not present a causal meaning in a speech formula, because speeches are among the most locally motivated elements in these narratives.

What follows from locating *kótos* at moments in early Greek mythology as important as the beginning of the Trojan War? For one thing, *kótos* shows itself to be at the heart of an archaic ethical system. Take, for example, the notion of *thémis*, where those who have violated the social boundaries represented by this term are subject to *kótos*. For a set of examples, I point to passages where a god is *kotessámenos* in relation to a group of mortals who have violated *thémis*.[68]

I examine this use of *kótos* first by returning to *Il.* 5.174–78, where Aeneas exhorts Pandarus to shoot his arrow at Diomedes:

> ἀλλ' ἄγε τῷδ' ἔφες ἀνδρὶ βέλος, Διὶ χεῖρας ἀνασχών,
> ὅς τις ὅδε κρατέει καὶ δὴ κακὰ πολλὰ ἔοργε
> Τρῶας, ἐπεὶ πολλῶν τε καὶ ἐσθλῶν γούνατ' ἔλυσεν·
> εἰ μή τις θεός ἐστι κοτεσσάμενος Τρώεσσιν
> ἱρῶν μηνίσας· χαλεπὴ δὲ θεοῦ ἔπι μῆνις.
> (*Il.* 5.174–78)

> But come, and with your hands outstretched to Zeus, shoot at the man who has control and has done much evil to the Trojans, because he has loosed the limbs of many and good [warriors]; unless he is some god with *kótos* against the Trojans, with *mênis* over sacred things; difficult is the *mênis* of a god.

This passage is ironic. Aeneas exhorts Pandarus to take aim at a prominent Achaean, not only on the grounds that he is a superior archer (*Il.* 5.171–73), but also because it is not a god's *kótos* that is at issue at Troy. But in fact the *kótos* of Zeus dooms the Trojans, although his anger is not motived by *hierá* ("sacred things").[69]

Zeus's *kótos* resembles Hera's *kótos* for the Trojans,[70] to which Zeus refers when he addresses Athena and Hera in these words:

> τίφθ' οὕτω τετίησθον, Ἀθηναίη τε καὶ Ἥρη;
> οὐ μέν θην κάμετόν γε μάχῃ ἔνι κυδιανείρῃ
> ὀλλῦσαι Τρῶας, τοῖσιν κότον αἰνὸν ἔθεσθε.
> (*Il.* 8.447–49)

> Then why are you two so upset, Athena and Hera? It can't be that *you* were worn out in the man-glorying battle, destroying Trojans, against whom you have set a terrible *kótos*.

Zeus characterizes Hera's motivation for *kótos*, without citing an explicit source. Now set this passage beside another earlier section where Zeus characterizes the wrath of Hera as not *kótos* but *khólos*.[71]

> δαιμονίη, τί νύ σε Πρίαμος Πριάμοιό τε παῖδες
> τόσσα κακὰ ῥέζουσιν, ὅ τ' ἀσπερχὲς μενεαίνεις
> Ἰλίου ἐξαλαπάξαι ἐυκτίμενον πτολίεθρον;
> εἰ δὲ σύ γ' εἰσελθοῦσα πύλας καὶ τείχεα μακρὰ
> ὠμὸν βεβρώθοις Πρίαμον Πριάμοιό τε παῖδας
> ἄλλους τε Τρῶας, τότε κεν <u>χόλον</u> ἐξακέσαιο.
> (*Il.* 4.31–36)

> Bold one, how many evils have Priam and the children of Priam done to you, that you rage incessantly against them to sack the well-built citadel of Ilium? I suppose if you had arrived at the gates and great walls and had eaten Priam and the children of Priam and the rest of the Trojans raw, then you would have cured your <u>*khólos*</u>.

Here and in *Il.* 8.447–49 Zeus challenges female divinities who are supporting the Greeks. And in both cases he suggests that anger has gone far enough. But in the passage from *Iliad* 4 (*Il.* 4.31–36), immediately after the duel between Paris and Menelaus, Zeus cites Hera's *khólos*; in *Il.* 8.447–49 he refers to a *kótos* shared between Hera and Athena.

Are *khólos* and *kótos*, at least in this doublet, to be taken as synonyms? On the contrary, these two passages, when read together, reproduce the concern felt by Calchas for the anger of the *basileús*; the parallels corroborate Calchas's definition in the following manner.

In Book 4, Zeus introduces the grisly image of cannibalism, where Hera's *khólos* can be satisfied by consuming the population of Troy.[72] Such a concept is intimately tied up with *khólos*, as defined by Calchas. Note that, as Zeus formulates it, this idea is in harmony with the image Calchas used: "He digests his anger in a day's time."[73] In the second instance, in Book 8, Zeus addresses a different problem: both goddesses' *kótos*. We have already seen how Athena, as *obrimopátrē*, can have *kótos*. This *kótos* emboldens the goddesses to help the Greeks, despite the restrictions that Zeus has established. The doublet, then, reproduces the hierarchy of anger terms that Calchas relied on in his definition: *khólos* is a matter of corporeality. It can either be digested or satisfied as hunger is satisfied. *Kótos*, by contrast, is on a different plane because it threatens to destroy not merely the bodies of the Trojans but their culture as well.[74]

The quality of that difference can be noted in the conclusion of each scene. In the first scene, Zeus and Hera strike a grim deal. Each god will let the other manifest *khólos* in the destruction of one of the other god's favored cities.[75] In the second scene no bargain can be struck. Rather, Zeus resorts to threats (*Il.* 8.450–56). As we might expect from Calchas's definition, with *khólos* one can bargain, but with *kótos* negotiations of any kind are pointless.

On this interpretation, this doublet is hierarchically ordered. Just as Calchas first explicates the danger of the *khólos* of the *basileús*, so in the first scene of this pair, Homer has Zeus focus on Hera's *khólos*. In the second scene, Zeus confronts the queenly goddesses with the limits of their *kótos*, even as Calchas emphasized the severe danger that Agamemnon's *kótos* would mean for the prophet.

Furthermore, if *kótos* has a special meaning for the quarrel between Menelaus and Paris—and, hence, for the Trojan War—then it is reasonable to suppose that Hera and Athena might be involved with this potent form of anger.[76] If this is so, then the *kótos* of Zeus in Aeneas's speech to Pandarus is meant to allude to the severe kind of anger that is to cause the fall of Troy.

Support for this last point is available in the controversial passage in which the second line of Group 3 occurs:

> πρόσσω ἱέμενοι, ἐπὶ δ' Ἕκτορι κέκλετο θυμός·
> ἵετο γὰρ βαλέειν· τὸν δ' ἔκφερον ὠκέες ἵπποι.
> ὡς δ' ὑπὸ λαίλαπι πᾶσα κελαινὴ βέβριθε χθὼν
> ἤματ' ὀπωρινῷ, ὅτε λαβρότατον χέει ὕδωρ
> Ζεύς, ὅτε δή ῥ' ἄνδρεσσι κοτεσσάμενος χαλεπήνῃ,
> οἳ βίῃ εἰν ἀγορῇ σκολιὰς κρίνωσι θέμιστας,
> ἐκ δὲ δίκην ἐλάσωσι, θεῶν ὄπιν οὐκ ἀλέγοντες·
> τῶν δέ τε πάντες μὲν ποταμοὶ πλήθουσι ῥέοντες,
> πολλὰς δὲ κλιτῦς τότ' ἀποτμήγουσι χαράδραι,
> ἐς δ' ἅλα πορφυρέην μεγάλα στενάχουσι ῥέουσαι.
> ἐξ ὀρέων ἐπὶ κάρ, μινύθει δέ τε ἔργ' ἀνθρώπων·
> ὣς ἵπποι Τρῳαὶ μεγάλα στενάχοντο θέουσαι.
> (*Il.* 16.382–93)

> [Achilles' horses] pushing forward, and his spirit drove [Patroclus] against Hector. For he was eager to shoot; but the swift horses carried him away. Just as under a storm the whole dark earth is oppressed on an autumn day, when Zeus pours down the fiercest torrent, since with *kótos* he bears it ill against those men, who violently make crooked judgments in the public space, and who then drive out justice, not heeding thus the consideration of the gods. Their rivers, all of them, are jammed in their flow, and the ravines cut through many a hillside, and greatly roaring they flow to the purple sea, straight down from the mountains, and human affairs are diminished. Thus the Trojan mares loudly groaned in their rushing.

Zeus's *kótos* here results in the destruction of mortal culture in a broad sense: *minúthei dé te érg' anthrṓpōn* ("and the works of mortals are diminished").[77] This theme is in perfect accord with Agamemnon's prediction that Troy will fall because of the breaking of the oaths; the mention of Zeus's *kótos* here is a clear allusion to the *kótos* of Zeus Xenios. In fact, this destructive anger of Zeus is also referred to by Aeneas in his exhortation to Pandarus (*Il.* 4.168).[78]

Finally, the relevance of the simile to its context is striking, given the *kótos* of Zeus in Book 4, as we have just studied it. Zeus's storm, instigated by a community's violation of *díkē*, causes the river to rush and flood, signaling the diminution of the *érga anthrṓpōn*; so too Patroclus pursues Hector and the Trojan horses who are pushed to the breaking point. The simile provides a reference to the *kótos* that will finally engulf the Trojans, even though within the *Patrocleia*, Troy comes to have the upper hand.[79]

An important question arises: If *kótos* is so important—if it is the driving force behind so much that is crucial to the story of Troy—why does the term play so small a role in the vocabulary of the *Iliad*, especially in comparison with *khólos*? The answer is the same as that to a similar question about the story of the fall of Ilium and its relation to the story of Achilles. The tradition has supplied the singer with a full range of events and consequences, within which he preserves the plan of the particular song. Thus, the particular performance chooses to highlight one aspect of the tradition.[80]

So Zeus's *kótos*, stemming as it does from a violation of a divinely sanctioned human institution, must not take precedence over his plan with regard to Achilles. Thus his *kótos* is not stressed. In fact, it is only directly mentioned once in the *Iliad* and then only by Agamemnon, who often doubts his own ability to read divine facts. Instead, the *kótos* against the Trojans is handled by Athena and Hera as in, for example, *Il.* 8.448–49 and *Il.* 18.367. Meanwhile, the passages where Zeus has *kótos* point to the traditional history outside the *Iliad*'s plot.

The next passage, the third example of *kotessámenos* in Group 3, is the last line of a conversation between Zeus and Hera just before Hephaestus is asked by Thetis to make the shield of Achilles. As the two gods watch the ritual preparation of the body of Patroclus (*Il.* 18.343–55), Zeus suggests to Hera that there must be some connection between Hera and the birth of the Achaeans for events are moving so in their favor that Achilles is about to return to battle. Such words—tokens of praise—ring hollow in the funereal context, but Hera's rejoinder makes use of *kótos* in a way that clarifies how she perceives this anger. *Kótos*, as we remember from Calchas's definition, needs to have its *télos*, which in the case of Ilium, means the destruction of the city of Priam. So Hera emphasizes the need for a *télos* in life's endeavors. Why, even mortals need to have a *télos* (*Il.* 18.362)! Furthermore, while Zeus is king of the gods, the elder sister and wife of Zeus should be able to weave evils against those for whom she has *kótos*:

> πῶς δὴ ἔγω γ᾽, ἥ φημι θεάων ἔμμεν ἀρίστη,
> ἀμφότερον, γενεῇ τε καὶ οὕνεκα σὴ παράκοιτις
> κέκλημαι, σὺ δὲ πᾶσι μετ᾽ ἀθανάτοισιν ἀνάσσεις,
> οὐκ ὄφελον Τρώεσσι <u>κοτεσσαμένη</u> κακὰ ῥάψαι;
> (*Il.* 18.364–67)

How is it that I, who boast to be the best of the goddesses, in two ways, both by birth and because I am your wife, and you rule over all the immortals—how ought I not weave evils for the Trojans, kotessaménē ("seeing that I am enraged")?

We see here the major themes of *kótos* engaged by Hera to make her point about her prerogatives regarding the Trojan War. Her right to make trouble for the Trojans through *kótos* is parallel to Zeus's role as *ánaks* (*Il.* 18.366), and it is also related to her authority as the *theáōn arístē* ("best of the goddesses"). As far as *kótos* goes, the queen's role is as important as the king's in determining anger's victims.[81]

Kótos in its Verbal Forms: the Reduplicated Perfect

In Group 6 (Appendix 1) we see the perfect participle of *kotéō* presenting a stative meaning (see Chantraine 1927, 22; see also Monro 1891, §28). Note that the active desinence, the *o*-grade of the root, along with its reduplication, put *kekotēṓs* in a class of old perfects (Chantraine 1927, 22). As to the form, the perfect is based on the present *kotéō*, a form still in need of explanation (Chantraine 1927, 24); for parallels to *kekotēṓs*, see *bebarēṓs*, and *kekorēṓs* (Chantraine 1927, 25, 38). Chantraine goes on to cite, as appropriate to the stative meaning of the perfect, certain emotion words, "verbes qui exprime un sentiment, joie, souffrance, crainte, colère . . . *kekhólōmai* 'je suis irrité,' *odōdustai* 'il est en colère,' *kekotēṓs* 'plein de ressentiment.'"[82] *Kekotēṓs*, thus, although poorly attested, shows an expected parallel with an old class of verbs expressing emotion. This fact, along with the formulaic status of the phrase in Group 6, merits analysis to determine whether its phraseology presents deeply traditional material.[83]

In terms of traditional notions of the formula, the *kótos* phrase used most often is *kekotēóti thumôi*. This phrase fills the entire second half of the line from the hephthemimeral caesura. As it happens, the perfect participle is fixed in the hexameter in a way that positions the root *kót-* in the same metrical slot as the noun (see Groups 1 and 2). For words shaped ¯˘ this position (O'Neill's position 10) is less likely to be used other than in (O'Neill's) position 8,[84] so that I can suggest that the positioning of [-]*kot-* in the substantive and in the old perfect displays a feature of the regularity of Homeric phrasing, that is to say, of formulaic style. The stative perfect participle form always occurs in modification of *thumôi* and always immediately after the main verb of its clause.

Now these four passages have the phrase *kekotēóti thumôi*—hardly more than an expanded way of saying *kótōi*. I have already shown how *thumós* is used in such passages, generally as "seat of the emotions."[85] In fact, this formula inverts the way the noun-epithet combination, according to Parry's famous formulation, conveys the "given essential idea." Here the adjectival part of the noun-participle combination conveys the "idea," while the noun seems relatively subordinate.[86]

Discussion of Phrases

The repeated phrase *kekotēóti thumôi* ("with a heart full of wrath") refers the narrative to the larger significance of the Trojan War outside the *Iliad*'s specific concern with the quarrel between Achilles and Agamemnon. When *kótos* occurs in the *Iliad* it can refer to the fall of Troy, or to the events that lead up to the fall, or to the cause of Troy's destruction. When it occurs three times in the *Odyssey*, its reference is to that poem's overarching concern with the potential fall of the house of Odysseus.

Let me begin with the one occurrence of *kekotēóti thumôi* from the *Iliad*. Here Poseidon recalls for Apollo that they both served the Trojans in the building of the wall:

> νηπύτι', ὡς ἄνοον κραδίην ἔχες· οὐδέ νυ τῶν περ
> μέμνηαι, ὅσα δὴ πάθομεν κακὰ Ἴλιον ἀμφὶ
> μοῦνοι νῶι θεῶν, ὅτ' ἀγήνορι Λαομέδοντι
> πὰρ Διὸς ἐλθόντες θητεύσαμεν εἰς ἐνιαυτὸν
> μισθῷ ἔπι ῥητῷ· ὁ δὲ σημαίνων ἐπέτελλεν.
> ἤτοι ἐγὼ Τρώεσσι πόλιν πέρι τεῖχος ἔδειμα,
> εὐρύ τε καὶ μάλα καλόν.
> (*Il.* 21.441–47)

Foolish one, how unthinking is your heart! And you do not even remember those very things that we suffered, the number of ills, around Ilium, we two alone of the gods, when we slaved for man-leader Laomedon, having arrived here from Zeus, for a year's time and for set pay. And he made it clear and he gave the orders. Yes, it was I who built the wall around the city for the Trojans, both wide and truly good.

Thus, Poseidon builds a wall for Troy and Apollo tends the flocks (*Il.* 21.446–49). But Laomedon cheats the gods:

> νῶι δέ τ' ἄψορροι κίομεν κεκοτηότι θυμῷ,
> μισθοῦ χωόμενοι, τὸν ὑποστὰς οὐκ ἐτέλεσσε.
> (*Il.* 21.456–57)

But we two gods went on back with a *thumós* full of *kótos*, angry for the payment, which he had promised us but had not delivered.

One could hope for no more explicit explanation of the meaning of *kótos* than that displayed by this scene. The failure of Laomedon to meet the agreed-upon fee (*misthòs rhētós*, *Il.* 21.445) is parallel to the earlier breaking of the oaths in

Iliad 3–4; the connection with *télos* is continued in *etélesse*, in its special meaning of "pay." Here and in *Iliad* 4, contracts or oaths are violated or left unfulfilled, with the further implication in this passage that a promise (*hupostás*, *Il.* 21.457) has been broken. Moreover, the promise and contract, whose dissolution provokes *kótos*, takes place in the context of human work, the building of a city's fortifications and the resolution of conflict through a duel between the most interested parties. *Kótos* turns out to be a political term, such that, even when the gods are involved, the center of attention is human culture, the activities of human actors in the real world.[87] Furthermore, the *kótos* is lodged between two members of two different levels related to each hierarchically, as they are within Calchas's definition. Compare here, for a parallel that supports this reading, the passage in Group 6, from *Odyssey* 19, where Melantho thinks that, as the social superior, she can berate her supposed inferior, the disguised Odysseus. Instead he gets the best of her by invoking the *kótos* both of Penelope (her true superior in the household) and of a soon-to-be-revealed Odysseus. So too Laomedon mistreats two gods who are in thralldom to him but who are, in fact, superior to him by virtue of their divinity. Thus the gods' epiphany in the *Iliad* is parallel to the inversion of social roles effected by Odysseus's disguise.[88]

To continue with the passage from *Iliad* 21, Poseidon argues that it is not right, given this shared *kótos*, for Apollo to help the Trojans:

> τοῦ δὴ νῦν λαοῖσι φέρεις χάριν, οὐδὲ μεθ' ἡμέων
> πειρᾷ, ὥς κε Τρῶες ὑπερφίαλοι ἀπόλωνται
> πρόχνυ κακῶς, σὺν παισὶ καὶ αἰδοίῃς ἀλόχοισι.
> (*Il.* 21.458–60)

> You are grateful to his people now, nor will you try with us to have the contemptuous Trojans perish totally, badly, along with their children and virtuous wives.

For the tone, we need only look back to Agamemnon's lament for Menelaus's wound. For the destructive result, the anger must be *kótos*, the anger that reaches easily back across the generations to Laomedon and, in its attachment to cause and violation, responds to the breaking of the contract: thereby will his people suffer for generations later, men, women, children—all. And just as the doom of Troy was sealed by *kótos* in response to Paris's abduction of Helen, so too Poseidon here metes out general punishment for the deception of Laomedon.[89]

To summarize, the stative perfect participle points to the situation in which the gods find themselves with respect to Laomedon's violation: the gods are in a state of *kótos* against him. This situation is precisely what Calchas feared from Agamemnon: an anger that must reach a *télos* will drive the *basileús* to bear a grudge against him; and this will last a long time. It need hardly be said that the *basileús* ("king") is to the "lesser man" of *Il.* 1.80 as the gods are to mortals. Here the anger that will level Troy seems to have its roots not only in Paris's violation of *xenía* ("guest friendship") but also in the remote past haunted by Paris's ancestor; and its terrible fulfillment is yet to come: *metópisthe . . . óphra teléssēi* ("in the future . . . until he fulfills it").[90]

Another example of the profound nature of an action performed in a state described as *kekotēóti thumôi* occurs at *Od.* 22.477. Melanthius is the last man killed in the battle in Odysseus's hall:

χεῖράς τ᾽ ἠδὲ πόδας κόπτον κεκοτηότι θυμῷ.
οἱ μὲν ἔπειτ᾽ ἀπονιψάμενοι χεῖράς τε πόδας τε
εἰς Ὀδυσῆα δόμονδε κίον, τετέλεστο δὲ ἔργον.
(*Od.* 22.477–79)

His hands and feet they cut-off in their state of *kótos*. But having washed their own hands and feet, they went to Odysseus's house, and the deed had reached its *télos*.

The hero's destruction of the suitors, thus, is capped by a reference to *kótos* and the explicit notation that the *télos* ("goal") of Odysseus's effort has been reached. The emphasis is on the completion of the action with the pluperfect *tetélesto* (*Od.* 22.479). Calchas's definition here finds its validity in action, where the *télos* is marked by an act of extreme violence motivated by *kótos*, not by any particular hatred against Melanthius but rather by the desire to conclude the entire *kótos*. With this passage in mind, one need not wonder at Calchas's fear of *kótos*. For the violence displayed here is that of a long-standing anger that has accrued throughout the entire *nóstos* of Odysseus, so that when the *basileús* has *kótos* its fulfillment is on record even before the final, terrible moment.

This passage further supports another part of Calchas's definition: the slaughter of the suitors is the reassertion of Odysseus as *basileús* ("king").[91] This interpretation is reinforced when we see a goatherd ("a worse man") as vengeance's final victim, after the twelve maidservants. Furthermore, in *Od.* 22.466–79, it is the collectivity that mutilates Melanthius, after which they return to the domicile.[92] And the final use of the passive voice, with the resounding *tetélesto*, caps the act by calling to mind Calchas's own definition: *óphra teléssēi*.

Thus far we have seen how the phrase *kekotēóti thumôi* occurs in passages that highlight a deep-seated rancor bringing out themes that Calchas had earlier told us were crucial for *kótos*, especially the hierarchic sense of the term and its focus on the *télos* of its activity. The remaining two instances of the phrase can be handled quickly now that we have this background. First let us look at *kótos* as it effects Melantho, the namesake of her brother, the ill-fated Melanthius.[93]

δαιμονίη, τί μοι ὧδ᾽ ἐπέχεις κεκοτηότι θυμῷ;
ἦ ὅτι δὴ ῥυπόω, κακὰ δὲ χροῒ εἵματα εἷμαι,
πτωχεύω δ᾽ ἀνὰ δῆμον; ἀναγκαίη γὰρ ἐπείγει.
τοιοῦτοι πτωχοὶ καὶ ἀλήμονες ἄνδρες ἔασι.

καὶ γὰρ ἐγώ ποτε οἶκον ἐν ἀνθρώποισιν ἔναιον
ὄλβιος ἀφνειὸν καὶ πολλάκι δόσκον ἀλήτῃ,
τοίῳ, ὁποῖος ἔοι καὶ ὅτευ κεχρημένος ἔλθοι·
ἦσαν δὲ δμῶες μάλα μυρίοι, ἄλλα τε πολλὰ
οἶσίν τ' εὖ ζώουσι καὶ ἀφνειοὶ καλέονται.
ἀλλὰ Ζεὺς ἀλάπαξε Κρονίων· ἤθελε γάρ που·
τῶ νῦν μήποτε καὶ σύ, γύναι, ἀπὸ πᾶσαν ὀλέσσῃς
ἀγλαΐην, τῇ νῦν γε μετὰ δμῳῇσι κέκασσαι·
μή πώς τοι δέσποινα κοτεσσαμένη χαλεπήνῃ
ἢ 'Οδυσεὺς ἔλθῃ· ἔτι γὰρ καὶ ἐλπίδος αἶσα.
(*Od.* 19.71–84)

Now why are you, bold as your are, abusing me in this way, your *thumos* filled with *kótos*? Is it that I am squalid, and that I wear trashy clothes on my skin, and that I beg throughout the community? Yes, necessity is compulsion. Such are beggars and vagrants. For, in fact, I once inhabited a house among men, a wealthy man and a rich home, and I was often generous to the beggar, whatever kind he might be and with whatever need he came; and there were very many servants and other things with which one lives well and is called wealthy. But Zeus, son of Kronos, has brought it to ruin. For so was he willing. Therefore now do not lose everything, my good woman, all your radiance, with which now you are outstanding among the maids, lest your mistress—having come to have *kótos*—take it ill, or lest Odysseus come home. For there is yet a measure of hope.

Why should Odysseus claim that Melantho's upbraiding (*enénipe*, *Od.* 19.65) is done *kekotēóti thumôi*? Melantho had already insulted Odysseus in Book 18 (*Od.* 18.321–36), so we might be tempted to say that her antagonism against him refers to something that seems to transcend their momentary encounter. But a reason more firmly in keeping with the value of *kótos* is at hand. Odysseus identifies this anger as *kótos* partly because he observes that there is no immediate cause for, say, a *khólos* that Melantho might direct against the beggar. Instead, his suggestion that the anger is *kótos* points to a kind of class bias that he detects in her: as a servant she thinks of herself as better than a beggar and thus wants him to sleep outside (*éxelthe thúraze* "go out to the door," *Od.* 19.68). Her anger turns out to be based on a violation of social decorum. From this perspective, to act in this manner is to risk losing her *pâsan aglaíēn* ("all her bright-radiance," *Od.* 19.81–82),[94] or her privileged status (*têi nûn te metà dmōêisi kékassai* "by which you are outstanding among the servants," *Od.* 19.82). The social context of *kótos* in this situation is precisely in accord with the terms of Calchas's definition: she is *kotessaménē* against a "worse man."

Odysseus further emphasizes the notion of *kótos* by suggesting that she will reap what she sows: Penelope as queen is capable in her turn of having *kótos* against a woman of lower class. Now we have seen that Odysseus, in his disguise as a beggar, chides Melantho for abusing him by trying to expel him from Penelope's presence (*Od.* 19.66–69). At this point, Odysseus explains his circumstances by the vicissitudes of fortune (*Od.* 19.71-80) and the compulsion of necessity (*Od.* 19.73) together with the will of Zeus (*Od.* 19.80), all of which is to prepare the ground for his claim that Melantho had better be careful lest she incur the wrath of her mistress; that wrath is *kótos* in part because it is the wrath of a superior against an inferior, in particular, of a queen against her servant. Thus it is not surprising that Odysseus the beggar suggests to Melantho that Odysseus the king might return. Finally, he asserts that even if Odysseus does not return, Telemachus is now old enough to take over (*Od.* 19.86–87). In these ways, this passage underscores the notion that the *basileús* can come to have *kótos* and that whatever Melantho does, she is on the bottom rung of the hierarchical ladder, with respect to Odysseus and Penelope.

Since *kótos* is significant in the punishment of the suitors, especially in the way that it motivates the extremity to which Odysseus and his party go in carrying out their mission, this scene may resonate with the death of the suitors. And, indeed, there are indications that the scenes are doublets. The last of the suitors' party is Melanthius, the feminine form of which name is Melantho. In addition Melanthius and Melantho are siblings, both being children of Dolius.[95] Both of them have a special relationship to one of the most important suitors: Melanthius is partial to Eurymachus (*Od.* 17.257); Melantho is Eurymachus's lover (*Od.* 18.325). And both Melanthius and Melantho provoke Odysseus.

Thus, if *kótos* is important for Odysseus's revenge against the suitors, the narrative marks it as such, beginning with the insult of Melantho. Indeed, the potential *kótos* of Penelope against Melantho is completed by the *kótos* of the house of Odysseus against Melanthius at the end of Book 22.

By now we have seen, in a number of contexts, two parts of Calchas's definition at work in the Homeric use of *kótos*. First, we have seen that *kótos* is a kind of anger that endures. Moreover, as in the most recently discussed cases of the phrase *kekotēóti thumôi*, the social status of the person enraged is an element that helps provoke anger. Clearly, these two features of *kótos* (duration and social status) may be engaged independently of one another. Thus, as we will see below, the social status of the principals need not be at issue in every instance. (Indeed, equals may have *kótos* against one another.[96]) Additionally, as to the notion of time, how long *kótos* threatens to last may remain implicit within any given passage.

From Group 6 of Appendix 1, one last dramatic example puts into relief the phrase *kekotēóti thumôi* ("with a *thumós* filled with *kótos*"). In Book 9 of the *Odyssey*, Odysseus confronts the Cyclops at just that moment when he reveals his name, so as to prompt Polyphemus's recollection of a seer's prophecy. Since we have seen the phrase *kekotēóti thumôi* occur as a dramatic climax to the killing of the suitors, what similarity between Polyphemus and the suitors is here being exploited? In particular, does the term *kótos* indicate something about the relationship between Odysseus and the Cyclops that can be triggered by using *kekotēóti thumôi*?

Just before Odysseus reveals his name, he and the survivors among his crew are almost free of the Cyclops when Odysseus feels the need to taunt him:

> ἀλλ' ὅτε δὴ δὶς τόσσον ἅλα πρήσσοντες ἀπῆμεν,
> καὶ τότε δὴ Κύκλωπα προσηύδων· ἀμφὶ δ' ἑταῖροι
> μειλιχίοις ἐπέεσσιν ἐρήτυον ἄλλοθεν ἄλλος.
> (*Od.* 9.491–93)

> But when we had traversed the sea twice as far, even then I addressed the Cyclops; but around me my companions with soothing words restrained me one from one side, another from another.

But they fail in their attempt to stop Odysseus from continuing his taunt:

> "σχέτλιε, τίπτ' ἐθέλεις ἐρεθιζέμεν ἄγριον ἄνδρα;
> ὃς καὶ νῦν πόντονδε βαλὼν βέλος ἤγαγε νῆα
> αὖτις ἐς ἤπειρον, καὶ δὴ φάμεν αὐτόθ' ὀλέσθαι.
> εἰ δὲ φθεγξαμένου τευ ἢ αὐδήσαντος ἄκουσε,
> σύν κεν ἄραξ' ἡμέων κεφαλὰς καὶ νήια δοῦρα
> μαρμάρῳ ὀκριόεντι βαλών· τόσσον γὰρ ἵησιν."
> ὣς φάσαν, ἀλλ' οὐ πεῖθον ἐμὸν μεγαλήτορα θυμόν,
> ἀλλά μιν ἄψορρον προσέφην κεκοτηότι θυμῷ.
> (*Od.* 9.494–501)

> "Fool, why do you wish to enrage the wild man? Even now he has shot a missile seaward and has lead our ship again to the shore. Look, we believe we'll die here. And if he hears someone's call or someone addressing him, he will crack together our heads and the ships timbers, with a shot from a sharp boulder. For he can throw this far." Thus they spoke, but they did not move my great *thumós*, but I spoke back to him with my *thumós* filled with *kótos*.

Their question is a good one. What motivates Odysseus' bravado here? From the point of view of character, Odysseus's provocative trickster persona consistently cannot resist "claim[ing] authorship of the deed."[97] But is *kótos* consistent with the kind of anger that such a scene entails? Furthermore, is there an implicit contrast between the *kótos* of Odysseus at *Od.* 9.500 and the *khólos* of the Cyclops just before he launches his treacherous missile?[98] Is the meaning of *kótos* that we have been tracing, based on Calchas's definition, consistent with what happens here?

The answer lies partly in the thematics of *kótos*. First, the Cyclops has violated principles in such a way that he comes to represent the class of mortals who make *skholiàs thémistas* ("crooked judgments"). Second, the revelation of Odysseus's name thrusts to the foreground of the scene the seer who had predicted Cyclops's fate (*Od.* 9.507–21).

When Odysseus and his crew first arrive, Polyphemus questions their presence (*Od.* 9.252–55); then Odysseus responds by identifying them as Achaeans on their *nóstos* (*Od.* 9.259–66). In addition, he identifies himself and his crew as suppliants:

> ἡμεῖς δ᾽ αὖτε κιχανόμενοι τὰ σὰ γοῦνα
> ἱκόμεθ᾽, εἴ τι πόροις ξεινήιον ἠὲ καὶ ἄλλως
> δοίης δωτίνην, ἥ τε ξείνων θέμις ἐστίν.
> ἀλλ᾽ αἰδεῖο, φέριστε, θεούς· ἱκέται δέ τοί εἰμεν.
> Ζεὺς δ᾽ ἐπιτιμήτωρ ἱκετάων τε ξείνων τε,
> ξείνιος, ὃς ξείνοισιν ἅμ᾽ αἰδοίοισιν ὀπηδεῖ.
> (*Od.* 9.266–71)

> And we in our turn approach you and take your knees, on the chance you might give us a guest-friendship token or that you might otherwise give us a gift, which is the right thing for guest-friends. But respect the gods, oh best one; we are here as suppliants. And Zeus the protector of suppliants and guest-friends, Zeus Xenios, attends at the same time to honorable guest-friends.

The language, shot through with the key terms for early Greek values (forms of *xein-* [5x]; *thémis; hikómetha, híketai, hiketáōn*;[99] *tímē* in *epitimḗtōr*; *doíēs dōtínēn;* and forms of *aid-* [2x]), is crafted by the master of rhetoric and disguise to locate his request in the ethical particulars of early Greek thought.

But Polyphemus disdains the terms of Odysseus's argument ("*nḗpios eis, ō xeîn*" "You are a fool, stranger," *Od.* 9.273). Polyphemus flaunts his vice as a virtue both by addressing Odysseus as a *xeínos* and by making explicit his own peoples' defiance of the rules. In light of the passage from *Iliad* 16, the defiance of the Greek institution of *xenía* and suppliancy by the Cyclops as well as the participation in this act of *húbris* by the entire nation of Cyclopes may be enough to launch *kótos* as a justifiable reaction against Polyphemus.

These indications of the appropriateness of *kótos* to the Cyclops's story in the *Odyssey* are capped at the end of the scene, immediately after Odysseus's companions have tried to persuade him not to provoke the Cyclops. In refusing their advice, Odysseus, as he narrates this scene, identifies *kótos* as the driving force behind revealing his name to Polyphemus:

> ὥς φάσαν, ἀλλ᾽ οὐ πεῖθον ἐμὸν μεγαλήτορα θυμόν,
> ἀλλά μιν ἄψορρον προσέφην κεκοτηότι θυμῷ.
> (*Od.* 9.500–501)

> Thus they spoke; but they did not sway my great heart; but I spoke back at him with a *thumós* full of *kótos*.

The formula here points to a wrath larger than the crew's appeal to reason can counteract; it is the kind of wrath that Calchas fears coming from his own irate king. Remember that Odysseus, qua character, is presented as doing something very foolish by Odysseus, qua narrator, who motivates the act through the notion of *kótos*. In contrast to Polyphemus, who is motivated in his rage by mere *khólos*, Odysseus as captain of his crew is committed to his action because of a *kótos*, which must reach its *télos*. The Cyclops's *khólos* (*Od.* 9.480–86), which leads to his violent attack, cannot be more different from Odysseus's verbal assault. Odysseus, as presented in the narrative in the Phaeacian court, acts out of a *kótos* fueled by the Cyclops's extravagant violation of *xenía*, just as he is to punish the suitors later: in both cases the action is taken *kekotēóti thumôi.*[100] But there is more. Polyphemus's recollection of the seer's prophecy introduces terms even more consistent with the notion of *kótos*. The prophecies are **palaí**-*phata thésphata* (*Od.* 9.507) ("anciently spoken decrees"), and they come to have a *télos* ("completion") in the future (**tel**-*eutēsesthai* **opís**-*sō*, *Od.* 9.511), thereby recalling Calchas' *met*-**ópis**-*then* . . . **tel**-*éssēi (Il.* 1.82) ("he will accomplish it in the future"). Finally, Odysseus, the narrator, by presenting his authority in this way mirrors the relationship of Calchas to Agamemnon in Book 1: Odysseus is the *basileús* ("king") who can be driven by *kótos*, in contrast to the one recalling the prophecy, who is an *anēr kheirōn* ("a lesser man," cf. *Il.* 1.80) and—in the calculations of the Odyssean narrative—the lowest creature on the social scale.[101]

To summarize, the phrase *kekotēóti thumôi* is used in both the *Iliad* and the *Odyssey* to refer to the outer limits of anger: in the *Iliad*, Poseidon's and Apollo's *kótos* seals the fate of the city of Troy because of Laomedon's broken promise, as in the *Odyssey* the mutilation of Melanthius, *kekotēóti thumôi*, signals the *kótos* of Odysseus's struggles with the suitors over who is to be the *basileús*; and the struggle of Odysseus (as beggar) with Melantho, the sister of Melanthius, continues the discourse of the *Odyssey* regarding the kingship of Odysseus—it is the anger of the king that Melantho, and the suitors, should fear. Moreover, the use of this phrase in the Cyclops episode shows the way that *kótos* crystalizes the thematics of authority as it distinguishes between Polyphemus and the returning hero, with the Cyclops's uncivilized response to the institution of hospitality punished by the *kótos* of Odysseus.

Kótos in its Verbal Forms: The Present Stem and Isolated Forms

The present stem (notably all in the *Iliad*, as seen in Appendix 1, Groups 7, 8, and 9) shows a series of various forms that tend to cluster at major line breaks. For example, *kotéonte* and *kotéousin* are at line-end in Group 7, while the main caesura serves a function similar to line-end in Group 8 (see below). The remaining two instances of the present stem (Group 9) are unique in both form and placement.

The derivational history of *kótos* with regard to these forms is in dispute. The present stem behaves as if derived as a denominative from an *s*-stem,[102] which shows a future in *-ésō*, and an aorist in *-éssa*.[103] Chantraine classifies *kotéō* as one of a set of "irregular" forms showing stems with *-e*.[104] In the *Grammaire,* he calls to mind an analogy with *pothéō*,[105] which suggests that *kotéō* might not be denominative after all.[106]

If the verbal forms were derived from a thematic stem we would expect a denominative relationship, such as obtains between *philéō/phílos*,[107] including future *ḗsō*- and aorist *-ḗsa*. Given the meaning that emerges for *kótos* in the previous chapters, I suggest that *kótos* might continue an old formation, specifically that of *-éō* verbs reflecting a *PIE* iterative-intensive formant, with *o*- vocalism of the root.[108] If *kótos* presents are thus derived, such a process is consistent with the sense of duration implicit in *kótos*.

Discussion of Words and Phrases

In Appendix 1, Groups 7–9, my collection of the present tense verbal forms related to *kótos* shows a surface phraseology of striking variety. Yet, despite the differences among these *kótos*-phrases, the *Iliad* displays these examples with a regularity of placement that argues for their traditional status. It has been shown that phrases at the end of the line are related to those at the main caesura.[109] To put this in terms of the Homeric traditional phrase, a phrase set at line-end is formulaic with the same phrase at the caesura. Compare, for example,

Il. 3.350 = 17.46 Ἀτρείδης Μενέλαος ἐπευξάμενος <u>Διὶ πατρί</u>
Il. 4.23 = 8.460 σκυζομένη <u>Διὶ πατρί</u>, χόλος δέ μιν ἄγριος ᾕρει

where the phrase *Diì patrí* occurs either at the end of the line or at the main caesura.[110] So too for the verbal forms of *kótos*, when the stem and desinence exhibit the same form of metrical patterning as *Diì patrí*, with the present form of the verb occurring at the end of the line or at the main caesura. In fact, the pattern depends on the underlying structure of these forms. To elaborate, setting aside the two participial forms (at *Il.* 10.517, *Il.* 23.391), the present form occurs either at the end of the line or at the main caesura. In this way, the present dual participle (for imperfect) *kotéonte* (*Il.* 3.345) and the present *kotéousin* (*Il.* 14.143) are related to the imperfect *kotéonto* (*Il.* 2.223) and the present participle *kotéontos (Il.* 1.181); further, even the present participle *kotéōn* (*Il.* 4.168) is drawn into the group despite its being shorter by one syllable than the other forms, as is revealed by the placement of the form at caesura and line-end. Thus, the set of verbal forms presented by *kotéō* behaves in the systematically elegant manner characteristic of Homeric practice, despite the variety of forms that it displays.

The formulaic quality of the present tense forms of *kótos* is also supported by the underlying forms of *kotéousin* and of *kotéousa*, since *kotéousin* comes from **koteio-nti-n* and *kotéousa* from **koteio-nt-ia*. Thus, with two exceptions (*Il.* 10.517, *Il.* 23.391), every present form of the iterative-intensive present *kotéō* occurs at line-end or at the main caesura, and all these forms have either as a surface feature or as an underlying feature a morpho-phonological resemblance (-e-i-on-[t]).[111] To put the matter schematically, the following collocation suggests a schema for the surface features as derived from the underlying features.

(a.) [2x] κοτεον# (*Il.* 3.345, 14.143)
(b.) [3x] . . . κοτεον[το/τος] || (*Il.* 1.181, 2.223, 4.168)

These regularities in phrasing argue for the traditional status of this system.

The middle imperfect *kotéonto* is the only form of the present to show other than an active diathesis. This pattern continues an old feature of Greek, shared by parallel phenomenon in Indo-Iranian, thoroughly examined by S. Jamison. Her conclusion about the morphological development of middle endings in Indic *-áya-* verbs leads to a discussion about the middle in the imperfect of *kotéō* and similar verbs: "When semantic and/or metrical conditions encourage it, the act[ive] form is replaced by the corresponding med. form, which has the advantage of being metrically identical to the act[ive] prim[ary] form. Note that the replacement probably happened in many cases before the dialectal change *-οντι > -ουσι, when the characterizing -ντ- was still visible in the prim[ary] ending. Hence the tendency for these replacements to occur in old formulae."[112] Keeping Jamison's analysis in mind, I conclude that the imperfect middles in their prosody as well as their morphology point to the fundamental antiquity of *kótos* in Homeric poetics.

Discussion of Context

Earlier we examined the passage containing *Il.* 3.345, when Paris and Menelaus engage in single combat. This duel alludes to the central conflict of Greek epic narrative, the abduction of Helen by Paris. The anger appropriate to this passage is *kótos*, not *khólos*, because it is motivated by an event outside the immediate context and at its foundations. Neither Menelaus nor Paris has done anything to the other on the battlefield, so they have no immediate reason to be angry with each other. But the term *kótos* can extend over time and must reach a *télos*. Because of this longevity, it is possible to find oneself facing one's opponent over an issue that happened elsewhere in time and space.[113] It is in this sense that Paris and Menelaus can have *kótos* against one another.

Furthermore, oath-taking provides a serious context for justifying *kótos*. To elaborate, mishandling *thémistes* ("judgments") can lead to the *kótos* of Zeus (*Il.* 16.386–87), and, in a similar fashion, Odysseus's use of the formula *kekotēóti thumôi* ("with a *thumós* filled with anger") suggests a connection with the world of prophecy and authority. So too the oaths here provide the lofty context for which *kotéonte* is apt, a use consistent with the function of *kótos* once the oaths have been violated (*Il.* 4.168, *Il.* 5.177). Indeed, the classification of the present forms of *kotéō* as iterative-intensive is most appropriate for the anger of Paris and Menelaus, the two agents of anger in the conflict between the Trojan and the Mycenaean lords. In short, this occurrence of *kotéō* carries an enormous weight with reference to the origin of the war and the abiding enmity of Paris and Menelaus. But the term's force might have been easily missed; were we not told at the beginning of the poem, in a way that now seems programmatic, that a clear distinction exists between *khólos* and *kótos*.

In the previous example, it would be difficult for anyone to question that Paris and Menelaus are angry with each other, so that the particulars of that anger—the abduction of Helen, the violation of *xenía*—are underscored by the poet's use of *kotéonte*. In the next example, Apollo's *kótos* against Athena in *Il.* 10.517, no specific reason is given for the anger of Apollo against Athena, and the commentaries do not deem the term itself worthy of explication. But spurred on by Calchas's definition, we cannot help but wonder why the term is used here. Might Apollo's *kótos* be said to rely on a motive to the side of the immediate battle?

That this *kótos* is consistent with antagonisms outside the immediate context is clear from the conflict in *Il.* 23.383–91, where Apollo and Athena are engaged in helping mortals. At this point in the horse race, the mares of Diomedes are about to gain on the horses of Eumelos, when Apollo intervenes:

> καί νύ κεν ἢ παρέλασσ' ἢ ἀμφήριστον ἔθηκεν
> εἰ μὴ Τυδέος υἷι κοτέσσατο Φοῖβος Ἀπόλλων,
> ὅς ῥά οἱ ἐκ χειρῶν ἔβαλεν μάστιγα φαεινήν.
> (*Il.* 23.382–84)

> And now he [Diomedes] would have driven past him or he would have made the contest a draw, had not Phoebus Apollo had *kótos* against the son of Tydeus, who threw from his hands the gleaming whip.

Apollo comes in from out of the blue here and his "anger" at Diomedes seems unmotivated had we not known that *kótos* itself tends to *seem* unmotivated. The driving force for this kind of anger comes from the conflictual history of the two parties. In this case, Ameis-Hentze (at 383) points us to *Il.* 2.766, where we find out an important detail about the horses of Eumelos:

> Ἵπποι μὲν μέγ' ἄρισται ἔσαν Φηρητιάδαο,
> τὰς Εὔμηλος ἔλαυνε ποδώκεας ὄρνιθας ὥς,
> ὄτριχας οἰέτεας, σταφύλῃ ἐπὶ νῶτον ἐίσας·
> τὰς ἐν Πηρείῃ θρέψ' ἀργυρότοξος Ἀπόλλων
> (*Il.* 2.763–66)

> The mares of the son of Pheres were by far the best, those which Eumelus drove, swift footed, bird-like, alike in coat and age, even along their backs in a line; these mares in Pereia were bred by Apollo of the silver bow.

Thus to understand the anger of Apollo in Book 23, one must understand the rivalry between the mares of Eumelos, ultimately Apollo's, and the mares of Diomedes. We further see that Apollo's *kótos* is answered by Athena's *kótos*:

> οὐδ' ἄρ' Ἀθηναίην ἐλεφηράμενος λάθ' Ἀπόλλων
> Τυδείδην, μάλα δ' ὦκα μετέσσυτο ποιμένα λαῶν,
> δῶκε δέ οἱ μάστιγα, μένος δ' ἵπποισιν ἐνῆκεν·
> ἡ δὲ μετ' Ἀδμήτου υἱὸν <u>κοτέους</u>, ἐβεβήκει
> (*Il.* 23.388–91)

> Nor did Apollo in his confounding of the son of Tydeus escape Athena's notice, but very quickly she hastened after the shepherd of the people and gave him his whip, and inspired his horses. And she in turn, <u>having *kótos*</u>, made her approach against the son of Admetus.

Here Eumelos, the son of Admetus, is the object of Athena's rage,[114] while Diomedes is the object of Apollo's rage. In each case *kótos* is seen as a response to the other god helping a mortal. So where Athena helps Diomedes steal the Trojan horses, Apollo *(kotéōn)* joins the Trojan host; where Apollo hurts Diomedes, Athena (*kotéousa)* attacks Admetus's son. Thus, by means of the implicit loyalties of the gods, this passage positions the anger of *kótos* as a reciprocal social force and one that is consistent with Calchas's definition. It is impressive to see that *kótos* is an unseen but crucial motivating force behind the conflict in this scene, because in an understated way it confirms the information from Calchas that *kótos* is worse than *khólos,* that it can be operational even where no obvious motivation impels loyalties towards aggression. Since, in this passage, no specific source is indicated for *kótos*, we have to search elsewhere for the source of such conflict here, just as we have had to assume that the source of strife between Menelaus and Paris motivates their duel in Book 3. In the latter case, the discord between Paris and Menelaus is so much a part of the tradition as we know it that we do not have to search for it for long, whereas to know that Apollo raised Eumelus's horse belongs to those best versed in the tradition, the performers and the audience of Homeric narrative.

Just as nothing in the chariot race itself triggers Apollo's *kótos* at the moment when Diomedes appears to be on the verge of passing the leader, the remaining passage from Group 9 (*Il.* 10.517) shows similar motivation at a distance. In Book 10, Apollo keeps watch over Trojan interests, which Athena harms by helping Diomedes steal the horses of Rhesus. Because of such loyalties, he comes to have *kótos* against Athena who is helping one Greek in particular, Diomedes. *Kótos,* thus, can be the anger that gods have with one another simply because they are allied with different mortals in conflict. In fact, Diomedes, as an old ally of Athena's, can be an object of Apollo's anger. Furthermore, Eumelos, as the son of Admetus, in turn has a special relationship with Apollo.[115] That is to say, Apollo's alliance with Eumelus crosses generational boundaries, so that Apollo is not so much harming Diomedes as helping Eumelos. The same applies to Athena who is harming Admetus's son for the sake of Diomedes.

Finally, the anger (*kótos*) between Diomedes and Eumelus has its origin in their rivalry over Helen. Now the suitor-list in Apollodorus shows Eumelus's name, in addition to that of Diomedes. Indeed *kótos* takes its place again at the foundational loyalties and conflicts of Helen's legend.[116] Structurally, *kótos* in the passages just reviewed describes the wrath between individuals who may be called equals (god vs. god, warrior vs. warrior). But the origin of this wrath is not any animosity between the characters who, at the moment, are said to have *kótos*, be they gods or mortals. Rather some founding moment—in the *Iliad*'s narrative, the social issues surrounding Helen: her marriage, her abduction or flight—needs to be unearthed in order to understand *kótos*.

The *kótos* that gods have with one another comes about in the context of human conflict and can cross generational boundaries, as does the *kótos* of Apollo in defense of Eumelos, the son of Admetus. Apollo, against the Greeks and on behalf of the Trojans, has *kótos* in regard to Athena, who in turn has *kótos* against the Trojans on behalf of the Greeks. Moreover, the connections have ultimately led us to Helen. The divine-mortal nexus positions *kótos* at the center of the system of anger represented in the Homeric poems.

Two forms remain to discuss. Though each occurs only once, they both continue of *kótos* entailed in Calchas's definition. For convenience I reproduce here the lines in question from Appendix 1 (Group 10):

Group 10 (Isolated forms)

Il. 5.191 ἔμπης δ' οὐκ ἐδάμασσα· θεός νύ τίς ἐστι κοτήεις
Il. 3.220 φαίης κε ζάκοτόν τέ τιν' ἔμμεναι ἄφρονά τ' αὔτως

As to the first example, Diomedes is in his *aristeia* when Aeneas tries to get Pandarus to shoot down the rampaging warrior. The passage contains not merely the form *kotēeís* but also a number of other anger terms, beginning at *Il.* 5.177–78:

εἰ μή τις θεός ἐστι κοτεσσάμενος Τρώεσσιν
ἱρῶν μηνίσας· χαλεπὴ δὲ θεοῦ ἔπι μῆνις.

Unless some god has come to have *kótos* against the Trojans angry over offerings; anger of a god is difficult to deal with.

This passage is to be compared to *Il.* 5.184–86:

> εἰ δ' ὅ γ' ἀνὴρ ὅ φημί, δαΐφρων Τυδέος υἱός,
> οὐχ ὅ γ' ἄνευθε θεοῦ τάδε μαίνεται, ἀλλά τις ἄγχι
> ἕστηκ' ἀθανάτων, νεφέλῃ εἰλυμένος ὤμους.
>
> But if this is a mortal as I declare, the brilliant son of Tydeus, he still does not rage so apart from a god, but someone of the immortals has stood near him, covered as to his shoulders with a cloud.

The above two examples provide a context for Diomedes' anger in *Il.* 5.190–91:

> καί μιν ἔγωγ' ἐφάμην 'Αιδωνῆι προϊάψειν,
> ἔμπης δ' οὐκ ἐδάμασσα· θεός νύ τίς ἐστι κοτήεις.
>
> And I thought to hurl him to his doom, but still I did not defeat him; now it is a god that has *kótos*.

The tangle of anger words here is worth unraveling. Aeneas and Pandarus are operating in the realm of speculation and hypothesis, just as were Achilles and Calchas when Calchas went through the possible kinds of anger that might result from his revelation of Agamemnon's folly in *Iliad* 1. If this passage is consistent with the meanings that I have outlined for *kótos*, we should take *kotessámenos* (*Il.* 5.177) as causal—"some god, *because* he or she has *kótos* against Trojans, has *mênis* over *hierá*" (*Il.* 5.178). That is to say, the *kótos* drives the *mênis* forward.[117] The difficulty in which the Trojans find themselves leads Pandarus to speculate about what possible explanation can account for Diomedes' success and the failure of his bow. Such remoteness is available most easily through the culturally based notion of *kótos*, one that we have seen calls to mind the social rupture that has caused the war. The most powerful reading for Pandarus's allusion to the *kótos* of a god is that he recognizes what Aeneas denies: it is not so much that rituals have been violated, but rather that the foundations on which those rituals are built have been irreparably damaged. In effect, Pandarus dismisses Aeneas's speculation about a god, *hierōn mēnisas* ("angry over sacrificial offerings") and points to a much more horrifying prospect: that things are going wrong now because of *kótos*.[118]

To summarize these points, in fact no ritual violation has taken place. Rather the poem is moving ahead in the direction of the fulfillment of the original plan of Zeus, to be temporarily set aside for Thetis's son, Achilles.[119] In the larger tradition, the abuse of Hera and Athena by Paris coupled with the violation of *xenía* ("guest-friendship") against Menelaus provoked the *kótos* of Zeus. So too was Zeus's wrath provoked in a simile in *Iliad* 16 (385–92), one that describes an injustice in the *agorḗ* ("the assembly"); so too in Books 3, 4, and 5 the breaking of the oaths provides a context in which to remember the *kótos* that is at the root of the Trojans' troubles.

Finally, I will examine here one of the most famous passages in the *Iliad*, as influenced by the concept of *kótos*. The words are those of Antenor as he describes Odysseus:

> ἀλλ' ὅτε δὴ πολύμητις ἀναΐξειεν Ὀδυσσεύς,
> στάσκεν, ὑπαὶ δὲ ἴδεσκε κατὰ χθονὸς ὄμματα πήξας,
> σκῆπτρον δ' οὔτ' ὀπίσω οὔτε προπρηνὲς ἐνώμα,
> ἀλλ' ἀστεμφὲς ἔχεσκεν, αἴδρεϊ φωτὶ ἐοικώς·
> φαίης κε ζάκοτόν τέ τιν' ἔμμεναι ἄφρονά τ' αὔτως.
> (*Il.* 3.216–20)

> But whenever many-minded Odysseus darted up, he would stand, and he would look down with a gaze fixed on the ground, then he gesticulated with the staff neither backwards nor forwards, but he would hold still, like a man with no clue; you'd say he was deep in *kótos*, and with no mind at all.

Kirk's summary of the content of this scene omits that Odysseus's character is typed as *zákotos*:

> Now comes the most dramatic and effective part of Antenor's speech, to which the rest is preliminary in a sense: whenever Odysseus leapt to his feet he would just stand there with his eyes fixed on the ground. His staff held motionless as though he were a fool.[120]

Not just any fool, but one who has *kótos*. That is to say *kótos* is not the anger of the fierce warrior, violent, extravagant in gesture and speech; rather Odysseus's anger is masked with silence; it is an anger that plays the fool so as to catch its victim off guard. As it turns out this is the anger of feud.[121] The intensive prefix *zá-*, highlights how Odysseus is characterized by this kind of anger, an anger that Achilles is only once said to have. For Achilles' anger, as we have seen in Book 1, does not fix its eyes on the ground nor does it keep still. When Achilles' anger is *kótos,* it is so only in the fantasy of Agamemnon as he imagines Achilles at home with a successful *nóstos*:

> Μυρμιδόνεσσιν ἄνασσε· σέθεν δ' ἐγὼ οὐκ ἀλεγίζω
> οὐδ' ὄθομαι κοτέοντος·
> (*Il.* 2.180–81)

> Rule over the Myrmidons; I can hardly care about you, nor can I worry about your *kótos*.

But Achilles is to have no *nóstos* nor is he to have the privilege of being a powerful *ánaks*. The anger that Calchas has told us is the prerogative of kingship can only belong to Achilles in Agamemnon's worst nightmare. Yet, as Antenor tells us, it is a part of Odysseus's personality to have *this* kind of anger, the kind drenched in the gore in Ithaca when Odysseus's soldiers destroy the last suitor, *kekotēóti thumôi* (*Od.* 22.477).[122]

Notes

1. These and subsequent examples are gathered together in Appendix 1, in an order reflecting my presentation.

2. See O'Neill 1942. Thus *kótos* follows Beekes's useful explanation of the causes of word localization in the Homeric line: "Rule 2: Word end desired at O'Neill's position 8" (Beekes 1972, 2).

3. O'Neill 1942: Table 2.1 shows that, for words shaped ˘ ˘ , position 8 is greatest in frequency (36.7% for the *Iliad*) against position 4 (19.4%), followed by positions 2, 6, and 10. The point here is that *kótos* is regularized in this position. This is one example of the paradigmatic features of Homeric formular practice (Martin 1989, 165); Parry puts the point succinctly, when he talks about the way Homer uses *mênis* (Parry 1971, 433), "The word is sufficiently uncommon, and yet . . . its position is prescribed." Groundbreaking work in localization and formulas has been undertaken in Visser 1987, 1988.

4. See Eustathius at *Il.* 1.82; I will cover *Il.* 14.111 with the other exceptions in a separate study on *khólos* and *kótos* in the manuscript tradition. See above p. 14 and n. 23 below; also p. 33 and p. 124, n. 4. For Diomedes's speech, see Lowenstam 1993, 84–85 and Lohmann gives it brief mention (1970, 93–94).

5. The stative value will be important in establishing the force of Calchas's meaning, and I will return to this topic below.

6. Compare here also *Od.* 19.71, *daimoníē, tí moi hōd' epékheis kekotēóti thumôi?* ("Lady, why thus do you hold a vehement grudge against me?").

7. As for its usage with anger terms, *ainós* occurs also with *khólos* (*Il.* 22.94) but only once in the *Iliad* and *Odyssey*; but see *H. Dem.* 350, 354; it is also found with *mênis* in the *H. Dem.* 350–51, and 410. See Watkins 1977a, 192 and Mawet 1979, 316. *Ainós* is the only epithet shared by *khólos* and *kótos* (cf. Paraskevaides 1984, 69). See also its use with with *khṓomai* (*Il.* 8.397 and *Il.* 20.29) and *ménos (Il.* 17.565).

8. For *phúlopis* see *Il.* 4.15, 65; *Il.* 5.496; *Il.* 6.105; *Il.* 11.213; *Il.* 16.256; *Il.* 16.677; *Od.* 24.475; and for *dēiotḗs* see *Il.* 3.20 [= 7.40, 51]; *Il.* 13.207; *Il.* 13.603; *Il.* 15.512; *Il.* 22.64; *Od.* 11.516; Od. 12.257; Od. 22.229. Cf. *LfgrE* s.v. *ainós*, B.1.

9. See note 7 above.

10. It is tempting to think of *kótos* and *khólos* as representing a binary pair that can manifest itself in different ways across the Homeric texts. In this regard it is significant that *tetíēsthon* at *Il.* 8.447 plays the role that *khólos* did in Calchas's definition. For *tetíēsthon* as anger, see Slatkin 1991, 98–99 n. 10: "In Homer the formula *tetiēménos êtor* ("disturbed at heart") when it is used to describe the gods always means "angry." In *Iliad* 16, Hera warns Zeus about the divine anger of the *athanátoi*, as Calchas warned Achilles of Agamemnon's royal *kótos*. See Richardson 1993 at 24.23–30 and the literature there for the controversy surrounding allusions to the judgment of Paris in the *Iliad*. Cf. 1990, 18–20. If Calchas's definition of *kótos* is accepted, this anger term provides more evidence for such an allusion to the distant beginning of the conflict.

11. Cosset 1990, 7–8.

12. See Alcman (Page) 1.13–14 and Palmer 1950 with Watkins 1983, 39.

13. For *kótos* and feud see Chapter 5.

14. On the importance of *ákhos* to the thematics of the *Iliad*, see Nagy 1979, 69–93 with Mawet 1979, 293–349. We will return in Part II to the subject of *ainós* as an epithet shared by both *khólos* and *kótos*.

15. "Dans quelques cas, ἐπί souligne le sentiment qui provient de tel ou tel événement. . . ." Chantraine 1953, 106 (§151).

16. See, for example, *epíkotos stásis* in Pindar, *Frag.* 109.4 (Snell-Maehler) and *epikótea mḗdea* in Aeschylus, *Prometheus Bound* 601; cf. *aràs epikótous* in Aeschylus, *Seven against Thebes* 786, with *epikótōs* in *Prometheus* 163; these may be an extension of *epí* with accusative signifying "duration" (cf. Chantraine 1953, 111 [§156]).

17. *Ékhō* thus strengthens the perfective sense of the perfect participle *kekotēóti*. Such an example shows an early stage in the development of *ékhō* as an auxiliary with a participle to give a perfect sense. Cf. *LSJ* s.v. *ékhō* IV. The notion of duration is also part of *ékhō*'s perfectivizing function (*LSJ* s.v. *ékhō*, IV.2 and A.8). In Homer, *khólos* is never the object of any form of *ékhō*. On *kekotēóti*, see Chantraine (1973a, 428 [§204]).

18. Important for understanding *télos* is Ambrose 1963 and 1965, with the study of Waanders 1983.

19. See Muellner 1992, 18–19, and above Chapter 1.

20. See also *Il.* 9.436, 14.50, 14.207, 406, 15.155, 16.206, etc. On *thumós* in the dative see Sullivan 1980, 142–44. On *thumós* with verbs for anger see now Caswell 1990, 39–40, who senses the importance of *kótos* (see §56 on "unusual ways of describing anger"); Caswell is in agreement with Jahn (1987) in seeing synonymity for the major terms for consciousness (*thumós, phrēn, kēr, prapídes, kradiē, êtor*) in Homeric poetry. For Caswell (1990, 50) *thumós* is identified as the "neutral bearer of emotion"; see also 39. This encourages us to see *thumós* as playing little role in the definition of *kótos* and *khólos*. Cf. Clarke 1999.

21. For the poetics of such a dichotomy, cf. Watkins 1970.

22. See, for example, *Il.* 4.161: *eí per gár te kaì autík' Olúmpios ouk etélessen, / ék te kaì opsè teleî* ("For if in fact the Olympian has not accomplished it, he will accomplish it at length, even if late").

23. The nature of *kótos* is important to the force of Athena's claim at *Od.* 13.342. However we see the rhetorical force of Athena's statement in this passage (cf. Clay 1983, 44), her voice is made even stronger when she introduces the *kótos* of Poseidon into her speech. Note that this passage is one of the few (cf. *Il.* 14.111 and *Il.* 24.584) that show a variant reading of *khólos* for *kótos*. *Kótos* is also used of Poseidon's wrath against Odysseus at *Od.* 11.102. Here compare Poseidon's *kótos* at Odysseus's treatment of Polyphemus with his *khólos* at his grandson's death in battle (*Il.* 13.206). We will see that the death of one's *phíloi* ("one's nearest and dearest") is a typical source of *khólos*. Thus, for *kótos* to be styled as Poseidon's anger in the *Odyssey* is an indication of the particular character of the god's wrath; indeed, the actions of Odysseus, in this case, are seen as the fulfillment of a prophecy. (For a general discussion, cf. Düntzer 1872.) Furthermore, Odysseus's actions, in violation of *xenía*, are related to transgressions that lead to *kótos*, as in the lengthy duration of the anger of Poseidon (predicted by Teiresias at *Od.* 11.100–103). In the light of what is to be said about *kótos* and notions such as *díkē*, I quote J. Lidov (1977, 235n.9): "What is important is that in the *Odyssey* Homer sets Poseidon's angers in a context that gives them a moral value," where I read "moral" as a term that points to violations of a social code that threaten the social order.

24. Cf. Ebeling's *immitto* for *entíthesthai* and *eniénai*.

25. Cf. *Il.* 10.361, 364; *Od.* 9.386, 21.69. P. Chantraine discusses this phrase in an article on sigmatic compounds (1975, 83–85). *Emmenés* is composed of *en* + *ménos* with *en* indicating "que le sujet est rempli de *ménos*" (84). Originally there is no connection to *ménein*: "mais il n'est pas impossible que le vieux composé *emmenès aieí* ait subi dans cette formule l' influence de *ménō* . . ." (84).

26. The careful reader will note the place of *khṓomai* in Calchas's definition. Since the matter is complex, I will turn to that term for anger in a separate study. It must suffice to say for now that *khṓomai* is often coupled with *khólos*. For a discussion of the richness of Homer's vocabulary for anger, see my Introduction and n. 18 below.

27. It should be kept in mind here that *khólos* never occurs with *emmenés aieí*, as noted above.

28. Chantraine (1975) cites Aratos 339: *Lagōòs emmenès ḗmata pánta diṓketai* and, using J. Martin's translation, "le Lièvre (constellation) sans arrèt, continuellement échappe à la poursuite" (83). The hunting image is transferred to the description of the stellar night. The parallels to the hunting simile in *Iliad* 10 include the image of the hare as well as the use of *diṓketai*.

29. For the translation see Russo et al. 1992 ad loc. to the effect that "the verb governs both *tóde dôma* and the two infinitives, which are consecutive or final"; but see Merry 1892, who takes *dôma* as the direct object of *esthiémen* (citing the parallel in *Od.* 4.318) with an intransitive main verb: "you who have set yourselves to eat and drink this house. . . ." This latter version is compatible with LSJ's rendering, s.v. *kráō* (A).

30. On the development, see Chantraine 1927, 21–24; 1973, §289.

31. The locus classicus for reticence in naming is the opening of the *Odyssey*. See Clay 1983, 26–29, 54–68. "The omission of the hero's name from the prologue . . . points to an important thematic component of the *Odyssey*" (29). I expand this observation to include, besides Clay's comment on the thematics of the *Odyssey*, the parameters of Homeric style, where naming conventions can be highly formal: see Muellner 1976, 74–75 n.9, outlining another restriction on naming. Furthermore, names can also be spoken when they ought not be: see Lycaon's disastrous use of Hector's name at *Il.* 21.95–96, the close of his supplication to Achilles; cf. Odysseus's boast to Polyphemus (*Od.* 9.504–5).

32. Note that the suppression of the dative object coincides with the expression *tó ge thumôi*, one of the only three expressions signifying a (physical or mental) location for *kótos*. On the way pronominal usage can be tied to the social context of the speech, see Muellner 1992, 126 and 1975, 74–75 n. 9.

33. For the notion of "family" in understanding the intricate patterns of traditional language, see Nagler 1974, especially Chapters 1 and 2. Valuable use has been made of this concept by Kahane 1994, esp. 13–14.

34. On nucleus and periphery see Bakker 1991 and for metrics Visser 1987 and 1988. The systematic analysis of language as to relationship between center and periphery is originally developed in Prague school linguistic theory. In Homeric study, the new applications of the model to formulaic theory appear to veer off from Parryan formulaics, but it remains premature to assess the theoretical implications of this model. A promising connection can be made to Nagler's (ultimately Wittgenstein's) notion of "family" (cf. Nagler 1974, 15 for an important quotation from the *Philosophical Investigations*); cf. Nagler 1966, 457.

35. *Il.* 2.599, *Il.* 2.195, *Il.* 3.413, *Il.* 4.391, *Il.* 6.205, *Il.* 9.538, *Il.* 15.68, *Il.* 20.253, *Il.* 21.479, *Il.* 23.482, *Il.* 24.55; *Od.* 12.348, *Od.* 16.25.

36. *Il.* 4.501; *Od.* 8.227.

37. See Nagy 1974, 35–36, 99. See also the use made of this observation in Muellner 1976, 45–46.

38. See Watkins 1977a, 191–92.

39. The point of method here is stated by Nagy 1976b, 211 n. 21: "In studying the semantic range of forms in formulaic diction, it is methodologically important to distinguish derived forms from basic forms, since the two will not have the same range of applications."

40. See note 38.

41. See the important qualification of Turpin 1988 with Muellner 1992, 136–35; and now see Muellner 1996.

42. Watkins 1977a, 203; the connection has been furthered in his later work, especially 1987a. I will return to this word in my discussion of *khólos* below.

43. On the metaphors of "crooked" vs. "straight" and *díkē*, see Nagy 1990a, 184; cf. 311–12, where the tradition of correlating natural phenomena with human events is elucidated.

44. On the derivation of *epopizéō* < *opid-* see Watkins 1977a, 204; and on the implications of a word for anger coming from a word of perception (*h_3ek^w-), see pages 204–9 and Part II below.

45. On the omission of names as a stylistic feature: Muellner 1992, 126 and 1976, 74–5 n. 9; cf. Clay 1983, 26–29.

46. Irmscher 1950, 32; Arend 1933, 95; Nagler 1974, 55; this arming is singled out by Armstrong in one of the classic studies of type-scenes (1958, 342 n. 11). Although he refrains from analyzing it with the other arming scenes that he studies ("it is a special arming"), he notes that the spear in being described as *brithù méga stibarón* is equivalent to Achilles' spear (*Il.* 16.141, *Il.* 19.388) and to that of Patroclus (*Il.* 16.802).

47. On the differences between the two scenes see Fenik 1968, 73–74 and Kirk 1990 at *Il.* 5.747.

48. Stanford emphasizes that the line is generic, as can be seen from the use of generic *te* with the gnomic aorist. His translation is "heroes, whoever are of the kind that she is accustomed to be angry with" (Stanford 1947–1948 at 1.101).

49. At the level of a narrative sequence or a speech we could call this "ring-composition." However, at the level of a short, epigrammatic sequence this kind of closure has many parallels; in the Indo-European realm see the Irish *dúnad* (cf. Murphy 1961, 86).

50. On the possessive compound *obrimopátrē*, see Chantraine *DELG* 2:864 ("au père puissant"), with his discussion of *óbrimos* at p. 772 (s.v.); and Frisk II, 345. *Brithù méga stibarón* occurs three other times in the *Iliad* (*Il.* 16.141 = 19.388, 16.802) each of which refers to the spear of Achilles, wielded in Book 16 by the doomed Patroclus. This asyndetic formula primarily applies to Achilles and Athena, presenting us with another collocation that links the gods with Achilles, besides the well-known association of the gods and Achilles through *mênis* (see Watkins 1977a, 189, "En effet le seul humain pour lequel le substantif *mênis* est prédiqué dans le corpus homérique et hésiodique est précisément Achille [4 fois sur 12 dans l'*Iliade*; dans l'*Odyssée mênis* apparaît 4 fois, dans Hésiod et les Hymnes 3 fois, toujours à propos d' un dieu]"). Cf. now Muellner 1996 for full treatment of the role of *mênis* between gods and mortals.

51. See Burkert 1985, 141–49 on Athena's martial aspects, her "primitive ferocity."

52. On *stíkhas andrōn*, Kirk (1990 at 5.745–7) doubts that "subduing the ranks of heroes" is traditional. Yet *stíkhas andrōn* often occurs in places where a leader is putting

subordinates in line; cf. Agamemnon at *Il.* 3.196; or where, as does Diomedes in Book 5, a warrior is decimating the *stíkhas andrōn* (*Il.* 5.166). The collocation implies hierarchical relations.

53. On the syntax of *toîsin* see Chantraine 1953, 168, with reference to the variant *hoîsin*. In either case the generic nature of the statement is clear.

54. Frisk 1960–1970, s.v. *óbrimos*, "das ὀ- macht grosse Schwierigkeiten." See *ópatros* and *óbrimopátrē* in Sommer 1948, 141–49.

55. See note 54.

56. For the wrath of Athena see Clay 1983, especially 46–53; Athena's anger has special significance for the *Odyssey*. Clay 1983, 46–53; see Irmscher 1950, 69–71.

57. The usual pattern for the last three items is shield, helmet, and spear (Armstrong 1958, 344). But as Armstrong points out (342 n. 11), Athena's arming substitutes her aegis for the shield. That her aegis presents an ecphrastic display makes it an allomorph of the warrior's shield.

58. Martin 1989, 28. *Kótos* is linked with promises in *Il.* 21.456–57, where Poseidon and Apollo, cheated by Laomedon, are *kekotēóti thumōi, misthoû khōoménoio, tòn <u>hupostàs ouk etélesse</u>*. The notion of promising points to the future as much as does the unfulfilled *télos*. That payment and debt are intimately bound up with the notion of feuding is stressed by Black-Michaud 1975, 80–85.

59. Such a neat one-line summary of both poems (the *Iliad* = *Ílion ekpérsant' euteíkheon* ["having sacked well-walled Ilium"]; the *Odyssey* = *aponéesthai*) occurs also earlier at *Il.* 1.19: *ekpérsai Priámoio pólin, eû d' oíkad' hikésthai*. Cf. *Il.* 2.453-54; *Il.* 1.151; *Od.* 2.342–43, etc. For a partial list of such passages, cf. Walsh 1999: 160-161. This kind of self-reference is an important feature of the Homeric poetic technique of allusion.

60. See Frame (1978, 82, 99, 110–11) for the name "Nestor" presenting a transitive meaning: "he who brings [his people] home."

61. Muellner 1992, 128, with examples (p. 127) *Il.* 15.122, *Od.* 5.146–47, *H. Aphr.* 290, *Il.* 16.711, *Il.* 5.444; cf. now Muellner 1996.

62. Chantraine *DELG* II, s.v., (772); and *DELG* I s.v. *brímē* and *briarós* (196).

63. Chantraine *DELG* II, s.v. *óbrimos*.

64. Frisk's caution on this passage ("sehr fragliche Konjektur," s.v. *brímē*) is not relevant, since the variant *hup' ombrímēs* would yield the same result for our purposes.

65. See Frisk on *brímē*-, Frisk 1960–1970: I.269.

66. The only loquitur formula including a *kótos*-form is at *Od.* 9.501, where the *kótos*-phrase is circumstantial rather than causal. Significantly this passage occurs in the apologue, where Odysseus as narrator may be thereby expressing an interest by so identifying his anger.

67. The one exception might be *Il.* 4.168.

68. See Group 3, Appendix 1. The mortals referred to in Group 3 are twice explicitly the Trojans and once a hypothetical group of men, analogous to the Trojans, who have violated *thémis*.

69. See my discussion of *Il.* 4.164–68 above, p. 23–25.

70. See O'Brien 1993 for the wrath of Hera in the *Iliad*. O'Brien argues that the wrath of Zeus and Hera are opposed, the latter serving as the model for Achilles' savagery, while Zeus's *khólos* is part of a process which leads ultimately to Zeus' "divine pity" (1993, 77–111).

71. As Kirk 1990 suggests at *Il.* 8.457–62.

72. On cannibalism in this passage and elsewhere in the poem see O'Brien 1993, 78–81; and see her Chapter 4, "Hera's Iliadic Venom and its Source," for Hera's rage.

73. I will return to this important concept in Chapter 6.

74. Cf. *Il.* 16.384–92, especially 392: *minúthei dé te érg' anthrōpōn* ("and the works of mortals are diminished").

75. *Il.* 4.51–57, and note *atéleston* ("unfulfilled") at 57.

76. In the *Iliad* the basis of *kótos* is Paris's original choice, which is mentioned only once at the end of the *Iliad* (24.27–30). The referents of *sphin* are Hera, Athena, and Poseidon (*Il.* 24.25–26). See Reinhardt 1938 for an influential discussion of Homer's minimal reference to the judgment of Paris, with a crucial reevaluation in Stinton 1990, 18–20. Richardson 1993 at *Il.* 24.23–30 presents a strong argument for the judgment of Paris as "part of the original poem." From a traditionalist's point of view the evidence for the thematics of *kótos* suggests that the judgment of Paris is fundamental to the long history of Homeric performance. See also Griffin 1978, 15 and n. 49.

77. Note that Nagler (1974, 149–50) shows the mythic resonance of this passage; flood myths tend to suggest provocations by errant human beings of gods charged with maintaining order. See also Lloyd-Jones 1983, 6 with the literature cited there.

78. Janko 1992, at *Il.* 16.384–93 points to the agricultural context for this destruction; I take *érg' anthrṓpōn* as metonymic for the culture of those who have thwarted *themis*.

79. On interaction of storm similes with their context, see Petegorsky 1982, Chapter 1. On the simile, see Janko 1992 at *Il.* 16.384–93, who compares *Il.* 21.522–24, "where a Trojan rout is likened to a city destroyed because of the gods' anger; here the Trojans are linked with wrong doing, and the poet comes near to an open justification of Troy's fall."

80. On the notion of "plan" and its importance to oral composition, see Thornton 1984, Chapter 3.

81. On the anger of Hera, see above n. 74.

82. Chantraine 1927, 8; so too Monro 1891, 32 (§28).

83. Although *kotéō* is usually understood as denominative, it is good to keep in mind that: "le problème de la distinction entre les déverbatifs à vocalisme *o* et les dénominatifs de substantif à vocalisme *o* ne se pose pas au niveau de grec" (Chantraine 1973b, 240 [§287]). The paucity of occurrences of the noun *kótos*, and then only in the accusative case, and the seeming antiquity of the verbal forms make a plausible case for a deverbative development of this root. This issue is relevant to the etymology of *kótos* (see Chapter 6).

84. O'Neill 1942, 145, Table 18.

85. In addition to these references, see also Onians 1951, 49–56, where Onians relates both *khólos* and *kótos* to the *thumós*. Important for the meaning of *thumós* in Homer are Jahn 1987, with the earlier work of Böhme 1929, 19–23 and Sullivan 1980. See also Claus 1981, 37, with Renehan 1984. *Thumós* eventually changes from meaning "seat of anger" to "anger", see LSJ, s.v. *thumós* II.4; cf. Webster 1957, 153, 154; with Thalmann 1986, *Il.* 494–506, where the variety of emotions that the *thumós* can feel is made clear: "The *thumós* . . . can feel anger, fear, zeal, love . . . and battle fury . . . it is probably also aroused by hatred, sudden shock, and envy, and it plays a part in premonition" (499). On anger and *thumós* see also Bremmer 1983, 54–55, and on *thumós* and Homeric psychology Adkins 1970, 15–19, as well as Harrison 1960, 66–68; 71–72; 74–75; cf. Caswell 1990. Further references can be found at Sullivan 1988, 69 n. 73. M. Clarke's *Flesh and Spirit in the Songs of Homer* (Oxford: Clarendon Press, 1999) appeared too late to include in my discussion.

86. Here we can apply the notion of nucleus and periphery, as presented by Visser 1987, 1988, and Bakker 1991, Bakker and Van den Houten 1992. The linguistic feature of center and periphery can be traced to Prague School linguistics.

87. Cf. *Il.* 16.392

88. *Il.* 21.457, presents the same kind of cluster of anger words that obtains in *Od.* 5.146–47. The *kótos* determines the depth of the anger in both these cases, and the other anger term functions to mark the emotional level accompanying the *kótos*. It is important to remember that of all the anger words used in such clusters, *khólos* is never used with *kótos*.

89. The use of *etélesse* in line 457, responding to *misthoîo télos* in line 450, suggests the goal implicit in *kótos*. For the use of *télos* and time see Ambrose 1965, 53; for a contrary view, see Waanders 1983, 53 (§41); 43 (§34). Whichever lemma we choose, the poetic relationship of *télos* and *kótos* is certain.

90. That this move into ancient Trojan history happens in Book 21 is no accident, since in this book we have Achilles fight with the river, "the climax of the *Iliad* on its mythic level of organization" (Nagler 1974, 152), especially in its presentation of disorder on a massive scale. Poseidon's conflict with Apollo over Laomedon's swindle is another sign of this pervasive abnormality.

91. Compare how Eurymachus describes Antinoos's perfidy: not so much that he wanted to marry Penelope as "in order that *he himself be king* in the community of well-built Ithaca" (*Od.* 22.52). On the mixed blessing of Odysseus' return as king see Nagler 1990, 231–35.

92. Throughout the punishment of Melanthius, the verbs are plural with no named subject: *êgon* (474), *támnon* (476), *exerúsan* (476), *kópton* (477), *kíon* (479); note too the participle *aponipsámenoi* (478) and the infinitive *dásasthai* (476). Far from the act of an individualistic hero, the destruction of the suitors is portrayed as an act of the *oîkos* as a whole.

93. On the meaning of the names, see Vidal-Naquet 1981, 153; on a connection between "black" and anger, see Padel 1995, Chapter 5, but note that this feature is relevant to *khólos* and not *kótos*. On the mythological valence of "black" see Fontenrose 1960, 233–246; there may be an implicit contrast between the servile family of Dolius and king Odysseus being worked out along the lines of Calchas's opposition of *khólos* to *kótos*. Moreover, a name like *Mélanthos* can be associated with Poseidon, cf. Usener 1948, 221. More on darkness and anger can be found in Sullivan 1988, 44–48 (with a focus on *phrénes*) and Slatkin 1991, 90–98, as applied to Thetis and Demeter.

94. With a play on her name *Melanthṓ* ("the dark one") and *aglaíē* ("bright-radiance").

95. I know of no other case where brother and sister in Greek literature are so named. Again see Vidal-Naquet (n. 13).

96. I use "equals" loosely to mean characters that are not socially positioned in a hierarchical relationship.

97. Heubeck and Hoekstra 1989 at 9.500–5.

98. *Od.* 9.480: *ho d' épeita khólōsato kēróthi mâllon* ("When he came to be the more angry in his heart"). On this formula, see Part II.

99. Muellner 1976, 88 argues that the relationship of these words is "not only etymological but still felt." On institutions of reciprocity see Donlan 1982, Schwartz 1982 and 1985.

100. It is worth noting that of the four passages in Group 6, each involves a *télos*: for *Il.* 21.456, see *Il.* 21.450 (*mistoîo télos* "the time for payment") and 455 (*tòn hupostàs ouk etélesse* "[the payment] which he promised he did not accomplish"); for *Od.* 9.501, see *Od.* 9.512 (*teleutḗsesthai opíssō* "to be fulfilled in the future"); for *Od.* 22.477, see Od. 22.479 (*tetélesto de érgon* "and the deed was accomplished"). The concept *télos* is also implicit in the context of *Od.* 19.71 and *Od.* 19.88–89.

101. There is an implicit ethical claim on Odysseus' part when he uses *kótos* here; this claim is in tension with a reading of the poem that questions the violations of *xenía* by Odysseus and his crew in the Cyclops's cave. That tension is part of the effect of the narration presented by Odysseus as the narrator of his own tale in the Phaeacian court. The context of the tale as understood by an audience, perhaps even the one in Phaeacia, might call this narrative into question, if it critically evaluates Odysseus' crew's uninvited feasting in Cyclops's cave. It is precisely these kinds of complex social questions that *kótos* brings to mind.

102. Chantraine 1973a, §164.

103. Chantraine 1973b, §281; see also Monro 1891, §39, p. 41.

104. Chantraine 1973b, §289, with Monro 1891, §39.

105. Chantraine 1973a, §164.

106. Although Chantraine and the handbooks so classify it (Chantraine 1973b, §289; Monro 1891, §39, 41). On *kotéō* as denominative, see Chantraine 1928, 24, deriving *ketkotḗōs* < *kotéō* based on the thematic noun.

107. Chantraine 1973b, §288, with examples.

108. Chantraine 1973b, §287.

109. For interchange between phrases placed at line-end and caesura Nagy 1974, 66, 94; see Muellner 1976, 63, for the notion of the metrical transposition of formulas from line end to caesura.

110. Cf. previous note.

111. See Chantraine 1973a, §163.

112. Jamison 1981, 180–81, with Jamison 1977, Chapter 8, 285-287. Jamison goes on to point out that these replacements generally involve "words of emotion or mental activity . . . to stress the subject's involvement in the action."

113. Compare the way that Glaucus and Diomedes in Book 6 discover their common bond in *xenía*. It is worth suggesting that *kótos* is a kind of reverse *xenía*. In the final chapter of Part I, *kótos* will emerge as a way of talking about feud. See Black-Michaud 1975 for an introduction to the literature on feuding; W. I. Miller elaborates on the distinction between feuds and other kinds of violence (1990, 180–81); his definitive discussion of the feud in Icelandic saga has as yet no parallel in Homeric studies, for its systematic analysis of vengeance and feud in a narrative tradition (Miller 1990, especially 179–220). See also Byock 1982.

114. The prepositional phrase *met' Admḗtou huión* follows *ebebḗkei*, leaving *kotéous(a)* without an explicit object; that object may indeed be Apollo but the *result* of the *kótos* is her aggression against Eumelos. This kind of ambiguity, we will see, is what we can expect from the anger of feud, where the focus is on the loyalties of the victim, and not the victim as an individual. On the syntax see Chantraine 1953, 118 (§167).

115. On the legend of Admetus and Apollo see Dale 1954, vii-xiii. This passage should be added to the list of sources found there.

116. Apollodorus 3.10.8 gives us Eumelus's name as a suitor of Helen.

117. Indeed, Muellner (1996, 48–51) sees the use of *mênis* here as "generic," because "it is not possible to claim with confidence . . . [that] *mênis* is a sanction for the violation of the reciprocal exchange in connection with the abduction of Helen." It is now possible to make such a claim with the confidence provided by what we have found out about *kótos*, that it can typically bring to mind the abduction of Helen; indeed, its reference outside the immediate context is liable to make it seem "generic," when its reference is quite particular, namely, the motivation for the entire Trojan War.

118. For a parallel to this scene see Achilles' suggestion in *Iliad* 1 that Apollo's plague is caused by some ritual violation (*Il.* 1.64–67, with the anger word *ekhṓsato* [64]). Here too Calchas needs to correct the erroneous interpretation of Achilles, as I think Pandarus in *Iliad* 5 tries to change Aeneas's immediate and incorrect suggestion. I will analyze *khṓomai* in a subsequent study, but let me say now that it should be read as closely related to both *khólos* and *mênis*, so that it is in essence a different kind of anger from *kótos*.

119. See now Slatkin 1991.

120. Kirk 1985 at *Il.* 3.216–23.

121. See again Black-Michaud 1975 and my remarks at the end of Part I, below.

122. The scene at the wall continues by telling us that Odysseus' silence anticipates a rhetorical flourish: *all' hóte dḕ ópa te megálēn ek stḗtheos eiē / kaì épea niphádessin eoikóta kheimeríēisin. . . .* (*Il.* 3.221–22) "But when he sent his voice forth from his chest and words like winter snows. . . ." The Achillean hero, relying on *khólos* and *mênis*, is presented in bold opposition to Odysseus and his reliance on voice (*ópa*, 221) and words (*épea*, 222) as well as disguise (*polúmētis*, 216, "many-minded," masquerading as *áphrōn* [220]—perhaps the most self-reflexive trick of *mêtis*).

Chapter Three

Κότος and Social Status

At the beginning of this study, I suggested that *kótos* was identified in Calchas's definition both by the length of time that it lasts and by the social status of the angered party. We have seen that the use of *télos, metópisthen*, and other related terminology gives *kótos* a sense of extraordinary duration. The issue of the term's relation to social status now demands attention.

Calchas's definition focuses on Agamemnon's potential *kótos* against the prophet as the rancor of a superior, a *basileús* in this case, against a social inferior (*Il.* 1.80–83). That *kótos* characterizes especially the anger of kings suggests that *kótos* may apply also to relationships between different categories of superiors and subordinates.

The following scheme classifies *kótos* with reference to Homeric social hierarchies.

Gods against mortals:

In each of these cases, a god or gods has *kótos* against (or in reference to) a mortal.

Il. 4.168 Zeus's *kótos* at mortals for breaking oaths.
Il. 5.177 Speculation about a god's *kótos*.
Il. 5.191 Speculation about a god's *kótos*.
Il. 5.747 = *Od.*1.101 = *Il.* 8.391 Athena's *kótos* at mortals (*hērṓōn*).
Il. 8.449 Hera's and Athena's *kótos* at men.
Il. 14.143 A god's (potential) *kótos* at Agamemnon.
Il. 16.386 Zeus's *kótos* at a city (in a simile).
Il. 18.367 Hera's *kótos* at Trojans.
Il. 21.456 Poseidon's and Apollo's *kótos* at Laomedon.
Il. 23.383 Apollo's *kótos* at Diomedes.

Il. 23.391 Athena's *kótos* at Eumelus, the son of Admetus.
Od. 1.101 = *Od.* 8.391 = *Il.* 5.747 Athena's *kótos* at mortals (*hērṓōn*).
Od. 11.102 Poseidon's *kótos* at Odysseus.
Il. 13.342 Poseidon's *kótos* at Odysseus.

Gods against other gods:

Il. 14.191 Aphrodite's *kótos* at Hera (concerning competing allegiances to the Trojans and Achaeans; cf. *Il.* 23.391).
Il. 16.449 Zeus's (potential) *kótos* at immortals (concerning the sons of the immortals).
Od. 5.147 Zeus's (potential) *kótos* at Calypso (over Odysseus).
Il. 10.517 Apollo's *kótos* at Athena (concerning competing allegiances to the Trojans and Achaeans).

Mortals against mortals of subordinate status:

Od. 9.501 Odysseus and the Cyclops.
Od. 22.477 Odysseus' *oîkos* and Melanthius.
Od. 19.71 Melantho and Odysseus.
Od. 19.83 Penelope and Melantho.
Il. 2.223 Achaeans and Thersites.

Mortals against mortals of comparable status:

Il. 1.181 Achilles and Agamemnon (over Briseis).
Il. 3.345 Paris and Menelaus (over Helen).
Il. 13.517 Deiphobos and Idomeneus (over Helen).

In a number of these cases, the interpretation of *kótos* depends on the weight attached to Calchas's assertion that *kótos* implies antagonism across social strata. In particular, structuralist method provides one approach to understanding this data. In the cultural code of aggression, *kótos* can play a particular role, namely, to mediate conflict between the cultural categories of divine and mortal, master and slave, man and woman. Within each of these categories *kótos* involves conflict between rivals, especially in cases where cultural categories are crossed or where rivalries derive from loyalties within categories.

Of all the circumstances in which *kótos* is used, only five are clear instances of *kótos* between equals (gods: *Il.* 14.191, *Il.* 10.517; mortals: *Il.* 1.181, *Il.* 3.345, and *Il.* 13.517). All of these examples relate directly to the fundamental questions of the *Iliad*: four instances point directly to the central conflict of the Trojan War (*Il.* 3.345, *Il.* 10.517, *Il.* 13.517, *Il.* 14.191, while the fifth (*Il.* 1.181) relates to the quarrel between Achilles and Agamemnon. A brief review of these instances will show how central this kind of anger is to the story of the *Iliad*.

In *Il.* 3.345, Paris and Menelaus engage in single combat. This single combat alludes to a fundamental source of conflict in Greek epic narrative, the abduction of Helen by Paris. The anger here described is *kótos*, not *khólos*, because, as we have seen, it is motivated by an event outside the immediate context. As I have shown, in the narrative neither Menelaus nor Paris has done anything to the other on the battlefield, so that no immediate motivation exists for either to be angry with the other. In this way, *kótos* can extend over time in order to reach a *télos* ("conclusion"), so that it is possible to find oneself facing one's opponent over an issue that happened elsewhere in time and space.[1] In this sense, Paris and Menelaus can be said to have *kótos* against one another.

The *kótos* between Deiphobus and Idomeneus has its origin in their rivalry over Helen (as in *Il.* 13.517 ff.); so too does the *kótos* of Athena and Diomedes in *Il.* 10.517 and *Il.* 23.391. Structurally, *kótos* in the passages just reviewed describes a wrath between individuals who may be viewed as equals (for example, a god vs. a god, a warrior vs. a warrior). But the origin of this wrath is not any particular and immediate grievance between the characters. Rather some founding moment, often but not always involving members of another social stratum, must be unearthed in order to understand *kótos*. Table 3.1 displays the way the conflict between and within social strata provides motivation for *kótos* in such cases.

Table 3.1 *Kótos* between Equals

Social Stratum	*Equals*	*Cause*
God vs. god	Hera vs. Aphrodite (*Il.* 14.191)	**Old rivalry**: οὕνεκ' ἐγὼ Δαναοῖσι, σὺ δὲ Τρώεσσι ἀρήγεις
	Apollo vs. Athena (*Il.* 10.517)	**Old rivalry**: ὡς ἴδ' Ἀθηναίην μετὰ Τυδέος υἱὸν
Mortal vs. mortal	Paris vs. Menelaus (*Il.* 3.345)	**Past outrage**: Ἀλεξάνδροιο τοῦ εἵνεκα νεῖκος ὄρωρεν
	Deiphobus vs. Idomeneus (*Il.* 13.517)	**Old rivalry**: Σ: ὡς ἀντεραστὴς Ἑλένης
	Achilles vs. Agamemnon (*Il.* 1.180–82)	**Future rivalry (of kings)**: Μυρμιδόνεσσιν ἄνασσε

Some important features emerge to amplify our view of *kótos*. In *Il.* 14.190–92 Hera prepares for the seduction of Zeus by seeking Aphrodite's assistance:

ἦ ῥά νύ μοί τι πίθοιο, φίλον τέκος, ὅττι κεν εἴπω,
ἦέ κεν ἀρνήσαιο, <u>κοτεσσαμένη</u> τό γε θυμῷ,

οὕνεκ' ἐγὼ Δαναοῖσι, σὺ δὲ Τρώεσσιν ἀρήγεις;
(*Il.* 14.190–92)

Would you obey me at all, my child, in what I tell you, or would you refuse, because of <u>*kótos*</u> in your heart about the fact that I help the Danaans and you the Trojans?

Here, as in Hermes' warning to Calypso, a god is styled as having *kótos*, potentially, against another god; indeed we have observed divine *kótos* working against mortals in those cases that concern violations on the human level. Here it is a god's *kótos* that is rooted in the all-too-human Trojan War (*Il.* 14.192): *hoúnek' egṑ Danaoîsi, sù dè Trṓessin arḗgeis* ("that I help the Greeks and you the Trojans").

The change in emphasis from a god's *kótos* against a mortal to a god's *kótos* against another god because of mortal concerns is marked by a change in phrasing. Each instance of *kotessámenos* in the *Iliad* is accompanied by a dative object immediately preceding, at the trochaic caesura, or following *kotessámenos*. But here the cause of the *kótos* is specified and expanded upon in the next line (*Il.* 14.192).

Here, the *kótos* is not merely Aphrodite's against Hera; rather, her *kótos* is due to the separation and opposition of the two mortal groups. The Trojan War makes it possible for Aphrodite to deny Hera's request because of conflicting loyalties across social segments. That is to say that the *kótos* alluded to in *Iliad* 14 finds its genesis in the origins of the Trojan War, since Aphrodite possesses *kótos* because of the loyalties of the subordinate groups, here groups of mortals (the Trojans and the Greeks). Moreover, the *kótos* that may prevent Aphrodite from helping Hera is the very anger alluded to in *Il.* 24.27, which arose because of Paris' *átē* ("moral blindness") in regard to *makhlosúnē* ("lust"). Thus *kótos* has as its source something outside the immediate context, especially in reference to foundational experiences, the greatest one being the *neîkos* that leads to the Trojan War.

In many cases, *kótos* involves characters from the same social level, with conflict occurring at the same time on another social level. For example, when Hera warns Zeus that he would be challenging fate by saving Sarpedon, the *kótos* she refers to is that of the immortals against men:

αἴ κε ζῶν πέμψῃς Σαρπηδόνα ὅνδε δόμονδε,
φράζεο μή τις ἔπειτα θεῶν ἐθέλῃσι καὶ ἄλλος
πέμπειν ὃν φίλον υἱὸν ἀπὸ κρατερῆς ὑσμίνης·
πολλοὶ γὰρ περὶ ἄστυ μέγα Πριάμοιο μάχονται
υἱέες ἀθανάτων, τοῖσιν <u>κότον αἰνὸν</u> ἐνήσεις.
(*Il.* 16.445–49)

If you wish to send Sarpedon, alive, to his own home, think whether anyone of the gods thereafter might wish to send his own son from the strong conflict; for

> many are fighting around the great city of Priam, many sons of the Achaeans, among whom you will hurl a grievous *kótos*.

This *kótos* is comparable to that at *Il.* 14.191 and *Il.* 10.517 because it emerges from an alliance of gods and warriors. In addition, when Hera sees the gods enraged at Zeus because the gods' sons have died in battle, she presents a figure analogous to that of Agamemnon imagining the *kótos* of an Achilles returned to Phthia (*Il.* 1.181), an image that Agamemnon, in a fit of bravura, dismisses out of hand. *Kótos* is used in such passages as a kind of a fortiori argument because of its long duration and its intrinsic need to reach a *télos*, as well as the implication (made explicit in *Il.* 16.449) that the anger is not that of an individual but of a social group. *Kótos* is the most dangerous thing to be feared when considering another's anger because it may involve much more than a personal grievance. In effect, what Hera is telling Zeus here is that his actions might precipitate a *feud* among the gods.

When Agamemnon fantasizes about Achilles' *kótos* (as discussed above), he does so because of loyalties relating to subordinates (here the Myrmidons) in the context of Achilles as their sovereign:

> οἴκαδ' ἰὼν σὺν νηυσί τε σῇς καὶ σοῖς ἑτάροισι
> Μυρμιδόνεσσιν ἄνασσε, σέθεν δ' ἐγὼ οὐκ ἀλεγίζω,
> οὐδ' ὄθομαι κοτέοντος. ἀπειλήσω δέ τοι ὧδε.
> (*Il.* 1.179–81)

> Go homeward with your ships and your companions, rule over the Myrmidons, but I won't trouble myself about you, nor will I take heed of your *kótos*; but I will threaten you in the following way.

Now, it may be said that the structural relationship is the same in this as in the previous examples: *kótos* between two equals over a conflict concerning a subordinate. Just as the gods' *kótos* against one another concerns mortals, so Agamemnon and Achilles can potentially have *kótos* against each other because of their captives.

As to Thersites, these lines remain problematic:

> ὀξέα κεκλήγων λέγ' ὀνείδεα. τῷ δ' ἄρ' Ἀχαιοὶ
> ἐκπάγλως κοτέοντο νεμέσσηθέν τ' ἐνὶ θυμῷ.
> (*Il.* 2.222–23)

> Shrilly he spoke sharp reproaches; now the Achaeans had *kótos* deeply against him, and they were indignant at him in their hearts.

In the light of Calchas's information, the anger appropriate to the Achaeans and their feelings toward Thersites[2] can be styled *kótos* because their hatred is based on Thersites' quarrels with kings (*Il.* 2.214: *erizémenai basielûsin*). In this scene, his conflict is with Agamemnon (*Il.* 2.221–23: *tót' aût' Agamémnoni diōi / oxéa keklḗgōn lég' oneídea* ("Then in turn with a sharp cry he reproached Agamemnon"). Thus, the Achaean warriors have *kótos* against one of their own because of their superiors, namely, the *basilêes* mentioned in 214 (cf. 220) and, specifically, Achilles, Odysseus, and Agamemnon.[3]

Moreover, the *kótos* that Thersites inspires in the Achaeans is related to the *éris* he causes the *basilêes* and to the *neîkos* involving Agamemnon, Achilles, and Odysseus.[4]

> [Θερσίτης] ὅς ἔπεα φρεσὶ ᾗσιν ἄκοσμά τε πολλά τε ᾔδη,
> μάψ, ἀτὰρ οὐ κατὰ κόσμον, ἐριζέμεναι βασιλεῦσιν,
>
> . . . .
>
> ἔχθιστος δ' Ἀχιλῆι μάλιστ' ἦν ἠδ' Ὀδυσῆι·
> τὼ γὰρ νεικείεσκε· τότ' αὖτ' Ἀγαμέμνονι δίῳ
> ὀξέα κεκλήγων λέγ' ὀνείδεα. τῷ δ' ἄρ' Ἀχαιοὶ
> ἐκπάγλως κοτέοντο νεμέσσηθέν τ' ἐνὶ θυμῷ.
> (*Il.* 2.213–14; 220–23)

> [Thersites] who knows in his mind words, many of them and unseemly ones, unfortunate, and indeed not appropriate, for contending with kings. . . . And he was especially hateful to Achilles and to Odysseus; for he used to provoke them; and then he took to making sharp reproaches shrilly against godly Agamemnon; now the Achaeans had *kótos* deeply against him, and they were indignant at him in their hearts.

The series of imperfects here emphasizes the longevity of *kótos*, that persistance being highlighted by the frequentative in *-sk-* (of *neikeíe-sk-e*) and by *kotéonto*, which is based on an old iterative-intensive formation.[5] Finally, note that Odysseus, involved as he is in *kótos* with respect to the Cyclops, Melantho, Melanthius, and the rest of the suitors, goes after Thersites with a similar streak of violence, and with an emphasis on Thersites' subordinate status:

> ἴσχεο, μηδ' ἔθελ' οἶος ἐριζέμεναι βασιλεῦσιν.
> (*Il.* 2.247)

> Hold and don't wish alone to contend with kings.

> τῶ οὐκ ἂν βασιλῆας ἀνὰ στόμ' ἔχων ἀγορεύοις,
> (*Il.* 2.250)

> Don't mouth off about kings in your declamations.

These are statements of principle because they refer beyond the particulars of the offensive speech that Thersites has just made. In this regard, Odysseus's comments resemble the remarks he will make to Melantho in the *Odyssey*. Finally, the display of violence against Thersites clearly shows us why Calchas has asked for protection against a king's *kótos*.

Odysseus enforces the *kótos* that the body of Achaeans feels against Thersites.[6] So too Odysseus enforces *kótos* in the *Odyssey*. Since (1) Odysseus plays the role of enforcer in the Thersites episode by providing a theory of kingship (*Il.* 2.246–64) and the enactment of violence that it justifies (*Il.* 2.265–69); since (2) Antenor remarks on his demeanor as being *zákotos* "very angry"; and since (3) his *oîkos* "household" caps the violence in Odysseus's homestead *kekotēóti thumôi* "with an angry heart" (*Od.* 22.477), I suggest that Odysseus is the hero of *kótos*—the anger of feud—in contradistinction to Achilles, whom Agamemnon can only imagine as having *kótos* in the future, of course, in his own *oîkos* among the Myrmidons.[7]

Achilles, thus, is only in a peripheral sense denoted by *kótos* in the *Iliad*. His anger is both *mênis* and *khólos*, while *kótos* is reserved to the background of the *Iliad*, where it has special reference to the beginning and the end of the war. We have already seen that Achilles is only once referred to as having *kótos* (*Il.* 1.178–81).[8] This reference is part of Agamemnon's view of Achilles, coming as it does at the height of the quarrel, when Agamemnon's insult almost drives Achilles to murder. Agamemnon might well fear Achilles' *kótos*, especially if Achilles takes his place as a *basileús* ("king") after a *nóstos* ("return") to Phthia. In this case, Achilles' status as a *basileús* is clearly involved in Agamemnon's dismissal, a fortiori, of *kótos*.

Furthermore, Agamemnon needs to dismiss Achilles' *kótos*, precisely because of the substance of the threat he has just made. For not only is Agamemnon contemplating Achilles as a returned king; in addition, he is about to rob him in full view of those over whom Agamemnon holds sway. Thus, the entire process of dealing with Achilles' anger depends upon the hierarchical structure of Achaean society as represented in Greek epic, from the king in battle with his army to the successful return–hero, now at home and in power. Moreover, in so far as both the plot of the warrior–hero and that of his returning counterpart effectively involve contractual relationships among the Achaeans, abrogation of those relationships constitutes a kind of crooked *thémis* ("judgment"), and hence potentially a locale for *kótos*.[9] Finally, in this threat, Agamemnon ranks Achilles below himself:

ὄφρ' ἐῢ εἰδῇς
ὅσσον φέρτερός εἰμι σέθεν, στυγέῃ δὲ καὶ ἄλλος
ἶσον ἐμοὶ φάσθαι καὶ ὁμοιωθήμεναι ἄντην.
(*Il.* 1.185–87)

. . . so that you might well know how much better I am than you, and so that another might hate to call himself equal to me and to square off against me.

One of the most important features of *kótos* is called into play here, namely, a superior's anger against an inferior. And in projecting Achilles' kingship to a time after his imagined *nóstos* to Phthia, Agamemnon assumes, rightly, that any *kótos* resulting from his public violation of Achilles' due could be protracted in its devastating consequences.

But Achilles has no *nóstos* ("return") and no future, apart from the *kléos* ("fame") provided by song. Hence, *kótos* will never again be referred to when the subject of Achilles' anger comes up. Rather, as in the *Iliad*'s proem, his anger is *mênis*, or, most often, as we will soon see, *khólos*. In fact, in the very next scene, Achilles is about to kill Agamemnon when Athena comes down and restrains him. Here his anger is *khólos* (*Il.* 1.192, 1.217) and *oú pō lêge khóloio* (*Il.* 1.224) "and he did not yet let go of his *khólos* ('anger')."

Before we turn to the wrath of Achilles, our pursuit of Calchas's definition provides us with questions that need to be answered comparatively, in two senses. First, from the point of view of comparative historical linguistics, I will provide a history of *kótos*. Second, with the comparative insights provided from the ethnography of the feud, I will demonstrate the typological foundation for this kind of anger.

Notes

1. Compare again the way that Glaucus and Diomedes in Book 6 discover their common bond in *xenía* ("guest-friendship").

2. I take it to be Thersites that is referred to here. On this reading, I see 216–22 as digressive, to be resumed by *tôi d'* (222), picking up from 212–16. Others take Agamemnon as the referent; see Thalmann 1988, 18 and notes 44 and 45 for support of that position. To say that the Achaeans have *kótos* against Agamemnon makes no sense in the light of the implications of Calchas's definition.

3. There has been substantial work on the Thersites episode recently, and issues of class and social status are foremost. My study of *kótos* need not secure the ultimate status of Thersites, except to say that he is not on an equal plane with the *basilêes*. See Thalmann 1988; for Thersites as a poetic figure see Nagy 1979, chapter 14. If Thersites is a blame poet and the representative in the *Iliad* of the Hellenic tradition of blame poetry, he presents an interesting parallel to Calchas, whose skill in divination also belongs to the verbal arts. Certainly Thersites' aggressive stance toward Agamemnon is the mirror image of Calchas's deferential approach to his superior.

4. See again Nagy 1979, Chapter 14 and, for *neîkos*, Chapter 12. And see now Nagler 1990 and Martin 1989, 68–69. On *éris* see Hogan 1981 and Nagler 1988, and 1992 with Gagarin 1990.

5. See Part I, Chapter 2; consult Jamison 1981, 180–81 for an account of this mediopassive. Compare also the use of *-sk-* forms in Antenor's description of Odysseus as *zákotos* (*Il.* 3.213–23); cf. *Il.* 2.271, as discussed at the end of Chapter 2.

6. See Thalmann 1988 for a review of the complex issues involving the ideological character of this relationship.

7. In this way, I suggest that the *mênis* of Achilles is kept separate from *kótos*. On *mênis*, see Muellner 1996.

8. On *mênis* and *kótos*, see Muellner 1996, 7 and 30 n. 50.

9. See *Il.* 16.386–88.

Chapter Four

Anger's History: *Κότος* and Etymology

With Calchas as my guide, I have shown *kótos* to be an anger, that, in the *Iliad*, relates to the fall of Troy, while in the *Odyssey* it calls to mind Odysseus's vengeance against the suitors. The method, thus far, has been to focus on the diction of Homeric poetry, its phraseology and narrative contexts. In the remaining two chapters of Part I, I turn to two methods that can illuminate this area in a manner external to the text. In this chapter, the comparative method will be used to help throw light from cognate languages on this species of Homeric anger, and in the next chapter, I apply to these problems the notion of the feud as developed in the social sciences. I turn here to the comparative method in order to produce evidence for the semantic force of this important word that, when placed beside our findings from the *Iliad* and the *Odyssey*, indicates how deeply rooted is Calchas's definition of *kótos*.

The evidence from historical analysis points to a meaning consistent with Calchas's explanation of *kótos*, but before the analysis presented here, there was little systematic support from Greek to the effect that *kótos* means anything other than "wrath" (or "grudge") as opposed to "mere anger." Now it is possible to view the cognates from five Indo-European branches (Celtic, Germanic, Anatolian, Indo-Iranian, and Slavic) as providing corroboration for the profound implications of Calchas's definition, namely, that *kótos* is a term with a specific denotation within the terminology of conflict displayed in the Homeric poems and descended from the earliest strata of the tradition that produced those poems. My own investigation of *kótos*, we will find, strengthens the case for the connections between *kótos* and the cognates suggested in the literature.

Both Frisk and Chantraine propose connections for *kótos* with certain Celtic and Germanic forms referring to conflict, specifically to "battle, combat, etc.,"[1] found, for example, in *Catu-rīges* (Gaulish name), *Hadu-brand* (Old High

German name);[2] cf. Old Norse *hǫð* "battle."[3] The first element of these compounds presents evidence for a Celtic and Germanic root **katu-* "fight, quarrel." In *Catu-rīges*, the second element of this name (*-rīg-*) has cognates in other Celtic languages, in Latin, and in Sanskrit (cf. Old Irish *rí*, Lat. *rēx*, Skt. *rāj-*, all "king," or "ruler" [*IEW* 855]) which connection reminds us that for Calchas, *kótos* has a special connection to the *basileús* or *ánax*.[4]

Sanskrit *śát-ru-* "enemy" (with *-ru-* suffix) is connected by Mayrhofer to the Celtic and Germanic forms just cited, and he also confidently compares Old Church Slavic *kotora* (translating *mákhē*).[5] However, Mayrhofer finds Greek *kótos* questionable as a comparandum, presumably on the semantic grounds that *kótos* does not mean "battle." Mayrhofer here is in harmony with Frisk[6] among others who find Greek *kótos* difficult to connect with a word for "battle." There is indeed room to question—however attractive the formal connections—how a word for "battle" is related to a word for "anger," so that the semantic connection can be accounted for in a systematic fashion. In this regard, the Anatolian branch of the Indo-European language family adds important evidence, specifically Hittite *kattawatar* and Cuneiform Luvian *kattawatnalli*. Both forms will be important as we delve further into two problems related to the cognates of *kótos*.

First, the morphological variation between the Greek, Germanic, Celtic, Slavic, Anatolian, and Indo-Iranian terms can be reconciled, if we bring into play the notion of a Caland-system root with a series of suffixes including stative verbal forms with *-ē-* (cf. *kot-ḗ-eis, ke-kot-ē-óti*), and nominal forms with *-u-* (e.g., Old Irish *cath*), *-ru-* (e.g., Skt. *śát-ru-*), and a neuter *-es-* stem noun.[7] In Greek, the verbal forms survive and are still productive through the conservative platform of Homeric epic, but the noun is reanalyzed, so that an inherited neuter noun in *-es-* was reinterpreted as thematic, perhaps in the epic tradition itself, thereby producing a thematic back-formation based on the *o*-grade of the stative perfect.[8]

Thus, it may not be best to see the verbal forms related to *kótos* as recent denominative formations, especially since at least some of the verbal forms point to old inherited classes consistent with the basic meaning of such a verb: for example, the present stem looks to continue an iterative category inherited from Indo-European, with expected *o* vocalism of the root, and stem in *-ei̯o-*;[9] in addition to the present forms, the perfect forms also belong to a class that has vital claims to antiquity; note that the term itself ceases to be productive after the archaic period in favor of other terms for anger (including *khólos*, but also *orgḗ*, and *thumós*).[10]

Second, let us turn to the Anatolian forms, since they have given some problem to those seeking cognates for *kótos*.

(1) Consider here Hittite *kattawatar* in the next example from Mursilis' prayer to the sun goddess (Lebrun 1980, 162–63 [A 49–53]):

> ki-nu-na a-ra-ah-zé-na-an-te-eš [ud-ni-an-t]e-eš
> hu-u-ma-an-te-eš KUR ^{URU}KÙ.BABBAR-ti

[w(a-al-h)]a-an-ni-eš-ki-u-wa-an da-a-ir.
na-at *ANA* ᵈUTU ᵁᴿᵁA-ri-in-na kat-ta-wa-a-tar nam-ma
ki-i-ša-ru.

And now the neighbors of foreign lands all of them took to attacking Hatti. Thus may it be once more a *kattawatar* for the Sun-goddess of Arinna.[11]

Now the Hittite word *kattawatar* refers to the anger of the goddess on seeing the neighboring cities attacking Hatti, and it occurs in a prayer of great antiquity[12] performed in a context of social crisis.[13] Lebrun's translation of *kattawatar* as "un motif de vengeance" suggests a value similar to the one that we have found for *kótos* in the Greek contexts. Further this passages points to a long-standing relationship (here between countries, "neighbors of foreign lands") of the kind that we will see (in the next chapter) is required for a feuding relationship. Moreover, Mursilis continues his prayer through the notions of anger that he thinks come into play with respect to the goddess's *kattawatar* (Lebrun 1980, 163 [A 54–56]):

nu *ANA* DINGIR.MEŠ ku-iš kar-pí-iš kar-tim-mi-ya-az
ku-iš DINGIR.MEŠ-na-aš *U-UL* na-ah-ha-an-za na-aš-ta le-e
a-aš-ša-u-e-eš i-da-a-la-u-wa-aš an-da har-kán-zi

This wrath, violent anger for the gods, it is not respectful of the gods; let not the good and evil perish together.[14]

After the mention of the goddess's vengeance, this passage shows two other words for anger in Hittite, both representing a more generalized form of wrath, *karpís* and *kartimiyaz.* The order is iconic, with the word for the divine revenge heading a list of anger-terms. Recall here the way that *kótos* could be used in clusters with other Homeric terms for anger: *ei mḗ tis theós esti kotessámenos Trṓessin / hirōn mēnísas; khalepè dè theoû épi mênis,* "Unless it is a certain god that has *kótos* with the Trojans, being enraged over sacrifices; difficult is the rage of a god" (*Il.* 5.174–78); *mḕ pṓs toi metópisthe kotessámenos khalepḗnēi / hoútō nûn apópempe, Diòs d' epopízeo mênin* "lest with *kótos* in the future, he (Zeus) take it ill, give now (to Odysseus) passage home, and take heed of the rage of Zeus" (*Od.* 5.146–47).[15] In both Homeric cases, *kótos* seems to be the more grave form of anger, and in both cases, a god's anger is the focus. In Mursilis' prayer, the sun goddess's *kattawatar*, a marked term, is the central request, with other (unmarked) more conventional terms for anger following in its wake.

(2) Now the form *kattawatar* is an abstract with the suffix *-atar*, attached to the root *katu-*, like *idāluātar* ("evil" based on *idālu-*) "bad,"[16] and we have, with different suffixal material, the same root in an important Cuneiform Luvian word, *kattawatnalli-* "vindicatif."[17] In Cuneiform Luvian the word *kattawaatnallinza*, for example, is in the following phrase (KUB XXXV.45.ii.18):

^{LÚ}KÚR^{MEŠ}-in-zi kat-ta-ua-at-na-al-li-in-za ú-ud-na-as-si-in-za "the enemies, the *kattawatnallinza*, the lords of the land" (Davies).[18] Since *kattawatnalli* is an attribute of the word for enemy,[19] and since Hittite *kattawatar* designates an anger of the divinity that can be called upon to exact vengeance on an enemy, I suggest that the stem **katu-*[20] presents us with a significant comparison point for Greek anger and in particular for *kótos*. Indeed, the parallels to Homeric narrative can be multiplied, as when Mursilis asks the sun goddess that she inflict plague and pestilence on the enemy, just as does Chryses of Apollo in Book 1 of the *Iliad*, at which point the Hittite king suggests, in the context of his prayer, that the goddess distinguish between good (*a-aš-ša-a-u-e-eš*) and bad (*i-da-a-la-u-wa-aš*).[21]

In 1965, Laroche argued for a connection between the Anatolian forms and Greek *kótos*, but more recently, Melchert is reluctant to accept Laroche's suggestion that the Anatolian and Greek words are connected.[22] Although the morphological variation between the Greek thematic noun and the Germanic, Indo-Iranian, Celtic, and Anatolian *u*-stems can be referred here to Caland morphology, the semantics remain a problem. But that problem can be resolved by a closer look at the evidence from early Greek narrative. For example, such forms as Gaulish *Catu-rīges*, where the derivative of the root that yields Greek *kótos* is coupled with the element *rī-*, meaning king, make a striking parallel to the connection of *kótos* with the *basileús* in Homeric Greek. Moreover, if there is an anger term that invokes both military aggression (as in the Luvian passage) as well as military encounters ("battles," etc., as in Germanic, Celtic, and Slavic), that term may also refer us to the clear and well-defined sense of anger displayed, as shown above, by Greek *kótos*. The Homeric evidence makes a striking argument in favor of reaffirming the connection of *kótos* to its most likely congeners.[23]

Moreover, the Anatolian forms come to be of special interest, in light of the definition of Calchas. For the Achaean prophet, *kótos* is presented as primarily social in that it is based on violations of the social code. The Anatolian forms encompass socially volatile concepts such as vengeance and reciprocal violence, just as does Greek *kótos*. A reasonable conclusion is that the Anatolian passages show forms based on *katu-* in a way that establishes an undeniable semantic fit between terms for this kind of anger in Greek and Anatolian.[24] For example, Luvian *kattawatnallinza* (discussed earlier) is used as an adjective modifying the word for enemy, with a clear comparison here to Sanskrit *śátru-* "enemy," but not just any kind of enemy: the magical sequence that provides us with a Luvian cognate of *kótos* includes the formula *^{LÚ}KÚR^{MEŠ}-in-zi kat-ta-ua-at-na-al-li-in-za ú-ud-na-as-si-in-za*,[25] whose meaning encompasses vengeance, violence and society, a meaning forcefully consistent with the kind of feuding enmity firing the Trojan War.

A semantic process links these terms together. An inherited word referring to some aspect of the feud as an institution in the pastoral or seminomadic stage of development of the Indo-European world is retained in some of the daughter languages, often in ways that refer to the old institution of the feud. In Greek the cognate refers to an accompanying "emotion," namely *kótos*; in Germanic, Celtic and Slavic it is the violent event that marks moments in the course of an ongoing feud (for example, a "battle"); the Anatolian languages earmark the general institution itself with words that refer to "vengeance-seeking," "vendetta," or an aggrieved party ("plaintiff").[26]

My focus on the meaning of *kótos* as a term that reflects social ruptures serious enough to precipitate the Trojan War resolves the semantic problems surrounding the relation of the Greek term to its cognates. By metonymy, *kótos* and its congeners come to indicate various aspects of feuding conflict. The basic sense of this term involves political hostility of a severe nature, severe enough to involve divinities, plagues, and disputes between distinct political entities. As we have seen, it is in the Anatolian evidence with its social context that we find a meaning that comes very close to the notion of feud. Succinctly, Piero Meriggi glosses Hittite *kattawatar* as "vendetta."[27]

In conclusion, the Homeric material provides a good reason to see the Hittite term *kattawatar* as resonant with the characteristics of *kótos* in Homer, especially with regard to the violation of Laomedon's contract, the destruction of Troy, and the restoration of Odysseus's kingship. The notion of vendetta certainly is attractive in its association with Greek *kótos*, given what we know of its duration over time and that it is related to kingship. In fact, the Greek case provides a secure link between the notion of a legal violation and a battle, both meanings evident in the Indo-European cognates of *kótos*, the latter meaning manifest in Celtic and Germanic and the former in Anatolian. The semantic difficulties seen as blocking a connection between the Hittite and Cuneiform Luvian forms and *kótos* in Greek disappear when the anger of the king and the relationship of *kótos* to *díkē* (see again *Il.* 16.384–92) is set alongside the startling conjunction of *kótos* with the origins of the Trojan war and with the denouement of Odysseus's *nóstos*. I hope that such a conclusion leads to further research into the Indo-European vocabulary for aggression and the institutions of violence that surround the proto-society's warrior figures. But now I turn to the ethnographic literature on feuding to elucidate the kind of anger that is *kótos*.

Notes

1. Frisk 1960–1970 s.v., Chantraine 1968–1980 s.v.

2. Indeed *katu-* shows up in many proper names in Germanic and Celtic: an early form is Runic *HaðulaikaR* [Kjølevig c. 500, Krause Nr. 61, cited in de Vries 1961 s.v. *hǫð*]; cf. the warrior's name *Hǫðbroddr* also cited in de Vries; cf. Old English *Heaðulāc*. De Vries proposes an etymology different from the one elaborated below. For Celtic names, see Vendryes 1959– s.v. *cath*.

3. De Vries, s.v.: cf. Old English *heaðu-*, Old Saxon *hathu-* with Old High German *hathu-*, *hadu-*. De Vries dismisses a connection with Old Church Slavic *kotora*.

4. In this regard, look also to other Celtic cognates, where *katu-* is identical to the ancestor of Old Irish *cath* (*u*-stem, masc., gen. *catha*, Lewis-Pedersen 1961, 170; *DIL* s.v. *cath* "battle," cf. Welsh *cad* "battle," and the Gaulish onomastic element *catu-*. See *IEW* 534, with Vendryes 1959– s.v. *cath*).

5. The variation in initial consonant is accounted for through "Gutturalwechsel" (* *k*' ~ *k*), Mayrhofer 1986– s.v. *śátru-*.

6. See Frisk (note 1) with his comment, "keine überzeugende Etymologie."

7. For the connection with *-u-* and *-r-* stems, see *DELG* s.v. *kótos*; cf. Frisk s.v. *kótos*; for a clarification of the morphology see Tucker 1990, 40–41. I am grateful for a valuable suggestion made to me by Calvert Watkins regarding the applicability of Caland's Law to these forms (interview, 1988).

8. On the possible origin of *kótos* as an old neuter in *s*, see W. Schulze 1892, 404.2, with Fraenkel 1909–1910. See now Tucker 1990, 35, "The thematic noun *ho kóto-* (Hom.) "anger" has probably replaced an inherited *-s-* stem **tò kótos*," with her note to Fraenkel's suggestion that we should "assume *s*-stem with the expected vocalism, namely, **tò kétos*." Such a transformation would present no metrical problems in the only nominal case attested in Homeric epic, the accusative case (with the exception of the doubtful reading *kótōi* in *Il.* 14.111).

9. With *o* vocalism, cf. *pothéō, póthesan,* with *thésssasthai*; *phobéō*, *ephóbēsa* "faire fuir" with *phébomai*; *phoréō*, *ephórēsa*, *phérō*; *potéomai*, *pepótēmai,* as listed in Chantraine 1973a, 348–49, where he also tells us that "les itératifs à vocalisme *o* se confondent dans beaucoup de cas avec les dénominatifs en *-έω* tirés de noms thématiques," a confusion that might well apply to the verbal forms of *kótos*. Note that *DELG* (s.v. *kótos*) leaves the matter open ("verbe probablement dénominatif"). In my opinion, *kótos* belongs with *pothéō*, etc. as a true deverbative.

10. After Pindar and Aeschylus we have no instances in drama, apart from a passage in Euripides' *Rhesus* (828) and some late prose (*DELG* s.v. *kótos*).

11. My rendering of the A text in Lebrun follows his translation ("Mais maintenant l'ensemble des [pay]s voisins a commencé à attaquer le pays hittite; que cette situation devienne une fois de plus un motif de vengeance pour la déesse Soleil d' Arinna" [Lebrun 1980, 170]). I thank Carol Justus for drawing my attention to this passage.

12. Lebrun 1980, 155.

13. "Une prière adressée par le roi Mursili II à la déesse Soleil d' Arinna à la suite de l' épidémie de peste dévastatrice et de difficultés extérieures" (Lebrun 1980, 155).

14. After Lebrun's "Tel (est *un objet*) *d' irritation*, *de violente colère* pour les dieux, [55–56] tel n'est pas respectueux des dieux; aussi, que les bons ne périssent pas avec les mauvais" (Lebrun, 1980).

15. And note *erízetai* on l. 172.

16. Cf. Friedrich 1960, §83; the comparison to *idālu-* is made by Laroche (1965, 51).

17. *DLL* s.v.; H. Craig Melchert (1987, 188–90); see also Davies (1986, esp. 142), who carefully explores the meaning of the word (Hieroglyphic Luvian) KATUNI—including a possible connection with *kótos*—on the Karkamiš inscriptions (A6 and A7), eighth century; and Weitenberg 1984, 116–17.

18. *KUB* XXXV 45ii18, as cited in Davies 1986, 142, from a ritual text, Starke 1980, 152. Davies elaborates upon the placement of *kattawatnallinza* next to ^{LÚ}KÚR^{MEŠ}-

in-zi "enemies"; cf. Rosenkranz 1952, 22; cf. 70–72 ("Die rachesuchenden Feinde des Landes").

19. Cf. Weitenberg 1984, 117.

20. Davies 1986.

21. See Lebrun 1980, 178–79, with the text on p. 163 (A 56).

22. Melchert 1987, 190 n. 20; Laroche 1965, 51; reluctant also is Mayrhofer 1986;

23. See also the comments by O. Szemerényi (1992, 1592), where he says "At least as important as the data of Celtic, Germanic, and Slavic, are the Hittite forms recognized as cognate by Laroche (1965, 51): *kattawatar* 'vengeance, rancune', and the adjective *kattawannalli*—based on an unattested **katu-* 'haineux, rancunier' immediately comparable to κότος."

24. Rosenkranz 1952, 22.

25. With Davies' translation (above), rendered by Rosenkranz (1952, 71) "die rachesuchenden Feinde des Landes."

26. Melchert 1994, 232; see also 1979, 268–71, where he carefully reviews the glosses translating Hittite *kattawatar*, including "revenge, retribution, reparation; object of revenge, grounds for revenge," and the juridical connotations of "(legal) grounds for a quarrel, compliant, plaintiff." Cf. Laroche's gloss of *kattawanalli-* as "vindicatif" *DLL* 55, with Rosenkranz's translation of the same term as "Rachesuchender" (1952, 71). The institution of the feud involves a wide range of categories, from the quasi-legalistic issues surrounding the resolution of conflict, to the emotions generated by that same conflict; especially salient for *kótos* are the "legal connotations" of *kattawatar*, given *skholiàs . . . thémistas* "crooked judgments" (*Il.* 16.387) and *ek . . . díkēn elásōsi* "they drove out justice" (388) in the context of *Zeùs . . . kotessámenos* (386).

27. Meriggi 1980, 304 ff.

Chapter Five

Anger's Aggression: The Wrath of Feud

I began this study with a close look at the terms of Calchas's definition (*Il.* 1.80–83), especially because he uses three categories to define the two different kinds of anger, *khólos* and *kótos*. Those three categories were time, social status, and the body. We proceeded to examine the features of Homeric diction that characterize *kótos* in the *Iliad* and *Odyssey*, as revealed to us through an overview of formal characteristics such as grammatical class and regularity of phrase with special attention to context. Through all this discussion, I have championed Calchas's culturally informed definition by pointing to the category of time—the long duration of *kótos*—and its consistent refusal to be part of any immediate quarrel: *kótos* has typically highlighted the anger that comes into play from beyond the particulars of the narrative proper. We have also seen that hierarchy, the role of the *basileús* in particular, has a special place with reference to *kótos*, although that feature of Calchas's definition remains to be further delineated. Finally, we looked at potential congeners of *kótos*, and found that the compelling series of cognates can best be grouped and analyzed by bringing what we know of Homeric *kótos* to bear on the linguistic evidence. By doing so, I developed the idea that Greek *kótos* continues an old feature of IE **kot-*, with reference to the anger that accompanies a particular kind of violence.

But to come to terms with that violence, we need to turn to the literature of comparative ethnography, where the taxonymy of violence in diverse cultures has been explored. What *kind* of violent, aggressive impulse and behavior might *kótos* refer to, if that question is asked with a view to typological comparison?

The term *kótos* refers to a special kind of anger in a way that invites comparison to the sociological notion of the feud.[1] But the feud has not been explored in Homeric studies; we have Hammond's (1985) comparison of the trial scene on the shield of Achilles to the Albanian blood feud, as described in

Hasluck (1954); and we have the dated and idiosyncratic study *Poine* (1923) by H. J. Treston.[2] But recently no systematic study of the cultural category of the feud as represented in the Homeric epic has yet emerged from our observations on violence and aggression in early Greek literature.[3] It is important to note this lack, since, for example, in the study of Old Norse saga, feuding mechanisms have long been recognized as a crucial topic for analysis.[4]

Because of my exclusive focus on *kótos* and *khólos*, I cannot claim to strike the definitive note on the topic of feuding in Homeric narrative beyond its particular relationship to *kótos*, but the conclusions that have emerged from the study of Calchas's definition of *kótos* lead directly to the social conception of the feud and its relevance to Homeric anger. In particular, what anthropologists know about the feud presents an answer as to why *kótos* involves the notions of duration and hierarchy.

Hammond points out that "blood-feud is very rarely mentioned in the *Iliad*,"[5] where blood-feud is strictly taken to mean vengeance exacted for a single act. So the potential killing of Phoenix's father, Patroclus's homicide of his agemate in a dice-game, and the like all can potentially function as part of a blood-feud mechanism. So too one can add the imagined situation that Ajax presents to Achilles in *Iliad* 9 (628–42), where Achilles is shown in Ajax's evaluation to be unjustified in his behavior, given the social mechanisms available even to one whose brother or son has died (632–33).

A classic study of feud is that of Jacob Black-Michaud, in which he criticizes many of his predecessors for failing to distinguish more carefully between homicides of various kinds and the feud *per se*.[6] In particular, Black-Michaud is at pains to underscore the social context of feuding and to highlight, in addition, that the idea of blood-price is not to be taken as the *sine qua non* of the feuding mechanism. In and of itself, this means that we must do more than catalogue instances of blood-price if we are to treat Homeric practices comparatively.

Black-Michaud's study, in its critique of earlier literature on feuds, presents his own synthetic theory, so as to to place the notion of feud in certain kinds of societies and to establish the kinds of conflicts that are defined by the term "feud." In Black-Michaud's analysis, previous writers have fallen short of seeing the full implications of feud over time (86), in part because they stressed too strongly the idea that feud could have a built-in machinery for the conclusion of hostilities. Understandably, such theorists were not able to see a feud as in existence when there was no such conciliatory mechanism. Black-Michaud comes to the conclusion that such conciliatory mechanisms are not central to the feud.

The details of Black-Michaud's study come from the tribal societies that practice feud in the Mediterranean and Middle-East, which he subdivides into those societies that have herding as their primary means of subsistence (and are primarily nomadic), and those that subsist primarily through agriculture (and hence are sedentary). Furthermore, these societies are primarily egalitarian, so that the individual members of the social order see few means by which they can gain a position of social supreriority over another (150).

Black-Michaud proceeds to present two problems that face the ethnographer in dealing with these societies: how do leaders arise to fulfill indispensable functions despite a "fiercely egalitarian ideology" (191)? And why does there exist a marked difference between the frequency and intensity of feuds in sedentary agricultural societies and nomadic pastoral groups" (191), in that the sedentary societies have much more devastating feuds than do the nomads?

Now the care with which Black-Michaud makes his argument cannot easily be captured in a brief summary, but the usefulness of the author's analyses and conclusions for our understanding of *kótos* should be clear. Black-Michaud argues against those who see compensation or vengeance as bringing a feud to an end (15–16). Such activities, as he puts it, can "arrest but not terminate" a feud (16). He quotes E. Evans-Pritchard on this point (1940, 154): "in spite of payments and sacrifices a feud goes on for ever, for the dead man's kin never cease to have war in their hearts." Black-Michaud follows Peters (1967)[7] in seeing feud as "eternal" and as leading to sequences of hostilities. Feud, moreover, constitutes "a set of relationships" (23); it is a means of affirming authority in the absence of an institutionalized power structure. In a "fiercely egalitarian" society the necessity for leaders is met by the institution of the feud.

The basic outline of Black-Michaud's conclusions is that feud is a social system *per se* (169) and not to be identified merely with homicide nor with revenge killing. In defining the social phenomenon of the feud, Black-Michaud describes the externals that mark its course, especially in the way that feud arises in what he calls a "fiercely egalitarian ideology," and also in the differences that are present between the intensity and frequency of feud in sedentary agricultural societies and in those that are nomadic pastoral groups (191). Feud partakes of a ritual "language" that "succeeds in conveying the messages of 'cohesion and superordination'" (241); in the societies identified as "feuding" societies, the feud is not a part of the social life of these people; the feud, rather, *is* the social system itself, because it defines the leaders and identifies the coherence of the groups within the social structure.

More importantly for our purposes, Black-Michaud stresses that although previous thinkers have emphasized the methods by which feuding can be brought to an end, these methods—a successful vengeance killing, the act of compensation, or any other element in the system of action and response—can only "arrest but not terminate" the feud. Feud, in contrast with vengeance killing, is political because it provides the foundations for internal political hierarchy and because it establishes external ties of temporary dominance.

With reference to *kótos* there are three elements that articulate how Black-Michaud's analysis of the feud is relevant to Homeric practice. First, feud, like *kótos*, has a relationship to time. In the case of feud, the time is infinite; feud is everlasting, which puts us in mind immediately of *Il.* 13.517, where *kótos* was "steadfast forever" (*emmenès aieí*). But remember also Calchas, who told us that feud will last until it reaches its *télos*. Does having a *télos* contradict the notion of everlastingness in Black-Michaud's analysis? No. Rather the *télos*, for Homer, is something in the hands of gods. No human action can put an end to a *kótos*, although Zeus can bring it to some kind of fruition by destroying culture (*Il.* 16.392); or Homeric narrative can imagine the fall of Troy as bringing the feuding to closure (*Il.* 8.449). But even here in such a case the feuding mechanism dictates that hostilities continue, as symbolized by Hera and Zeus's deal to exchange Troy for a Mycenaean citadel (to be specified later, *Il.* 4.51–57). Here, as we have seen above, Zeus has styled Hera's anger as *khólos* specifically to make it manageable; but her own interpretation of her anger is that it is *kótos*, precisely because of her status in the divine hierarchy.[8]

Here is where our use of ethnography must take good care. The gods in Homer are as real as the human actors, and Homer has ways of talking about events with the gods in mind that must be accounted for. Indeed, *kótos* is "everlasting" with reference specifically to human activity. No human action can bring it to an end until its *télos* comes to be reached and that particular work is in the purview of the gods. Thus, Zeus can spur on his *kótos* against the city of wrongdoers, but the duel between Paris and Menelaus fails to bring it to an end; indeed, the entity that will bring the feud of Menelaus and Paris to an end is Zeus Xenios. Thus, *kótos* as an anger term is similar to feud because its temporal dimension is limited only by some sense of coming to an end but only outside of human agency.[9]

Black-Michaud also stresses that feud forces an egalitarian social ideology to produce leaders. In this case, we have an apparent contradiction with the Homeric situation. Surely Calchas's anxiety involves the power of an established *basileús*! And no one would claim that Homeric society is egalitarian in the way of the feuding peoples studied by Black-Michaud, Peters, and others. Despite these facts, for *kótos* to be the anger of feud, Homeric society need not show a complete "feuding social system." Instead, Homeric narrative might show us some of the remaining vestiges of feuding social activity, brought in with the introduction of Greek culture and, no doubt, intermingled with the social systems of the Near Eastern cultures with which the early Greeks interacted.[10]

Even if Homeric "society" is not a feuding social order, the role of kingship in Calchas's definition can be clarified by means of reference to the anthropology of the feud, for the Homeric text conserves structures from many different cultural moments. Thus, when Calchas invokes the anger of feud, he suggests that if Agamemnon engages that kind of anger, it threatens to capsize the balance among the kings of the Achaeans. Agamemnon thus threatens to assume a hierarchical position by consolidating his power with reference to others: he becomes more than a *primus inter pares*. Thus the egalitarian subculture of Athenian kings promotes the threat of feud. Agamemnon, in fact, reverses this threat in his attempt to neutralize what ought to be his greatest fear, that Achilles' anger will rise to the level of *kótos*: (*Il.* 1.180–81): *Murmidónessin ánasse, séthen d' egȍ ouk alegízō, / oud' óthomai kotéontos,* "Rule over the Myrmidons, but I don't care about you, nor do I have regard for your *kótos*."

Black-Michaud highlights the ritual quality of the feud. In a provocative discussion of ritual (Chapter 5: 208–41), Black-Michaud is at pains to draw parallels between what we know of ritual and what we know of aggression. For Black-Michaud, the "feud is a form of communication frequently suffused with a strong admixture of ritual concommitants"; he goes on to call it a "ritual of social relations." The ritual perspective on feud helps Black-Michaud amalgamate a distinction that is very important for understanding feud as opposed to homicide, raiding, warfare, or other kinds of social violence. Black-Michaud asks us to understand realistic conflict as that oriented toward a goal; there are specific demands, estimates of gains, and all activity is directed at an object. Nonrealistic conflict is not oriented toward the attainment of specific goals. For example, a thief is violent in a way that can be styled realistic, but one seeking to establish one's honor is engaging in behavior that is nonrealistic. Now the ritual perspective puts feuding squarely in the heart of nonrealistic activity. In this way, Black-Michaud brings to light from his research on nomadic feuding relationships a crucial concept for our understanding of *kótos*. As with the feud, *kótos* refers to something extrinsic to the particular conflict, something not realistic. Nonetheless, we need to distinguish the *télos* of *kótos* from Black-Michaud's notion of the goal. Rather the *télos* that Calchas refers to is the end of the entire process, the destruction of the feud itself. For Menelaus and Paris to try to end the *kótos* through a duel, only to fail, shows that no simple goal can bring the feud to its *télos*: *kótos* is fundamentally nonrealistic. It will take Zeus to exterminate the Trojan city, to bring a formal end to the *kótos*, as is clear from the storm simile in *Iliad* 16 (384–93, already discussed).

Thus, in the case of the duel between Paris and Menelaus, they can be said to be fighting *kotéonte* (*Il.* 3.345) because the duel is a ritual act, promising to bring the fighting to an end, but instead, as failed ritual, prolonging it, in Black-Michaud's terminology "everlastingly."[11] When Zeus, in that same storm simile from Book 16, has *kótos* against the people who make *skholiaì thémistes* ("crooked judgments"), the anger suggests a context. There is no specific violation that Zeus is angry about; the basic social structure has turned out "crooked" and Zeus's storm is about to "straighten" things out, apocalyptically, ritually. And when Deiphobus and Idomeneus meet on the battlefield in *kótos*, it is a symbolically laden moment, since these were once rivals for Helen's hand and the social bond represented by this kind of conflict is styled best with the term *kótos*, since it is in fact to last forever.[12]

Finally, by introducing ritual, and nonrealistic aggression, Black-Michaud paves the way for one of the most vital parts of his analysis. Feuding over honor is devastating, because to feud over honor is to engage in the most powerful of nonrealistic violent acts. And to do so also brings into play the role of women in these turbulent interactions. For Black-Michaud, the honor of men is contrasted to and parallel with the notion of shame in women.[13] Just as feuds over the nonrealistic motive of honor of men tend to be worse than feuds over realistic goals, so too feuds over the comparably nonrealistic goal of the shame of women tend to be exaggerated in their scope of violence.

These considerations introduce the important idea that feuds provide a way for women to participate in a defining social institution (Black-Michaud 1975, 217–19), even though this participation seems passive to outside observers (Black-Michaud 1975, 218–19). As to their passivity, we can see that women are instead active in preserving the memory of the feud:

> The only activity connected with feud in which women could legitimately indulge was incitement to vengeance: it was the womenfolk of the victim whose duty it was to keep his memory alive by singing funerary dirges, lacerating their faces until they bled and keeping relics such as a blood-soaked shirt, to show provocatively to the heirs of the victim when they were grown old enough to bear a rifle.
>
> (Black-Michaud 1975, 219n)

Indeed, it seems as if the women are the keepers of the traditions of violence:

> If feud expresses the varying quality of relationships between groups over interminable periods of time, *the events of generations past must be remembered* in order that the history of outrage and homicide may serve as a mould in which to cast the pattern of present relations. Largely preliterate feuding societies have consequently created a number of crude devices which serve to record the events of feud and to "awaken" successive generations to take vengeance for their forbears. In Somaliland, southern Greece, Albania, and Corsica it is customary practice for the women to incite the dependents and close kin of the victim to wash the stain of blood from their house by spilling the blood of the killer or his near agnates. *These dirges express ferociously blood-thirsty sentiments and are frequently the work of women endowed with outstanding poetical gifts*. They are remembered by the kin of the victim over whose bier they were sung and are repeated by their womenfolk for years after the event to instill into the male heirs of the deceased, who may have been infants at the time of the killing, the necessity to bring vengeance when they grow old enough to bear arms.
>
> (Black-Michaud 1975, 78–79 [my emphases])

If these vivid passages from *Cohesive Force* put us in mind of the Muses keeping the memory alive, both because they were there (*Il.* 2.485) and because they can recall who fell first in a rout, and who fell last, Black-Michaud's words certainly should stimulate our thinking about Helen's weaving her robe the first time we see her, in *Il.* 3 (125–27):

> ἡ δὲ μέγαν ἱστὸν ὕφαινε,
> δίπλακα μαρμαρέην, <u>πολέας</u> δ' ἐνέπασσεν <u>ἀέθλους</u>
> Τρώων θ' ἱπποδάμων καὶ Ἀχαιῶν χαλκοχιτώνων.

She was weaving a great web, double-folded, bright, and she wove into it the numerous conflicts of horse-taming Trojans and bronze armored Achaeans.

The sublimity of this passage is often noted,[14] but from the perspective of feuding, the sublimity is shot through with a sinister implication. Helen is the weaver of conflict in her role as the woman whose shame, in the technical sense, is the center of the conflict, so that she, as the center of the feud, also plays a role as the inciter to vengeance. There is one activity that women during a feud have as their own, the creation of narratives to emboss in cultural memory the violations that provoke revenge. To use the terms of Aristotelian rhetoric, Helen's robe may be more deliberative than epideictic. After all, in the very middle of her speech to Paris when he returns to her chamber, after he has been rescued by Aphrodite, she gives this chilling order:

ἀλλ' ἴθι νῦν προκάλεσσαι ἀρηΐφιλον Μενέλαον
ἐξαῦτις μαχέσασθαι ἐναντίον·
(*Il.* 3.432–33)

But come now and challenge Menelaus, beloved to Ares, again to a duel.

This is the core of her speech, around which we have her ironic wish for Paris to have met his doom on the field of Troy that day (*Il.* 3.428–29) and her advice not to dare do such a foolish thing (*aphradéōs*, *Il.* 3.436). As it turns out then, her task—as the woman over whom the war is fought—is to incite the men to fight *for* their own honor and *because of* her shame.

I think here too of the moving songs—laments, after all—for Hector as his corpse is returned to Troy. Although Homer has Cassandra (*Il.* 24.704–6), Andromache (*Il.* 24.725–45), Hecabe (*Il.* 24.748–59), and, significantly, Helen (*Il.* 24.762–75) all mourn for Hector in a way that emphasizes his gentleness, this loss, as Achilles discovers, can spur on great deeds of violence, since keeping the memory of the deceased alive can easily lead to a renewal of conflict. Can sublime laments become the stuff of vigorous calls to battle?

ଌ

This kind of anger, *kótos*, entails the social motivations for human actions, as they are seen on a grand scale. The presence of compelling parallels in cultural congeners, most securely in Indic, Celtic, Germanic, Anatolian, and Greek make it possible to suggest that the source of Greek *kótos* is a term designating a kind of violence comparable to the feud. In the taxonomy of violence displayed by the Indo-European languages, such a term would have constituted one word among many to indicate kinds and levels of conflict. In the *Iliad*, for example, *kótos* takes root in the source of the conflict that informs the narrative, namely, the abduction of Helen. In Homeric practice, *kótos* is used much less frequently than *khólos*, in part for the same reason that direct view of the abduction of Helen is suppressed within the narrative. The *boulḗ* of Zeus, in the *Iliad*, works *within* the larger scheme of the retribution of the Achaeans against the Trojans. The Homeric poems are not about the abduction of Helen but about the world as it looks afterwards. Gazing over the expanse of the Homeric tradition, I see *kótos* located at the horizons that mark its limits, not on the dust and the blood of the battlefield.

For the anger that lives in that dust and that blood, I draw our attention in Part II to a study of the other element in Calchas's definition, *khólos*.

Notes

1. See Black-Michaud 1975 and Otterbein 1994 for overviews of the literature.

2. In this vein, note that neither of the recent commentaries lists "feud" in the indices.

3. See now the brief remarks on vendetta by Segal 1994, 218–20, with an identification of *khólos* and *kótos* at 218; and Lowenstam 1993, 101 for blood-price. For feud and Athenian culture, see Cohen 1995. Seaford (1994, 25–29) shows a connection between reciprocity and vengeance. The careful distinctions made by Black-Michaud among these various terms (feud, revenge, vendetta, and so on) need to be maintained. For the Homeric poems, not all acts of vengeance are provocative of feud, a linguistic border protected by the semantic distinction between *khólos* and *kótos*.

4. See, for example, Miller 1983, 1990; Byock 1982, 1993. Studies of Greek "values" or morality have tended to focus on the Homeric tradition as antedating a full-blown morality. Hence the important ways in which traditional cultures organize action and behavior tend to be placed in the background. See Adkins 1960 with the important reply of Long 1970; the well-known studies of *díkē* and other terms for justice certainly participate in this favoritism toward posttraditional social configurations, cf. Lloyd-Jones 1983, 1987; Gagarin 1973, 1987; Adkins 1987. D. Cohen's work on Athenian social practices (1991, 1995) in its theoretical orientation to practices and their relation to symbolic effects holds some promise for a study of these issues in the Homeric texts. In particular the comparative method promoted by Cohen seems to me crucial for a body of work that does not have the historical controls available for Athens or other well-documented societies.

5. Hammond cites in particular *Il.* 9.448–77, *Il.* 23.85–90, *Od.* 15.272–76.

6. Black-Michaud 1975. For a discussion of definitions and models of the feud, see W. I. Miller 1990, 179–89; see too Cohen's application of the feuding model to Athenian society (Cohen 1995).

7. Black-Michaud 1975, 19.

8. See *Il.* 18.364–67.

9. Compare the following statement from *Cohesive Force*: "Feud survives the death of both principals and continues down the generations until physical distance or extermination bring about a permanent cessation of hostilities" (Black-Michaud 1975,

74), with the deal made by Zeus and Hera at the beginning of Book 4, where the death of "both principals" is schemed for by the divinities. Cf. also Black-Michaud 1975, 78–80, where poetry and song are identified as elements in perpetuating the feud; compare Helen's weaving the *poléas . . . aéthlous / Trṓōn th' hippodámōn kaì Akhaiôn khalkokhitṓnōn* (*Il.* 3.126–27), to Hera's comment regarding weaving evils for the Trojans at *Il.* 18.364–67.

10. It is worth remembering that *kótos* as an active part of the Greek vocabulary for anger all but disappears after Aeschylus.

11. Black Michaud on the duel (1975, 228): "Insofar as duels can be said to express the tenor of relationships by nonrealistic means, they may be described as rituals of social relations."

12. As is implied by the adverbial phrase *emmenès aieí*, *Il.* 13.517. Again, remember that the meeting of Deiphobus and Idomeneus has as its counterpart and opposite number the meeting between Glaucus and Diomedes in *Il.* 6: feud and *xenía* ("guest-friendship") turn out to be opposite sides of the same coin, one of the highest value in Homeric social currency.

13. Cf. Abu-Lughod 1986 and often in the literature.

14. On the association of Helen with textuality, see Thalmann 1984, 166, with Clader 1976. See also Segal 1994, 125, who emphasizes the particular Homeric touches that distinguish Helen from Andromache.

Part II

Fighting Words

Chapter Six

Helen's Cure and the End of Anger

In Part I, I surveyed and analyzed the language of *kótos* to show the validity of Calchas's definition in *Il.* 1.80–83; in addition to confirming Calchas's formulation, I concluded that comparative evidence locates this term for anger in the institution of the feud. Since only part of Calchas's formulation has been elucidated, in Part II I turn to the other part of that definition, namely, *khólos*. The difference between the two terms shows itself immediately in their dissimilarity with respect to quantity of attestation, a difference that is understandable if referred to the structural linguistic feature of assymetric relationship called markedness:[1] in terms of distribution the unmarked term is more widely distributed than the marked term.[2] For our purposes, we certainly need to account for the features of a term that occurs nearly four times as often as *kótos*. Indeed the numbers tell a significant part of the story.

In contrast to the 27 instances of *kótos*,[3] *khólos* is used (in both its verbal and nominal forms)[4] 138 times in the Homeric poems. For those 138 instances of *khólos*, Achilles' anger provides the most frequent reference, 30 times;[5] the next most often cited reference is the anger of Zeus, 14 times.[6] Thus, of mortals, Achilles has the most *khólos*; the god who has *khólos* the most is Zeus. Besides these, other mortals who have *khólos* are Agamemnon (8 times) and Odysseus (7 times),[7] with Hera and Athena among gods showing *khólos* in 5 instances.[8]

Besides the frequency of distribution that marks the difference between *khólos* and *kótos*, the terms do different kinds of work in our texts. Where *kótos* is only used once of Achilles' anger and there only in Agamemnon's fantasy,[9] the anger of *khólos* is most frequently the anger of Achilles. Both Achilles and Zeus take the lion's share of the *khólos*, reinforcing Whitman's conclusion that the relationship between these two is central to the thought of the *Iliad*.[10]

Moreover, *khólos* is both the most frequently used word for anger and the one whose usage is marked by a variety of epithets[11] (8 of these 11 being used only once) and by numerous contexts across both texts,[12] each of which needs accounting for.

At this point, we can be grateful for our informant's folk definition, since Calchas has indicated the features of *khólos* that begin to identify it in contrast to *kótos*. Indeed, we can confidently build our notion of *khólos* by looking specifically for the ending and beginning of *khólos*. As we proceed to inquire after Calchas's definition, more indications of the fundamental importance of *khólos* will be brought to bear on the argument, indications that will forcefully deepen for us the insight of our learned informant. As we have seen, the core of Calchas's definition is that *khólos* and *kótos* are to be distinguished because *kótos* cannot be brought to an end as can *khólos*; I take this to mean that *khólos* is more in the hands of the human actors on the Trojan plain than is *kótos*. Moreover Calchas pointed to *khólos* through the use of figurative language (e.g., *autêmar katapépsēi*), something quite alien to the abstract world of *kótos* that we have just finished examining. That feature of *khólos*, its robust way with Homeric metaphor and figure, will inform the semantic analysis in Chapter 7. And with *kótos* delineated as the anger of the *basileús* can we expect any kind of restriction along class lines for *khólos* or is it, because unmarked, available to all? Before too long we will see that the unmarked character of *khólos* does not stop the Homeric poems from giving it a shape and texture of its own. I will begin, as I did for *kótos*, by presenting a passage that corroborates some part of the definition proferred by the prophet of the Achaeans in order to encourage us to proceed once again in the direction pointed out by Calchas's definition, this time to track down and meet head on Homeric anger's most frequent term.

The noun *khólos* is made into a negative adjective, with the addition of the α-privative, only once. In this passage Helen provides for her guests in Sparta an intoxicant, one that is described with a telling set of *hapax legomena*:

> ἔνθ' αὖτ' ἄλλ' ἐνόησ' Ἑλένη, Διὸς ἐκγεγαυῖα·
> αὐτίκ' ἄρ' εἰς οἶνον βάλε φάρμακον, ἔνθεν ἔπινον,
> νηπενθές τ' ἄχολόν τε, κακῶν ἐπίληθον ἁπάντων.
> ὃς τὸ καταβρόξειεν, ἐπὴν κρητῆρι μιγείη,
> οὔ κεν ἐφημέριός γε βάλοι κατὰ δάκρυ παρειῶν,
> οὐδ' εἴ οἱ κατατεθναίη μήτηρ τε πατήρ τε,
> οὐδ' εἴ οἱ προπάροιθεν ἀδελφεὸν ἢ φίλον υἱὸν
> χαλκῷ δηιόῳεν, ὃ δ' ὀφθαλμοῖσιν ὁρῷτο.
> (*Od.* 4.219–26)

There in turn godborn Helen took thought of other things; immediately she threw a drug into the wine that they were drinking, one that allays grief, and anger, and causes forgetfulness of all ills. The one who swallows it, whenever it is mixed in the mug, would not that day cast down a tear from his cheeks, not even if his own mother died or his father, nor if before his very eyes they cut down a brother or beloved son.

The drug with which Helen doses the wine is characterized as "banishing anger (*khólon*),"[13] but also as stilling suffering (*nēpenthés*) and inducing forgetfulness (*epílēthon*). Turning first to *ákholon*, I note that in meeting the test of Calchas's definition, *khólos* indeed must be banishable, or, in his words, if one comes to have anger, then *khólon ge kaì autêmar katepépsēi* (*Il.* 1.81). But what kinds of things cause one to have *khólos*? Helen gives two examples of the experiences that can result in *khólos* and that, therefore, her *phármakon ákholon* can soothe: if one's mother and father die or if the enemy slaughter one's brother or son. A limiting case, that is to say, is the death of a member of one's *phíloi* before one's eyes in an act of violence.

Now the importance of this description of a soothing drug comes clear when we turn to the phrasing of *Od.* 4.221, in which are highlighted themes crucial to the poetics of the *Iliad* and the *Odyssey*. For now, note that this *phármakon* ("drug") is *nēpenthés* ("soothing of sorrow"), a word that also responds to the thematics of Homeric diction through the traditional notion of *pénthos*.[14] We will shortly see that the death of a loved one at enemy hands stimulates *khólos*, a situation available to hand in any *kótos* context. In the *Iliad*, *pénthos* along with *ákhos*, is one of the terms that "designate the grief of Achilles over his loss of *tīmē*."[15]

In the *Odyssey*, *pénthos* further designates the grief that Penelope has when she contemplates Odysseus's absence (*Od.* 1.342). In this passage the singer Phemius has failed, through song, to do what Helen succeeds in doing through drugs. Instead of forgetfulness of grief (*kakôn epílēthon hapántōn* "providing oblivion for all evils"), he instills unforgettable grief (*pénthos álaston*). The play of opposites, then, in *Od.* 4.221 is striking, as if the tradition is presenting the possibility of stopping its entire world as represented by the two traditions: the death of one's *phíloi* at the hands of the enemy (*Od.* 4.225), deaths of the kind that fill the *Iliad*, in addition to the *Odyssean* grief that attends the passage of time and death of one's homebound friends, here represented by father and mother (*Od.* 4.224).

Od. 4.221 presents three Homeric *hapax legomena*, each of which negates traditional themes. The most neglected of these three terms is *ákholon* ("stilling anger"), but it should be noted that *nēpenthés* ("stilling suffering") is the negative of one of the most important of Homeric themes, alongside the all important theme of memory, here negated by *epí-lēthon* ("inciting oblivion of," where the adjective is built on *lēth-*, indicating forgetfulness.). This link between memory and pain has not gone unnoticed, and I point to a particularly useful exposition when I quote G. Nagy in reference to the important thematics involved in *nēpenthés* and *epílēthon*:

> As for unforgettable grief, πένθος ἄλαστον, the only way to forget it is by magic. Thus the φάρμακον of Helen, which she puts into the wine (δ 220ff) is νηπενθές and κακῶν ἐπίληθον ἁπάντων, "without grief" and "without memory of any evils" (δ 221). He who drinks this potion would not even mourn the death of his father and mother (δ 224) or of his brother or of his son: no, he would not mourn, not even if they were killed before his very own eyes (δ 225 f).
>
> (Nagy 1974, 258[16])

Thus far I have stressed the semantics of *pénthos* and *epílēthon* and related forms. But what about the third *hapax legomenon*, *ákholon*? Indeed, this term goes largely unremarked in the literature, although here it stands in relief between pain and memory.[17] If unforgettable grief attends such painful events as deaths within one's family, why is it necessary, in addition, to quiet *khólos*? Is there indeed a relation between the idea of forgetfulness and *khólos*?[18] From this passage, let us continue our probing of Calchas's definition with the hypothesis that the anger signified by *khólos* can be that anger that directly attends the deaths of one's *phíloi*, most especially if such deaths happen before one's very eyes. That anger, tied to its sad occasion, is capable of being soothed, deep though it be. Indeed, we will see that putting an end to *khólos* is a major concern of early Greek poetry.

Khólos in Homeric poetry

In this section, I consider the meanings of *khólos* suggested by its poetic use in the Homeric texts. In Appendix 2, Groups 1–3, you can see a cumulative list of *khólos* forms as needed for my argument in this part of the study. That appendix contains all the Homeric attestations of the noun *khólos* referring to the cessation of anger.[19] The extent of this list is immediately useful because we can make a direct link to Calchas's definition. Just as Calchas declared, *khólos* indeed can come to an end, but the means for stopping *khólos*, in their variety, demand attention, in contrast to *kótos*, which shows no means for its control apart from reaching its cosmically appointed *télos*. As we begin to probe the variety of *khólos* contexts, another immediate observation can be made, namely, that the occurrences of *khólos* in the accusative case always (with one exception, *Il.* 14.50) refer to the cessation of *khólos*. We will see that the nominative and dative cases have a significantly different distribution.

In Group 1 (Appendix 2) we are reminded of Helen's concern with stopping *khólos* when we see that the accusative of *khólos* occurs with forms of *paúō* four times (at the bucolic diaeresis; a similar collocation occurs twice more in the first half of the line, Group 2), so that its immediate context in all cases but one (*Il.* 14.50) concerns the cessation or restraint of anger.

Further, we see that at the bucolic diaeresis, the system of Homeric language produces a number of formulas worth interrogating, one of which is *paú- khólon*. Taking the placement of *paúō* + *khólon* directly at the bucolic diaeresis as a regular expression, the exceptions to this metrical placement in Book 9 are striking. The variation occurs at the collocation of *-paúō* and *khólon*, in Group 1, specifically in the phrase *paúe' éa dè khólon thumalgéa* ("Stop and set aside this heart-paining *khólos*") *Il.* 9.260, a phrase that displays the middle imperative of *paúō* moved to the front of the line, only to be then supplemented by *éa* (in the sense of "let go"). Significantly, this line ends Odysseus's proem as he addresses Achilles in the embassy scene of *Iliad* 9, just before he begins to quote directly Agamemnon's offer of gifts to Achilles. In the event, he ends his introduction with an unusual collocation, both because the *paúō* occurs usually alone with *khólon*, and not as here with another imperative (*éa*), as well as because the formula *khólon thumalgéa* usually occurs with the figurative verb, *-péssō* (*Il.* 4.513, and *Il.* 9.565).

Now *paúō* at the beginning of the line is expressive, as can be seen in

> ἀλλ' ἤ τοι μὲν ἐγὼν ἀποπαύσομαι, εἰ σὺ κελεύεις,
> παυέσθω δὲ καὶ οὗτος· ἐγὼ δ' ἐπὶ καὶ τόδ' ὀμοῦμαι. . . .
> (*Il.* 21.372–73)

> But yet I will stop, if you order me; but let this man stop. And in response I too make the following oath. . . .

where Scamander begs Hera to have Hephaistos stop burning the river; or when Halitherses contemplates stopping the suitors' outrages:

> ἀλλὰ πολὺ πρὶν
> φραζώμεσθ', ὥς κεν καταπαύσομεν· οἳ δὲ καὶ αὐτοὶ
> παυέσθων· καὶ γάρ σφιν ἄφαρ τόδε λώϊόν ἐστιν.
> (*Od.* 2.167–69)

> But long before this let us consider how we will bring an end to it. Let them cease. For this would be instantly better.

In both of these passages, the line-initial imperative emphasizes the importance and possibility of stopping the action, while concluding a major part of the speaker's argument.[20] Similarly Odysseus's speech has as its entire point bringing to an end the anger of Achilles that has led to his withdrawal.

The second variation to the placement of *paú- khólon* at the bucolic diaeresis occurs with *paúseien* in *Il.* 1.192, presenting us with the only appearance of *khólon* after the first long of the second foot and the only occurrence of *paúseie* in this position.[21] That Aristarchus athetized this passage adds to the sense that it shows something unexpected, an innovation emerging from the performer's display of a dramatic moment, Achilles' contemplation of the murder of Agamemnon. Once again the *paúō* is complemented by a second predicate indicating restraint of anger (*erētúseie thumón*), as we saw *éa* function above. For our purposes, we see the narrative producing another way of demonstrating the restraint of anger, this time introducing another word, *thumós*, that is, in a special way, linked *to khólos*.

Thus far we have seen that the cessation of anger can be expressed with the formula *paúō khólon* at the bucolic diaeresis, with variations possible for expressive effect. What is the context for the regular phrase *-paú- khólon* in Homer? In the first two lines of this set, a god causes a mortal's anger to stop. The third instance inverts this pattern: through ritual, a mortal causes a god's anger to stop.

Consider the way that Achilles' anger is highlighted through this variation. In *Il.* 9.459 and *Il.* 15.72, Homeric narrative shows us how gods work to end human anger. In particular, Zeus stipulates when he will put an end to Achilles' anger and why he must wait that long before intervening:

> τοῦ δὲ χολωσάμενος κτενεῖ Ἕκτορα δῖος Ἀχιλλεύς.
> ἐκ τοῦ δ' ἄν τοι ἔπειτα παλίωξιν παρὰ νηῶν
> αἰὲν ἐγὼ τεύχοιμι διαμπερές, εἰς ὅ κ' Ἀχαιοὶ
> Ἴλιον αἰπὺ ἕλοιεν Ἀθηναίης διὰ βουλάς.
> τὸ πρὶν δ' οὔτ' ἄρ' ἐγὼ παύω χόλον οὔτε τιν' ἄλλον
> ἀθανάτων Δαναοῖσιν ἀμυνέμεν ἐνθάδ' ἐάσω,
> πρίν γε τὸ Πηλεΐδαο τελευτηθῆναι ἐέλδωρ,
> ὥς οἱ ὑπέστην πρῶτον.
> (*Il.* 15.68–75)

> And godly Achilles will kill Hector, out of *khólos*. After this I will make thereupon a retreat from the ships continual and immediate, until such point as the Achaeans might take steep Ilium through the counsels of Athena. But I do not stop *khólos*, neither do I allow any other of the immortals to defend the Danaans, before the wish of the son of Peleus has been accomplished, as first I promised him.

In this passage, Zeus refers to Achilles' anger, not his own.[22] In contrast to the restraint displayed here by Zeus, in *Il.* 9.459 Phoenix credits an immortal with halting his *khólos* against his own father:

> τὸν μὲν ἐγὼ βούλευσα κατακτάμεν ὀξέι χαλκῷ·
> ἀλλά τις ἀθανάτων παῦσεν χόλον, ὅς ῥ' ἐνὶ θυμῷ
> δήμου θῆκε φάτιν καὶ ὀνείδεα πολλ' ἀνθρώπων,
> ὡς μὴ πατροφόνος μετ' Ἀχαιοῖσιν καλεοίμην.
> (*Il.* 9.458–61)

> Him did I plan to kill with sharp bronze; but one of the immortals stopped the *khólos*, who placed in my heart the community's gossip and the extensive

reproaches of men, so that I should not be called a patricide among the Achaeans.

Here we have a mortal's account of a divine event, the god in question being referred to by the indefinite *tis*. Since Phoenix is concerned to make an exemplum in his speech, the implication might be that it is in fact Zeus who is in charge of these matters, as indicated when Zeus stops the *khólos* of Achilles in Book 15.

The gods' *khólos* figures prominently in *Od.* 4.583, in an example that is contextually distinct from the others. Here a mortal brings a god's anger to a halt through ritual. Menelaus describes to Telemachus his propitiation of the gods' anger:

ἂψ δ' εἰς Αἰγύπτοιο, διιπετέος ποταμοῖο,
στῆσα νέας, καὶ ἔρεξα τεληέσσας ἑκατόμβας.
αὐτὰρ ἐπεὶ κατέπαυσα θεῶν χόλον αἰὲν ἐόντων,
χεῦ' Ἀγαμέμνονι τύμβον, ἵν' ἄσβεστον κλέος εἴη.
(*Od.* 4.581–84)

And back to Egypt's rain-swollen river, I beached the ships, and I prepared finished hecatombs. And when I had stopped the *khólos* of the everliving gods, I set up a funeral-mound for Agamemnon that there be unquenchable fame.

This example is formally distinct from the others in two ways. The bucolic diaeresis here is only a metrical break and not also—as in the other three instances of this category (Group 1)—a syntactic break. *Theôn aièn eóntōn*—the phrase that joins these two segments of the line—is part of a formulaic system that declines in the following way:

Nominative: θεοὶ αἰὲν ἐόντες (*Il.* 1.290, *Il.* 1.494, *Il.* 21.518, *Il.* 24.99; *Od.* 5.7 = 8.306 = 12.371 = 377)
Genitive: θεῶν . . . αἰὲν ἐόντων (*Od.* 3.147, 4.583)
Accusative: θεοὺς . . . αἰὲν ἐόντας (*Od.* 1.263, 1.378 = 2.143, 8.365)

The formulas in the genitive and accusative cases have a heavy second syllable ending with a consonant. Since words shaped ˘¯ ending in a consonant, such as *theôn* and *theoús*, cannot occur before the bucolic diaeresis, the nominative of the formula remains intact, while the oblique forms, all ending in a consonant, distribute part of the formula elsewhere.[23] The difficulty this situation poses is reflected in the frequency with which the nominative case is found (4 times in the *Iliad*, and 4 times in the *Odyssey*, in three instances of a whole-line formula), with only two cases of the genitive (in the *Odyssey*) and 4 cases (1 repeated whole-line formula) of the accusative, each with a different innovating segment interposed between the first part of the formula and the second.

I have proceeded to detail the system in which the formula *theoì aièn eóntes* operates in order to suggest that a similar process is at work in the formulas based on *paúō khólon*. Since the oblique cases of *theoì aièn eóntes* end in a consonant and hence cannot be shortened, they must—if the formula is to be used without contraction—be separated from *aièn eónt-*. Similarly, the formula *paúō khólon*, in the case of *Od.* 4.583, presents us with the *khólon* of the phrase *paú-khólon* occurring between *theôn* . . . *aièn eóntōn*. The result is a complex phrase consisting of two formulaic units dovetailed together. This variation, a good example of the flexibility of Homeric poetics, signals a further semantic distinction.[24] This formular complexity coincides with the contextual uniqueness of *Odyssey* 4.583, in which Menelaus puts an end to the *khólos* of the gods through sacrifice. Thus, the phrases used when a god stops human anger are distinguished from those used when a human being halts a god's *khólos* through ritual.

When Menelaus has stopped the anger of the gods in *Odyssey* 4, he uses ritual means to accomplish his purpose, but what means can be used to stop the *khólos* of Achilles? The last example of *paúō* with *khólos* at the bucolic diaeresis (Appendix 2, Group 1) echoes Zeus's stipulation of the proper moment to put an end to Achilles' anger. In this case, Achilles puts an end to his quarrel with Agamemnon in the context of a speech that I will examine carefully. For now, this line (*Il.* 19.67) accomplishes what Zeus promised in *Il.* 15.68–75 (quoted above). Here we have promise and fulfillment displayed in the use of the formula *paúō khólon*—the promise belonging to Zeus, the fulfillment to Achilles. The *khólos* phrase is in the same metrical position in both passages and signals how closely Zeus and Achilles are related, as demonstrated by Whitman.[25] The link here is reinforced by the fact that only Achilles, of mortals, refers to ending his own *khólos*.[26]

Athena intervenes to stop the *khólos* between the gods (Ares and Zeus), just as she prevents it between the Achaeans (Agamemnon and Achilles) in Book 1. There she physically restrains Achilles by grabbing his hair before he can draw his sword and violently attack Agamemnon. Here she physically restrains Ares by grabbing his helmet, shield, and sword, and by verbally indicating the profound trouble that will be stirred should he put his *khólos* into action:

> ὦρτο διὲκ προθύρου, λίπε δὲ θρόνον, ἔνθα θάασσε,
> τοῦ δ' ἀπὸ μὲν κεφαλῆς κόρυθ' εἵλετο καὶ σάκος ὤμων,
> ἔγχος δ' ἔστησε στιβαρῆς ἀπὸ χειρὸς ἑλοῦσα
> χάλκεον . . . .
>
> (*Il.* 15.124–27)

She rushed from the outercourt and left her seat, where she sat, and took from off his head his helmet and the shield from his shoulders, and grabbing it she stowed the sword, after taking it from his thick hand, the bronze sword. . . .

In the case of both Achilles and Ares, Athena restrains the *khólos* of one who is righteously angry. But she approaches the two situations differently. In the case of Achilles she pronounces her order succinctly (*all' áge lêg' éridos, Il.* 1.210 "but, come, cease from strife"); clearly the present situation may require a different strategy from that required in the human domain—we are in the world of the immortals and not the potentially tragic human world. Nevertheless, in speaking to Ares she dilates on the consequences should Ares pursue his vengeance, in a passage that resembles Nestor's criticism in *Il.* 1.254–84.

> ἦ ἐθέλεις αὐτὸς μὲν ἀναπλήσας κακὰ πολλὰ
> ἂψ ἴμεν Οὔλυμπόνδε καὶ ἀχνύμενός περ ἀνάγκῃ,
> αὐτὰρ τοῖς ἄλλοισι κακὸν μέγα πᾶσι φυτεῦσαι;
> αὐτίκα γὰρ Τρῶας μὲν ὑπερθύμους καὶ Ἀχαιοὺς
> λείψει, ὁ δ' ἡμέας εἶσι κυδοιμήσων ἐς Ὄλυμπον,
> μάρψει δ' ἑξείης ὅς τ' αἴτιος ὅς τε καὶ οὐκί.
> τῶ σ' αὖ νῦν κέλομαι <u>μεθέμεν χόλον υἷος ἑῆος</u>.
> (*Il.* 15.132–38)

> Do you wish, after having endured many woes, to come back to Olympus and, though forced to grieve, to establish a great evil for all the rest [of us]? For immediately he will leave the haughty Trojans and Achaeans, and he will come enraged against us to Olympus, and he will snatch in order both the blameworthy and the innocent; therefore I order you <u>to stop your anger over your son</u>.

Athena here argues that it is expedient for Ares to cease lusting for vengeance, because of the harm that will come to guilty and innocent alike if Zeus learns of Ares' *khólos*. As with Achilles in *Iliad* 21, Zeus's *khólos* does not discriminate as to guilt or innocence: all will pay the *tísis*.

These too are the terms that Nestor uses to condemn the *khólos* between the best of the Achaeans in *Iliad* 1. Nestor, it can be said, provides the mortal version of Athena's divine concerns:

> ὢ πόποι, ἦ μέγα πένθος Ἀχαιΐδα γαῖαν ἱκάνει·
> ἦ κεν γηθήσαι Πρίαμος Πριάμοιό τε παῖδες
> ἄλλοι τε Τρῶες μέγα κεν κεχαροίατο θυμῷ,
> εἰ σφῶιν τάδε πάντα πυθοίατο μαρναμένοιιν,
> οἳ περὶ μὲν βουλὴν Δαναῶν, περὶ δ' ἐστὲ μάχεσθαι.
> (*Il.* 1.254–58)

> O my, a great woe reaches the Achaean land; yes, Priam and the children of Priam would rejoice, and the other Trojans greatly would be grateful in their hearts, if they should see you two contending in all these ways, those who are best at counsel of the Danaans and those of you who are best at fighting.

Nestor's *méga pénthos* corresponds to Athena's *kakòn mége* (*Il.* 15.134; cf. also *pâsi* with *Akhaiída gaîan*). Moreover the relation of *pénthos* to *khólos* sends us back to Helen's drug: *pénthos* and *khólos* are central to the heroic epic warrior's world. Furthermore, Athena's order (*kélomai*) that Ares resist *khólos* corresponds with Nestor's entreaty (*líssomai*) that Achilles restrain his own anger (*Il.* 1.283).[27] The formula *methémen khólon* means subtantially the same thing as *paúō khólon*, but with the implication of "self-restraint"—a god or man can order (*kélomai*) or entreat (*líssomai*), but the action is to be taken on one's own. Both scenes displaying *methémen khólon* show that direct means can be taken to halt an anger already in progress; in each case the speaker attempts to suggest some way, outside the actual grievance, to bring matters to an end. In Book 15, Athena claims that the community of gods will suffer if Ares pursues his *khólos*. In the first book, Nestor argues before the Achaeans that their community will suffer if Achilles pursues his *khólos*. Because—according to Calchas's definition—*khólos* has no *télos* of its own, Nestor and Athena are free to seek "diplomatic solutions" to the conflict.[28]

Just as the best of the Achaeans is Achilles, so the most powerful god is Zeus. As Achilles' support of Calchas tests Agamemnon's power, so Ares challenges Zeus, to the extent that the supreme god's *khólos* threatens to emerge as a possible reaction to Ares' vengeance:

> ἔνθα κ᾽ ἔτι μείζων τε καὶ ἀργαλεώτερος ἄλλος
> πὰρ Διὸς ἀθανάτοισι χόλος καὶ μῆνις ἐτύχθη,
> εἰ μὴ Ἀθήνη πᾶσι περιδείσασα θεοῖσιν
> ὦρτο διὲκ προθύρου.
>
> (*Il.* 15.121–24)[29]

> There a still great and more painful *khólos* and *mênis* would have been made by Zeus against the immortals, had not Athena rushed in fear for all the gods from the outercourt.

Thus far we have observed how the cessation or restraint of anger is expressed in the Homeric poems with *paúō* and *methémen*, with formulas that tend to cluster at the bucolic diaeresis. It is worth noting at this point that in two of these cases—both in the *Iliad*—this use of *khólos* marks the passages as thematically significant. In the first instance (*Il.* 15.138) Zeus predicts that he will end the anger of Achilles, which is in the second instance soon to be called to a halt by Achilles himself (*Il.* 19.67).[30] We will see in Chapter 3 that *khólos* in fact has special meaning in Greek epic that helps motivate such usage.

There is another important occurrence of *methíēmi* with *khólos* outside the *Iliad*; it demonstrates nicely the possibility for *khólos* to be brought to a conclusion by divine or human will. The anger of Poseidon at the blinding of Polyphemus clearly qualifies as *khólos* because he is enraged by the calamity that has befallen his son. The blinding of the Cyclops, then, leads to the anger of

Poseidon that Athena must allay before Odysseus can be given safe passage home.[31] Zeus tells Athena that "Poseidon is the cause, unrelenting in his anger for the blinding of his son Polyphemus" (Peradotto 1990, 60). If this anger is *khólos* then the problem of placating Poseidon[32] can be brought under the social mechanisms surrounding *khólos*. When Zeus, after his own disgruntled complaint about human beings and their *atasthalíai* (*Od.* 1.32–43), acquiesces to Athena's reasonable request that Odysseus, blameless as he is, (*Od.* 1.60–62), be allowed to come back home, he styles the anger of Poseidon in a manner consistent with the passages we have looked at above:

> ἀλλ᾽ ἄγεθ᾽ ἡμεῖς οἵδε περιφραζώμεθα πάντες
> νόστον, ὅπως ἔλθῃσι· Ποσειδάων δὲ μεθήσει
> ὃν χόλον· οὐ μὲν γάρ τι δυνήσεται ἀντία πάντων
> ἀθανάτων ἀέκητι θεῶν ἐριδαινέμεν οἶος.
> (*Od.* 1.76–79)

> But come let us all here consider the *nóstos*, how he might wish it. And Poseidon will relax his own *khólos*. For he will never be able against the will of all the immortal gods to make a contention alone.

For Zeus, the *nóstos* of Odysseus, thus, depends on the end of the *khólos* of Poseidon; as with the anger of Ares and the anger of Achilles, Zeus understands that this kind of wrath can be brought to a conclusion. The council of the gods, here as in *Iliad* 15, is specifically concerned with bringing about an end to a *khólos* that impedes the action.[33]

The sense of bringing *khólos* to an end clearly has thematic value in the *Iliad*,[34] a point that is underscored as we turn to the 7 instances of the genitive, 5 of which occur in contexts referring to the cessation of *khólos* in the *Iliad*.[35] One of the two passages from the *Odyssey* is in an explicitly Iliadic context: the anger of Ajax over the arms of Achilles, *Od.* 11.554. The other instance from the *Odyssey* (*Od.* 21.377) shows an extension of the phrase *methémen khólon*, when the suitors ease from their *khólos* "in deference to Telemachus" (*LSJ*).[36] Here the suitors react to a threat by Telemachus. The speech is clearly meant to rouse their anger (*apeilḗsas*, *Od.* 21.368; *biḗphi te phéreteros eíēn*, *Od.* 21.373). Such a speech typically might provoke *khólos*. Instead the suitors are consumed with laughter, and as the language emphasizes (*kaì dḗ*),[37] they have a reaction opposite to the expected one, namely, they cease from *khólos*, since, I suggest, they cannot accept Telemachus as an Iliadic threat.

To return to the *Iliad*, of the 7 instances of the genitive of *khólos*, the genitive occurs 5 times at line-end, where we expect the older genitive in *-oio* (the *-ou* genitives finding their place in the less conservative part of the line at *Il.* 10.107 and *Od.* 11.554).[38] Of these all the examples in the *Iliad* refer to the anger of Achilles. Not only that, but three of those four examples occur in the highly charged embassy scene, Book 9 of the *Iliad*. The significance of *khólos* in the *Iliad* comes to light in Homeric use of the formula *metallḗksanti khóloio* (3 times) in *Iliad* 9, where Agamemnon's desire to still Achilles' *khólos* is managed by the ambassadors he has sent to the tent of the best of the Achaeans.[39]

When Odysseus quotes Agamemnon's offer to Achilles he modifies Agamemnon's rhetorical approach to Achilles. Agamemnon asks:

> ταῦτά κέ οἱ τελέσαιμι μεταλλήξαντι χόλοιο.
> (*Il.* 9.157)
>
> I would accomplish these things for him, on his yielding from *khólos*.

This statement occurs at the very end of the list detailing what will be given Achilles if he desists from his *khólos* (*Il.* 9.120–56). Odysseus picks up on the formula but uses it to frame the list of items, at

> ἄξια δῶρα δίδωσι μεταλλήξαντι χόλοιο.
> (*Il.* 9.261)
>
> He would give these worthy gifts to you on your yielding from *khólos*.

and

> ταῦτά κέ τοι τελέσειε μεταλλήξαντι χόλοιο.
> (*Il.* 9.299)
>
> He would accomplish these things for you on your yielding from *khólos*.

Odysseus thus uses the phrase *metallḗksanti khóloio* as a ring-compositional frame for the offer made to Achilles. The editing of Agamemnon's offer, as is clear from the research into this passage by Whitman, Nagy, and others is crucial to the meaning of this scene. Nagy's summary states the matter clearly:

> By taking the lead among the emissaries, [Odysseus] puts himself in the position of being the one who actually delivers the terms of compensation proposed by Agamemnon for settlement with Achilles (9.260–99). . . . In doing so, Odysseus makes a significant adjustment to Agamemnon's original message by failing to repeat Agamemnon's reaffirmation of social superiority over Achilles (9.160–61).[40]

It has yet to be noted, however, that what Odysseus substitutes for Agamemnon's "reaffirmation" (*dmēthḗtō*, *Il.* 9.158) is a further focus on the aspect of *khólos* highlighted in Calchas's definition, that *khólos* can be set aside. Thus Odysseus's framing locution *metallḗksanti khóloio* is used to highlight a point that Odysseus is here trying to secure, that Phoenix will succeed in making explicit in the story of Meleager, and that finally Ajax will make in an aside—that a necessary part of a justifiable *khólos* is knowing when to give it up.[41] Thus, where Agamemnon stresses Achilles' surrender, Odysseus (later joined by Phoenix and Ajax) stresses the proper role of one so enraged: he should yield from it under certain culturally acceptable—we might, from a literary stance, say "conventional"—circumstances.

A closer look at the differences between the two speeches demonstrates Odysseus's rhetorical strategy and the different ways in which Agamemnon and Odysseus frame the offer made to Achilles that evening.

Agamemnon:

ὡς νῦν τοῦτον ἔτεισε, δάμασσε δὲ λαὸν Ἀχαιῶν.
(*Il.* 9.118)

Now he has honored this man, and he has subdued the host of Achaeans.

ταῦτά κέ οἱ τελέσαιμι μεταλλήξαντι χόλοιο
δμηθήτω—Ἀίδης τοι ἀμείλιχος ἠδ' ἀδάμαστος.
(*Il.* 9.157–58)

I have accomplished these things for him, if he yield from his *khólos*; let him be subdued—it's Hades that is unpropitiable and unsubduable.

Odysseus:

ὣς ἐπέτελλ' ὁ γέρων, σὺ δὲ λήθεαι. ἀλλ' ἔτι καὶ νῦν
παύε', ἔα δὲ χόλον θυμαλγέα· σοὶ δ' Ἀγαμέμνων
ἄξια δῶρα δίδωσι μεταλλήξαντι χόλοιο.
(*Il.* 9.259–61)

Thus did the old man enjoin, but you've forgotten, still even now make an end of it, and leave off your heart-hurting *khólos*; and Agamemnon gives worthy gifts to you, if you yield from your *khólos*.

ταῦτά κέ τοι τελέσειε μεταλλήξαντι χόλοιο.
εἰ δέ τοι Ἀτρείδης μὲν ἀπήχθετο κηρόθι μᾶλλον,
αὐτὸς καὶ τοῦ δῶρα, σὺ δ' ἄλλους περ Παναχαιοὺς
τειρομένους ἐλέαιρε κατὰ στρατόν, οἵ σε θεὸν ὣς
τίσουσ'·
(*Il.* 9.299–303)

He would accomplish these things for you, if you yield from your *khólos*; but if the son of Atreus is so hateful to you the more in your heart, himself and his gifts, still, pity the rest of the Panachaeans in their plight in the army, who will honor you like a god.

Odysseus does more than merely suppress Agamemnon's tactless remark (*dámasse* in 118 picked up by *dmēthḗtō* in 158, with a further jab in the remark about Hades): Odysseus has to restructure the rhetoric of Agamemnon's speech so as to avoid the insult that Agamemnon has encoded in the rhetorical and poetic device of ring-composition. Odysseus revises the speech so that the framing device no longer underscores Achilles' submission but points instead to the major theme of the diplomatic mission: the malleable nature of *khólos*. He does this by repeating *khólos* twice in two lines, in a manner distinctive within the formulaic systems for *khólos*.[42] This restructuring may well be what we are to imagine comes out of the huddle that Nestor calls in *Il.* 9.179–81, where no doubt the ambassadors debated the means of persuasion:

> τοῖσι δὲ πόλλ' ἐπέτελλε Γερήνιος ἱππότα Νέστωρ,
> δενδίλλων ἐς ἕκαστον, Ὀδυσσῆι δὲ μάλιστα,
> πειρᾶν, ὡς πεπίθοιεν ἀμύμονα Πηλεΐωνα.
> (*Il.* 9.179–81)

> Gerenian horseman Nestor ordered many things to them, giving the details to each one, and most especially to Odysseus, to make the attempt to persuade the blameless son of Peleus.

The master rhetorician might have told each of them to highlight *khólos*, each in his own way, as the object of their rhetorical invention. Phoenix and Ajax handle the matter differently, but Odysseus begins by exploiting Agamemnon's phrase and manipulating the diction for *khólos* in such a way that Achilles has to contemplate the possibility of bringing it to an end.

Another passage earlier in the *Iliad* shows *khóloio* used once again with a form of *lḗgō* in a way that reflects the *khólos* theme. I list it here (Group 4) as an exception to the contextual pattern because it presents an anger that Achilles will not control:

> Πηλεΐδης δ' ἐξαῦτις ἀταρτηροῖς ἐπέεσσιν
> Ἀτρεΐδην προσέειπε, καὶ οὔ πω λῆγε χόλοιο·
> (*Il.* 1.223–24)

> And the son of Peleus in turn spoke with deadly words to the son of Atreus, and he did not yet stop from his anger.

This use of *khólos*, in contrast to the other three uses, does not occur in a speech. In this case, the text gives us Achilles' refusal to stop having *khólos* against Agamemnon just after Athena has kept him from killing the king. No better example could be found of the social management of Homeric *khólos*. The situation is put in terms of the choice of Achilles either to kill Agamemnon or restrain himself and that restraint is seen as the restraining of *khólos*:

Ὣς φάτο· Πηλεΐωνι δ' ἄχος γένετ', ἐν δέ οἱ ἦτορ
στήθεσσιν λασίοισι διάνδιχα μερμήριξεν,
ἢ ὅ γε φάσγανον ὀξὺ ἐρυσσάμενος παρὰ μηροῦ
τοὺς μὲν ἀναστήσειεν, ὃ δ' Ἀτρεΐδην ἐναρίζοι,
ἦε χόλον παύσειεν ἐρητύσειέ τε θυμόν.
(*Il.* 1.188–92)

Thus he spoke and the son of Peleus was aggrieved, and the heart in his chest was split two ways, whether having drawn the sharp sword from his thigh he might dismiss the group and slay the son of Atreus, or whether he should put an end to his *khólos*, and restrain his heart.

Yet when Athena gives her order to Achilles, she does not use the word *khólos*, but *ménos* (*Od.* 1.207). In particular, Athena refrains from using a phrase containing *lḗge* + *khólos* to use instead as the centerpiece of her speech to Achilles *lḗgō* with *éridos*: *all' áge, lêg' éridos, mēdè ksíphos hélkeo kheirí* (*Il.* 1.210) "But come, stop your *éris*, and don't draw the sword with your hand." As if to indicate what Athena is really talking about, Achilles introduces the notion of *khólos* as his main topic:

"χρὴ μὲν σφωίτερόν γε, θεά, ἔπος εἰρύσσασθαι
καὶ μάλα περ θυμῷ κεχολωμένον· ὣς γὰρ ἄμεινον.
ὅς κε θεοῖς ἐπιπείθηται, μάλα τ' ἔκλυον αὐτοῦ."
(*Il.* 1.216–18)

It is necessary to attend to your word, goddess, even in my heartfelt *khólos*. Thus it would be better; the one who obeys the gods, they listen to him the more.

This use of *khólos* helps explain why Athena's request that strife be put aside is fulfilled through the two phrases: *all' áge lêg' éridos* (*Il.* 1.210) "but come stop your *éris*"; *oúpō lêge khóloio* (*Il.* 1.224) "don't yet leave off *khólos*." For Achilles has indeed put an end to the *éris* represented by the exchange of speeches in *Iliad* 1. But the *khólos* is another matter. Achilles knows that he can maintain his *khólos* with Agamemnon at the level of words, even if slaying him outright is forbidden. And *khólos* itself can be used with great, even deadly, force in the realm of words as is demonstrated by its intricate relationship to speech. Thus, the line Athena speaks at *Il.* 1.211 (*all' ḗtoi épesin mèn oneídison, hōs ésetaí per* "but reproach him with words, the way it will in fact be") leaves the door open for *khólos*. Although it is one thing to say that *éris* may be stopped, *khólos* need not belong to the world of action.[43] For Achilles, the consequences seem to lie in the sphere of verbal indignation (cf. *atartēroîs epéesin*, 223 "with harsh words"). The opening of the *Iliad* provides a ripe context for the formula *meta- lêge- khóloio* and other phrases that point to the malleability of *khólos*, because here the narrative sets in motion a kind of anger that can be waged as much with words as with deeds.

Notes

1. See Moravcsik and Wirth 1986, 3.

2. Besides distribution, markedness also affects syntagmatic structure and paradigmatic complexity.

3. Excluding *Il.* 14.111 and *Il.* 3.220.

4. I read *khólōi* at *Il.* 14.111 against Allen and van Thiel. West (2000) omits this variant.

5. *Il.* 1.192, 1.217, 1.224, 2.241, 4.513, 9.157, 9.260, 9.261, 9.299, 9.436, 9.523, 9.565, 9.646, 9.675, 9.678, 10.107, 14.367, 15.68, 15.72, 16.30, 16.61, 16.203, 16.206, 17.710, 18.111, 18.337, 19.16, 19.67, 23.23, 24.395, excluding the generic reference in 18.108.

6. Not counting *Il.* 15.217, a reference to the reciprocal *khólos* of Zeus and Poseidon, we have *Il.* 4.42, 5.421, 5.762, 8.407, 8.421, 14.310, 15.122, 15.155, 15.210, 15.223, 20.301, 24.114, 24.135; *Od.* 24.544.

7. Agamemnon's *khólos*: *Il.* 1.78, 1.81, 1.283, 1.387, 2.195, 4.178, 4.241, 9.33; Odysseus's: *Il.* 4.494, 4.501; *Od.* 7.309–10, 8.205, 18.20, 22.59, 22.369.

8. Hera: *Il.* 4.24, 4.36, 8.461, 21.479, 24.55; Athena: *Il.* 4.23, 8.460; *Od.* 3.145, 22.224, 22.225.

9. *Il.* 1.181, and see above, Part 1.

10. Whitman 1958, 183–87.

11. In order of frequency, *ágrios Il.* 4.23, 8.460, *Od.* 8.304; *thumalgḗs Il.* 4.513, 9.260, 9.565; *argaléos Il.* 10.107, 18.119; *ainós Il.* 22.94; *aipún Il.* 15.223; *anḗkestos Il.* 15.217; *deinós Od.* 5.145; *drimús Il.* 18.322; *epizáphelos Il.* 9.525; *kakós Il.* 16.206; *khalepós Od.* 21.377.

12. The distribution of *khólos* points to the generic distinction between the *Iliad* and the *Odyssey*: 36 times in the *Odyssey* and 102 times in the *Iliad*. Cf. Walsh 1999: 160–61.

13. Heubeck et al. 1988 at *Od.* 4.220ff.

14. Crucial to understanding this word is Nagy 1979, 94–102; along with the indispensable study of Mawet (1977, Chapter IV, 253–91).

15. Nagy 1979, 94.

16. Further on *lēth-* and Homeric poetics can be found in Nagy 1990a, 59–60, with literature.

17. The recent literature on this passage tends not to dwell on *khólos* even while attending closely to the other characteristics of this drug; see Nagy 1974, 258–60; Nagy 1979, 99–100; Heubeck et al. 1988 at 4.207. See Bergren 1981; Clader 1976, 32–33. An exception is Collins 1988, 50–51, who connects *khólos* (and *pénthos*) to the death of a *phílos*. That this passage resembles "similar language concerning the effects of song" (Thalmann 1984, 166) will be relevant to our consideration of *khólos* and the genre of the *Iliad*, and see Lowenstam 1993, 230, n. 197.

18. These passages suggest that the relationship is close: *Od.* 11.102 and 553; if Calchas is right, forgetfulness may be one method by which *khólos* can be brought to an end.

19. For "stopping" verbs and *mênis*, see Watkins 1977a, 195–99.

20. Compare *Od.* 6.173–74.

21. *Od.* 5.492 shows *hína min paúseie tákhista / dusponéos kamátoio* . . . and *Il.* 21.249 gives *hína min paúseie pónoio*.

22. Janko 1992 at *Il.* 15.72–73, along with many commentators and translators (including Lattimore and Fagles), takes the *khólon* here to refer to the anger of Zeus; so too does Watkins 1977a, 197–99. But line 68 and line 72 easily refer to Achilles' wrath, especially since the *khólos* of Zeus has little to do with the *Iliad*; it is the *boulḗ* ("plan") of Zeus at *Il.* 1.5, with respect to the anger of Achilles, that drives the plot of this poem. Indeed there is a parallel reference in line 71 to the *Athēnaíēs boulás* ("Athena's plan") directed at the end of the war and the destruction of Troy. The plan of Athena to destroy Troy complements the plan of Zeus to honor Achilles, as indicated by Zeus's allowing his (Achilles') *khólos* to rage. Thus, *kholōsámenos* (*Il.* 15.68) and *khólos* (*Il.* 15.72) are linked, with Zeus referring to the same anger in each case, specifically to Achilles' *khólos* and not his own. To be sure, a god can stop a mortal's *khólos*, as is seen from *Il.* 9.459; one can also stop one's own *khólos* (*Il.* 19.67). But the *khólos* of Zeus is not the driving force of the *Iliad*. Even with a less precise definition of *khólos* than I am attempting here, can one really say that Zeus remains "angry" until the death of Hector? Note that the textual variant *paúsō* (for *paúō*, 72) keeps the parallel with *eásō* in 73, for which point recall the correlation of *paúein* and *eân* in *Il.* 9.260.

23. In the *Hymn to Demeter* 325 *theoús* is contracted so as to maintain the contiguity of the formulaic elements. In the earlier Homeric passages, the formula is less likely to need this kind of strategy to maintain its integrity. Chantraine 1973a indicates that "certaines prononciations monosyllabiques paraissent particulièrement artificielles" (*Gr. Hom.* I. §26, 66); I only add that the artifice may have to do with the relationship of the performer to the tradition: the passages from a period secure in its diction can afford to be flexible; if *Demeter* is late, the singers may feel the need to buttress the traditional quality of the line by preserving the unity of the phrase.

24. See Hainsworth 1968, 110–28 for the issue of creativity and formulaic regularity, with Nagler 1974, Chapters 1 and 2.

25. Whitman 1958, 225–30.

26. Clearly Achilles' special relation to *khólos*, because only he speaks of ending his own *khólos*, is parallel to the stricture that the noun *mênis* only refers to the anger of Achilles and that of the gods (cf. Watkins 1977a and Muellner 1996, 189–94; Muellner argues for more caution in understanding the notion of taboo with reference to *mênis*; since *khólos* is not a taboo word, but rather one of the variants of *mênis* expected in a taboo situation, poetic constraints on its use may loom as large as social contexts). It is this special handling of *mênis*, *khólos*, and other words for wrath that mark the *Iliad*'s view of wrath in contradistinction to that of the *Odyssey*. I agree with Clay that wrath is important in both poems (Clay 1983, 67), but the poetry of the *Iliad* sees it as a central focus and handles the formulaic system a special way depending on which of the wrath words is employed.

27. As to whether the *khólos* here is that of Achilles or Agamemnon, see van Bennekom 1984, with Eisenberger 1985. Leaf 1886 (comparing *Od.* 21.377) takes *Akhillêi* as a dative of interest, so that the *khólos* is that of Agamemnon, and see Merry (1892) at *Od.* 21.378, with *Od.* 11.553; Muellner 1996, 111 also reads Agamemnon as the party with *khólos*. More attractive to me is the notion that Nestor is "addressing" Achilles in the third person, as happens in the embassy scene in Ajax's speech; for Achilles addressed in the third person see Muellner 1996, 151 and 165.

28. Compare here the passage where Phoenix acknowledges the *phátis dḗmou* ("popular opinion"). In this case other concerns—his personal reputation—overrides his *khólos* against his father.

29. On *khólos kaì mênis,* cf. Watkins 1977a, 192–93, and see especially Muellner 1996, 97 n. 10.

30. On the relation of Zeus to Achilles see Whitman 1958, 228–31.

31. On the anger of Poseidon, see Lidov 1977. The anger of Poseidon is styled with differing words throughout the *Odyssey*: *menéainen* 6.330; *kóton*, 13.342, *khṓomenos*, 13.343. As elsewhere, I am concerned to establish that it can be a *khólos* but not exclusively a *khólos*. For the various types of divine wrath in the *Odyssey* see Clay 1983, 51 n. 89; her further comment (230) that "his motive is simply to avenge his son—brutal and impious though he may be" is consistent with notion of *khólos* as an immediate and direct rage.

32. Peradotto 1990, 75, and n. 16; Woodhouse 1930, 39. Peradotto goes on to say that "in the system of verisimilitude that controls the Homeric poems, wrath appears to be a social and political response, not a passing tantrum. It requires compensation." As we have seen, the compensation is *tísis*, which, with a *khólos* type of anger, can be brought to a conclusion through the action of the angered person. *Kótos*, as I argued in Part 1, is very different because once it is set in motion, it must reach a *télos* that even the participants might not live to experience.

33. It is tempting to suggest that when Thersites characterizes Achilles as *methḗmōn* (*Il.* 2.241) he is saying that he is likely to restrain his *khólos*, a gross misunderstanding of the *Iliad*'s angry hero. If, as Nagy suggests (1979, 253–64), Thersites calls forth the tradition of blame-poetry, what worse thing can one call a *khólos*-hero than *methḗmōn*, easy to calm? The only other character in the Homeric narratives who gets this epithet is Nausikaa, at *Od.* 6.25, where the meaning seems to be "unheedful."

34. Just as the end of *mênis* has thematic value, Watkins 1977a, 195–97.

35. The passages are listed in Appendix 2, Group 4.

36. See also Leaf 1886 at 1.283.

37. Denniston (1995, 248) explains the function of *kaì dḗ* here: "In Homeric narrative *kaì dḗ* usually corresponds to the later *kaì dè kaí*. It introduces something similar in kind to what has preceded, but stronger . . . and makes a kind of climax." In this case it clarifies the following as the full statement of the meaning of this laughter—they have no *khólos*.

38. Both these occurrences of the *-ou* genitive of *khólos* can be resolved to their older variant (*khóloio*). On *-oio/-ou* genitives see Chantraine 1973a, §18, 63, and 80.

39. Watkins 1977a, 192.

40. Nagy 1979, 52 and Whitman 1958, 191–92 as cited in Nagy.

41. It is indeed an essential feature of *khólos*, unlike *kótos*, that it can be "given up."

42. There are two other occurrences *khólos* in contiguous lines in the doublets *Il.* 4.23 and 24 and *Il.* 8.460 and 461, with a number of other examples of *khólos* repeated (the rhetorical figure of *polyptoton*) in close proximity in *Il.* 9 (9.523 and 525, 9.565 and 566, and 9.675 and 678), as well as in *Il.* 13.203 and 206, with *Od.* 22.224 and 225.

43. This relationship between *éris* and *khólos* is exploited in *Il.* 18.107–8.

Chapter Seven

The Beginning of *Χόλος*

As we have seen, *khólos* comes to be identified by its endpoint, a feature that accords well with Calchas's indication that it can be consumed "in a day" (*autêmar, Il.* 1.81). Can we also expect that it can be located as to its *beginning*, the moment at which a character comes to be angry? And will we also find moments to designate the continuation of the state of anger, that is to say, a point somewhere between beginning and end? In fact, just as, when the narrative presents the end of *khólos*, the phraseology involves a form of *khólos* in the accusative case, so the beginning of *khólos* is linked to a phrase that displays the nominative case. Moreover, I will show that the process of *khólos* is carefully handled by Homeric diction in a way that is foreign to the notion of *kótos*.

In Appendix 2 (Group 6a-d), I have listed all the forms of nominative *khólos*, (23 in all) in both the *Iliad* and the *Odyssey*, with a further breakdown according to formulaic phrases involving a specific set of verbs, namely, *édu, lában, hḗrei, émpese,* and *híkoi.* There are clear examples of formulas with nominative *khólos* referring to the inception of *khólos*. It is important that central figures of the narrative are involved in this group, in particular Achilles (*Il.* 19.16), Hector (*Il.* 22.94, by way of a simile) and Meleager (*Il.* 9.553).

There are three cases of the phrase *édu . . . khólos* where the narrator pinpoints the beginning of anger as that moment when *khólos* "enters into" the angered party. Book 19's example of this phrase highlights one of the most dramatic moments in the *Iliad*, when Achilles receives the newly made armor from his mother, Thetis. It is often noted that his response presents him as somehow infused with a kind of anger, but we should note that this kind of anger is specifically *khólos*:

αὐτὰρ Ἀχιλλεὺς
ὡς εἶδ', ὥς μιν μᾶλλον ἔδυ χόλος, ἐν δέ οἱ ὄσσε
δεινὸν ὑπὸ βλεφάρων ὡς εἰ σέλας ἐξεφάανθεν·
(*Il.* 19.15–17)

As for Achilles, when he saw [the armor], just so did *khólos* enter him the more, and his eyes, as if a lightning flash, shone terribly beneath his brow.

Coincident with the viewing of his armor is the manipulation of his *khólos*; we will see that the use of *khólos* here is poetically motivated within the context of the *Iliad*. *Khólos* typically involves images or metaphors concerning visual perception.

Another character whose *khólos* "enters" him in this way is Meleager, in Phoenix's exemplum. As the narrator of the story of Meleager, Phoenix links the *khólos* of Meleager with the moment at which the evils begin for the Aitolians:

ὄφρα μὲν οὖν Μελέαγρος ἀρηΐφιλος πολέμιζε,
τόφρα δὲ Κουρήτεσσι κακῶς ἦν,
. . . .
ἀλλ' ὅτε δὴ Μελέαγρον ἔδυ χόλος,
. . . .
ἤ τοι ὃ μητρὶ φίλῃ Ἀλθαίῃ χωόμενος κῆρ
κεῖτο παρὰ μνηστῇ ἀλόχῳ, καλῇ Κλεοπάτρῃ,
(*Il.* 9.550–51; 553; 555–56)

While Meleager, then, beloved of Ares continued to fight, so long did it go badly for the Kouretes. . . . But when *khólos* entered into Meleager . . . indeed out of anger in his heart at his beloved mother, he lay beside his lawful wife, lovely Kleopatra.

The narrator makes his scene dramatic by pointing to the effects of the *khólos* scenario, in which the warrior comes to be absent from war and refuses to fight, and his absence comes at just the moment (*hóte dḗ*, 554) that anger "enters" him.[1] In both cases, the reception of the armor and the story of Meleager, the arousal of *khólos* marks a turning point in the description (*Il.* 19.16) or the narrative (*Il.* 9.554). Furthermore, that Achilles responds in just the way Meleager responded comments on this stage of his wrath. In Nagler's words:

The onset of Achilles' (second) anger represents his personal, psychological response to the terrible *charis* which the god has put into the armor, and which the hero seems to *absorb and then project through his eyes*. . . . In the act of "returning" to the military responsibilities of the convenership Achilles "withdraws" a step further from rationality, and from the normal social aspects of leadership. His *charis* is so great that his own attendants, far from gazing at him in admiration, shrink back in fear.[2]

The importance of this observation for my discussion is that it announces *khólos* as a mark of "withdrawal."

The simile of the serpent in Book 22, indicating the (short-lived) ferocity of Hector as he takes his last stand against Achilles, does not single out the temporal aspect of the beginning of *khólos*, but the serpent's gaze here calls to mind the passage from *Iliad* 19, when Achilles sees his armor:

> ὡς δὲ δράκων ἐπὶ χειῇ ὀρέστερος ἄνδρα μένῃσι,
> βεβρωκὼς κακὰ φάρμακ', ἔδυ δέ τέ μιν χόλος αἰνός,
> σμερδαλέον δέ δέδορκεν ἑλισσόμενος περὶ χειῇ.
> ὣς Ἕκτωρ ἄσβεστον ἔχων μένος οὐχ ὑπεχώρει.
> (*Il.* 22.93–96)

And as a serpent of the mountain in his lair awaits a man, and he has consumed evil drugs, and a terrible *khólos* entered him, and he gazed with terror, winding in his hole, thus Hector with unquenchable *ménos* ("rage") was not yielding.

Although the discussion of the metaphor will have to wait until Chapter 11, note that the onset of *khólos* is marked by the ingestion of *phármaka* ("drugs") , in a manner resembling how *khólos* is taken in through Achilles' eyes at the beginning of *Iliad* 19 (15–18).[3]

Thus far we have seen three examples of nominative *khólos*, two pointing to the moment when the hero becomes angry. A similar value can be attached to the formula *khólos láb-(en/oi)* (Appendix 2, Group 6b), where two of the instances clearly point to the onset of anger, with the third (*Il.* 16.30) embedded in a negative wish. Thus, when Achilles characterizes the quarrel that he has just had with Agamemnon, he tells his mother

> αὐτίκ' ἐγὼ πρῶτος κελόμην θεὸν ἱλάσκεσθαι·
> Ἀτρεΐωνα δ' ἔπειτα χόλος λάβεν, αἶψα δ' ἀναστὰς
> ἠπείλησεν μῦθον, ὃ δὴ τετελεσμένος ἐστί.
> (*Il.* 1.386–88)

Immediately I first ordered that we propitiate the god; but *khólos* then took hold of Agamemnon and immediately he stood up and made a threatening speech, which came to pass.

As Richard Martin has shown, this entire speech is characteristic of Achilles' rhetorical style, especially in showing how he uses the recollection of past events, where it is pointed out that in these lines Achilles "intrudes as narrator" by characterizing the speech of the son of Atreus as a threat (*epeílēsen mûthon*, *Il.* 1.388).[4] I only add here that Achilles is the first to use *khólos* of Agamemnon;[5] certainly in the quarrel proper there was frequent reference to the *khólos* of Achilles (*Il.* 1.192, 217, 224, 283), but Agamemnon's anger was only alluded to indirectly.[6]

Moreover, Agamemnon's *khólos* is presented as responding to Achilles' speech-act with another speech-act, a *muthos*, which, as Richard Martin has shown, signifies an authoritative speech.[7] What is important to remember is that this is Achilles' account of the quarrel in that he puts his own interpretation on the event. Achilles' act, as he tells Thetis, was an order to propitiate the god; it is to this pious speech-act[8] that Agamemnon responds with *khólos*, one of the possibilities that Calchas envisions in his request for protection from Achilles (*Il.* 1.74–83). This is the only place in either poem where *khólos* is seen as resulting from an order to propitiate the gods: we have already seen that threats are related to *khólos*, as at *Od.* 21.377, where *khólos* results from a *muthos* characterized as a threat (*ēpeílēsen mûthon* "he threatened him in a *muthos*" *Od.* 21.388). That is to say, Achilles makes Agamemnon into a villain by giving his motive for *khólos* as irrational—denying as he does the sensible and appropriate propitiation of a god—and by characterizing his authoritative speech, his *muthos*, as containing a threat, and one calculated to provoke nothing less than *khólos*—all this justifying Achilles' own anger through that of Agamemnon.[9]

Indeed, Patroclus prays that *khólos* will not infect him as it has Achilles, in a famous passage from his own personal embassy to the withdrawn leader: *mḕ emé g' oûn hoûtós ge láboi khólos, hòn sù phulásseis* (*Il.* 16.30) "But as for me, at any rate, let not *this khólos* take me, that anger which you cherish." Through an emphatic use of diction, Patroclus focuses on distancing himself from what Achilles has made of *khólos*. First, the line opens with *emé*, the emphatic personal pronoun, to be followed, second, with one of only two examples of *g' oûn* in Homer;[10] next the formulaic elements are reversed, so that *khólos láben* goes to *láboi khólos*, with the accumulation of particles and the "busy" use of demonstrative pronouns as an indication that some transformation has taken place;[11] third, the caesura occurs between two words that are (typically contiguous) elements of a formula (*láboi khólos*); finally, the insertion of the demonstrative pronoun (*hoûtos*) makes a complete predication ending at the hephthemimeral caesura, with a strong pause between the two formulaic segments. Patroclus, it seems, brings all his rhetorical art to bear on his theme, the *khólos* of Achilles.[12]

Patroclus identifies *khólos* here as belonging to Achilles (*hòn sù phulásseis*). It is hard to imagine *kótos* belonging to any one character in this way. One has the sense that these characters respond to this emotion in ways that reveal both cultural convention and their own character traits, even as does Glaucus when he tells the story of Bellerophon. Here (*Il.* 6.161–65) Proitos, believing Anteia's lie, becomes angry. It is important that, as in Achilles version of the quarrel in Book 1, Anteia's speech-act (in this case a lie, *pseusaménē,* 163) produces *khólos* in Proetus (*Il.* 6.166):

ὣς φάτο, <u>τὸν δὲ ἄνακτα χόλος λάβεν</u> οἷον ἄκουσε.

Thus she spoke, <u>and *khólos* took hold of that king</u> when he heard such a thing.

It will become significant later that Anteia's request and Proetus's response is to kill Bellerophon (*káktane,* 164; *kteînai,* 167), but for now it is sufficient to underscore the *immediacy* of this kind of anger as it is manifest in prompt and dramatic action, in both of the formulaic contexts that we have just seen (*khólos láben* and *édu khólos*).

The three instances in Group 6c point to the *khólos* of a god, twice Hera (in a repeated line) and once Hephaestus in the song of Demodocus about Aphrodite and Hera. Although this latter scene is comic, Hephaestus's discovery of the pair of lovers trapped in his net is given a dramatic presentation: Helius keeps close watch. He announces that the trap has been sprung (*Od.* 8.303). Then Hephaestus returns home, bitterly enraged (*tetiēménos êtor,* 303).[13] With Hephaestus standing in the doorway, his *khólos* enters him to dominate his rebuke:

> ἔστη δ' ἐν προθύροισι, χόλος δέ μιν ἄγριος ᾕρει·
> σμερδαλέον δ' ἐβόησε, γέγωνέ τε πᾶσι θεοῖσι.
> (*Od.* 8.304–5)

> He took his stand in the doorway, and savage *khólos* took hold of him, and he gave a tremendous cry, and shouted to all the gods.

Once again the notion of *khólos* is used to characterize the force of the subject's response. Moreover, we have a new element added to our picture of the inception of *khólos*: instead of coming as a result of words, of a threat or other kind of speech act, here Hephaestus's anger is in direct response to the sight of Ares and Aphrodite caught *in flagrante delicto*. Characteristic here is the immediacy of *khólos*, with the production of anger directly connected to the sight of the provoking action. So, although Hephaestus *had* been angry, his rage only reaches full steam when he is standing in the doorway watching the trapped pair of lovers. Thus, quite different from *kótos*, *khólos* is visceral and shows itself as a direct response to a disturbance, be it word or deed..

The phrase *khólos dé min ágrios hḗirei* ("now a wild *khólos* was taking hold of him")—along with the formula in Appedix 2 (Group 6d) [*epeì*] *khólos émpese thumôi*—occurs in situations displaying the inception of *khólos*; these phrases occupy the second half of the hexameter line from the trochaic caesura to the end of the line. In the other two cases from Group 6c, we have a repeated whole line formula. Each case refers to the anger of Athena. Most importantly these forms occur in a context that shows *khólos* in the accusative referring to the anger of Hera.[14] Zeus has just spoken to Hera and Athena in words that are meant to be goading (*kertomíois epéessi* "with contentious words"; *parablḗdēn agoreúōn, Il.* 4.6, "speaking with provocation"); in fact it is made clear that he is trying to arouse their anger (*autík' epeirâto Kronídēs erethizémen Hḗrēn*, *Il.* 4.5, "straightway he tried to anger Hera") by suggesting that they can put an end to the war, here and now (*Il.* 4.13–19). In the goddesses' less-than-pleased response to all this, there is a clear contrast between the reaction of Hera and Athena, precisely with respect to *khólos*.

In the first place, Athena represses her anger; although her immediate response is to want to speak, she maintains silence:[15]

> ἤ τοι Ἀθηναίη ἀκέων ἦν οὐδέ τι εἶπε,
> σκυζομένη Διὶ πατρί, χόλος δέ μιν ἄγριος ᾕρει·
> (*Il.* 4.22–23)

> Still Athena was silent and she did not say a word, resentful as she was to Zeus her father, but savage *khólos* took hold of her.

Here the text points to the anger of Athena as it continues to hold sway over her, although its effects are something she keeps under control. Moreover, the very next line shows a failed attempt to control *khólos* on Hera's part, and the poetic artistry takes pains to make the contrast as stark as possible, with the enjambement functioning as a kind of pun (*hḗirei/ Hḗrēi*). The repetition of *khólos*, with the metrically identical (but diathetically distinct) forms (*khólos/khólon*) are positioned so that they are sequentially incremented (*khólos* [23] at O'Neill's position 7 and *khólon* [24] at position 8); the complex artistry is completed with the chiastic arrangement of formulaic elements, with the *khólos* formula at the end of 23 and at the beginning of 24:

> σκυζομένη Διὶ πατρί, χόλος δέ μιν ἄγριος ᾕρει·
> Ἥρῃ δ' οὐκ ἔχαδε στῆθος χόλον, ἀλλὰ προσηύδα.
> (*Il.* 4.23–24)

> Resentful as she was to Zeus her father, and savage *khólos* took hold of [her], but Hera's chest did not restrain her wrath, but spoke out.

The same can be said for the doublet at *Il.* 8.457–61, where Zeus once again challenges Athena and Hera (*Il.* 8.447–56), with Hera characteristically failing to restrain her anger (in the accusative), while Athena's *khólos* maintains its hold on her, although she keeps from speaking. It needs to be added that the use of the formula *khólos dé min ágrios hēirei* at *Il.* 8.460 follows Zeus's observation of the two goddesses being angry in a different way:

> τίφθ' οὕτω τετίησθον, Ἀθηναίη τε καὶ Ἥρη;
> οὐ μέν θην κάμετόν γε μάχῃ ἔνι κυδιανείρῃ
> ὀλλῦσαι Τρῶας, τοῖσιν κότον αἰνὸν ἔθεσθε.
> (*Il.* 8.447–49)

> Why thus are you angry, Athena and Hera? Aren't you tired of killing the Trojans in this man-glorying war, those against whom you bear a grievous *kótos*?

The accumulation of anger terms here puts Calchas's definition into perspective. The godesses are maintaining a long-standing *kótos* against the Trojans that Zeus in no way can assuage. Rather, he threatens them by reminding them that they cannot defy his will (*Il.* 8.450–56); as is in keeping with the definition of *kótos*, there is no suggestion here that they can bring the war to an end. It is this threat with its implications that they might be tired (*kámeton*) of doing what is after all their duty (enforcing *kótos*) that causes the *khólos* of the goddesses.

Thus far we have seen that *khólos* in the nominative case consistently refers to the inception or continuation of *khólos*, that is to say, to an ongoing anger, but one that remains potentially interruptable, as we saw to be possible in the previous chapter. The remaining examples of *khólos* (Group 6d in Appendix 2) display the same feature of *khólos* as an anger whose continuation or inception is in the hands of the subjects of anger, be they human or divine. In each of these cases from Group 6d, the formula *epeì . . . khólos émpese thumôi* "When anger came to fall into the heart" shows that *khólos* is located in the *thumós*. See for a formulaic parallel the accusative of *khólos* with *bállō* at *Il.* 14.50 (*en thumôi bállontai emoì khólon*) and with *-tithēmi* at *Il.* 6.326 (*daimóni' ou mèn kalà khólon tónd' éntheo thumôi*), where *én* (either as preverb or preposition, in tmesis) + a verb of placing (*píptō*, *títhēmi*, or *bállō*) + *thumôi* provides a coherent picture of *khólos* as an emotion rooted in bodily experience.

That *khólos*, as an ongoing anger, is of crucial import to Phoenix in his address to Achilles is made clear when we look at *Il.* 9.436. Here, Phoenix begins his speech to Achilles by invoking the disastrous consequences that have come to be *since* (*epeí*) the warrior's *khólos* dropped into his heart:

οὐδέ τι πάμπαν ἀμύνειν νηυσὶ θοῇσι
πῦρ ἐθέλεις ἀΐδηλον, ἐπεὶ χόλος ἔμπεσε θυμῷ,
(*Il.* 9.435–36)

And you are not willing at all to ward off completely the deadly fire from the swift ships, since *khólos* has come to fall in your heart.

The phrase *khólos émpese thumôi* functions clearly as a narrative marker, to indicate the exact moment at which the present situation came to be. This part of his argument, thus, links nicely to Odysseus's recollection of Peleus's advice to Achilles before he left for Troy (*Il.* 9.252–58). The idea is that *khólos* can, indeed, come to an end:

παύε', ἔα δὲ χόλον θυμαλγέα· σοὶ δ' Ἀγαμέμνων
ἄξια δῶρα δίδωσι μεταλλήξαντι χόλοιο.
(*Il.* 9.260–61)

Stop, and don't move forward this heart-wrenching *khólos*. Now Agamemnon gives you worthy gifts, if you relax your *khólos*.

It is as if Odysseus and Phoenix had divided up the topic of *khólos*, with Odysseus focusing on its conclusion (a theme again at *Il.* 15.299) and with Phoenix looking to its inception.[16]

The temporal focus of this use of *khólos* demarcates the period of inception and then the continuation of anger as can be seen in the *Diòs Apátē*, when, as Hera emphasizes to Aphrodite, discord arises among the old folks (Tethys and Ocean) beginning with an old *khólos*:

> ἤδη γὰρ δηρὸν χρόνον ἀλλήλων ἀπέχονται
> εὐνῆς καὶ φιλότητος, ἐπεὶ χόλος ἔμπεσε θυμῷ.
> (*Il.* 14.206–7 = *Il.* 14.305–6)

> For already they keep from one another for quite a long time, from their bed and their love, since *khólos* has come to fall into their hearts.

This doublet presents Hera's request for Aphrodite's help in seducing Zeus (*Il.* 14.198–210). The temporal specification *dēròn krónon* ("a lengthy time") makes clear that the formula *khólos émpese thumôi* is inceptive, to the effect that both Ocean and Tethys have been estranged *from that moment when khólos* separated them.[17] Moreover, Hera's deceptively claims that both Tethys and Oceanus will be persuaded to reconcile, even after their long-held *khólos*:

> εἰ κείνω γ᾽ ἐπέεσσι παραιπεπιθοῦσα φίλον κῆρ
> εἰς εὐνὴν ἀνέσαιμι ὁμωθῆναι φιλότητι,
> αἰεί κέ σφι φίλη τε καὶ αἰδοίη καλεοίμην.
> (*Il.* 14.208–10)

> If these two I could sit down and with words persade their dear hearts, to share a bed in love, then would I be declared forever worthy of their love and respect.

Both here and in *Iliad* 9,[18] *khólos* can be mollified by persuasion. The long duration of *khólos* (*dēròn krónon*, 206) does not make it resemble *kótos*, since unlike *kótos*, it has no intrinsic *télos* ("conclusion"); rather, the cultural expectation is that the power of persuasion can effectively be brought to bear on it—despite the failures such efforts meet in Achilles' tent or in the dwellings of the gods.

Let us return to Phoenix's speech, where he indicates the moment that Achilles abandoned the cause. In *Il.* 9.436, Phoenix points to the condition in which Achilles' *khólos* has left them:

> εἰ μὲν δὴ νόστον γε μετὰ φρεσί, φαίδιμ᾽ Ἀχιλλεῦ,
> βάλλεαι, οὐδέ τι πάμπαν ἀμύνειν νηυσὶ θοῇσι
> πῦρ ἐθέλεις ἀίδηλον, ἐπεὶ χόλος ἔμπεσε θυμῷ,
> πῶς ἂν ἔπειτ᾽ ἀπὸ σεῖο, φίλον τέκος, αὖθι λιποίμην
> οἶος; σοὶ δέ μ᾽ ἔπεμπε γέρων ἱππηλάτα Πηλεύς
> (*Il.* 9.434–38)

> If you are considering return in your heart, glorious Achilles, and you are not willing to ward off destructive fire from the ships, since *khólos* has fallen into your heart, how, my child, am I to be left here alone; it was on your behalf that horse-driving Peleus, in his old age, sent me here.

Here a critical moment in the embassy has arrived, with the refusal of Agamemnon's offer still hanging in the air. Phoenix sets up an opposition that gets to the heart of Homeric poetry—the difference between a *νόστος* (*Il.* 9.434) and a *khólos* (*Il.* 9.436). Apart from the link between *khólos* and the burning of the ships, *khólos* is now being opposed to *philótēs* (*phílon tékos*, *Il.* 9.437) made flesh in Phoenix. That is to say, the *withdrawal* of Achilles entails an implicit *abandonment* of *philótēs*. This particular point, which to his sorrow Achilles is unable to assimilate, fuses with the *khólos* that spurs the withdrawal.[19] As to the force of the phrase *khólos émpese thumōi*, it functions to indicate both cause and time-within-which. Like Hera's description of the *khólos* between Tethys and Ocean, the anger locates a point in time from and during which certain kinds of activity stop: what ceases for Ocean and Tethys is their sexual relationship (a social obligation), and for Achilles, what is at stake is his primary social obligation (certainly an affective state as well), namely, the warding off of destruction from the other Achaeans.

Is there any way we can be more certain that the formula *khólos émpese thumōi* presents an aorist indicating the temporal limits for anger? Consider the two other words used with this adonic cadence. In the *Iliad*, besides *khólos*, we find *déos* after a speech by Meriones as he urges Idomeneus to beat a hasty retreat:

> Ὣς ἔφατ', Ἰδομενεὺς δ' ἵμασεν καλλίτριχας ἵππους
> νῆας ἐπὶ γλαφυράς· δὴ γὰρ δέος ἔμπεσε θυμῷ.
> (*Il.* 17.624–25)

> Thus he spoke, and Idomeneus whipped the fair-maned horses to the hollow ships; for truly fear came to fall in his heart.

The swift withdrawal that the pair must make is emphasized by the particles and by the *s*-aorist marking "the entrance into that state [*khólos*] or the beginning of that action."[20] The other example of *émpese thumōi*, besides the four with *khólos*, takes place in the *Odyssey*, and it is tempting to think that the connection between that example and *khólos* is abandoned here, since instead of a word denoting emotion, we have *épos* at the moment when Odysseus hears the terrible lowing of the slaughtered cattle of the sun as he recalls Teiresias's prophecy:

> δὴ τότ' ἐγὼν ἔτι πόντῳ ἐὼν ἐν νηὶ μελαίνῃ
> μυκηθμοῦ τ' ἤκουσα βοῶν αὐλιζομενάων
> οἰῶν τε βληχήν· καί μοι ἔπος ἔμπεσε θυμῷ
> μάντιος ἀλαοῦ, Θηβαίου Τειρεσίαο,

Κίρκης τ᾽ Αἰαίης, οἵ μοι μάλα πόλλ᾽ ἐπέτελλον
νῆσον ἀλεύασθαι τερψιμβρότου Ἠελίοιο.
δὴ τότ᾽ ἐγὼν ἑτάροισι μετηύδων, ἀχνύμενος κῆρ.
(*Od.* 12.264–70)

At that moment, still on the black ship in the sea, I myself heard, the lowing of the penned cows and the bleating of the sheep. And a word came to fall into my heart, that of the blind prophet Theban Teiresias, and of Aeaean Circe, both of whom strongly enjoined me to avoid the island of mortal-delighting Helius. At that very moment I spoke to my companions, because I was grieving at heart.

The frame provided by *dè tót' egṓn* secures the temporal notion[21] that just at the moment of hearing the noise of the animals, the words of Teiresias come to mind.

The last example of *khólos* in the phrase *khólos émpese thumōi* not only reaffirms the importance of Calchas's reference to the inception of *khólos*, but presents *khólos* in a scene crucial to the anger of Achilles. In *Iliad* 16, Achilles imagines the Myrmidons saying:

σχέτλιε Πηλέος υἱέ, χόλῳ ἄρα σ᾽ ἔτρεφε μήτηρ,
νηλεές, ὃς παρὰ νηυσὶν ἔχεις ἀέκοντας ἑταίρους·
οἴκαδέ περ σὺν νηυσὶ νεώμεθα ποντοπόροισιν
αὖτις, ἐπεί ῥά τοι ὧδε κακὸς χόλος ἔμπεσε θυμῷ·
(*Il.* 16.203–6)

Troublesome son of Peleus, with *khólos* your mother nursed you, pitiless, you who keep by the ships your unwilling companions; surely let us go homeward with our sea-crossing ships again, since in fact this is the way that an evil *khólos* has come to fall into your heart.

Here is another occasion where *khólos* is made thematic, in this instance framing a four-line sequence quoting the "voice of the people," Achilles' Myrmidons. Remember that the voice of the people was also a determining factor in Phoenix's *khólos* against his father:

ἀλλά τις ἀθανάτων παῦσεν χόλον, ὅς ῥ᾽ ἐνὶ θυμῷ
δήμου θῆκε φάτιν καὶ ὀνείδεα πόλλ᾽ ἀνθρώπων
ὡς μὴ πατροφόνος μετ᾽ Ἀχαιοῖσιν καλεοίμην.
(*Il.* 9.458–61)

But some immortal stopped the *khólos*, by putting into my heart the report of the people and the many reproaches of men, so that I not be called a patricide among the Achaeans.

Achilles' troubled imagination internalizes the *tis athanátōn* of Phoenix's account, and the Myrmidons' evaluation of their leader replaces the quite stark possibility of patricide on Phoenix's part; also changed is the moment in the process of *khólos* that Achilles emphasizes: where Phoenix, for rhetorical purposes, focused on the end of *khólos*, Achilles glares at its inception. And the constant here is *khólos*.[22]

Khólos has a beginning, a development, and an end, a process that Homeric characters can affect in such a way as to magnify, diminish, or end the *khólos*. Now good sense can be made of what seems to be the one exception to the preceding analysis of *khólos*, namely, *Il.* 14.49–51:

> ὢ πόποι, ἦ ῥα καὶ ἄλλοι ἐυκνήμιδες Ἀχαιοὶ
> ἐν θυμῷ βάλλονται ἐμοὶ χόλον, ὥς περ Ἀχιλλεύς,
> οὐδ' ἐθέλουσι μάχεσθαι ἐπὶ πρύμνῃσι νέεσσι.

> Alas, the rest of the well-greaved Achaeans, consider in their heart a *khólos* against me, just as Achilles is also not willing to fight by the ship's sterns.

Now this is the only attested use of *bállō* with *khólos* and is the only case of *khólos* in the accusative case to signify the inception or continuation of *khólos*. The context presents Agamemnon imagining the *khólos* of other Achaeans—so complete is his mental distraction—as they join with Achilles after Hector sets fire to the ships.

This fear on Agamemnon's part deserves our notice because Agamemnon fears exactly the opposite of what Achilles has threatened:

> οὐ γὰρ πρὶν πολέμοιο μεδήσομαι αἱματόεντος,
> πρίν γ' υἱὸν Πριάμοιο δαΐφρονος, Ἕκτορα δῖον,
> Μυρμιδόνων ἐπί τε κλισίας καὶ νῆας ἱκέσθαι
> κτείνοντ' Ἀργείους, κατά τε σμῦξαι πυρὶ νῆας.
> (*Il.* 9.650–53)

> For never will I think of bloody war, before luminous Hector, flame-heartened Priam's son, reaches the huts and ships of the Myrmidons, as he continues to kill Argives, and with fire sets the ships completely ablaze.

This concession Odysseus fails to report to Agamemnon (*Il.* 9.677–93).[23] It can be argued that Odysseus deliberately connives to conceal the change in Achilles' attitude in *Iliad* 9.[24] In any case, Agamemnon misunderstands Achilles: fighting by the ships is precisely what Achilles *will* do.

To summarize, Agamemnon is mistaken in thinking that the other Achaeans, at the sight of the burning ships, will side with Achilles; Agamemnon's mistake is an exact inversion of Achilles' threat; and this mistake accompanies Odysseus's failure to report Achilles' final position as relayed to the embassy, namely, that he will fight at the ships. It only remains to be noted that Agamemnon's startling vision of Achaeans fleeing the Troad following Achilles' own withdrawal—a vision that makes subconscious his conscious exhortation in

Iliad 2—houses an anomalous use of *khólos*, since traditional phrasing would display the cessation of *khólos* in this position and in just this form. Indeed, within the poetics of the *Iliad* we expect fire at the ships to betoken the *end* of Achilles' *khólos*, since fire is a signal of the end of Achilles' anger as at *Il.* 9.650–53. Both this passage and Achilles' version of the Myrmidons' criticism (*Il.* 16.203–6) are clear examples of Homeric concern with the "gaze of the other" or intersubjectivity. The singer and the audience all know the traditional contexts of fire and anger, so Agamemnon's anomalous use of *khólos* here presents one more symptom of his mistaken sense of things.[25]

Notes

1. See Denniston 1975, 219, on *dḗ* with relative temporal adverbs ("precisely when," "just when").

2. Nagler, 1974, 140–41, my emphases.

3. The role of eating *phármaka* here should be set beside the *phármaka* of Helen (discussed in Part II, Chapter 1), presented in a potion that is *ákholon* ("stilling anger"). On a possible parallel between Achilles and Hector here (through *khólos*), see Lowenstam 1993, 117.

4. Martin 1989, 141; and set this threat beside that of Telemachus, which the suitors decline to be angry about, in *Od.* 21.376–88 (with *apeilḗsas,* ["having threatened him"] at *Od.* 21.368).

5. Apart from the reference made by Calchas at *Il.* 1.78.

6. My argument for taking 283 as referring to Achilles' anger will appear separately (for which controversy see van Bennekom 1984, Eisenberger 1985); as to *Il.* 1.78 and 81, these lines refer only generally to the anger of a king, as Agamemnon's claim that a man will be angry is potential at 1.139.

7. See Martin 1989, 22 on this speech.

8. Certainly referring to *tharsḗsas mála eipè theoprópion hó ti oîstha*, *Il.* 1.85 "With this strong encouragement speak the prophecy, as you know it."

9. Besides this instance of *kelómēn* (*Il.* 1.385 "I gave an order"), the other four others instances of the form take place in the *Odyssey*. Each of the *Odyssey's* examples are in a narration by Odysseus, where the fate of the crew depends on the execution of the leader's orders. In *Od.* 9.100, Odysseus orders his remaining crew to escape the fate of those who ate the lotus; and in *Od.* 14.259, in a story to Eumaeus, Odysseus recalls ordering his crew to watch the ships only to see them succumb to temptation and raid the Egyptians, with the same contrast between wise leader and foolishly disobedient followers appearing in *Od.* 17.428; in the remaining example, *Od.* 9.193–96, Odysseus tells the Phaeacians how he assigned part of his crew the task of staying to guard the ship, even as he chose others to follow with him to explore Cyclops's island. In each of these cases, the leader's orders are pivotal to the fate of the crew. In the only example from the *Iliad*, Achilles' wise order to propitiate Apollo (*Il.* 1.98) is contrasted with the *khólos* of Agamemnon at *Il.* 1.387, culminating in Agamemnon's threat (*ēpeílēsen*, *Il.* 1.386 "he made a threat") occurring in a rare and hence emphatic line-initial position. Thus, Achilles in his address to his mother establishes the rhetorical contrast he seeks to make

between Agamemnon's failed leadership, marked by his inappropriate *khólos*, and Achilles' wise stewardship of matters human and divine. The entire speech is crafted by Achilles to persuade his audience, Thetis, that his anger is justified.

10. Denniston 1975, 448 and 45.

11. Cf. Muellner 1976, 19 and note 5.

12. One result of this formulaic caesura is that the second half of the line (*khólos, hòn sù phulásseis*) functions as a gloss on *hoûtos*.

13. On the interpretation of this phrase as "angry," see Slatkin 1991, 98–99.

14. On Hera's anger, see O'Brien 1993, 77–111. She links Hera's savage anger to certain stages of Achilles' anger (79). I agree that Achilles and Hera share certain aspects of anger as they are manifest in *khólos*.

15. Cf. *Od.* 11.565.

16. I return to the issue of *Iliad* 9 and *khólos* in Chapter 8. For now, note that speculation as to how Nestor instructed the ambassadors ought to begin with how he set up the means of persuasion, as described at *Il.* 9.179–81.

17. Chantraine's formulation of the aorist aspect is instructive here: "l'aspect de l'action pure et simple étant essentiel et l'idée que le procès verbal est réalisé d' un coup mise en lumière" (Chantraine 1963, §272, 184).

18. E.g., *Il.* 9.179–81.

19. On these issues see Nagler 1990, 228–29 and Collins 1990, 45–50.

20. I quote Smyth's elegant summary of this often ignored function of *s*-aorists in Greek (Smyth 1956, §1924) and see §1925 for the observation that "most of the verbs in question are denominatives." The profile matches *khólos*.

21. "Homer never opens a sentence or clause with *dḗ*, except when it precedes a temporal adverb or *gár*" (Denniston 1975, 228). Although Denniston downplays the temporal force of *dḗ* (203), both our examples of the formula *émpese thumôi* without *khólos* focus tightly on the moment at which something is realized by the subject.

22. Note also that Achilles has generalized Patroclus's criticism to the extent that it seems to come from all his companions (*Il.* 16.203–6).

23. See Nagy 1979, 51–52.

24. See Martin 1989, 64.

25. For a modernist use of such intersubjectivity see, for example, Devlin 1989. For other warriors exhibiting such behavior, see Diomedes' words in *Il.* 8.149–50. The notion that anomalies of poetic usage can be correlated with the manner in which speakers deal with their language and culture has been thoroughly developed in the Homeric context by Nagler (1990; cf. 1988, 82); his work here examines how the narrative's lapses are joined to moments of ideological conflict. As Martin (1989) has demonstrated, the narrative and the narrative's characters "speak the same language." This clearly is something that the performer could exploit: in this passage Agamemnon's misunderstanding of the problem posed by Achilles' *khólos* demonstrates a feature of Agamemnon's character, namely, that he is, as Richard Martin has argued, a "deficient rhetorician" (cf. Martin 1989, 113–20, especially 119).

Chapter Eight

Fighting Words

In his definition, Calchas suggests that *khólos*, unlike *kótos*, can be brought under control. In this chapter, I will elaborate on the limitations of that control, by showing that certain kinds of speech may stimulate *khólos*, whereas for *kótos* that is an impossibility. First, responses to *khólos* can be styled as formal challenges, often in the manner of the invective. Second, I will show that besides such speech acts, actions of an immediate and violent nature can just as likely result from *khólos*.

Taunting Gods, Taunting Heroes

The verbal derivatives of *khol-* primarily occur in the aorist and the perfect,[1] with each class showing participial forms more than 50 percent of the time.[2] There are formulaic patterns and thematic associations among this large group of attestations. The lines presented in Appendix 2, Group 8 occur in contexts where the aorist participle always signals that an invective has provoked a decisive challenge that the original speaker must either accept with a counter-challenge or reject by backing down.

The clearest example of this motif occurs in Helen's encounter with Aphrodite in Book 3 of the *Iliad*. The line exhibiting *khólos* in this passage (*Il.* 3.413: *tḕn d' kholōsaménē prosephṓnee dî' Aphrodítē* "And godly Aphrodite, in a state of *khólos*, addressed her") had already been identified by Parry as marking the rhetorical force of the following speech, that is to say, as belonging to "the series of expressons whose essential idea is 'X' spoke to him in a certain tone or with a certain gesture."[3] As to *khólos* in this passage, it will be clear that features of Helen's previous speech (*Il.* 3.399–412) have provoked the *khólos* of Aphrodite.

Helen here participates in a clearly defined scenario by which a speech provoking anger is followed with a speech inspired by *khólos* leading, in turn, to a threat or a challenge. For Helen has insulted Aphrodite by ironically suggesting that the goddess abandon her divine status in order to consort with Paris. She caps the insult by suggesting that Aphrodite take up as his wife (*álokhon*, *Il.* 3.409) or slave (*doúlēn*, *Il.* 3.409). This provocation, not surprisingly, leads to Aphrodite's *khólos*. As a result, she responds to this speech with her own threat, one that highlights the anger that she is levelling against Helen:

> Τὴν δὲ χολωσαμένη προσεφώνεε δῖ' Ἀφροδίτη·
> "μή μ' ἔρεθε, σχετλίη, μὴ χωσαμένη σε μεθείω,
> τῶς δέ σ' ἀπεχθήρω ὡς νῦν ἔκπαγλα φίλησα."
> (*Il.* 3.413–15)

> And bright Aphrodite having come to be angry (*kholōsaménē*), addressed her: "Do not challenge *(érethe*, cf. *éris*, 'anger') me, bold one, lest in anger (*khōsaménē)* I cast you out. I can hate you, as much as now I excessively love you."

The agglomeration of anger words often is controlled by one key word.[4] Here *khólos* serves that function, with Aphrodite's threat providing the manifestation of her anger.

Helen incurs Aphrodite's wrath when she rejects her with these words:

> κεῖσε δ' ἐγὼν οὐκ εἶμι—νεμεσσητὸν δέ κεν εἴη—
> κείνου πορσανέουσα λέχος.
> (*Il.* 3.410–11[5])

> There will *I* not go—it would be regrettable—to clamber onto *his* bed.

Indeed Helen's refusal of Aphrodite's enticement (*Il.* 3.390–94) could be specifically designed to incur a god's wrath; first, on seeing through Aphrodite's disguise, Helen notices (*enóēse*, *Il.* 3.396) the parts of her appearance that Aphrodite could not brook to conceal (*Il.* 3.396–97; cf. *thámbēsen*, *Il.* 3.398 and *daimoníē, Il.* 3.399). Helen suggests that the goddess shun immortal haunts (*Il.* 3.406) and tend to Paris as his (mortal) wife.[6] In this passage, Helen thus calls to mind, in her challenge to Aphrodite, a potent part of the *Iliad*'s mythology, and a painful part of Aphrodite's own mythical narrative in her marriage to Anchises (*Il.* 3.408–9). At least it is so taken by Aphrodite, who responds with a kind of anger that is to be associated with verbal display: she responds with a threat motivated by *khólos*, as quoted above (*Il.* 3.413–15). The vocative *skhetlíē,* directly preceding the threat (*Il.* 3.414), presents Aphrodite's *khólos* as a product of Helen's impulsive slight, an insult that damages Aphrodite's honor. By treating Aphrodite as if she were the Lacedaemonian maidservant that is her disguise, Helen thus slights Aphrodite's sense of honor in a way that leads to *khólos*. All this is underscored by an accumulation of wrath-terms including the prohibition in *mḗ m' érethe* (*Il.* 3.414, "do not enrage me") and *khōsaménē* (*Il.* 3.414, "having come to be angry").[7] All of this anger is sufficient to motivate Helen, out of fear (*éddeisen*, *Il.* 3.418, "she feared"),[8] to yield to Aphrodite's request (*Il.* 3.418–20).[9]

The same kind of *khólos* is engaged in the chariot race in *Iliad* 23 when there is a dispute between Idomeneus and Oilean Ajax about who is leading the field (*Il.* 23.457–98). The Achaeans have been watching the chariot race when Idomeneus notices what he thinks is the winning team:

δοκέει δέ μοι ἔμμεναι ἀνὴρ
Αἰτωλὸς γενεήν, μετὰ δ' Ἀργείοισιν ἀνάσσει,
Τυδέος ἱπποδάμου υἱός, κρατερὸς Διομήδης.
(*Il.* 23.470–72)

And this man seems to me to be best, an Aitolian by birth, but he rules over the Argives, the son of horse-tamer Tydeus, strong Diomedes.

At this misjudgment, Oilean Ajax taunts Idomeneus harshly (*aiskrōs enénipen, Il.* 23.473), and he presents a straightforward critique of Idomeneus's speech, repeating the rare *labreúomai* ("to talk boldly," *Il.* 23.474) to characterize it.[10] He follows with a criticism of Idomeneus's age (*oúte neṓtatós essi met' Argeíoisi* "you are not the youngest among the Argives," *Il.* 23.477); all this is parallel to the specialized invective of Iros in *Odyssey* 18, as I will discuss below (*molobrós* "glutton," *Od.* 18.26; *epitrokhádēn* "torrentially," "garrulously," *Od.* 18.26; *grēì kaminoî* "female kitchen worker," *Od.* 18.27).

When Ajax disputes Idomeneus's contention that Eumelus's horses have come to grief, he does so in a manner that picks on Idomeneus's style of speech: "*Idomeneû, tí páros labreúai*" "Idomeneus, why do you continue to babble?" (*Il.* 23.474; cf. *Il.* 23.478, *Il.* 23.479). In the same way as Helen's pointed criticism, so too Ajax's reproof stimulates *khólos* (*tòn dè kholōsámenos Krētōn agòs antíon ēúda*, *Il.* 23.482), which leads to Idomeneus's insult and challenge, quoted below (*Il.* 23.483–84). This insult is followed by a suggestion with which Idomeneus hopes to best Ajax, to set up a wager with Agamemnon as a judge over the race (*Il.* 23.486–87) so that Ajax will end up paying for his insult (*hína gnoíēs apotínōn*, *Il.* 23.487). Both in Book 3 and Book 23 *khólos* demarcates a challenge, where the angered party responds by threatening to change the social circumstances so that the insulter will somehow be "paid back." In Helen's case, she will cease to be the pet of Aphrodite, where Idomeneus hopes to secure Ajax's downfall by formalizing the prize of judgment.[11]

Thus in both the *Odyssey* and the *Iliad* a verbal contest arouses *khólos*, which in turn leads to an invective laced with specialized language. In the passage from *Iliad* 23, as mentioned, Ajax directly criticizes his manner of speaking, in response to which Idomeneus becomes infuriated, to the extent that he replies to Ajax with a slight followed by a direct challenge, all of this posed in the form of a wager:

> Τὸν δὲ χολωσάμενος Κρητῶν ἀγὸς ἀντίον ηὔδα·
> "Αἶαν, νεῖκος ἄριστε, κακοφραδές, ἄλλα τε πάντα
> δεύεαι Ἀργείων, ὅτι τοι νόος ἐστὶν ἀπηνής.
> δεῦρο νυν, ἢ τρίποδος περιδώμεθον ἠὲ λέβητος,
> ἴστορα δ' Ἀτρεΐδην Ἀγαμέμνονα θείομεν ἄμφω,
> ὁππότεραι πρόσθ' ἵπποι, ἵνα γνώῃς ἀποτίνων."
> (*Il.* 23.482–87)

> Having come to have *khólos*, the leader of the Cretans spoke in address to him, "Ajax best at contention, ill of intention, you are lacking in all things among the Argives, in that your mind is mean. Come now, either let us bet a tripod or cauldron, and make Agamemnon the son of Atreus the judge for us both, as to whichever pair of mares is ahead, in order that you might learn, when you have paid up."

Thus, Homer uses *kholōsámenos* in the context of a dialogue of a kind that involves invective accompanied by judgment. In such "fighting words" passages, an exchange such as this can lead to a direct confrontation, whether it be between Helen and her patron goddess, or a wager proposed by Idomeneus, or fisticuffs on Ithaca (as in the fight between Irus and Odysseus).

In *Od.* 18.25, when Irus, the beggar, becomes enraged at Odysseus, his reaction to Odysseus's previous speech is characterized through the participial form *kholōsámenos*; here Odysseus refuses Irus's order that he leave the doorway (*Od.* 18.9–12), going on then to make it clear that he will resist him even to the point of violence (*Od.* 18.20–21); in fact, he specifically points to the cause of *khólos* as being a public challenge (*Od.* 18.20: *khersì dè mḗ ti líēn prokalízeo, mḗ me kholṓsēis* "And lest you contend with me physically, don't make me angry"). As in Helen's speech to Aphrodite, the invective has spurred on the *khólos* of Iros,[12] so that Irus's subsequent speech is given with the rhetorical force appropriate to *khólos*, despite Odysseus's attempt to deflect that reaction.[13] Irus's angry speech continues the challenge by including a threat along with the invective:[14]

> τὸν δὲ χολωσάμενος προσεφώνεεν Ἶρος ἀλήτης·
> "ὢ πόποι, ὡς ὁ μολοβρὸς ἐπιτροχάδην ἀγορεύει,
> γρηῒ καμινοῖ ἶσος· ὃν ἂν κακὰ μητισαίμην
> κόπτων ἀμφοτέρῃσι, χαμαὶ δέ κε πάντας ὀδόντας
> γναθμῶν ἐξελάσαιμι συὸς ὣς ληιβοτείρης.
> ζῶσαι νῦν, ἵνα πάντες ἐπιγνώωσι καὶ οἵδε
> μαρναμένους· πῶς δ' ἂν σὺ νεωτέρῳ ἀνδρὶ μάχοιο;"
> (*Od.* 18.25–31)

With *khólos*, Iros, the beggar, spoke to him, "Oh my, how roughly this bum runs off at the mouth, like some hag at her cooking! Him I would treacherously plot against, trouncing him with both of these, and to the ground I'd send his teeth, all of them, from his jaws, like some crop-gourging sow. Gird up now, so that all of these here might come to know us as we fight. How would you fight a younger man?"

As in the other instances of the participle *kholōsámenos*, a provocative speech (that of Odysseus) leads to a threatening challenge (from Iros).[15] Because Irus's speech, following from his *khólos*, includes a threat and a challenge, it bears comparison with Aphrodite's speech to Helen as well as with the speech of Idomeneus to Ajax.[16] And in the *Odyssey*, Irus's angry response to the disguised Odysseus includes boldly insulting invective and a challenge to fight.

Hera's anger at Artemis in *Iliad* 21 is a little more complicated. Here Apollo has backed down from a challenge by Poseidon, in which the perfidy of the Trojans is thrown in Apollo's face (*Il.* 21.455–60), so that he is made to withdraw and leave the Trojans to their fate (*Il.* 21.462–63). In response to this, Artemis taunts Apollo,

φεύγεις δή, ἑκάεργε, Ποσειδάωνι δὲ νίκην
πᾶσαν ἐπέτρεψας, μέλεον δέ οἱ εὖχος ἔδωκας·
νηπύτιε, τί νυ τόξον ἔχεις ἀνεμώλιον αὔτως;
μή σευ νῦν ἔτι πατρὸς ἐνὶ μεγάροισιν ἀκούσω
εὐχομένου, ὡς τὸ πρὶν ἐν ἀθανάτοισι θεοῖσιν,
ἄντα Ποσειδάωνος ἐναντίβιον πολεμίζειν."
(*Il.* 21.472–77)

Do you flee, I say, far-worker, and cede the entire victory to Poseidon, and have you given an idle boast to him? Senseless one, why thus do you now have a bow that is useless? Let me now hear you no longer in the halls of your father, giving a boast, as before among the immortal gods, that you can fight one-on-one with Poseidon.

This has much in common with Helen's taunting of Aphrodite, including the rhetorical question (*Il.* 3.399 ~ *Il.* 21.474); a teasing vocative (*daimoniē*, *Il.* 3.399 ~ *nēpútie*, *Il.* 21. 474); a proposal for future action ("woo Paris yourself," *Il.* 3.406–9 ~ "boast no longer," *Il.* 21.475–77). Moreover, the focus on idle discourse has much in common with Ajax's taunting of Idomeneus (*méleon . . . eûkhos, Il.* 21.473, cf. *Il.* 21.475–76 ~ *tí páros labreúai*, *Il.* 23.474, cf. *Il.* 23.478–79).

I would expect Apollo to respond aggressively, but since he has already withdrawn, Hera steps into the breach and it is *her khólos* that is aroused. The text emphasizes this by making it clear that Apollo's silence is unexpected after Artemis' taunt:

῞Ως φάτο· τὴν δ'οὔ τι προσέφη ἑκάεργος Ἀπόλλων,
ἀλλὰ χολωσαμένη Διὸς αἰδοίη παράκοιτις
νείκεσεν ἰοχέαιραν ὀνειδείοις ἐπέεσσι.
(*Il.* 21.478–80)

Thus she spoke; but far-working Apollo said nothing at all to her, but Hera, came to have *khólos*, Zeus's wife, and challenged the arrow-shooter [Artemis] with contentious words.

This passage shows the flexibility of Homeric poetic practice, where the context shifts together with the formal structure accommodating the shift. The pattern should, in other words, call for Apollo to respond to Artemis's taunt, but Hera takes the initiative instead, as she does one other time with Apollo.

At the beginning of *Iliad* 24, though Hera refrains from directly calling out to Apollo, her speech pits Achilles' *timḗ* ("honor") and that of Hector against one another, as she insults Apollo directly (at *Il.* 24.63).[17] Hera's scolding has the familiar characteristics that we can attribute to the speeches marked by *khólos* in this context, including a kind of Homeric epideictic high-style:

Τὸν δὲ χολωσαμένη προσέφη λευκώλενος Ἥρη·
"εἴη κεν καὶ τοῦτο τεὸν ἔπος, ἀργυρότοξε,
εἰ δὴ ὁμὴν Ἀχιλῆι καὶ Ἕκτορι θήσετε τιμήν.
Ἕκτωρ μὲν θνητός τε γυναῖκά τε θήσατο μαζόν·
αὐτὰρ Ἀχιλλεύς ἐστι θεᾶς γόνος, ἣν ἐγὼ αὐτὴ
θρέψα τε καὶ ἀτίτηλα καὶ ἀνδρὶ πόρον παράκοιτιν,
Πηλέι, ὃς περὶ κῆρι φίλος γένετ' ἀθανάτοισι.
πάντες δ' ἀντιάασθε, θεοί, γάμου· ἐν δὲ σὺ τοῖσι
δαίνυ' ἔχων φόρμιγγα, κακῶν ἕταρ', αἰὲν ἄπιστε."
(*Il.* 24.55–63)

And having come to be angry white-armed Hera addressed him. "This word of yours would be true, silver-bowed one, if you give equal honor to Achilles and Hector. Hector, a mortal, nursed at a woman's breast. But Achilles is the offspring of a goddess, whom I myself nursed and reared and gave as wife to a mortal, Peleus, who was beloved in their heart to the immortals. All of you gods attended the marriage. There you were a guest, with your lyre, companion of evils ever untrustworthy."

As in the other examples of this kind of speech, the rhetoric is remarkable. Note the playful alliteration in lines 57–59 (*thḗsete / thnētós / thḗsato / theâs / thrépsa*) as well as the placement of *thḗsete / thḗsato* in the dactylic portion of the adonic clausula of successive lines. In keeping with the rhetoric of the *khólos* passages under discussion, Hera's challenge to Apollo consists of questioning the notion that mortals and immortals should be equally judged (*Il.* 24.57–61). Finally, the characteristic scolding vocatives occur at the end of the speech.

In summary, the aorist participle derived from *khólos* can indicate that anger has provoked certain types of invective or taunts that arise specifically from a character's speech. That kind of anger in this case leads not to action but to a kind of social challenge, whether it be regarding status (as in, for example, Aphrodite's threat to Helen), or a judgment (as when, for example, Ajax threatens Idomeneus).

A Taunting Formula: *kholōtoîsin epéessin*

That *khólos* marks certain kinds of verbal discourse is made even more clear in the passages identified by Group 8a in Appendix 2. These four lines consist of the verb *neikeiō* ("to quarrel") followed by a dative form of the adjective *kholōtós* ("displaying anger") modifying the noun *épea* ("words"). The formula *kholōtoîsin epéessin* occupies the slot from the trochaic caesura to the end of the line. *Khólos* is closely associated with *neîkos* ("quarrel"), as for example, when Idomeneus (*kholōsámenos* "having come to be angry") challenges Ajax, he calls him *neíkei áriste* (*Il.* 23.483, "best at contention"), and when Hera challenges Artemis in *Iliad* 21 she does so also in a *neîkos* (*Il.* 21.479–80, discussed above).

A verbal challenge based on *khólos* leads to strife (e.g., a *neîkos* "quarrel").[18] As it turns out, *khólos* is one of a number of ideas that characterize a speech by means of adverbial expressions designed to indicate the style and content of that speech.[19]

Consider the following lines (Appendix 2, 8a):

Il. 4.241 τοὺς μάλα νεικείεσκε <u>χολωτοῖσιν</u> ἐπέεσσιν·
Od. 22.26 νείκειον δ' Ὀδυσῆα <u>χολωτοῖσιν</u> ἐπέεσσι·
Od. 22.225 νείκεσσεν δ' Ὀδυσῆα <u>χολωτοῖσιν</u> ἐπέεσσιν·
Il. 15.210 νεικείεν ἐθέλῃσι <u>χολωτοῖσιν</u> ἐπέεσσιν.

The lines have *neikeíō* 3 out of four times in line-initial position, with a structure of the type: #Verb + Object + Dative.[20] The traditional phrase structure, featuring a verbal form of *neik-* at the beginning of a line, with *kholōtoîsin epéessin* concluding the line, varies in response to a local phenomenon, namely, the syntax of the surrounding utterance. In this case note the syntax of antecedent and resumptive in:

<u>Οὕς</u> τινας αὖ μεθιέντας ἴδοι στυγεροῦ πολέμοιο,
<u>τοὺς</u> μάλα νεικείεσκε χολωτοῖσιν ἐπέεσσιν.
(*Il.* 4.240–41)

<u>Whomever</u> he saw holding back from the dreadful war, he would chide <u>them</u> the more with words of *khólos*.

The object, a resumptive pronoun, based on *ho, hē, tó*, or the like, syntactically comes first in its clause, thereby pushing the verb (here *neikeíeske*) back from the front of the line. The adverb *mála,* in following Wackernagel's law, leaves the verb as the third element in the line, in what G. Holland has called a modified sentence initial position: the variation between the two lines from *Odyssey* 22 and *Iliad* 4 are, that is to say, directly related to features of archaic Greek syntax and poetics.[21] Thus, though we can say that *Il.* 4.241 is a variation of the traditional phrase, the variation itself is based on old syntactic patterns.[22]

Agamemnon's review of his troops presents our first example of this phrase as part of a sequence of speeches, each speech varying in style depending on whether Agamemnon is speaking to troops who are reluctant to enter battle or those who are enthusiastically preparing for war. As Martin has shown (1989, 69–77), in this scene Agamemnon is trying to get his troops to fight by using the kind of speech act that speech-act theorists call "directives."[23] But Agamemnon's directive speech-acts, though all functioning in a similar fashion, have different surface representations.[24] For those troops who are moving forward, the directive comes as encouragement (*tharsúneske*, *Il.* 4.233, "he would rouse them"), but for those who are "holding back" (*methiéntas*, *Il.* 4.240), a scolding is appropriate (*neikeíeske*, *Il.* 4.241, "he would rile them"); for those whose preparations, please him, sweet words are the reward (*meilikhíoisin*, *Il.* 4.256, "with sweet [words]"); when he finds the two Ajaxes, Agamemnon speaks (with joy *gḗthēsen, Il.* 4.283, "he rejoiced") winged words to them,[25] as he does again to Nestor at *Il.* 4.311–12, when he finds him rousing the Pylians. But Menestheus and Odysseus fare worse in getting Agamemnon's blame (*neíkessen* "he riled them," and cf. *épea pteróenta, Il.* 4.337, "winged words"), which succeeds in angering Odysseus.[26] This is the same treatment afforded to Diomedes and Sthenelus (*Il.* 4.418), the last of the ranks treated to Agamemnon's attention.[27]

The variations possible within the speech-acts of this scene identify the rhetorical purpose of *khólos* within a given speech. In this context, *khólos* is part of the rhetoric of blame in that when Agamemnon blames one of his warriors for being less than he can be, he expects his reaction to be one of *khólos*, and that anger, as we will see below, is particularly to be identified with the warrior's violent function. Thus, in the orchestration of this passage, beginning as it does generally with a set of warriors that is moving forward in their preparations (*Il.* 4.232–39) and a second set that hangs back (*Il.* 4.240–49); the latter are blamed with words designed to instill *khólos* (see above *Il.* 4.240–41). And those words, as we saw in the loquitur formulas discussed above, include invective epithets (*Argeîoi ióm̄oroi, elenkhées* "Argive compulsive archers, deserving of reproach"),[28] and strong denunciation. I want to suggest here that this couplet (*Il.* 4.240–41) makes precise the kind of rhetorical approach that Agamemnon uses against the two groups of warriors of which he is critical, namely Odysseus and Menestheus and Diomedes and Sthenelus. Even more, the frequentative form of the verb *neikeíō* ("to chide," "to challenge"), as well as the indefinite relative (*hoús tinas*, *Il.* 4.240, "whomever") along with the structure of the past general condition are to be taken closely with the phrase *kholōtoîsin epéessin* "with words of *khólos*," as looking forward to Agamemnon's scolding of these last two groups of Achaeans.

There emerge the kinds of ideas that *khólos* is opposed to: at *Il.* 4.256, *meilikhíoisin* ("sweet") characterizes the *épea* ("words") of Agamemnon to Idomeneus, even as he rejoices (*gḗthēsen*) every bit as much as he does when encountering the Ajaxes (*Il.* 4.283) and Nestor (*Il.* 4.311). In these latter two cases we get no phrase specifying the kind of *épea* ("words") that Agamemnon profers to those with whom he is pleased, though *épea pteróenta* ("winged words," *Il.* 4.284 and *Il.* 4.312), as a phrase, continues to characterize the directive nature of the speech act.[29] Throughout the entire review only two phrases specify the force of Agamemnon's sequence of speeches (for negative discourse *kholōtoîsin epéessin*, and for positive discourse *meilikhíois epéessin*). It is a feature of Homer's style that the phrases are not repeated after the first instance (respectively, *Il.* 4.241, *Il.* 4.256): given the economy of Homeric style, the audience already knows that Agamemnon's speech is designed to arouse the anger of the warrior. Thus, when Agamemnon perceives the Athenians and Cephallanians holding back, the narrative presents Agamemnon's blame without an explicit reference to *khólos*, because the discourse has already been typed as an instance of the typical situation described at *Il.* 4.240–41.

Odysseus demonstrates that the warrior's *khólos* is at issue when he responds in anger, as indicated by the loquitur formula: *tòn d' ar hupódra idṓn proséphē polúmētis Odusseús* (*Il.* 4.350, "And looking darkly many-minded Odysseus addressed him").[30] And *hupódra idṓn* ("looking darkly"), closely associated with *khólos*, is repeated at the end of the review of the troops, when Sthenelus intervenes to defend Agamemnon against Diomedes' critique (*Il.* 4.404–10). The effect, then, of Agamemnon's review is to instill *khólos* in the reluctant troops, so that when the scene is over they are ready to fight, with the result that they form a fearful spectre before the enemy.[31] Thus the meaning of the formula *toùs mála neikeíeske kholṓtoisin epéessin* is "he blamed them with words that inspire *khólos*." In this case the *khólos* is something Agamemnon wants to instill in his lackadaisical warriors, just as in *Od.* 22.225, Athena tries with the same phrase to get Odysseus to fight: she rouses his *khólos* through a rebuke (*neíkessen*) that reminds him of his previous valor (*Od.* 22.226–35).[32] Earlier in the same book, the suitors rebuke the disguised Odysseus for killing Antinoos (*neíkeion d' Oduséa kholōtoîsin epéessin*, *Od.* 22.26, "They chided Odysseus with words that inspire *khólos*"). The passage from the *Odyssey* shows a different use of the formula from that of the *Iliad* in that the suitors are ignorant of the consequences of rousing the Odysseus's *khólos*. Homeric usage tells us right away that only out of their own ignorance (*tò dè nḗpioi ouk enóēsan*, *Od.* 22.32, "The fools did not realize this") have the suitors managed to enrage Odysseus. But that they have succeeded in rousing Odysseus's soldierly wrath is clear from the occurrence of the key phrase *toùs d' ár' hupódra idṓn, Od. 22.*34 "And he looked darkly at them."[33] Moreover, the relationship between *khólos* and *hupódra idṓn* is secured in the course of this exchange, when Eurymachus tries to strike a deal by forgiving Odysseus for his previous anger, if only he would accept bronze and gold as payment for their violations:

> "Χαλκόν τε χρυσόν τ᾽ ἀποδώσομεν, εἰς ὅ κε σὸν κῆρ
> ἰανθῇ· πρὶν δ᾽ οὔ τι νεμεσσητὸν κεχολῶσθαι."
> τὸν δ᾽ ἄρ ὑπόδρα ἰδὼν προσέφη πολύμητις Ὀδυσσεύς·
> (*Od.* 22.58–60)

> "We will compensate you with gold and bronze, until your very heart melts; before this, yes, there could be no criticism of your *khólos*." But looking darkly up spoke manyminded Odysseus.

Thus *khólos*, with its preeminent place in the warrior's vocabulary, as the anger of the warrior *par excellence*, is here inadvertently aroused in the suitors' worst nightmare, Odysseus, king and warrior both.[34]

In light of these passages, Poseidon's criticism of Zeus's rebuke in Book 15 seems odd, for here Iris has just conveyed Zeus's order that Poseidon refrain from helping the Achaeans, a message that includes a strong threat (*Od.* 15.160–61). This is another directive, of course, but what lies behind Poseidon's claim that Zeus's words prompt *khólos* in him?[35] As it turns out, Iris, after delivering Zeus's directive, including the threat,[36] is met with consternation by Poseidon,[37] who criticizes the rhetoric of Zeus's order with the suggestion that it is wholly inappropriate for Zeus to address him in this manner.[38] At this point, Iris modifies the rhetorical approach by making the tone conciliatory and practical:

> ἦ τι μεταστρέψεις; στρεπταὶ μέν τε φρένες ἐσθλῶν.
> οἶσθ᾽ ὡς πρεσβυτέροισιν Ἐρινύες αἰὲν ἕπονται.
> (*Il.* 15.203–4)

> Or will you retreat a bit? Malleable are the minds of the good. You know how the Erinyes constantly attend the elders.

Here *khólos* is softened through a speech of conciliation. Iris acknowledges Poseidon's *khólos* but emphasizes the propriety of retreat, just as the ambassadors of *Iliad* 9 try to persuade Achilles through acknowledging the propriety of his *khólos*, even as they ask him to yield in the culturally accepted manner.[39]

The Mounting Rage Sequence

Having reviewed *khólos* as part of a directive style of heroic speaking, I am ready to explore the kinds of *actions* that characterize *khólos*. I begin by looking at a set of passages that bridges both words and deeds. This transitional group shows how *khólos* can come from provocative speech and turn to inspire either angry speech or angry action or both. In terms of the rhetoric of Homeric discourse, the kind of violent action that follows such rhetorical display corresponds to *khólos* as deed does to word. In terms of the poetics of Homeric tradition, *khólos* turns out to be at the center of a motif-sequence[40] crucial for the poetics of the *Odyssey* in particular, one that otherwise has all but gone unnoticed.

This motif pattern can be called the "mounting rage" sequence, the identifying term for which is the aorist middle *kholṓsato* in lines that localize the word metrically, along with contextual markers of clear significance.[41] The pattern may be schematized as follows from the examples (See Appendix 2, Group 8b):

ἄρ᾽ ἔφη, ποταμὸς δέ
ὥς ἐφάμην· ὁ δ᾽ ἔπειτα
ὥς ἔφατ᾽ Αντίνοος δ᾽ (ἐ)χολώσατο κηρόθι μᾶλλον
ὥς ἔφατ᾽ Εὐρύμαχος δ᾽
ὥς φατ᾽᾽Αθηναίη δὲ

Calchas's informed definition reveals the significance of *mâllon* ("more") at the end of this phrase. The ability of human agents to affect and control *khólos* suggests that it can be described in terms of degree, unlike *kótos* which we have seen must exist until it reaches its *télos*. In these instances, a speech launches the addressee into a greater state of *khólos*.

Indeed, the differences in degree of *khólos* emphasize certain dramatic situations in the epic narrative. For example, at the beginning of the quarrel, Achilles uses the degree of his anger against Agamemnon to inform Athena of how sensible he is to obey her (*kaì mála per thumôi kekholōménon*, *Il.* 1.217, "even though angered the more in his spirit"). So too, when Odysseus is filled with the warrior's rage on the battle-field, the narrative tells us that it is so to a greater degree than before: *Oduseùs mála thumòn . . . kholṓthē* (*Il.* 4.494, "Odysseus became the more angered in his heart").[42]

This particular sequence shows the speech formula *hṑ (é)phatos* ("thus he [or she] spoke") preceding *(e)kholósato kēróthi mâllon* ("he became the more enraged in his heart"), a formulaic sequence that thereby marks the preceding speech as provoking another's wrath. The enraged party then commits an act of violence in response, against the speaker, who is located at a doorway or other liminal spot. The subsequent act of violence takes the form of a missile shot. The motif sequence has, thus, the following elements:

1. Provocation: Speech
2. Emotional response: Anger.
3. Location: Liminal area
4. Action: Missile shot

The most dramatic examples form a doublet in the Ithacan scenes of the *Odyssey*.[43] In Books 17 and 18 of the *Odyssey*, Odysseus is assaulted by suitors or their representatives. The first such assualt directly leads to this motif sequence, when Melanthius meets Odysseus and Eumaeus as they make their way into the city. Odysseus has already encountered his old dog, Argos, in a dungheap, before the gates of the house, a thematic point of some importance, as we will see. After this, Melanthius contemptuously predicts that the beggar, Odysseus in disguise, will meet with violence (*Od.* 17.230–33)

> αἴ κ' ἔλθῃ πρὸς δώματ' Ὀδυσσῆος θείοιο,
> πολλά οἱ ἀμφὶ κάρη σφέλα ἀνδρῶν ἐκ παλαμάων
> πλευραὶ ἀποτρίψουσι δόμον κάτα βαλλομένοιο.

> If he arrives at the house of Odysseus the godlike, throughout the house his ribs will wear out many stools, as he is hit about the head.

This prediction proves true as both Eurymachus and Antinoos will hurl furniture at Odysseus. As preparation for these scenes, Melanthius's scornful threat focuses both on the body of the victim (*plurai* "ribs") and on the location of the assault (*pròs dṓmat', dómon káta* "at the house," "throughout the house"). Much is made of the physical location that the beggar takes in the house of Odysseus,[44] a position that puts him just next to "outside the house," even as Argus is outside, in the household dungheap. Odysseus leaves this spot at Telemachus's and Athena's insistence (*Od.* 17.345–47; 360–64) in order to beg in a formal manner from the assembly.[45] The disorder of the household is clearly presented when Melanthius,[46] interrupts the beggar's process through the hall, thereby provoking Antinoos to chide Eumaeus for bringing him there in the first place. Even Antinoos's boorishness doesn't upset the ritual begging, so strong an institution must it be,[47] though both Eumaeus and Telemachus each get a confrontational word in against Antinoos (*Od.* 17.381–404).

At this point, Odysseus continues his ritual begging, and the others give him something (*Od.* 17.411), while the text prepares the scene for Antinoos's violent outburst by focusing attention on a footstool (*Od.* 17.409–10) that he is using to relax, ostentatiously not giving to the beggar. Clearly Antinoos is the last[48] in the ritual order, since Odysseus is turning back to the threshold (*Od.* 17.413) as he makes this request, ("*dós, phílos*," *Od.* 17.415, "give, friend"), including an extended lying speech (*Od.* 17.415–44), one that Antinoos mocks (*Od.* 17.446–52). Having made his formal request, only to be rejected by one suitor, Odysseus turns to a provocative four-line speech:

> ὢ πόποι, οὐκ ἄρα σοί γ' ἐπὶ εἴδεϊ καὶ φρένες ἦσαν·
> οὐ σύ γ' ἂν ἐξ οἴκου σῷ ἐπιστάτῃ οὐδ' ἅλα δοίης,
> ὃς νῦν ἀλλοτρίοισι παρήμενος οὔ τί μοι ἔτλης
> σίτου ἀποπροελὼν δόμεναι· τὰ δὲ πολλὰ πάρεστιν.
> (*Od.* 17.454–57)

> Ah, so your mind *doesn't* match your appearance. No, you would not give even salt from your own house's store, though you sit now with others' things without enduring to take and give a little bit from your plate. And there is a great deal left.

This is not a restrained speech, since it cuts to the core of the suitors' violation and irritates an already visibly provocable Antinoos. At this point, we get the central element of this motif-sequence, namely, the anger of Antinoos:

> ὣς ἔφατ', Ἀντίνοος δ' ἐχολώσατο κηρόθι μᾶλλον,
> καί μιν ὑπόδρα ἰδὼν ἔπεα πτεροέντα προσηύδα·
> "νῦν δή σ' οὐκέτι καλὰ διὲκ μεγάροιό γ' οἴω
> ἂψ ἀναχωρήσειν, ὅτε δὴ καὶ ὀνείδεα βάζεις."
> (*Od.* 17.458–62)

> Thus he spoke, but Antinoos came to be the more angry in his heart, and having looked darkly at him he spoke winged words. "But now no longer will you make a fair retreat from the hall, since in fact you have spoken words of reproach."

Antinoos's *khólos* displays those same elements we have seen accompanying *khólos* before, including the glowering look (*hupódra idṓn*) and the reproaching words (*oneídea*). But here the gesture and the speech is followed by action: Antinoos takes the footstool that he has only just recently set in place (*Od.* 17.409–10) and throws it at the beggar, hitting him in the right shoulder (*Od.* 17.463–65). With his ears ringing, Odysseus finally returns to his threshold seating place (*Od.* 17.464–65) and delivers a stinging speech against the suitors (*Od.* 17.468–75) only to elicit another threat from Antinoos (*Od.* 17.478–80), received in turn with some trepidation by the other suitors (*Od.* 17.480–87).

Taking the phrase *kholósato kēróthi mâllon* as an index marker for this motif sequence, I schematize the sequence in the following way:

> Motif 1: Flyting speech: a character at a liminal point between danger and safety challenges a character who seems more powerful. The liminal point may be expressed either literally or symbolically.
> Motif 2: Reaction of addressee: described in a speech formula + *kholṓsato kēróthi mâllon*; followed by a speech in which he denigrates the flyting speech as so much persiflage.
> Motif 3: Missile shot—addressee hurls an object, doing some—but not total—damage to the object of his attack.

Schematically Antinoos's outburst is congruent with the scene in Book 18, where Eurymachus hurls furniture at Odysseus.[49] The line that serves as an index to this sequence is *kholṓsato kēróthi mâllon*, with the elements of the scene easily identified from this example. After defeating Irus, Odysseus has returned to his position at the threshold (*Od.* 18.109), and following a digression in which Penelope comes to the hall in order to extract gifts from the suitors (*Od.* 18.159–306), Odysseus tries to dismiss the serving women (*Od.* 18.313–19); at this point Eurymachus insults Odysseus before the assembled suitors, with the claim that the hall can be lit from the gleam off the beggar's bald pate (*Od.* 18.352–56); he continues with a flyting speech directed to Odysseus, challenging him to work for a living instead of living off what he can get begging (*Od.* 18.338–65). Here begins Odysseus's response in his own flyting speech in which he boasts that he can best him in both work (*Od.* 18.367–76) and warfare (*Od.* 18.377–82), with a final fillip about his seating position at the edge of the social group:

> εἰ δ' Ὀδυσεὺς ἔλθοι καὶ ἵκοιτ' ἐς πατρίδα γαῖαν,
> αἶψά κέ τοι τὰ θύρετρα, καὶ εὐρέα περ μάλ' ἐόντα,
> φεύγοντι στείνοιτο διὲκ προθύροιο θύραζε.
> (*Od.* 18.384–86)
>
> Were Odysseus to come and return to his fatherland, right now these doors here, though they seem truly broad, would be too narrow for you to flee outside through the entrance.

With the beggar standing at the threshold, the vision of Odysseus's blocking the way out is the more powerful for the audience, especially with the threefold repetition of the root *-thúr-*.[50]

At this point, we have our key line followed by the same phrase that followed that line in *Odyssey* 17:

> ὣς ἔφατ', Εὐρύμαχος δ' ἐχολώσατο κηρόθι μᾶλλον,
> καί μιν ὑπόδρα ἰδὼν ἔπεα πτερόεντα προσηύδα·
> (*Od.* 18.387–88)
>
> Thus he spoke; and Eurymachus came to be angry the more in his heart and looking grimly spoke winged words to him.

The provocative speech obviously has gotten Eurymachus's goat and he accuses Odysseus of being drunk (*Od.* 18.391) and (continuing the second part of the sequence) prattling nonsense (*metamṓnia bázeis*, *Od.* 18.392). With that, Eurymachus takes a stool (*sphélas*, *Od.* 18.394) and hurls it at Odysseus who ducks just in time to miss it, though it hits a wine-steward (*Od.* 18.396).

In the doublet, displayed by these two scenes from the *Odyssey*, the notion of *khólos*, as provoked by a flyting speech, gives form to the tension mounting in Odysseus's home on Ithaca.[51] But *khólos* does more than this by connecting this scene to a crucial moment earlier in the *Odyssey*; the boorishness of the suitors has an analog in the uncouth manner in which the Cyclops has treated Odysseus, especially when Noman has almost gotten away.

Our indexical key for the Mounting Rage sequence (*kholṓsato kēróthi mâllon*) also occurs in *Od.* 9.480. The narrative has just shown Polyphemus talking to his lead ram, treating his animal tenderly and with compassion (*kriè pépon*, *Od.* 9.447, "good ram") at the beginning of the speech and giving closure to it with a violent image, one that Odysseus overhears:

> "τῷ κέ οἱ ἐγκέφαλός γε διὰ σπέος ἄλλυδις ἄλλῃ
> θεινομένου ῥαίοιτο πρὸς οὔδεϊ, κὰδ δέ κ᾿ ἐμὸν κῆρ
> λωφήσειε κακῶν, τά μοι οὐτιδανὸς πόρεν Οὖτις."
> ὣς εἰπὼν τὸν κριὸν ἀπὸ ἕο πέμπε θύραζε.
> (*Od.* 9.458–61)

> "So his brains would be sprinkled through the cave hither and thither, once he is struck at the threshold, and my heart would be relaxed of their evils, which this no-account Noman gave me." Thus having spoken he sent his ram off outside.

The scene is thus set for the motif sequence, with a character at the threshold (Odysseus) and a threat from a thug (Cyclops), though in this case the thug's speech is merely overheard by Odysseus.[52] Having established Odysseus as the man at the threshold, Odysseus and his crew scramble to their vessel and steal Polyphemus's livestock (*Od.* 9.469–70). As they are about to get away, Odysseus provokes the Cyclops:

> ἀλλ᾿ ὅτε τόσσον ἀπῆν, ὅσσον τε γέγωνε βοήσας,
> καὶ τότ᾿ ἐγὼ Κύκλωπα προσηύδων κερτομίοισι·
> "Κύκλωψ, οὐκ ἄρ᾿ ἔμελλες ἀνάλκιδος ἀνδρὸς ἑταίρους
> ἔδμεναι ἐν σπῆι γλαφυρῷ κρατερῆφι βίηφι.
> καὶ λίην σέ γ᾿ ἔμελλε κιχήσεσθαι κακὰ ἔργα,
> σχέτλι᾿, ἐπεὶ ξείνους οὐχ ἅζεο σῷ ἐνὶ οἴκῳ
> ἐσθέμεναι· τῷ σε Ζεὺς τίσατο καὶ θεοὶ ἄλλοι."
> (*Od.* 9.473–79)

> But when I was as far as one might be heard with a shout, even then I spoke to the Cyclops with scornful words: "Cyclops, you were about to eat savagely the companions of a powerless man in your hollow cave. Yes, evil deeds were truly to find you, wretch, since you did not take care about eating the guests in your house; therefore Zeus has paid you back, and the other gods too."

That Odysseus specifies that the distance between him and the Cyclops amounts to a restatement of the "threshold" element of this sequence,[53] where just as the principal character is about to get away, Odysseus cannot resist taunting the thug. The content of Odysseus's flyting speech, to the effect that the rules of *xenía* have been flaunted and retribution has been exacted by Zeus, resembles the beggar Odysseus's taunt of Antinoos's stinginess at *Od.* 17.454–57 (discussed above). Finally, unlike the suitors, the Cyclops does not speak a word,[54] but moves directly to the major action of this sequence, after the indexical phrase:

ὣς ἐφάμην, ὁ δ' ἔπειτα χολώσατο κηρόθι μᾶλλον,
ἧκε δ' ἀπορρήξας κορυφὴν ὄρεος μεγάλοιο,
κὰδ δ' ἔβαλε προπάροιθε νεὸς κυανοπρῴροιο
τυτθόν, ἐδεύησεν δ' οἰήιον ἄκρον ἱκέσθαι·
(*Od.* 9.480–83)

Thus I spoke, but thereupon he came to have *khólos* the more in his heart; he broke off and flung the peak of a great mountain, and cast it down before the dark-prowed ship, right near it, but it failed to reach the rudder's tip.

The violence of the missile shot[55] coupled with its ineffectuality[56] secures the parallel to the scenes in Odysseus's palace. The threshold motif emerges in a number of ways: at the cave, at the boundary between the sea and the shore, and at the tip of the rudder (*Od.* 9.483). Thus the parallel between the Cyclops' failure to practice *xenía* and the evil-doing of the suitors is bolstered by a doublet on Ithaca among the major suitors that clearly evokes Odysseus's escape from Polyphemus's island. As it is a doublet, the passage from *Odyssey* 9 is the most elaborated of the Mounting Rage sequences.[57]

For my primary interest in *khólos*, these passages show the role that this kind of anger has in a social context where there is dispute over behavior within the social codes. In each case, the defiant are pushed to the brink by someone who points out how wrong they are. The careful analogy that Homeric poetics builds between the monsters of the apologue and the suitors includes, thus, analogous tempers based on the notion of *khólos*.[58]

More can be said about this sequence, in particular since mounting rage characterizes a flyting speech of Athena's directed against Odysseus as the slaughter of the suitors proceeds to its conclusion. Here, in *Odyssey* 22, the doors are prominent, from the first line where Odysseus displays himself at the threshold, where only shortly before he had been cowering,[59] even while Melanthius, seized by Eumaeus and Telemachus at the threshold (182), is tied up (188–89) and the doors are closed on him (201). In this passage the mounting rage is that of Athena, who disguised as Mentor, has been recruited by Odysseus but is threatened by Agelaus (213–22) and responds with mounting rage and a rebuke, not to Agelaus but to Odysseus:

ὣς φάτ', Ἀθηναίη δὲ χολώσατο κηρόθι μᾶλλον
νείκεσσεν δ' Ὀδυσῆα χολωτοῖσιν ἐπέεσσιν·
(*Od.* 22.224–25)

Thus he spoke; but Athena came to be more angry in her heart, and she reviled Odysseus with words designed to anger.

Here a form of *khólos* is used twice, once of the response that Athena has to Agelaus's threat of violence against Mentor, and a second time of the response she wishes to elicit from Odysseus through her speech.

Thus the *Odyssey* makes use of a motif-sequence, marked by *khólos* in a formula repeated 4 times, a phrase poised at key thematic moments crucial to the revelation of Odysseus's identity, both in the apologue and in the Ithacan books, where this motif-sequence speech and violence play a crucial role: Homeric narrative uses a poetic tool to stitch together the relationship that provides a link between Odysseus's enemies, the suitors, and the Cyclops. From a post-traditional perspective, it is fair to say that the thematics of the *Odyssey preserve* this sequence, since the *Iliad* did not make use of the Mounting Rage sequence in the same overtly structured manner as did the *Odyssey*.

The Iliad has that formula only once at 21.136, where this motif-sequence is presented in a muted but effective way; Achilles has just slain Lycaon and launched an invective against him; this invective causes Scamander to have *khólos*. Note that Achilles speaks winged words to Lycaon at *Il.* 21.122–35, boasts again to Asteropaeus, and indirectly challenges Scamander (*Il.* 21.126–35 and again, later, at *Il.* 21.194–98); in Scamander's metamorphosis, he becomes angry—the mounting rage formula presenting itself at *Il.* 21.136—and as his rage increases he finally confronts Achilles, with an angry speech (*Il.* 21.212, *khōsámenos*) and violent missile shots, this time, grotesquely, in the form of Trojan corpses jettisoned from the river's waters (*Il.* 21. 235–37):

> πάντα δ' ὄρινε ῥέεθρα κυκώμενος, ὦσε δὲ νεκροὺς
> πολλούς, οἵ ῥα κατ' αὐτὸν ἅλις ἔσαν, οὓς κτάν' Ἀχιλλεύς·
> <u>τοὺς ἔκβαλλε θύραζε</u>,
>
> And he impelled in his turbulence all the streams, and pushed out the corpses,
> in their numbers, which were in him in a swarm—the ones Achilles had killed;
> <u>he threw them outside</u>.

The elements of the motif-sequence are all here, even where their denotation is metaphorical rather than literal, as in *thúraze*, the banks of the river pointing to the threshold motif in the Mounting Rage sequence The nonhuman creature (as in the Cyclops' case, or even in the suitors' case, where they have excluded themselves from human ways) is pushed into a state of rage by Achilles, the representative of human activity, so that the monster fires missiles (dead bodies) and provides a temporary setback to the hero's victory. Here Achilles has indeed gone too far, as Nagler clearly shows (1974, 147–66). Since we only have one example of this *khólos* phrase in the *Iliad*, it would be difficult to determine its rhetorical force within the Mounting Rage sequence, where we not to have the *Odyssey* passages. How many more such moments of Homeric artistry are only such potentially (as is *kholṓsato kēróthi mâllon* at *Il.* 21.136), waiting to be elaborated in their appropriate generic context, such as their own Odyssey or Iliad?

Notes

1. The aorist shows 26 examples, with the perfect having 27 examples.

2. The aorist active and the perfect (excluding the future perfect) each show 15 participles. The details are presented in Appendix 2, Group 7.

3. Parry 1971, 15–16; he goes on to discuss these predicate formulae as belonging to "a type consisting of pronoun-conjunction-participle-verb" followed by a "subject expresssion made up of a noun and one or two epithetic words" (15). "And finally, we could also establish in the case of these predicate expressions a formula type composed of a pronoun, a conjunction, a participle, and of προσέφη or προσέφης" (16).

4. See above Chapter 4.

5. Note the use of *némesis* here as above to indicate the last straw, the point beyond which one cannot go: to go this far has been bad enough but to go further, that would involve *némesis*. The word *némesis* frequently occurs in *khólos* contexts: *Il.* 6.335, *Il.* 9.523, *Il.* 16.541, *Il.* 8.407, 421, *Il.* 5.757–62 (in ring form); *Il.* 9.872, *Il.* 15.223, 227; *Il.* 15.103, *Il.* 15.208, 211, *Il.* 23.494, *Il.* 24.53–55; *Od.* 22.58. This list is not exhaustive. Ebeling takes the two concepts to be synonymous (Ebeling 1880–1885, 1137[2] s.v. *nemesízomai*). See the cautious statements on synonymy by Martin (1989, 14).

6. On a mortal male wedded to an immortal, see the example of Thetis (Slatkin 1991, 55–56, with 38–39, and on the relation of this mythic motif to Thetis' anger, see her Chapter 3).

7. On *éris* see Hogan 1981 and Nagler 1988 and 1992. As to *khṓomai*, it has a special relationship to *khólos*, especially in the light of this passage and many others where *khólos* seems related to *khṓomai* (e.g., *Il.* 21.136 with *Il.* 21.212; *Il.* 23.482 with *Il.* 23.489; and *Od.* 12.348 with *Od.* 12.376).

8. This is a comparable fear to that of Chryses in *Iliad* 1 (*éddeisen d' ho gérōn kaì epeítheto múthōi*, 33, "And the old man was taken with fear and obeyed the speech"), since in both cases the reproach is met with silent acquiesence when the defeated person leaves (cf. *Il.* 1.34, *bê d' akéōn* "He went off in silence" with *Il.* 3.419–20, *bê . . . sigêi* "He went off in silence" where the word for silence receives emphasis, through placement at the beginning of the line).

9. I will show that *khólos* frequently has its place in response to another speech: *Il.* 8.460: Hera's response to a speech of Zeus; *Il.* 4.24; *Il.* 6.166, a response to the false accusation of Proetus's wife against Bellerophon; cf. *Od.* 9.480; *Od.* 17.458 (=18.387; cf. *Od.* 22.224); and of course Calchas's fear is that Agamemnon will have *khólos* in response to proclamation as to the source of the plague (*Il.* 1.76–78).

10. 474, 478, and the compound *labragórēn*, 479; cf. Richardson's note at 473–81 (1993, 222), for a discussion of *labrós*, its derivatives and usage.

11. Note that in *Iliad* 23, Achilles steps in on hearing that Agamemnon is being set up as the judge. Indeed, throughout Book 23 and 24, Achilles is made to intervene in situations of anger.

12. Cf. *hupódra idṓn* "looking darkly," and *mḗ me kholṓsēis* "Don't make me angry," 20. See the discussion of *hupódra idṓn* below, Chapter 11.

13. Line 20, quoted above.

14. And for that matter with the Idomeneus's speech to Ajax discussed below.

15. Cf. *hupódra idṓn* and *mḗ me kholṓsēis*, 20.

16. This speech is consistent with the others just discussed in having an insult (*ho molobrós*), with the demonstrative used contemptuously as the Attic orators used *hoûtos* (*LSJ*, s.v., c.3); see also tragedy, e.g., Sophocles, *Ajax* 89.

17. See again the list of examples, Appendix 2, Group 8.

18. On *neîkos* see Nagy 1979, 223–24, with an explication of how the concept is deployed in Homeric speech in Martin 1989, 68–69 and 71–76.

19. As a formulaic phrase, *kholōtoîsin epéessi* can be compared with expressions such as: *oneideíois epéessi(n)* (*Il.* 1.519, *Il.* 2.277 [with *neik-*], *Il.* 16.628, *Il.* 21.480 [with *neik-*], *Od.* 18.326); *kertomíois epéessi(n)* (*Il.* 4.6, *Il.* 5.419, *Od.* 24.240); *ekpáglois epéessin* (*Il.* 15.198, *Od.* 8. 77); *atartēroîs epéessin* (*Il.* 1.223); *antibíoisi . . . epéessin* (*Il.* 1.304); *khalepoîsin . . . epéessi(n)* (*Il.* 23.492, *Od.* 3.148, cf. *Il.* 23.489); *aiskhoîs epéessi(n)* (*Il.* 3.38, *Il.* 6.325 [with *neík-*], *Il.* 13.768, cf. *Il.* 24.238 [*épess' aiskhroîsin*], *epéessin . . . stugeroîsin* (*Od.* 11.81, 465); *épesín te kakoîsin* (*Od.* 24.161); and contrasts with phrases such as *epéessi malakoîsin* (*Il.* 1.582, cf. *Il.* 6.337 [*malakoîs epéessi(n)*], *Od.* 16.286, *Od.* 19.5, *Od.* 10.422; and *Od.* 10.70 [*malakoîsi . . . epéessin*] with *Hymn Dem.* 336); *aganoîs epéessi(n)* (*Il.* 2.164, 180, 189, *Il.* 24.772); and *épessí te meilikhíoisi[n]* (*Il.* 9.113, *Il.* 10.542, cf. *meilikhíois epéessi[n]* in *Il.* 11.137, *Il.* 21.339, *Od.* 9.493, *Od.* 10.442, *Od.* 16.279, *Od.* 18.283, *Od.* 24.393, with *Od.* 6.143, 146, *Od.* 19.415 [*epéessin{n}* . . .] *meilikhíoisi[n]*.) The force of these phrases is clarified in Martin's study of the relationship between *mûthos* and *épos*. See Martin 1989, 20–22.

20. Instrumental, cf. Chantraine 1953, 76 (§102).

21. Wackernagel observed that sentence particles and enclitic pronouns tend to be placed after the first stressed element in the clause. See Wackernagel 1892. For modified sentence initials, see Holland 1980, 34; and note the structure of the relative clauses in *Il.* 12.265–69 and *Il.* 4.240–41. On the traditional and regular variation of formulas either at line beginning or at the main caesura, see Muellner 1976, 34–35 with n. 42.

22. On the special nature of *neîkos* in Homeric poetry, see Nagy 1979, 223–28. Most apt for the present discussion is the formulation that "the words *éris*/*neîkos* apply not only to the language of blame but also to the action of physical combat" (Nagy 1979, 228). I only add that the kind of anger that moves in this way between language excludes *kótos* but includes *khólos*.

23. Martin 1989, 31.

24. Martin 1989, 32.

25. On the directive function of *épea pteróenta*, see Martin 1989, 30–35.

26. Note *hupódra idṓn* at 349, and *khōoménoio* at 357. See also n. 7 above.

27. Note again that Diomedes' anger is aroused (*hupódra idṓn*, 411).

28. One can hold back from this kind of anger as one can from war. Resisting an aggressive action is associated with holding back from *khólos*, as in *tô s' aû nûn kélomai methémen khólon huîos heêos* (*Il.* 15.138, "Thus, I now order you to relax your *khólos* for your son"), *líssom' Akhilēi methémen khólon* (*Il.* 1.283, "I entreat Achilles to relax his *khólos*"); and cf. *methíete thoúridos alkês* (*Il.* 4.234 "you are relaxing from your raging valor").

29. Again see Martin 1989, 32–34.

30. As recognized by Agamemnon at *Il.* 4.357 (*hôs gnô khōoménoio*, "as he saw that he was angry"). As for *hupódra idṓn*, see Lakoff's summation (1987, 394): "Aggressive visual behavior stands for anger"; and in Homeric poetry see the close relationship of *khólos* to *hupódra idṓn* in *Od.* 8.165, with 205.

31. Cf. *Il.* 4.419–21, closing the scene with the notion of *déos* ("fear") (one result of the display of *khólos*) to be contrasted with *ptṓssein* and *ptōskazémen* (371, 372, "to cower"), characteristics of the coward. Note how the Diomedes and Odysseus sections respond to each other. In the former, Agamemnon rouses Odysseus by criticizing Menestheus, to whose defence Odysseus comes; in the second case, the narrator tells us Agamemnon chides Diomedes for being less than his father so that Sthenelus intervenes, only to have Diomedes close the scene (*hupódra idṓn* 411, "looking darkly"), by recognizing Agamemnon's rhetorical task (*otrúnonti mákhesthai*, 414, "rousing them to fight") for what it is, a pose to stimulate the slackers and encourage the bold. See Holoka 1983, 6.

32. To be discussed in the next section; and note the repetition of *kholṓsato* . . . *kholōtoîsin* in 224–25.

33. And note the fear at l. 42 (*déos heîle*).

34. Note that Eurymachus's rhetorical ploy is the same as that of Phoenix in *Iliad* 9, who also says *prìn d' oú ti nemessētòn kekholôsthai* (523), indicating that *khólos* is appropriate but only to the point of having received an offer of material goods in recompense for the slight that led to the anger. Both attempts are futile. The quality of *khólos* that Calchas originally singled out, its ability to be limited by human action, leads both Eurymachus and Phoenix to try to quell the warrior's *khólos*. In both cases, the warrior is given a way out of a troublesome situation only to reject it. For the conflictual situation posed by an act of violence by the head of the household in his *oîkos* see Nagler 1993.

35. *Il.* 15.157, *épea pteróenta proseū́da*, "he spoke winged words"; again see Martin 1989, 30–35.

36. *Il.* 15.176–83 quoting 160–67.

37. *Il.* 15.184; Scully (1984) presents a discussion of the formula, but mostly in the context of passages of deliberation.

38. And see the closure provided for this speech by the repeated critique of Zeus's rhetoric at *Il.* 15.197–98: *thugatéressin gár te kaì huiási kérdion eín / ekpánglois epéessin enissémen, hoùs téken autós*, "It would be better to criticize with outrageous words his daughters and sons, since he is their father."

39. Though, significantly, he points out that an uncurable *khólos* can still be an option (217).

40. I use the term in the manner of Thornton 1984 and Nagler 1974, 113–44.

41. Outside of this sequence we have only one other example of the third singular aorist middle of this verb (*Il.* 15.155), located in a different position (O'Neill's position 10), and requiring the augment after *idṓn*. All the examples of *kholṓsato* in this motif sequence can be produced with *dé* preceding the unaugmented form, with the exception of *Od.* 9.480.

42. See also, *Il.* 4.241, *Il.* 13.660, *Il.* 17.399, *Il.* 17.710, *Il.* 18.322, *Il.* 23.543; *Od.* 15.214, *Od.* 19.324; and compare also *Il.* 9.678, *Il.* 19.16, *Od.* 16.425 (*liēn*), *Od.* 19.324 (*mála*). On *kēróthi* with *khólos*, see Caswell 1990, 34, and 39 and see the useful list on 69. In a separate study, I explore *khṓomai* and its close relation to *khólos*. For now see *Il.* 21.305–6 and n. 7 above.

43. Nagler recognizes that the importance of this line at least partly resides in its implication of a "growing provocation" (1974, 148 and note). I emphasize again that such shifting parameters for the anger in question are characteristic of *khólos*, but not even possible for *kótos*. For now note that *(e)kholṓsato kēróthi mâllon* is an expansion of the formula *kēróthi mâllon*, which occurs otherwise 7 times in the *Odyssey*, one time in the *Hymns* and 2 times in the *Iliad*. At *Od.* 5.284 the verb is *ekhṓsato* ("he came to be angry"); *ákhos* ("grief" completes the phrase at *Od.* 11.208); forms of *philéō* occur in *Od.* 15.370 (*phílei dé me*, "and he loves me") and *H. Apoll.* 138 (*phílēse dé*, "he came to love me"). See also *apḗkhtheto* ("he was hated") at *Il.* 9.300.

44. As for example at *îze d' epì melínou oudoû éntosthe thuráōn, / klinámenos stathmôi kuparissínōi* (*Od.* 17.339–40), "He sat at the ash threshold within the doors, leaning on a post of cypress"; and again at 413 and 465.

45. The formal manner is for the beggar to go from left to right, begging from one man after another: *bê d' ímen aitḗsōn endéxia phôta hékaston* (*Od.* 17.365, "and he went to ask each man singly clockwise"), *after* he has consumed the portion given by the head of the household (which Telemachus presented to him through a known servant, Eumaeus (*Od.* 17.345–47; see *ḗsthei, Od.* 17.358, "he ate"). This domestic ritual is related to the "hero's portion," cf. *Il.* 7.50–51, 73–75, with the discussion at Nagy 1979, 133 n. 48.

46. As he sits near Eurymachus (*Od.* 17.256–57), where he is offered food (*Od.* 17.257–60).

47. Cf. Eumaeus's defence of the process, *Od.* 17.381–83.

48. But not worst, Odysseus says (*Od.* 17.415–16).

49. On Antinoos and Eurymachus as "character doublets" see Fenik 1974, 198–207, with discussion of the "throwing scenes" at 201–2 and 206 ("the throwing scenes characterize the suitors and show them losing the upper hand").

50. And note the demonstrative *tá* in *Od.* 18.385. There is a thematic contrast between the *nóstos* "return" of Odysseus as expressed doubly in two verbs of motion (*élthoi kaì híkoit', Od.* 18.384) and the narrowing of the passage way for Eurymachus as he flees (*pheúgonti, Od.* 18.386), possibly with an iconic figure in the juxtaposition of *prothúroio* "through the door" and *thúraze* "out the doorway." On the relation of expression with *pheúgō* "to flee" and the notion of *nóstos* "return," see Frame 1978, 91–92.

51. Again see Fenik 1974, Part II, for detailed discussion of how such doubling works in Homer.

52. Notice the wordplay on Odysseus's pseudonym and the word for threshold: *oúdei* at the bucolic diaeresis responded to by *Oûtis* at the end of line 460, supported by *outidanós* (noted by Rank, below) in the middle of line 460. (Add this to Louden's discussion of puns on Odysseus's name (1995, 34–37; cf. Rank 1951, 63–65). Compare the threefold repetition of *-thur-* at *Od.* 18.384–86; these grand flourishes of Homeric style highlight the thematic markers of the motif-sequence. The importance of wordplay of many kinds for early literature is developed in Schwartz's important work on Zoroaster's poetics (Schwartz 1986).

53. See the discussion of these types of phrases in Homeric usage in Nagler 1974, 29–37, presenting a full discussion of the "make oneself heard by shouting" family.

54. There may have been a felt incongruity with using *hupódra idṓn* to accompany the verb of speaking for the blinded Cyclops.

55. Note that the line initial verbs, *#hêke*, *#kàd d' ébale*, typical of a "sudden blow," are presented iconically (cf. *Il.* 1.52).

56. That Cyclops just misses the rudder anticipates Eurymachus's missing Odysseus as he ducks behind Amphinomos, only to hit the wine-pourer instead (*Od.* 18.394–96). Antinoos is more accurate, when he hits Odysseus with full force, with Odysseus, unlike the wine-pourer, withstanding the blow (*Od.* 17.460–65); also compare the fall of the wine-pourer (*pésen húptios en koníēisi*, *Od.* 18.398) with Odysseus returning to his place at the threshold (and note *oudòn* at *Od.* 17.465).

57. The second part of the doublet continues after the Cyclops' recognition of the identity of Odysseus. At that point, Odysseus presents a second flyting speech (*Od.* 9.523–25) to which Polyphemus responds with a prayer (*Od.* 9.528–35) introduced by a two-line loquitur formula including a gesture that signals a prayer (*Od.* 9.526–27):

> ὣς ἐφάμην, ὁ δ' ἔπειτα Ποσειδάωνι ἄνακτι
> εὔχετο, χεῖρ' ὀρέγων εἰς οὐρανὸν ἀστερόεντα·
>
> Thus I spoke, but thereupon he prayed to king Poseidon, stretching his hands to starry heaven

after which he hurls a far larger rock (*polù meízona lâan*, *Od.* 9.537), with initial placement of the verbs for throwing (*#hêk'*, *Od.* 9.539, *#kàd d' ébalen*, *Od.* 9.540) parallel to that of the first member of the doublet (at *Od.* 9.481–82, discussed above), and with the same result (*Od.* 9.540 = 483).

58. The use of *kótos* in the Cyclops passage at *Od.* 9.501 is discussed above in Part I.

59. *Od.* 22.2 *âlto d' epì mégan oudón*. Cf. *Od.* 22.72, where Eurymachus identifies Odysseus's spot as the *oudoû . . . xestoû* from which they must, to survive, drive him away: *eí ké min oudoû apṓsomen ēdè thuráōn, / élthōmen d' anà ástu, boḕ d' ṓkista génoito, Od.* 22.76–77 ("If we push him from the threshold and the door, let us then go through the city, and let the swiftest outcry arise" [Cf. the echo of this phrase at *Od.* 22.132–34]). The latter calls to mind the "contact" phraseology that signaled the threshold motif in the Cyclops passage, with *boḗ* signalling that point in their longed-for escape that the suitors need to reach if they are to attain safety and *génoito* a substitute for *gégōne* (see Nagler 1974, 30, n. 5). But the tables have been turned, and Odysseus and his team are the hunters with the suitors the hunted. The suitors trying to escape the *oîkos* of Odysseus are like Odysseus and his crew making their hairy escape from Polyphemus's cave, the passage way obstructed by the lord of the manor. Odysseus thinks it imperative that he stay at the doorway (*Od.* 22.107: *mḗ m' apokinḗsousi thuráōn* "lest they move me off from the doors"). Later on, a side door (*orsothúrē*, *Od.* 22.126) becomes important (and see *Od.* 22.132–34); cf. *Od.* 22.250, *Od.* 22.275.

Chapter Nine

Fighting Deeds

ἐπέων κεχολωμένος ἠδὲ καὶ ἔργων
(*Il.* 11.703)

In the preceding chapter, *khólos* emerged in the context of speeches in which a character speaks out of anger or where the speaker elicits an angry reply, or both. In these instances, the angered party has a specific motive derived from the immediate context. But, as we will now see, *khólos* does not always remain a matter of discourse; its most grave consequences take place in the world of action.

The Warrior's Anger

Indeed, *khólos* is the warrior's anger, *par excellence.* For example, at the end of Book 4, Odysseus, kills a Trojan, Democoon.[1] The encounter results from the death of Simoeisios, who was killed by Ajax;[2] the Trojan Antiphus attempts to kill Ajax to avenge Simoeisius, only to miss Ajax and hit instead Leucus. Odysseus responds, with *khólos*, to the death of his comrade:

τοῦ μὲν ἅμαρθ', ὁ δὲ Λεῦκον, Ὀδυσσέος ἐσθλὸν ἑταῖρον,
βεβλήκει βουβῶνα, νέκυν ἑτέρωσ' ἐρύοντα·
. . . .
τοῦ δ' Ὀδυσεὺς μάλα θυμὸν ἀποκταμένοιο χολώθη,
(*Il.* 4.491–92; 494)

He missed him, but instead he [Antiphus] hit Leucus, the good companion of Odysseus, in the groin, as he was dragging the corpse [of Simoeisios] to the other side. And with his death Odysseus became the more angry (*kholṓthē*) in his heart.

The anger of Odysseus is specifically *khólos*,[3] as is soon restated in line *Il.* 4.501, when Odysseus has shot into a crowd of scattering Trojans (*Il.* 4.496–98), only to hit the hapless Democoon, an illegitimate son of Priam :

ἀλλ' υἱὸν Πριάμοιο νόθον βάλε Δημοκόωντα,
ὅς οἱ 'Αβυδόθεν ἦλθε, παρ' ἵππων ὠκειάων.
τόν ῥ' 'Οδυσεὺς ἑτάροιο χολωσάμενος βάλε δουρὶ
(*Il.* 4.499–501)

But he struck the illegitimate son of Priam, Demokoon, who had come from Abudos, on swift horses. Odysseus hit him with his spear, out of anger (*khólōsámenos*) for his companion.

In contrast to *kótos*, *khólos* presents us with a scene from the heat of the battle, where Odysseus's surprise at the death of his companion leads him to display his anger at the Trojans, so that he turns then to hit not the man responsible for the death of Leucus, namely Antiphus, but some other Trojan who happens to be in the crowd at that moment. We are far here from the specific, long-lasting, distantly motivated *kótos*, one that cannot be satisfied with simply the expenditure of bodily energy. Here the rage rises from immediate circumstance—the death of a charioteer,[4] and it is dealt with in the thick atmosphere of wrath, by a killing, any killing. In a sense, *kótos* was delimited by the notion of complete revenge, down to the wiping out of an entire people:[5] it may mean killing *everyone*. *Khólos* is different: it may mean killing *anyone*—any Trojan will do, whereas for *kótos*, only all Trojans will do.[6]

What is the relationship, then, of *khólos* to the violence that characterizes Homeric narrative? I begin by looking at the forms of *khólos* that are linked to violent death. Consider the forms of the aorist participle in the context of killing.

In the first group (Appendix 2, Group 9a), *kholōsámenos* / *-ē* is used to provide motivatation for a killing. These lines are not typical of the way that Homeric poetry shows killing with the verb *kteínō*: usually participles are not used to provide any motive, and indeed precious little qualification is given of the ultimate act.[7] In the typical case, the Homeric narrator offers no direct expression of motive when he indicates, with *kteínō*, the act of killing, except in the speeches of his characters when they are recounting a narrative. I am interested in the examples that show the motivation for a killing specified by a form of *khólos*.

For a dramatic example, in the speech of Zeus, where the plot of the *Iliad* is recounted in brief by the king of gods (*Il.* 15.61–77), the result of Zeus's *boulḗ*, the death of Hector, is prophesied in the line *toû dè kholōsámenos kteneî Héktora dîos Akhileús* (*Il.* 15.68) "Thus having come to be angry luminous Achilles will kill Hector." This line, occurring in a brief summary by Zeus shows a causal participle sketching Achilles' entire motive for his vengeance.[8] So too, in *Il.* 6.205 where Glaucus quickly runs through his genealogy, Artemis' anger (*kholōsaménē*, *Il.* 6.205, "having come to be angry") provides the causal circumstance for the killing, in a narrative summary after a digression. In this passage, Glaucus's paternal aunt, Laodameia, is killed by Artemis:

> Ἴσανδρον δέ οἱ υἱὸν Ἄρης ἆτος πολέμοιο
> μαρνάμενον Σολύμοισι κατέκτανε κυδαλίμοισι·
> τὴν δὲ χολωσαμένη χρυσήνιος Ἄρτεμις ἔκτα.
> (*Il.* 6.203–5)

> And as for Isandros, his son, Ares insatiable of war killed him in the struggle with the glorious Solymi. And as for his daughter, Artemis of the golden reins killed her, out of *khólos*.

In both cases, the speakers are anxious to summarize the motive for the death. A form of *kteínō* is repeated twice in the space of two lines, in the style of a catalogue leading to a climax, the birth of Glaucus (*Il.* 4.206).[9] Thus the causal participle (at the main caesura) and the aorist (line-final) verb are placed for a strong rhetorical effect, signalling a transition to a new part of Glaucus's narrative, by setting aside two deaths in the family, the last one needing only the explanation that *khólos* motivated Artemis.

One other character directly suggests *khólos* as a motive for killing. Odysseus, after he hits the mark twice in his contest with the Phaeacian youth, mentions *khólos*, in two different contexts. The first is the kind of *khólos* that stimulates competition:

> τῶν δ' ἄλλων ὅτινα κραδίη θυμός τε κελεύει,
> δεῦρ' ἄγε πειρηθήτω, ἐπεί μ' ἐχολώσατε λίην,
> ἢ πὺξ ἠὲ πάλῃ ἢ καὶ ποσίν, οὔ τι μεγαίρω,
> πάντων Φαιήκων, πλήν γ' αὐτοῦ Λαοδάμαντος.
> ξεῖνος γάρ μοι ὅδ' ἐστί·
> (*Od.* 8.204–8)

> But of the others, whomever heart and soul encourages, let him come here and test me—since you have caused me to have excessive anger (*khólos*)—either in boxing, wrestling, or racing; not at all do I begrudge it of all the Phaeacians except of course Laodamas himself. For this man is my guest-friend.

That *khólos* can involve competition will be discussed later in this chapter, but certain kinds of competition are especially dangerous, as Thamyris finds out, when the Muses have *khólos* because of his boast that he can beat them in a singing contest (*Il.* 2.594–600, to be discussed below). But neither is Odysseus's bravado about his victory on Scheria innocent of threat, for in establishing his credentials as an archer, in moving from the field of games (boxing, wrestling, racing) to that of archery and its potential violent use, he recounts the story of

Eurytus who contended with the gods, and because of that contention aroused the *khólos* of Apollo:

> τῶ ῥα καὶ αἶψ' ἔθανεν μέγας Εὔρυτος, οὐδ' ἐπὶ γῆρας
> ἵκετ' ἐνὶ μεγάροισι· χολωσάμενος γὰρ Ἀπόλλων
> ἔκτανεν, οὕνεκά μιν προκαλίζετο τοξάζεσθαι.
> (*Od.* 8.226–28)

> Therefore great Eurytus died quite quickly, and old age did not come upon him in halls. For Apollo, with anger (*khólos*), killed him, because he challenged him at archery.

I take the placement of *éktanen* as emphatic in this context, where Odysseus's *khólos* was just mentioned, his prowess at archery praised to the heights, and the challenge posed by the Phaeacians presented as possibly a violation of *xenía*: if Odysseus turns out to be a god, his *khólos* could mean as much trouble for Euryalus, as it does for Eurytus.[10] That *khólos*—or indeed any modifier—should be so rare with *kteínō* makes the rhetoric of this passage a work of high artistry.[11]

Often *kholōsámenos* and related forms precede other kinds of violence than killing, as in the story of Thamyris.[12] For example, Odysseus at *Il.* 2.195 speaks euphemistically of what Agamemnon will do to Achaeans who hold back from the war,[13] or on the opposite end of the spectrum from generalized euphemism, we see the specific brutality of war:

> ὥς ῥα τὸν ὑψοῦ ἔχοντε δύω Αἴαντε κορυστὰ
> τεύχεα συλήτην· κεφαλὴν δ' ἁπαλῆς ἀπὸ δειρῆς
> κόψεν Ὀϊλιάδης, κεχολωμένος Ἀμφιμάχοιο.
> (*Il.* 13.201–3)

> Thus did the two Ajaxes holding him high strip him of helmeted armor. And from his soft neck Locrian Ajax cut off his head, out of anger (*khólos*) for Amphimachus.

Nor is the occurrence of *khólos* in this battle-book adventitious. Just a few lines later after the gruesome image of Imbrius's head tossed like a ball on the field (*sphairēdón*, *Il.* 13.204),[14] Poseidon pursues the Trojans in anger (*ekholṓthē*) for the killing of his grandson.[15] Finally at *Il.* 13.660, on the death of Eukhenor, Paris comes to have *khólos*.[16]

Sure action can attend *khólos*, as Glaucus warns Hector in *Iliad* 16:

> ἀλλά, φίλοι, πάρστητε, νεμεσσήθητε δὲ θυμῷ,
> μὴ ἀπὸ τεύχε' ἕλωνται, ἀεικίσσωσι δὲ νεκρὸν
> Μυρμιδόνες, Δαναῶν κεχολωμένοι ὅσσοι ὄλοντο,
> τοὺς ἐπὶ νηυσὶ θοῇσιν ἐπέφνομεν ἐγχείῃσιν.
> (*Il.* 16.544–47)

But, friends, stand by and let it be an offense to your heart to let the Myrmidons take the armor, and disfigure the corpse, in anger for the Danaans that have perished, whom we killed by the swift ships with our spears.

In fact, besides the outright killing of the victim, mutilation forms one of the characteristic responses to *khólos*,[17] whether it be the blinding of Thamyris, the beheading of Imbrios, or the potential defilement of Sarpedon's corpse.[18] Penelope herself makes clear the way that *khólos* can lead to outrageous acts of violence, when in anger she reminds Antinoos of the favor that Odysseus did for his father, when the Ithacans had thought to slay him, *out of anger*:

ἦ οὐκ οἶσθ' ὅτε δεῦρο πατὴρ τεὸς ἵκετο φεύγων,
δῆμον ὑποδδείσας; δὴ γὰρ κεχολώατο λίην,
οὕνεκα ληιστῆρσιν ἐπισπόμενος Ταφίοισιν
ἤκαχε Θεσπρωτούς· οἳ δ' ἥμιν ἄρθμιοι ἦσαν·
τόν ῥ' ἔθελον φθῖσαι καὶ ἀπορραῖσαι φίλον ἦτορ
ἠδὲ κατὰ ζωὴν φαγέειν μενοεικέα πολλήν·
(*Od.* 16.424–29)

Or do you not know about the time when your father came here in flight, out of fear of the populace? For indeed their anger had become very great, because he had followed Taphian pirates and had caused trouble for the Thesprotians. They were close to us. See they wanted to kill him and to tear out his heart, and to eat his livelihood, great as it is, pleasing as it is.

The subtext here is a persistent vision of cannibalism, every bit as suppressed in the realistic scenario at Ithaca, as it is prominent in the fantastic cave of Polyphemus, or as in Zeus's self-interested characterization of Hera's anger (as cited below). Thus far we have seen that to have *khólos* is to have the kind of anger that leads to direct violence, which can either be described as "killing" or as various forms of mutilation. We know that *khólos* can be modulated from the angry speech of an irritated interlocutor to the savagery of beheading or disfiguring of a corpse. And indeed, Penelope's complaint to Antinoos strays very closely to some of the most grim outcomes of *khólos*, namely, cannibalism. In the *locus classicus* Zeus accuses Hera of cannibalism in *Iliad* 4:

ὠμὸν βεβρώθοις Πρίαμον Πριάμοιό τε παῖδας
ἄλλους τε Τρῶας, τότε κεν χόλον ἐξακέσαιο.
(*Il.* 4.35–36)

Should you eat Priam raw, and the children of Priam, and the other Trojans, then you would cure your *khólos*.

Here the spectre of cannibalism is introduced into the already violent world of the *Iliad*.[19]

In distinction to *kótos*, *khólos* has proven to be a complex and multivalent emotion, especially in its results—speech, mutilation, killing. But as for its sources—what is thought to cause *khólos*—we have closely examined only speech and speech situations, the kind of discourse that Calchas was petrified to have Agamemnon hear (*Il.* 1.81–82). But the warrior's anger is not only subject to verbal discourse; it also responds to death and violence in the world of human action, even as, at the start of this chapter, we saw Odysseus respond to the death of Leucus. And even Helen, through her potion, tries to put an end to the kind of *khólos* that responds to someone's death.[20]

Instead of considering at this point a restricted set of causes for *khólos*, I put *khólos* in the context of the situations that produce it. The advantage to this contextually-based approach is that the narrative is not made to interrogate the culture for a logical sequence, a chain of causation whose putative goal is some predetermined definition of our subject of *khólos*. To do so would make it seem as if *khólos* had its own teleology on which the text is focused. More fruitful would be to see what kind of social circumstances stimulate the growth of wrath. So I would like to look to three kinds of category of Homeric events that can be called "sites" for *khólos*. One of these sites is that of competition and contention, as in a *neîkos* or in funeral games. Another one of these sites is the assembly. Finally death becomes a site for *khólos*, especially if it is the death of a *phílos*.

Site One: Contest and Challenge

For the first site, note that *khólos* arises frequently during competition, as already seen in the contest between Ajax and Odysseus, so tactfully alluded to in Odysseus's voyage to the underworld. Here I want to take the analysis further, by pointing out that there are three references to *khólos* in this scene (*kekholōménē*, *Od.* 11.544; *khólou*, *Od.* 11.553; *kekholōménos*, *Od.* 11.565), in order to suggest that the anger occurs because the contest takes place in a questionable manner. This passage is extremely valuable for us because Odysseus, both as narrator and as participant in the narrative, takes pains to explain how the contest over the arms provides a site for *khólos*.[21] What is it about that contest that produces *khólos*? In Odysseus's description of the event we see key words for the judgment:

> οἴη δ᾽ Αἴαντος ψυχὴ Τελαμωνιάδαο
> νόσφιν ἀφειστήκει, <u>κεχολωμένη εἵνεκα νίκης</u>,
> τήν μιν ἐγὼ <u>νίκησα δικαζόμενος</u> παρὰ νηυσὶ
> τεύχεσιν ἀμφ᾽ Ἀχιλῆος· <u>ἔθηκε</u> δὲ πότνια μήτηρ·
> παῖδες δὲ Τρώων <u>δίκασαν</u> καὶ Παλλὰς Ἀθήνη.
> ὥς δὴ μὴ ὄφελον <u>νικᾶν</u> τοιῷδ᾽ ἐπ᾽ ἀέθλῳ·
> τοίην γὰρ κεφαλὴν ἕνεκ᾽ αὐτῶν γαῖα κατέσχεν,
> Αἴανθ᾽, ὃς περὶ μὲν εἶδος, περὶ δ᾽ ἔργα τέτυκτο
> τῶν ἄλλων Δαναῶν μετ᾽ ἀμύμονα Πηλεΐωνα.
> (*Od.* 11.543–51)

> Alone did the soul of Telamonian Ajax stand apart, angry on account of the victory, which I won in the judgment by the ships concerning Achilles' arms. And his lady mother set it up, and the children of the Trojans and Pallas Athena determined the judgment. Would that for such a prize there had been no victory, since the earth claims such a man on account of these things—I mean Ajax, who in form and in action is superior to the rest of the Danaans after the blameless son of Peleus.

The language of competition with forms of *níkē* (*Od.* 11.543, 544, 547, "victory"), and *dikázō* (*Od.* 11.544, 546, "judge"), including *éthēke* (*Od.* 11.545, "set up") in its technical sense of setting up prizes in the games, underscores the social context of the *khólos*, namely a competitive arena. But what happens that forces *khólos*? Surely it can't be that *any* contest leads to anger?

In this case, Odysseus, very delicately, positions his praise of Ajax in a way that only gingerly explains the unfairness of the judgment—after all Ajax is second only to Achilles in both word and deed. The implication is that Ajax deserved the arms, since he was next in rank; thus, the judgment was made in favor of someone less deserving, namely, Odysseus. In such a case, the sense of an unfair outcome in a social context involving competition or conflict leads to *khólos*, on the part of the person perceiving that outcome as unfair or inappropriate. In this case, Odysseus, as narrator, sides with Ajax, perhaps in order to display a magnanimous spirit before the Phaeacians, before whom, after all, he had displayed a winning form in contests held just the day of this narrative performance, where *khólos* had also been at issue.[22]

We can return again to the *khólos* that we observed in the Scherian games as Odysseus is challenged by the island's youth. The first *khólos* phrase (*Od.* 8.205, discussed above) is spoken by Odysseus when he confronts the young men:

> δεῦρ' ἄγε πειρηθήτω, ἐπεὶ μ' ἐχολώσατε λίην,
> ἢ πὺξ ἠὲ πάλῃ, ἢ καὶ ποσίν, οὔ τι μεγαίρω,
> πάντων Φαιήκων, πλήν γ' αὐτοῦ Λαοδάμαντος.
> (*Od.* 8.205–7)

> But come let there be a competition—since you have angered me to excess—either boxing, or wrestling, or the foot-race, not at all do I begrudge it, of all the Phaeacians, except of course Laodamas.

Indeed, Odysseus had already become angry at Euryalos, who had challenged him with anger: *tòn d' aût' Eurúalos epameíbeto neíkesé te ántēn: "... oud' athlētêri eoikas* (*Od.* 8.158; 164) "Euryalus responded to him and challenged him directly ... 'You don't resemble an athlete.'"[23] That anger is then expressed in the discus throw (*peirḗsom' aéthlōn, Od.* 8.184, "I will contend in the games"),[24] after which, in the flush of victory, Odysseus takes the opportunity to establish his devotion to *xenía* ("guest-friendship"):

ξεῖνος γάρ μοι ὅδ᾽ ἐστί· τίς ἂν φιλέοντι μάχοιτο;
ἄφρων δὴ κεῖνός γε καὶ οὐτιδανὸς πέλει ἀνήρ,
ὅς τις ξεινοδόκῳ ἔριδα προφέρηται ἀέθλων
δήμῳ ἐν ἀλλοδαπῷ· ἕο δ᾽ αὐτοῦ πάντα κολούει.[25]
(*Od.* 8.208–10)

This man is my guest-friend. Who would fight a *philos*? One would be stupid and a man of no worth, to contend in strife over prizes with a host in a strange land; he cuts short all things from himself.

These are potent words indeed for our *Odyssey*, pointing to the basics of the guest-host relationship, even as they demarcate the limits of anger and response within such relationships. Here Odysseus indicates that the central value of the *Odyssey*, *xenía*, is also threatened by *khólos*,[26] but that it can be modified by human action, such as choosing whom to oppose in a contest, what events are appropriate, and so forth; nonetheless, his magnanimity here, as with Ajax, functions to show him being gracious in victory.

I have already shown that Odysseus presents an exemplum in which *khólos* is a threat during a contest or challenge. In that case, he refrains from comparing himself, even at the height of boasting, to his betters, when, after claiming to be no mean bowman, he points out that Philoctetes was better (*Od.* 8.219). Furthermore, he refuses to compare himself to figures of legend (*andrási protéroisin Od.* 8.223) "men of old," since this puts one close to challenging the gods themselves:

ἀνδράσι δὲ προτέροισιν ἐριζέμεν οὐκ ἐθελήσω,
οὔθ᾽ Ἡρακλῆι οὔτ᾽ Εὐρύτῳ Οἰχαλιῆι,
οἵ ῥα καὶ ἀθανάτοισιν ἐρίζεσκον περὶ τόξων.
(*Od.* 8.223–25)

I am unwilling to contend with the mortals of the past, certainly not Heracles, nor Eurytus from Oichalia, who used to contend even with the immortals in archery.

The very fact of contending with immortals is problematic, because *khólos* belongs to that world of contention, so that the *khólos* of a god might be deadly indeed, as Eurytus's experience clearly demonstrates in *Od.* 8.226–28 (cited above, 166). Here again the language of contest (for example, *prokalízeto*, *Od.* 8. 228) is used to explain the cause of *khólos*.[27]

This exemplum underscores the threat implied in *Od.* 8.205. Since Odysseus has not yet identified himself and since he may thus be in fact a god, it is dangerous for the Phaeacians to challenge him, as it was dangerous for Eurytus to challenge Apollo. And central to the danger in such a situation is the possibility that *khólos* will arise.[28]

This kind of *khólos* can result from a challenge across social boundaries. The contest may arouse *khólos* because the contenders inappropriately cross boundaries such as that between gods and mortals.[29] In a digression within the catalogue of ships, a leads to a *khólos*, when Thamyris, the Thracian singer, foolishly contends with the muses. As it happens, it was as Thamyris made his way back from Eurytus's Oichalian home that he made his fateful boast to the muses:[30]

ἔνθα τε Μοῦσαι
ἀντόμεναι Θάμυριν τὸν Θρήικα παῦσαν ἀοιδῆς,
Οἰχαλίηθεν ἰόντα παρ' Εὐρύτου Οἰχαλιῆος·
στεῦτο γὰρ εὐχόμενος νικησέμεν, εἴ περ ἂν αὐταὶ
Μοῦσαι ἀείδοιεν, κοῦραι Διὸς αἰγιόχοιο·
(*Il.* 2.594–98)

There the Muses, encountering the Thracian Thamyris stopped his song as he made his way out of Oichalia from Oichalian Eurytus; for he averred in a boast that he would win, even if the Muses themselves should sing, daughters of aegis-bearing Zeus.

Here the language of opposition (*antómenai, Il.* 2.595) and competition (*nikēsémen*),[31] coupled with the parallel fate of Eurytus, all make the outcome of Thamyris' foolhardy boast predictably bad. The muses' response to this challenge is to become angry and react violently:

αἳ δὲ χολωσάμεναι πηρὸν θέσαν, αὐτὰρ ἀοιδὴν
θεσπεσίην ἀφέλοντο καὶ ἐκλέλαθον κιθαριστύν·
(*Il.* 2.599–600)

But they out of *khólos* made him blind, and they took away his godly song and caused him to forget his instrument.

Here it is inappropriate to challenge the divinities, and the result is their *khólos,* which they express through divine violence, mutilating the singer and depriving him of his art.

Site Two: Dispute and Quarrel

The second site for *khólos* is that of the *neîkos* ("quarrel"). Words for contention, including *neîkos* ("quarrel"), *níkē* ("victory"),[32] and *éris* ("contention"),[33] as they relate to *khólos*, are an important part of the plot of the *Iliad. Neîkos* is the technical term for the quarrel that signals the theme of the death of Achilles in Iliadic epic.[34] In the song of Demodocus (*Od.* 8.72–82)

The *neîkos* and all else that happened thereupon are described as the Will of Zeus (*Od.* 8.72), which is the same traditional device that motivates the *neîkos*

> at the beginning of the *Cypria* (Proclus 102.13–14; *Cypria fr.* 1. Allen). Likewise at the beginning of our *Iliad*, the Will of Zeus (*Il.* 1.5) leads to *éris* 'strife' between Achilles and Agamemnon (ἐρίσαντε: I.6; ἔριδι: I 8), and this strife takes the form of a *neîkos* 'quarrel'
>
> (Nagy 1979, 130–31)

Such quarrels, typified in a specific way by the tradition, provide sites for *khólos*. Indeed, although Calchas mentions Apollo's *mênis* in his plea to Achilles (*Il.* 1.75), the poem opens by describing Apollo's motive for destroying the Greeks, the emotional locus of that motive being *khólos*:

> Τίς τ' ἄρ σφωε θεῶν ἔριδι ξυνέηκε μάχεσθαι;
> Λητοῦς καὶ Διὸς υἱός· ὃ γὰρ βασιλῆι χολωθεὶς
> νοῦσον ἀνὰ στρατὸν ὦρσε κακήν, ὀλέκοντο δὲ λαοί,
> οὕνεκα τὸν Χρύσην ἠτίμασεν ἀρητῆρα.
>
> (*Il.* 1.8–11)

> Now who among gods cast those two in strife to fight? The son of Leto and Zeus. For he came to have *khólos* against the king and roused an evil sickness along the camp, and the host died, because he had dishonored Chryses his priest.

This particular form of *khólos*—the reaction to inappropriate behavior as expected within the social code[35]—is the most common source of *khólos* throughout the *Iliad*. Thus a violation of the rules concerning *timḗ* is the primary motive for the quarrel between Achilles and Agamemnon in Book 1.[36] And this violation makes transgressions against social codes constitute a threat to the social order.[37] In this case, orderly relations between gods and mortals are threatened by the denial of a ransom duly asked for and assented to by the social body as a whole (*Il.* 1.220). And the response is the *khólos* of Apollo.[38]

Other examples of divine *khólos* against mortals occur in response to a violation of a social boundary or conventional practice. In essence, in such contexts there is a violation of the terms of the relationship, such as that between Aphrodite and Helen (*Il.* 3.413) or between Hera and the Trojans (*Il.* 4.36).[39] On the mortal level, issues of decorum and propriety can be a source of *khólos*, as when Laertes avoids Anticleia's wrath by not sharing a bed with Eurycleia (*Od.* 1.432–33); or when Odysseus carefully approaches Nausicaa so that he not rouse her *khólos* by touching her inappropriately (*Od.* 6.147).[40]

We have seen that the contest, be it the funeral games of Patroclus or the festive games on Scheria, are sites in which *khólos* might flare up, either between the participants, or as before Patroclus's pyre, among the spectators. Another site for this kind of anger is the assembly that breaks up in a quarrel, where the contest and competition is not in manual skill or dexterity but rather in verbal craft. Thus the assembly that meets Apollo's priest at the beginning of the *Iliad* is a most potent site for the manifestation of *khólos* headed for a *neîkos*. This observation leads me to present a review of the passages in Book 1 that show *khólos*.[41]

There are nine attested instances of *khólos* and related forms in the first book of the *Iliad*.[42] Apart from one reference to the *khólos* of Apollo at Agamemnon (*Il.* 1.9) for rejecting Chryses, all the other references in Book 1 are situated in the quarrel between Achilles and Agamemnon, four times in reference to Achilles,[43] with one reference to Agamemnon.[44] That these are all tightly focused on the quarrel, its inception at the dishonoring of Chryses and the subsequent verbal duel between Agamemnon and Achilles, contrasts with what Muellner has described for *mênis* in Book 1:

> The simple underlying structure of the whole narrative in Book 1 . . . consists of three intertwined instances of the μῆνις theme. First is the μῆνις of Apollo. . . . In fact, it is Achilles' μῆνις that Thetis persuades Zeus to validate. . . . In attempting to suppress [Hera's] foreseeable protest, Zeus threatens Hera with μῆνις, but the threat is averted by Hephaestus's cautionary narrative about Zeus' μῆνις against him. Thus, Apollo's μῆνις proceeds through a complete cycle, the incipient μῆνις of Achilles is incurred and validated by Zeus, but the potential μῆνις of Zeus against Hera is averted. The goal of the narrative in Book I, is to be sure, to set into motion the μῆνις of Achilles, but it also serves to reveal, in three thematically coherent and interlaced examples, how a μῆνις can be appeased, incurred, and averted, for those are the exact points at which each of these first instances of the μῆνις theme concludes. The μῆνις of Achilles is now clearly situated between its two models, that of Apollo and that of Zeus.
>
> (Muellner 1996, 128–29)

Beside the tripartite elegance of this analysis of *mênis* in *Iliad* 1, I set the tight focus of *khólos* in the same book, where it all hangs from the central narrative moment in the opening of the poem, the quarrel between Agamemnon and Achilles.

Thus when Agamemnon makes his first gestures towards taking a substitute for Chryseis, he suggests that the warrior he approaches will have *khólos*,[45] a result made concrete in the vivid presentation of Achilles' moment of truth, when he seems ready to yield to his *khólos* and—sword drawn—moves to slay Agamemnon, *ēè khólon paúseien erētúseié te thumón* ("or stop his *khólos* and restrain his spirit," *Il.* 1.192). Indeed, Athena's visitation here, coupled with her suggestion that the second of the alternatives is preferable, leads Achilles to underscore that it is her divinity that can overcome his anger, specifically *khólos*:

> χρὴ μὲν σφωίτερόν γε, θεά, ἔπος εἰρύσσασθαι
> <u>καὶ μάλα περ θυμῷ κεχολωμένον</u>· ὣς γὰρ ἄμεινον.
> ὅς κε θεοῖς ἐπιπείθηται, μάλα τ' ἔκλυον αὐτοῦ.
>
> (*Il.* 1.216–18)

O goddess, I must heed this command from both of you even though my heart is full of *khólos* to a high degree; for it's better that way. To obey the gods is to be heard by them the more.

As discussed above, *mála* and related words point to the degrees of *khólos*, thereby highlighting Calchas's definition that *khólos* is subject to modification. In the same way, Achilles' action with respect to anger is well within his power to modify. The scene also shows that Achilles can both obey Athena by not harming Agamemnon, even while he continues his *khólos: Pēleídēs d' exaûtis atartērois epéessin / Atreídēn proséeipe, kaì oú pō lêge khóloio* "And the son of Peleus once again addressed the son of Atreus with violent words, and he had not yet let go of his *khólos*."[46] In sum, Achilles' *khólos* is situated in a *neîkos*, whose prosecution has taken an unfair turn, so that even Agamemnon has to acknowledge that *khólos* will come to the fore because of his actions. And that *khólos* is seen to be under the control of the principal character, Achilles.

Thus far in Book 1 all the references to a specific mortal's *khólos* have been made in reference to Achilles, but there is one certain reference to the *khólos* of Agamemnon at *Il.* 1.387. This singular reference to his *khólos*—of special significance to the way one assigns responsibility for the quarrel—is made by none other than Achilles himself in his reply to his mother's inquiry (*Il.* 1.365–412), and thus is full of the rhetoric of persuasion. Achilles' mentions others' anger (Chryses' at *Il.* 1.380, Agamemnon's at *Il.* 1.387) but not a word of his own. His argument here indeed hinges on the issue of *timḗ* (*Il.* 1.407–12), but not on his response to being deprived of it. It is left then to Thetis to see through this ruse so as to identify the problem. She then will advise him to continue his wrath,[47] with the assurance that Zeus will attend to things:

ἀλλὰ σὺ μὲν νῦν νηυσὶ παρήμενος ὠκυπόροισι
μήνι' Ἀχαιοῖσιν, πολέμου δ' ἀποπαύεο πάμπαν.
(*Il.* 1.421–22)

But sitting by the swift ships now rage on at the Achaeans, and hold back totally from the war.

Where Achilles does not or cannot[48] mention his anger, Thetis names it its highest name, thereby sanctioning, in sacral and numinous terms, the depth of Achilles' passion, a gesture made even more powerful by her commissioning and delivering the arms of Hephaestus which will come to have the powerful result of injecting Achilles with *khólos*:

αὐτὰρ Ἀχιλλεὺς
ὡς εἶδ', ὥς μιν μᾶλλον ἔδυ χόλος,
(*Il.* 19.15–16)

And Achilles when he saw [the arms], then the, *khólos* entered him the more.

In sum, the last occurrence of *khólos* in *Iliad* 1 refers us to Agamemnon and his rage, but only through Achilles' eyes and as Achilles gauges the propriety of mentioning his own rage to his mother.

What we have seen of *khólos* in Book 1 tells us that the quarrel between Achilles and Agamemnon, and its locus in Chryses' dispute with Agamemnon—a dispute that stimulates the *khólos* of Apollo—is a traditional site for the expression of this specific kind of anger. The special relation of *khólos* to the *Iliad* is also supported by the overwhelming number of occurrences of the term in the *Iliad* as opposed to the *Odyssey*.[49] Moreover, in the *Iliad*'s ninth book, a major turning point in the story of the anger of Achilles, we find by far the greatest number of instances of *khólos* (16). But the greatest number of references to *khólos* throughout the *Iliad* is to Achilles' *khólos* against Agamemnon.[50]

Site Three: The Death of One Near and Dear

The third site for *khólos* to be examined in this chapter has to do with the death of a *phílos* ("one who is near and dear"). As I discussed above in Chapter 6, Helen's drug could quell *khólos*, even in the context of such a death. It should come, then, as no surprise to find a thick dossier on *khólos* in reference to the death or harm that comes to a *phílos*. There are 23 clear instances of *khólos* in this context, out of the 138 cases of *khólos* in Homer. Indeed, the first instance of *khólos* in an Iliadic battle scene leads to a death on the battlefield, when Odysseus avenges his charioteer in *Iliad* 4 (*Il.* 4.494, *Il.* 4.501). After this scene, this kind of *khólos* appears again only after *Iliad* 9, and, then, only in the battle books, specifically in *Iliad* 13 (203, 206, 660); next *khólos* for a dead *phílos* comes on in full force only in reference to the anger of Achilles, especially in Zeus's summary of the action that will take place in the last part of the *Iliad* (cf. *Il.* 15.68 and 72);[51] here too Achilles gets more than his fair share of *khólos* passages,[52] with no one else, except Odysseus, getting more than one.[53]

I begin by looking at who has *khólos* over the death of a *phílos* in the *Iliad*:

Mortals:

Odysseus (*Il.* 4.494, 501), for Leucus, his charioteer
Ajax Oiliades (*Il.* 13.203), for Amphimachus
Paris (*Il.* 13.660), for Euchenor
Achilles (*Il.* 15.72, 17.310, 18.337, 23.23), for Patroclus
Maris (*Il.* 16.320), a Trojan, for his brother, Atymnius
Myrmidons (*Il.* 16.546), for Danaans slain
Patroclus (*Il.* 16.585), for Epeigeus
Priam (*Il.* 24.584), potential *khólos* at Achilles for Hector

Gods:

Ares (*Il.* 15.138), for his son
Scamander (*Il.* 21.136), over the Trojans slain by Achilles
Poseidon (*Il.* 13.206), for his grandson

Three examples come from the *Odyssey*:

Suitors (*Od.* 22.26), for Antinoos (the only example concerning mortals, in the *Odyssey*)
Poseidon (*Od.* 1.69, 78), for Polyphemus
Helius (*Od.* 12.348), for his cattle

The special character of *khólos* over the death of a *phílos* sends the cultural notion of *khólos* beyond its site in games, contests, or quarrels to the field of aggression and its deadly result. Such a *khólos* is particularly a concern of the *Iliad*, but strikingly much less so for the *Odyssey*, where we really see only three examples of this kind of anger, that of Poseidon for Polyphemus (*Od.* 1.69 and 78), that of Helius for his cattle, and that of the suitors for Antinoos. As for the *Iliad*, besides the passage at the end of Book 4 (with which this chapter opened) the concern over the death of a *phílos* primarily applies to the great central battle books, where, moreover, it is a mortal who can respond in this way. As for the gods, their relation to this kind of *khólos* is limited to special kinship relations, for example, when Scamander has *khólos* over the excessive slaying of the Trojans in *Iliad* 21 (136), or Poseidon's *khólos* for his grandson Amhimachus in *Il.* 13.206–7 (cf. 185–87). Indeed, Poseidon seems particularly susceptible to the *khólos* that responds to harm that comes to others. For example, he monitors Zeus's potential *khólos* over the overturning of fate that Achilles would accomplish by killing Aeneas (*Il.* 20.293–308). In another case, his anger flares up over the damage Odysseus does to Polyphemus (*Od.* 1.69, 78).[54]

In the battle books, the narrative initiates a flurry of *khólos* surrounding the death of *phíloi* with a grisly reprisal by Oilean Ajax for the death of Amphimachus. This complex battle scene has Hector aiming for Teucer in revenge for Imbrios, only to kill Amphimachus in the process. Then, Hector, tugging at the helmet of Amphimachus as he strips him of his armor, is pushed back by Ajax, leaving the two corpses, one Greek and one Trojan, to be dealt with by the Greeks. Amphimachus's corpse is rescued by Greeks (*Il.* 13.195–96), the two Ajaxes carry out Imbrius's body, with a chilling simile preparing the ground for the *khólos* that drives Oilean Ajax to an extremity of Homeric violence:

Ἴμβριον αὖτ' Αἴαντε μεμαότε θούριδος ἀλκῆς·
ὥς τε δύ' αἶγα λέοντε κυνῶν ὕπο καρχαροδόντων
ἁρπάξαντε φέρητον ἀνὰ ῥωπήια πυκνά,
ὑψοῦ ὑπὲρ γαίης μετὰ γαμφηλῇσιν ἔχοντε,

ὥς ῥα τὸν ὑψοῦ ἔχοντε δύω Αἴαντε κορυστὰ
τεύχεα συλήτην· κεφαλὴν δ' ἁπαλῆς ἀπὸ δειρῆς
κόψεν Ὀιλιάδης, <u>κεχολωμένος</u> Ἀμφιμάχοιο,
ἧκε δέ μιν σφαιρηδὸν ἑλιξάμενος δι' ὁμίλου·
(*Il.* 13.197–204)

And after Imbrius [came] the two Ajaxes, both vigorous in their ferocious valor; and as two lions rip off and carry a goat from snaggle-toothed dogs to the thick undergrowth, lifting it high above the ground in their jaws, so did both helmed Ajaxes hold him high up and strip his armor. And his head from his soft neck, Oilean Ajax cut off, <u>out of *khólos*</u> for Amphimachus, and he cast it throwing it like a ball through the throng.

While this passage is one of the few instances of beheading in the *Iliad*,[55] this is also, after Odysseus' *khólos* for Leucus in *Iliad* 4, the first instance of *khólos* since *Iliad* 4, where *khólos* comes from a comrade's death.

Ajax's extreme action leads to a divine manifestation of *khólos* for the very same Amphimachus. Poseidon, in one of only two passages where an Olympian has *khólos* for the death of a *phílos*, comes to be angered about Amphimachus, whom Ajax had just avenged so brutally. After the beheading of Imbrius's corpse, this passage initiates a self-metamorphosis by Poseidon as Thoas to rouse Idomeneus (*Il.* 13.206–20). Now the motivation for Poseidon's challenge to the will of Zeus is the *khólos* he feels for the death of his grandson.

καὶ τότε δὴ περὶ κῆρι Ποσειδάων <u>ἐχολώθη</u>
<u>υἱωνοῖο πεσόντος</u> ἐν αἰνῇ δηϊοτῆτι,
βῆ δ' ἰέναι παρά τε κλισίας καὶ νῆας Ἀχαιῶν
ὀτρυνέων Δαναούς, Τρώεσσι δὲ κήδε' ἔτευχεν.
(*Il.* 13.206–9)

And just then in his heart Poseidon <u>came to have *khólos* for his grandson</u> who had fallen in the terrible fighting; and he went to go by the huts and ships of the Achaeans, rousing the Danaans, but he fashioned woes for the Trojans.

Amphimachus's roles as grandson of Poseidon and comrade of Ajax have had his death marked twice by *khólos*, once from his mortal *phílos* and once from a member of his family who is a god. But why is *khólos* in play at this point? Is there a sense that the death of someone who was *not* the target is unfair, as contests can be unfair or as Achilles might legitimately claim Agamemnon has been unfair?

Fenik compares Poseidon's rage here to that of Ares over his son Ascalaphus (with italics indicating my emphasis):

There is one similarity between the two passages [the death of Amphimachus (170–81) and (506) the death of Askalaphos] *which is probably accidental.* At N 185 the man killed is Amphimachus, a grandson of Poseidon. The god is

enraged at this (206) and incites the Greeks and Idomeneus again. At N 518 Ascalaphus is the man slain by mistake. He is a son of Ares, who at O 113 is enraged when he hears of it and wants to intervene and take vengeance.
(Fenik 1968, 127)

But the similarity is not accidental. In Book 13 the death of Amphimachus has moved two of his *phíloi* to action through *khólos*, and later in Book 13, at line 518, Ascalaphus perishes in a passage that featured prominently in my discussion of *kótos* in Part I:[56]

τοῦ δὲ βάδην ἀπιόντος ἀκόντισε δουρὶ φαεινῷ
Δηίφοβος· δὴ γάρ οἱ ἔχεν κότον ἐμμενὲς αἰεί.
ἀλλ' ὅ γε καὶ τόθ' ἅμαρτεν, ὃ δ' Ἀσκάλαφον βάλε δουρί,
υἱὸν Ἐνυαλίοιο· δι' ὤμου δ' ὄβριμον ἔγχος
ἔσχεν· ὃ δ' ἐν κονίῃσι πεσὼν ἕλε γαῖαν ἀγοστῷ.
οὐδ' ἄρα πώ τι πέπυστο βριήπυος ὄβριμος Ἄρης
υἷος ἑοῖο πεσόντος ἐνὶ κρατερῇ ὑσμίνῃ,
ἀλλ' ὅ γ' ἄρ' ἄκρῳ Ὀλύμπῳ ὑπὸ χρυσέοισι νέφεσσιν
ἧστο Διὸς βουλῇσιν ἐελμένος, ἔνθα περ ἄλλοι
ἀθάνατοι θεοὶ ἦσαν ἐεργόμενοι πολέμοιο.
(*Il.* 13.516–25)

And Deiphobus as he was stepping slowly back shot him with the shining spear. For indeed he had *kótos* against him always. But he missed him then, and instead he hit Ascalaphus, with his spear, the son of Enyalius. And through his shoulder stuck the heavy spear. And he took his fall in the dust grasping the earth with his hand. Not yet did loud strong Ares come to know this, that his own son had fallen in the strong combat. But he was rather sitting on high Olympus under golden clouds yielding to the counsels of Zeus, just where the other immortal gods were being kept from the war.

Here, it should be noted, the contrast between *khólos* and *kótos* could not be more stark. Where the Trojan Deiphobus's anger is based on the long-past rivalry among Helen's suitors, the immediate death of Ascalaphus is hidden from his divine god-father simply because he was not there to observe it and because, as an Olympian subordinate to Zeus, Ares has yielded to his supreme will. The comparison with Poseidon's reaction to the death of Amphimachus is invited by the parallel between line *Il.* 13.522 (underlined above) and *huionoîo pesóntos en ainêi deiotêti* (*Il.* 13.207) "his grandson having fallen in the grievous battle" and the misfortune of being the victim of a misdirected missile-shot. It will be two books before Ares is told of the death of his son, by Hera, in a treacherous move to arouse a revolt among the gods:

ἤδη γὰρ νῦν ἔλπομ' Ἄρηΐ γε πῆμα τετύχθαι·
υἱὸς γάρ οἱ ὄλωλε μάχῃ ἔνι, φίλτατος ἀνδρῶν,
Ἀσκάλαφος, τὸν φησὶν ὃν ἔμμεναι ὄβριμος Ἄρης.
(*Il.* 15.110–12)

For now I expect woe has been fashioned for Ares; for his son has perished in the battle, the closest to him among men, Ascalaphus, whom furious Ares declares to be his own.

Hera presents us with the central motifs of the theme of *khólos* before the death of a *phílos*, emphasized by the claim of Ares that Ascalaphus is indeed his son. This cruel revelation has its desired effect by eliciting Ares' immediate rage in a manner that traditionally indicates a deep but restrainable wrath,[57] explicitly identified by Athena as *khólos* in line 138 of this passage, as she keeps him from his rage against Zeus:

τῶ σ' αὖ νῦν κέλομαι μεθέμεν χόλον υἷος ἑῆος.
ἤδη γάρ τις τοῦ γε βίην καὶ χεῖρας ἀμείνων
ἢ πέφατ', ἢ καὶ ἔπειτα πεφήσεται· ἀργαλέον δὲ
πάντων ἀνθρώπων ῥῦσθαι γενέην τε τόκον τε.
(*Il.* 15.138–41)

So I order you know to desist from this *khólos* about your son. For already someone better in strength and hand than he has either died or will thereupon die. Difficult it is to save the tribe and offspring of all men.

Then, as Achilles' support of Calchas tests Agamemnon's power, so Ares challenges Zeus to the extent that the supreme god's *khólos* threatens to emerge as a possible reaction to Ares' vengeance:

ἔνθα κ' ἔτι μείζων τε καὶ ἀργαλεώτερος ἄλλος
πὰρ Διὸς ἀθανάτοισι χόλος καὶ μῆνις ἐτύχθη,
εἰ μὴ Ἀθήνη πᾶσι περιδείσασα θεοῖσιν
ὦρτο διὲκ προθύρου.
(*Il.* 15.121–24)

Thereupon a still greater and more difficult *khólos* and *mênis* could have been fashioned from Zeus against the immortals, had not Athena, out of fear for all the gods, rushed from the threshold.

Athena intervenes to stop the anger between the gods just as she intervenes between the Achaeans in Book 1. There she had physically restrained Achilles by grabbing his hair before he could draw his sword and violently attack Agamemnon. Here, in contrast, she restrains Ares from putting his *khólos* into action after getting him to doff his armor:

ὦρτο διὲκ προθύρου, λίπε δὲ θρόνον, ἔνθα θάασσε,
τοῦ δ' ἀπὸ μὲν κεφαλῆς κόρυθ' εἵλετο καὶ σάκος ὤμων,
ἔγχος δ' ἔστησε στιβαρῆς ἀπὸ χειρὸς ἑλοῦσα
χάλκεον· ἢ ἐπέεσσι καθάπτετο θοῦρον Ἄρηα·
(*Il.* 15.124–27)

> She rushed from the threshold, and left the throne, where she sat, and she took from his head the helmet and the shield from his shoulders, and she took and stood up the spear from his firm hand, the bronze spear; and she restrained quick Ares with words.

In both cases, Athena restrains the *khólos* of one who is righteously angry. But she approaches the two situations differently. In the case of Achilles, she pronounces her order succinctly (*all' áge lêg' éridos*, *Il.* 1.210, "But come, stop strife"); but in *Iliad* 15, the situation is pressing in a different manner—we are in the world of the immortals, where the potential for wrath can include the *mênis* of Zeus.[58] Nevertheless, in speaking to Ares she reviews the consequences should Ares pursue his vengeance, in a passage that resembles Nestor's criticism in *Il.* 1.254–84.

> ἦ ἐθέλεις αὐτὸς μὲν ἀναπλήσας κακὰ πολλὰ
> ἄψ ἴμεν Οὔλυμπόνδε καὶ ἀχνύμενός περ ἀνάγκῃ,
> αὐτὰρ τοῖς ἄλλοισι κακὸν μέγα πᾶσι φυτεῦσαι;
> αὐτίκα γὰρ Τρῶας μὲν ὑπερθύμους καὶ Ἀχαιοὺς
> λείψει, ὁ δ' ἡμέας εἶσι κυδοιμήσων ἐς Ὄλυμπον,
> μάρψει δ' ἑξείης ὅς τ' αἴτιος ὅς τε καὶ οὐκί.
> τῶ σ' αὖ νῦν κέλομαι μεθέμεν χόλον υἷος ἑῆος.
> (*Il.* 15.132–38)

> Or do you yourself wish, having had your full measure of evils, to go back forcibly to Olympus, though griefstricken, and then to plant a great evil among the rest of us, all of us? For immediately he will leave the bold Trojans and the Achaeans, but he will come to Olympus to rout us, and he will snatch us one after another, the blameworthy with the blameless. Therefore, I order you now to leave off this *khólos* about your son.

Athena here argues that it is expedient for Ares to cease lusting for vengeance because of the harm that will come to guilty and innocent alike if Zeus learns of Ares' *khólos*.[59]

But this is all about the death of a *phílos*, a theme introduced vitally in *Iliad* 13, with two examples of the *khólos* of divinities (Poseidon and Ares) and, thus far, one example of a mortal's *khólos* for a *phílos*, namely Ajax's for Amphimachus. But even Paris can have this kind of *khólos*. The case in question is the death of Harpalion at the hands of Meriones in *Il.* 13.643ff. This dead warrior was a guest friend of Paris, and—perhaps with irony—the text thus motivates the return of Paris against the Greeks:

> Τοῦ δὲ Πάρις μάλα θυμὸν ἀποκταμένοιο χολώθη·
> ξεῖνος γάρ οἱ ἔην πολέσιν μετὰ Παφλαγόνεσσι·
> τοῦ ὅ γε χωόμενος προΐει χαλκήρε' ὀιστόν.
> ἦν δέ τις Εὐχήνωρ, Πολυΐδου μάντιος υἱός,

. . . .
τὸν βάλ᾽ ὑπὸ γναθμοῖο, καὶ οὔατος.
(*Il.* 13.660–63; 671)

And Paris deeply in his heart came to have *khólos* over his dead companion. For he had been his guest-friend among the Paphlagonians; with anger over this man, he shot his bronze arrow. But there was one Eukhenor, the son of Poluidus the prophet. . . . He struck him between the jaw and the ear.

In such a passage, a clear example of the general case, we see the workings of *khólos* as it engages itself on the battlefield. When a *xenos* ("guest-friend") is killed, the reaction is *khólos*, with its immediate result being a violent act against the killer. The anger is experienced to an intense degree (*mála*).

Another example of *khólos* over the death of one near and dear occurs in *Il.* 16.320, where the death of a brother leads to a *khólos* that motivates an act of vengeful violence. Here Antilochus slays the brother of Maris, Atymnius. This murder causes Maris to seek vengeance, with *khólos* as the accompanying emotion. The *khólos* of Maris against Antilochus happens in Book 16, so that from Book 13 to Book 16 we have a climactic series that displays this kind of anger, from Ajax to Paris to Antilochus, all prefiguring (for the purpose of climax) the greatest example of wrath over the death of a *phílos*. Thus within the story of Patroclus, we have one clear example of *khólos* in response to a companion's death, one that anticipates the central example of this kind *khólos*, the anger of Achilles over the death of Patroclus.

Here, it is important to mark the relationship between the *khólos* that comes from a violation of *timḗ* in the context of a *neîkos* and the one that comes from the slaying of a *phílos*. *Khólos* locates three of the major movements of the *Iliad*: the *khólos* that arises from Agamemnon's appropriation of Briseis (a violation of Achilles' *timḗ*) precedes the *khólos* that marks Achilles' withdrawal from the Achaean camp, a sort of exile. Finally, the *khólos* that arises from the death of Patroclus causes Achilles to return to war for vengeance against Hector.[60]

In *Iliad* 18, Achilles says to his dead friend's corpse:

νῦν δ᾽ ἐπεὶ οὖν, Πάτροκλε, σεῦ ὕστερος εἶμ᾽ ὑπὸ γαῖαν
οὔ σε πρὶν κτεριῶ, πρίν γ᾽ Ἕκτορος ἐνθάδ᾽ ἐνεῖκαι
τεύχεα καὶ κεφαλήν, μεγαθύμου σοῖο φονῆος·
δώδεκα δὲ προπάροιθε πυρῆς ἀποδειροτομήσω
Τρώων ἀγλαὰ τέκνα, σέθεν κταμένοιο χολωθείς.
(*Il.* 18.333–37)

But now since I will go later than you beneath the earth, I will not perform the funerary ritual for you before bringing great-hearted Hector's armor and head—he was your murderer; and twelve shining children of Trojans will I slaughter before the pyre, because of my *khólos* for your death.

Here we can see the manner in which Achilles has magnified his *khólos*. Where Maris sought to slay only the individual murderer of his brother, Achilles drops the blame on the children of the Trojans.[61] It is the flexibility of *khólos* (as manifest in its capacity to identify individuals or groups as objects of its aggression) that makes it so powerful in the epic. Achilles' anger goes through different stages of metamorphosis and, unlike *kótos*, *khólos* presents variations that point to the epic's horrific source of a warrior's violence.

Summary

I have argued that the frequent references to *khólos* in Homeric discourse correspond to regular and traditional patterns of usage. Notably, Homeric poetics has typical ways to indicate the beginning and end of *khólos*. In the *Iliad*, one kind of anger is, as Calchas says, *autêmar* (*Il.* 1.81). It can catch fire immediately from the long-smoldering anxiety over one's honor or it can flame up at a violation coming—so it seems—out of the blue. Moreover, a singer who is to compose an *Iliad* uses traditional strategies for marking the moments at which this anger comes to be and passes away. Furthermore, the prominent effects of *khólos* are utterly different from the almost sublime nature of *kótos*: volatile speech or violent action characterize *khólos*, in a way that we did not see marked for *kótos*. To put it a different way, *khólos*, in contrast to *kótos*, can be rhetorically manipulated so that it is as possible for human beings to bring this violent emotion under control as it is to let it get out of control.

Thus, our most poignant example of *khólos* for the death of one near and dear is in *Iliad* 24, where we might expect it. But the light shot through the prism of *khólos* comes not from a warrior's wrath but from that of an old man, watched by the specimen of war's art that is Achilles.

In addition to affirming the ultimate grounding for *khólos* in the immediacy of the moment, *khólos* emerges where conflict, unfairness, and the death of *phíloi* present themselves. We are in a terrain that differs from that of the nearly cosmological *kótos*, whose goal is *díkē*, whose god is Zeus. *Khólos* is rooted in the physically and psychologically felt response of a human being to the loss of esteem (as in the loss of *timḗ*) or the loss of an esteemed other (as in the loss of a child or friend, one of one's *philoi*). Such concerns place *khólos* at the heart of the *Iliad*.

In the next chapter, my focus will turn to the central issues of the *Iliad*, where *khólos* puts into relief the embassy to Achilles and points to the central position of the *Iliad* within its tradition.

Notes

1. For this kind of battle scene, see Fenik 1968, 139.

2. An exemplary death, as argued by Schein (1984, 73–76); see also Friedrich 1956, 65–66.

3. And we should note the adjective of degree, *mála*, corresponding to the phrase *kholṓsato kēróthi mâllon* ("he came to be the more angry in his heart"), as discussed in Chapter 8.

4. There are other motives for revenge, for example, *ákhos* ("grief"), as in *Patróklōi d' ár ákhos géneto phthiménou hetároio*, *Il.* 16.581, "there was grief for Patroclus over his fallen comrade."

5. As in *Il.* 16.386ff.

6. One can see here a sort of mass/count distinction: Achilles is angry enough to kill 12 children of the Trojans out of *khólos* (*Il.* 18.336–37); but when Zeus has *kótos* the images of natural catastrophe come fast and furious and the summary statement puts the destruction of a culture into a mass: *minúthei dé te érg' anthrṓpōn*, *Il.* 16.392, "and the works of mortals decline." So too for the duel between Paris and Menelaus, where the death of one man is presented as the *télos* of the *kótos*, thus constituting the structural equivalent of all the Trojans, one sole representative stands for the group. In sum, *khólos* is about killing individual persons; *kótos* is about killing the people as a collectivity.

7. The few exceptions, apart from the lines being examined here, are banal: *eidóte khármēs*, *Il.* 5.608; *ephormēthéntes*, *Il.* 6.410 (in a speech); *daízōn*, *Il.* 24.393 (in a speech); *hupophthámenos*, *Od.* 4.547 (in a speech); *lokhḗsas*, *Il.* 22.53; *elthṓn*, *Od.* 24.429 (in a speech). The phrasing of expressions for killing have been meticulously studied by Visser (1987). See the important elaboration and corroboration of this method by Riggsby (1992).

8. This account presents another reason to read *khólon* in *Il.* 15.72 as that of Achilles and not of Zeus. Only the *khólos* of Achilles is a motive force for the death of Hector on the Trojan plain.

9. Notice that the form with the preverb precedes that without. On the repetition of *kteínō*, see *Il.* 18.309, *Od.* 1.299–300, *Od.* 11.411–12, *Od.* 16.400, 402, 404; and compare *Od.* 3.307, *Od.* 11.279–80, *Od.* 14.405.

10. Given the propensity for wordplay in the *Odyssey* (see Louden 1995), it makes sense to compare the name Euryalus to Eurytus and to make the connection to the suitors, to Eurymachus, and among the crew, the rebellious Eurylochus. As for the placement of *éktanen* ("he killed"), see *báll'* ("struck") at *Il.* 1.52 (at clause boundary), indicating dramatic violence.

11. Achilles once again shares the stage only with gods: just as *mênis* has a tendency to signal a connection between the gods and Achilles (Watkins 1977a, Muellner 1992), so too, *kholōsámenos* with *kteínō* is used only with Achilles among mortals, and among immortals, with Artemis and Apollo. For important qualifications of this principle, see Muellner 1996.

12. See Appendix 2, Group 9b.

13. *mḗ ti kholōsámenos rhéxēi kakòn huîas Akhaiôn*, *Il.* 2.195, "lest out of anger he do something bad to the sons of the Achaeans."

14. *Il.* 13.204, and see Janko 1992 at 204–5, who refers us to the games at *Odyssey* 6, where we have already seen *khólos* at work.

15. "Out of anger for his fallen grandson," *Il.* 13. 206–7, *ekholṓthē / huiōnoîo pesóntos*.

16. "And Paris came to be the more angry in his heart," *Il.* 13.660, *toû dè Páris mála thumòn apoktaménoio kholṓthē*.

17. On the mutilation of the corpse, see Segal 1971. He points out that the passage from Book 16 introduces "the verb *aeikízein* for the first time in the *Iliad*." Segal contends that the "brutality toward the bodies of the slain" (Segal 1971, 72) reaches a crescendo in Books 16–22 (and to be continued in the remainder of the poem); in the same way, *khólos* promotes a connection with the death of *phíloi* only in the second half of the poem.

18. On the maltreatment of the corpse see Segal 1971. As Muellner points out no one's corpse is so maltreated in the *Iliad* (Muellner 1996, 145).

19. See the discussion of this passage and issues relating to violence and cannibalism in O'Brien 1993, 81–94.

20. As seen above in Part II, Chapter 1.

21. "On account of victory," *Od.* 11.544, *heíneka níkēs* and "on account of armor," *Od.* 11.554, *heíneka teukhéōn*.

22. See *Od.* 8.109–233, esp. 165, 205. The narrative of Odysseus is in competition with that of the Phaeacian bard.

23. Signaled by *hupódra idṓn* ("glowering") in *Od.* 8.164 and the strong rebuke *xeîn' ou kalòn eeipes; atasthálōi andrì eoikas* ("Stranger you are speaking out of line; you are an uncivil sort," *Od.* 8.166), an echoing response to Euryalus's denunciation (*xeîne*, *Od.* 8.159 ~ 66; *éoikas*, *Od.* 8.164 ~ 66, cf. *eiskō*, *Od.* 8.159).

24. Note the parallel of *peirēthḗtō* (*Od.* 8.205) with *peirḗsom(ai)* (*Od.* 8.158).

25. *Koloúei* closes off this section of his speech with possible wordplay pun on *ekholṓsate* in *Od.* 8.205; for another example of such verbal artistry involving *khólos*, see Louden 1995, 30.

26. For the important and old cultural features manifest in the vocabulary of *xenía*, see the revealing article of M. Schwartz 1982 with 1985, 486–89 and 495–96. And for *éris*, see Nagler 1988, where contextual features are identified (especially 82–83); cf. Hogan 1981. Notice that both *kótos* and *khólos* can respond to violations of *xenía*. What distinguishes the two is the cultural understanding of the event that motivates the emotion. If we were interviewing living informants, we could ask them why violations of *xenía* sometimes lead to a violent but containable *khólos*, while at others such outrages yield *kótos* with dire consequences. Such a possibility makes Calchas's definition necessary in the first place.

27. Compare *hoúneka* with *heíneka níkēs* (*Od.* 8.544, "on account of victory") and *heíneka teukhéōn* ("on account of the arms"), all three in quoted speech.

28. For comparative purposes, consider the relationship between English, "host" and "guest" in the light of "host" (in the sense of an enemy army) as well as "hostile." For all these, see Skeat 1963, under "guest" and "host."

29. *Khólos* shares some of these categories with *mênis* and other terms for anger, such as *éris*. Note that Muellner (1996, 190, with the arguments presented in his Chapters 1 and 2) has secured the meaning of *mênis* as "the name of the sanction for fundamental transgressions of the cosmic order. . . . " See Muellner 1996, 83 for a use of *khólos* in Hesiod in just such a context. See also n. 38 below.

30. It is striking that both these passages invoke the story of Eurytus. Kirk (1985, 216) points out in passing that Philoctetes provides another digression in the catalog,

and, we may now add, he provides another exemplum of a better archer in Odysseus's address to the Phaeacian youth (*Od.* 8.219–20).

31. See in this context Nagy's comment that "the name of the competitive poet Thámuris . . . seems to be the embodiment of the social context for poetic competition" (1979, 311 n, with literature).

32. Despite Chantraine's cautions (*DELG* s.v. *níkē*), both Frisk (s.v.) and Pokorny (761) have good reason to associate the two words. For our purposes, it is clear that the theme of contention is being invoked in these passages through these words.

33. Cf. Nagy 1979, 224, "These words [*éris* and *neîkos*] are appropriate for motivating the Trojan War in particular and the human condition in general."

34. Nagy 1979, 130.

35. Namely, *ētímasen*, 11 ("he dishonored").

36. Cf. *Il.* 1.412; and see, among other examples, Phoenix's attempt to recruit Achilles through a focus on *tīmḗ*, *Il.* 9.601–5.

37. Cf. Riedinger 1976, 257, "la *tīmḗ* du héros, la *tīmḗ* en général, n' est pas celle qui est réclamée par l' individu. Elle est l' objet d' une réponse de la société, mesurée par elle. Plus exactement encore: l'aspect subjectif et l'aspect objectif de *tīmḗ* ne sont pas séparables."

38. See Muellner 1996, 83–84 and 111–12 for the way in which *mênis* and *khólos* interact. That the *mênis* of Apollo attends to major transgressions of the social code has affinities with this competitive notion of *khólos*. *Grosso modo*, *khólos* has at its core non-cosmic issues, such as competition, death on the battlefield, and so on, while *mênis* is centered on cosmic issues, such as violations of the boundary between divinities and mortals, failure to observe death ritual, and the like.

39. This last responding to the *neîkos* of Paris and the three goddesses.

40. See Alcinoos's reassurrance that Odysseus's behavior to his daughter has not led to *khólos* on her father's part, *Od.* 7.309–10.

41. For *mênis* in Book 1, see Muellner 1996, 94–132.

42. *Il.* 1.9, *Il.* 1.78, *Il.* 1.81, *Il.* 1.139, *Il.* 1.192, *Il.* 1.217, *Il.* 1.224, *Il.* 1.283, and *Il.* 1.387.

43. *Il.* 1.192, *Il.* 1.217, *Il.* 1.224, *Il.* 1.283.

44. In general terms at *Il.* 1.81, and specifically at 1.387. The remaining reference is generic, with an oblique reference to Agamemnon (1.139).

45. "He will become angry, the one I approach," *Il.* 1.139, *ho dé ken kekholṓsetai hon ken híkōmai.*

46. *Il.* 1.283 poses a number of problems; for now I suggest that it is well-taken to refer to Achilles' *khólos* and not Agamemnon's. For an outline of the problems see van Bennekom 1984, with Eisenberger 1985 in response. See also Lowenstam 1993, 60–61. The rhetorical force of this passage will be treated in a separate piece.

47. Here magnified to *mênis*.

48. The issue of the taboo against speaking one's own *mênis* comes up here (see Watkins 1977a, with a dissenting view in Turpin 1988; cf. Muellner 1996). Muellner's latest analysis presents a sophisticated view of taboo in regard to Homeric *mênis*, by linking *mênis* as a linguistic entity to the taboo behavior that it sanctions; see Muellner 1996, 191–94 for a careful analysis of this issue. Moreover, it must be noted that here Achilles can speak of no anger, not *mênis*, not even *khólos* as his own, though just a short while earlier he was proudly announcing his *khólos* to Athena (*Il.* 1.217).

49. The *Iliad* has 101 examples of *khólos* forms, with the *Odyssey* showing 36 examples, for a total of 137.

50. For example, *Il.* 1.192, *Il.* 9.157, *Il.* 9.260, *Il.* 9.261, *Il.* 9.299, *Il.* 9.436, *Il.* 9.523, *Il.* 9.646, *Il.* 9.675, *Il.* 9.678, *Il.* 10.107, *Il.* 14.367, *Il.* 16.30, *Il.* 16.61, *Il.* 16.203, *Il.* 16.206, *Il.* 18.111, and so on.

51. I take this passage as referring to the anger of Achilles.

52. At least 5: *Il.* 15.68, 72, *Il.* 18.337, *Il.* 20.301, *Il.* 23.23; perhaps to be included here are the related instances of Patroclus at *Il.* 15.585 and the Myrmidons at *Il.* 16.546.

53. The examples of Odysseus having *khólos* are in Book 4.

54. The only other example of this kind of *khólos* in the *Odyssey* is that of Helius concerning the death of his cattle (*Od.* 12.348), but can they, even in an otherworldly sense, be considered part of the sun's social group? Even if we grant this, remember that Eurylochus, the rebellious crew member, posits this *khólos*; he certainly means by *khólos* the anger of a god over violated *timḗ*. It is important to remember that *timḗ* and *philótēs* are closely bound together. See Riedinger 1976, Muellner 1996, 149–50.

55. The others are *Il.* 11.146, *Il.* 11.261, *Il.* 14.465–68, *Il.* 14.496, *Il.* 20.481; and potentially at *Il.* 17.126, *Il.* 18.176f (Hector's intent against Patroclus); and at *Il.* 18.334–35 (Achilles against Hector). See Fenik 1968, 84 and Janko 1992 at *Il.* 13.201–3. The taking of the enemy's head has a special relationship to anger and violence in many warlike cultures, for which see Rosaldo 1980, 56–57, and 158–59, where she recounts that among the Ilongot, "the celebration of beheadings is itself a sort of commentary on the experience of 'anger,' showing private and disruptive feelings to be part of a larger process that provides for an intense and satisfying collective life." The throng of warriors that frame the rescue of Amphimachus and the mutilation of Imbrios suggest such a collectivity in a sort of halo over Imbrius's head as it manifests its gruesome individuality.

56. See Part I, Chapter 2.

57. *Il.* 15.113–14 on which see Lowenstam 1981.

58. On *mênis* and Zeus see Muellner 1996, 123–29 as well as his chapter 1 for the *mênis* of Zeus among the gods.

59. This entire scene has received illuminating analysis by Muellner (1996, 6–7), where he shows that *mênis* can be rooted in group solidarity among the gods. "[Athena] has in mind not that Ares will act alone on behalf of his son but that all the gods will be roused to action by what Zeus has done to her and the Achaeans" (7). The *khólos* of Ares, located in the site of the death of a *phílos* may lead to a *mênis* that threatens group solidarity. Such a progression has much to do with the genre of the *Iliad* itself, as I hope to show in Chapter 10.

60. See Nagler's clarification of the withdrawal-devastation-return pattern in the *Iliad* (1974, 174). Based on my analysis of *khólos*, I now add to his analysis that the narrative uses the violation of *timḗ* to motivate the first two withdrawals and the death of a *phílos* as the motivation for the last withdrawal.

61. See above note 6.

Chapter Ten

The Embassy, *Χόλος*, and the *Iliad*'s Genre

Iota sings the Embassy
And brave Achilles' stern reply.
Chapman

With the epigraph from Chapman's translation of *Iliad* 9, I mean to turn our focus to the nature of Achilles' reply, what Chapman calls its sternness. This translator of the *Iliad* sees quite clearly the importance of *Iliad* 9: Achilles' reply is unyielding. But there seems to be an expectation of just the opposite—both form and feeling present us with a situation where Achilles just might yield. What does Achilles do by refusing the embassy?

The Achaeans have sent emissaries in the persons of Odysseus, Ajax, and Phoenix to persuade Achilles to relent from his anger. This occasion has caused students of Homeric artistry to take pause and note this turning point in the plot of the poem.[1] My concern with *khólos* leads me to steer the discussion toward Calchas's definition. If *khólos* occurs prominently in the embassy scene, where the goal of the embassy is that Agamemnon reward Achilles and that, reciprocally, Achilles will return, is the meaning of *khólos* relevant to the goal of the envoys to Achilles' tent? What kind of anger is it that the Greek emissaries think they are trying to assuage? After all, it certainly is not *kótos*—this word never shows up in Book 9, and we have seen in Part I the clearly demarcated boundaries within which the anger of feud functions in the *Iliad*. To what extent do the specific qualities of *mênis* apply to the goal of the ambassadors? After all, there are only two cases of *mênis* and related forms in the entire book.[2] If Muellner is right that *mênis* and *philótēs* are here being set beside each other, what has this to do with *khólos*? I will suggest that *khólos* presents a link between these two concepts.

First, in *Iliad* 9 there are more examples of *khólos* than in any other book of the *Iliad* or the *Odyssey*.[3] Second, *khólos* plays a major role in the speeches of the three Achaeans sent to placate Achilles, Odysseus, Phoenix, and Ajax; third, the use of *khólos* in these speeches prepares the ground for some larger claims about *khólos* within the epic tradition.[4]

Of the 16 citations of *khólos* in Book 9, nine of them refer directly to Achilles' anger. Five other individuals are named as having *khólos*, but except for Meleager, each only once.[5] Meleager, whose narrative is presented by Phoenix specifically to convince Achilles to abandon his *khólos*, has his anger identified as *khólos* 3 times.

Now, of the nine instances of Achilles' *khólos* in Book 9, four refer to the possibility that Achilles will set aside his anger, and three of them present instances of the end-line formula *metallḗksanti khóloio* "if he has removed his anger" (*Il.* 9.157, *Il.* 9.261, *Il.* 9.299), one of many phrases that indicate the control that Achilles has over the continuation of his *khólos*. Indeed, the theme of the continuation of *khólos* is repeated at the end of the book when Achilles (in the first example) and then Odysseus (in the last two) assess Achilles' final position at the end of the discussion:

9.646 ἀλλά μοι οἰδάνεται κραδίη χόλῳ[6]
9.675 ἢ ἀπέεειπε, χόλος δ᾽ ἔτ᾽ ἔχει μεγαλήτορα θυμόν[7]
9.678-79 κεῖνός γ᾽ οὐκ ἐθέλει σβέσσαι χόλον, ἀλλ᾽ ἔτι μᾶλλον
πιμπλάνεται μένεος[8]

As for the end of *khólos*, we have seen it to be a major theme of the *Iliad*, one that Calchas's definition prompts us to expect. But this is the first time we have seen both the end of *khólos* and its continuation presented in such a concentrated fashion within one short segment of the poem.

The themes of setting aside one's anger,[9] and of the degrees of *khólos*[10] — that it can be modulated, increased, or decreased—are familiar topics that appear here to refer directly to the anger of Achilles within the context of the ambassador's speeches,[11] beginning with Agamemnon's establishment of the entourage and his catalogue of gifts (*Il.* 9.157) and concluding with Odysseus' description of what went on in the dim light of Achilles' tent. Thus, a way to display the use of *khólos* in *Iliad* 9 is to focus on the mission itself, by looking at *khólos* in the context of each of the speeches in order to draw conclusions in the light of what we have seen in the preceding chapters.

The Speech of Odysseus

The central purpose of Odysseus's speech is to present Agamemnon's offer, but he does so only after a lengthy introduction, in which he tries to capture

Achilles' good will by describing the plight of the Achaeans (*Il.* 9.229–48), followed by a recollection of Peleus's advice to his son, which culminates in the recommendation that *philophrosúnē* ("regard for others") be valued more than anger. Through the end of this section, Odysseus is putting Agamemnon's offer in what he hopes is its strongest light, since the gifts that are being offered are presented as a supplement to the desperate plight of the Achaeans; it is their trouble that Odysseus first hopes will catch Achilles' ear, especially if placed in the mouth of his father. In the next 6 lines, Odysseus concludes the quoted words of Peleus (*Il.* 9.257–58), dovetails his own comment on anger (*Il.* 9.259–60) and ends the prologue by quoting Agamemnon's words exactly (*Il.* 9.255), with a concluding tag that introduces the catalogue of gifts (*Il.* 9.262–63):

> "ληγέμεναι δ' ἔριδος κακομηχάνου, ὄφρα σε μᾶλλον
> τίωσ' Ἀργείων ἠμὲν νέοι ἠδὲ γέροντες."
> ὣς ἐπέτελλ' ὁ γέρων, σὺ δὲ λήθεαι. ἀλλ' ἔτι καὶ νῦν
> παύε', ἔα δὲ χόλον θυμαλγέα· σοὶ δ' Ἀγαμέμνων
> ἄξια δῶρα δίδωσι μεταλλήξαντι χόλοιο.
> εἰ δὲ σὺ μέν μευ ἄκουσον, ἐγὼ δέ κέ τοι καταλέξω
> ὅσσα τοι ἐν κλισίῃσιν ὑπέσχετο δῶρ' Ἀγαμέμνων·
> (*Il.* 9.257–63)

> "And stop your *éris* that fabricates ill, in order that the young and old of the Argives can honor you." Thus the old man enjoined, but you have forgotten. But still even now stop, leave off your *khólos* that is painful to the spirit; yours are the worthy gifts Agamemnon proffers, for your cessation from *khólos*. But come listen to me, and I will list for you as many things as he has promised in the huts.

The rhetoric here is carefully crafted, even though the particulars of Achilles' case force this approach to fail.[12] For example, Odysseus introduces the notion of Achilles' anger by quoting Peleus and using the more neutral *éris* (*Il.* 9. 257), rather than leading with the *khólos* that is at the heart of the matter.[13] The honor (cf. *tíōsi*, *Il.* 9.258) that the Argives will bestow, based on their *philophrosúnē* (*Il.* 9.256, "thoughtfulness"), is parallel to the gift of the gods (*kártos . . . dṓsousi*, *Il.* 9.253–54, "They will give . . . strength"), mentioned at the beginning of this segment. Odysseus's admonition thus dovetails and magnifies that of Peleus. That is to say, by the time Odysseus is ready to introduce the gifts of Agamemnon he has pictured Peleus's approving reference to the gifts to the restraint of anger on the part of one who has *philophrosúnē* ("thoughtfulness"). And by the time Odysseus makes his central request—what the entire mission is about—in a striking stylistic maneuver (enjambed imperative, bold caesura, with a second imperative, *paúe', éa*), the ground has been carefully prepared for the two first instances of *khólos*, in successive lines (*Il.* 9.260, 261).

Moreover, the phrase *metallḗksanti khóloio* ("after having put aside *khólos*") at the end of Odysseus's preamble is used also at the end of his enumeration of Agamemnon's gifts. In this way he frames the quoted section by using a from of *khólos* to closes his speech:

> ταῦτά κέ τοι τελέσειε μεταλλήξαντι χόλοιο.
> εἰ δέ τοι Ἀτρείδης μὲν ἀπήχθετο κηρόθι μᾶλλον
> αὐτὸς καὶ τοῦ δῶρα, σὺ δ' ἄλλους περ Παναχαιοὺς
> τειρομένους ἐλέαιρε κατὰ στρατόν, . . .
> (*Il.* 9.299–302)

> These are the things he would accomplish for you, were you to set aside your *khólos*. But if the Atreid is hateful in your heart the more, himself and his gifts, you should pity the rest of the Panachaeans being bested along the camp. . . .

The *khólos* phrase frames the enumeration of the gifts (*Il.* 9.261 and *Il.* 9.299), thereby signaling the beginning and end of the formal offer from Agamemnon. In addition, Odysseus adds terms of degree (*all' éti kaì nûn*, *Il.* 9.259, "But still more even now" and *kēróthi mâllon*, *Il.* 9.300, "the more in his heart"), such as we have seen are important to the thematics of *khólos*. But the phrase *metallḗksanti khóloio* also marks an important moment in Odysseus's presentation, one that Achilles soon picks up: Odysseus has conspicuously left out Agamemnon's rhetorically disastrous coda to his offer. This omission on Odysseus's part has been rightly emphasized in recent studies.[14] I add that *khólos* is the key word that marks where Odysseus has made his editorial cuts in Agamemnon's speech. The positive impetus of the catalogue of gifts is dropped after Agamemnon realizes how intractable Achilles might turn out to be, even so as to launch into an aside about Achilles' extreme behavior.

As far as Achilles' anger is concerned, the important point to make is simply that it is within cultural norms and human expectations that his anger be relinquished. That the anger is *khólos* makes this possible and the terms of Agamemnon's offer address that possibility. Odysseus, the canny orator, notices immediately that the last words after his formal offer show Agamemnon magnifying his superiority (*Il.* 9.160) and pointing to the world of the gods where Hades alone is implacable (*Il.* 9.158); Odysseus, we can assume, suspects that the speech is rhetorically inept: not only does Agamemnon remind Achilles of his divine status, but he also demotes him to a king of the underworld. Instead of repeating this disastrous segment of Agamemnon's speech, Odysseus avoids it by using the frame *metallḗksanti khóloio* to bring closure to the catalogue of gifts. This puts *khólos* within Achilles' reach as an object that he can and should handle. The kind of *khólos* that comes from unfair dealings, culturally unacceptable practices that bring rewards to the underhanded can, on Odysseus's (and Agamemnon's) terms, be set aside. The final strategy of Odysseus's speech turns away from *khólos* and emphasizes grief (*apḗkhtheto*, *Il.* 9.300[15]) and pity (*eléaire*, Il. 9.302).

In sum, Odysseus uses *khólos* three times in his speech, twice repeating Agamemnon's own words, with the result that his rhetorical inventiveness is marked with the *khólos* phrase. Thus, he comes to emphasize the need to withdraw from anger by putting the directly quoted *khólos* phrase at the beginning and end of Agamemnon's offer, clearly using it to structure parts of the speech. In fact, the repeated phrase (*metallḗksanti khóloio* "after having put aside *khólos*") sets in the foreground the quality that he wishes to emphasize about *khólos*: that it is malleable. In a sense, Odysseus has taken Agamemnon's offer[16] and modified it so as to convince even an Achilles: Odysseus has invoked Achilles' father, the solidarity of the Achaean group, and finally, the valor of Achilles before the onslaught of Hector.[17]

The Speech of Phoenix

Anger is a central topic of Phoenix's speech,[18] when Phoenix begins the story of Meleager, a narrative within the genre of *kléa andrôn* "fames of men." The anger of Meleager is identified as *khólos*. In the passage quoted below, the prologue to the tale, Phoenix cedes to Achilles that there is no offence in having *khólos* until an offer from the offending party has been put on the table. That condition has now been met. But, he goes on to say, there are hero tales where the hero's *khólos* can be shown to overstep its bounds.[19]

The thematic link between the story of Achilles and that of Meleager is *khólos*, as can be seen from the proem to the song of Meleager:

> πρὶν δ' οὔ τι νεμεσσητὸν κεχολῶσθαι.
> οὕτω καὶ τῶν πρόσθεν ἐπευθόμεθα κλέα ἀνδρῶν
> ἡρώων, ὅτε κέν τιν' ἐπιζάφελος χόλος ἵκοι·
> (*Il.* 9.523–25)

> Before then there is no offense taken at *khólos*. Thus even among our ancestors have we heard of the fames [*kléa*] of heroic men, whenever excessive *khólos* reached them.

Thus Phoenix's tactic differs from that of Odysseus, who had gingerly introduced *khólos* as a transition from the quoted speech of Peleus (see above) to the catalogue of gifts. But even there the emphasis on the term was unmistakable when Odysseus repeated it twice in as many lines (*Il.* 9.260, *Il.* 9.261) as Phoenix here does within three lines.[20] So, too, when the narrative shifts from the story of the Kouretes and the Aitolians to Meleager's anger at his mother, *khólos* shows up three times (*Il.* 9.553, *Il.* 9.565, *Il.* 9.566).

Phoenix has introduced a parallel to Achilles' case that involves the withdrawal of the hero with his companion, the refusal to fight being part of that withdrawal. What I have to add to this often cited point, is that there is a technical term in the Homeric singers' vocabulary for the anger that accompanies that kind of action: that term is *khólos*. Put most strongly, what I am suggesting is that Phoenix is not only telling Achilles one of the *kléa andrôn* of those who have lived before, but that he also is telling a specific kind of song, to be identified with the term *khólos*. This word, *khólos*, is the technical term in the oral poet's vocabulary for the story of the withdrawn hero, who refuses to fight, seeks refuge with a companion, and returns only too late.

With this suggestion in mind and with a view to supporting this claim in the course of the rest of this chapter, I propose to continue with Phoenix's use of *khólos* in this speech. Phoenix has already given us some indication that *khólos* would play a major role in his task as envoy. He began, first, by responding to Achilles' rejection of Agamemnon's offer in these words:

> εἰ μὲν δὴ <u>νόστον</u> γε μετὰ φρεσί, φαίδιμ' Ἀχιλλεῦ,
> βάλλεαι, οὐδέ τι πάμπαν ἀμύνειν νηυσὶ θοῇσι
> πῦρ ἐθέλεις ἀΐδηλον, <u>ἐπεὶ χόλος ἔμπεσε θυμῷ</u>. . . .
> (*Il.* 9.434–36)

> If it is a <u>return</u> that you consider in your mind, glorious Achilles, and if you are unwilling at all to defend the swift ships against the ravaging fire, because <u>*khólos* has fallen into your heart</u>. . . .

Remembering that Achilles has just mentioned his own *mênis* (*Il.* 9.426),[21] note that, after a pause to collect his thoughts (*Il.* 9.432), Phoenix responds in a manner that alludes to the first word of the *Iliad* together with a reference to the genre of the *Odyssey*, through the word *nóstos* ("return").[22] Perhaps it is Achilles' reference to *mênis* that sets the stage for the tight concentration on anger and return in Phoenix's speech. Certainly *nóstos* is the first word out of Phoenix's mouth after the awkward silence that accompanied Achilles' rebuff of Odysseus. Phoenix may be putting Achilles in the wrong epic, especially after the speech of the most famous *nóstos* hero of them all.[23] Here we find a significant collocation of a key word for Homeric epic (*nóstos*) with *khólos*, a word that Phoenix turns to again and again throughout his speech.[24] Thus, Phoenix begins his presentation by juxtaposing the two generic terms for Homeric epic, *nóstos* and *khólos*, a point that will become even more important as the negotiations in Achilles' tent moves forward.

Phoenix positions *khólos* at pivotal moments in his speech to Achilles. For example, by juxtaposing it to *nóstos*, he shines the spotlight first of all on the *khólos* of Achilles, where Odysseus had gingerly mentioned it in the course of giving structure to his catalogue of gifts. In the first exemplum of Phoenix's speech, his autobiography,[25] in a passage that otherwise poses textual problems of some magnitude,[26] Phoenix uses the word *khólos* to indicate the anger that a god forces him to suppress so that he not be damned by his social group:

τὸν μὲν ἐγὼ βούλευσα κατακτάμεν ὀξέι χαλκῷ·
ἀλλά τις ἀθανάτων παῦσεν χόλον, ὅς ῥ' ἐνὶ θυμῷ
δήμου θῆκε φάτιν καὶ ὀνείδεα πόλλ' ἀνθρώπων,
ὡς μὴ πατροφόνος μετ' Ἀχαιοῖσιν καλεοίμην.
(*Il.* 9.458–61)

I wished to slay him with the sharp bronze, but one of the immortals put a stop to [my] anger, who brought to my attention the report of the polity and the many reproaches of men, so that I not be called a parricide among the Achaeans.

The parallel to Odysseus's *paúe', éa dè khólon* should not be missed, nor should the parallel to *Iliad* 1.[27] Of the numerous parallels between Phoenix's autobiographical anecdote and the details of the quarrel in *Iliad* 1, one feature stands out, namely, the use of *khólos*. It is precisely in the context of this kind of anger that Phoenix is trying to identify with Achilles, since they both had *khólos* at older authority figures and both had to be restrained by a divinity.

The Meleager Story and *Khólos*

In the tale of Meleager, *khólos* is used with its full force. Six of Phoenix's 7 uses of *khólos* are in that story (beginning at *Il.* 9.525), with all but one (*Il.* 9.538) referring to Meleager. The sequence begins with Phoenix's announcement that he is about to tell one of the *kléa andrôn* (*Il.* 9.524), further specified as belonging to the class that shows *hóte kén tin/ /epizáphelos khólos híkoi* (*Il.* 9.525) "whenever raging anger comes on one." That anger itself is thematic for Phoenix's tale has long been recognized and does not need to be argued here, nor am I interested in establishing the existence of a "Zorn des Meleagros" and its relation to a "Zorn des Achilleus."[28] More important for us is to ask whether *khólos* has a special status in such examples of early epic.

Here *khólos* functions as does *mênis* at *Il.* 1.1 and *ándra* at *Od.* 1.1.[29] A number of features highlight the analogy that I am making here. For example, after the initial mention of *khólos* (*Il.* 9.525), Phoenix begins the narrative by filling in the background to the *khólos* of Meleager. After pointing to the *mênis* of Achilles, the narrative begins by backing up and telling us about the anger of Apollo, specified in the phrase *hò gàr basilêi kholōtheís*, *Il.* 1.9, "for he had become angry with the king." It is not until the anger of Apollo is engaged that the quarrel between Achilles and Agamemnon comes into play, with *khólos* playing a crucial role. So, too, in the tale of Meleager, once the *khólos* of the hero of the past is invoked, Phoenix steps back to narrate the *khólos* of a god, here not Apollo, but that other offspring of Leto, Artemis:

καὶ γὰρ τοῖσι κακὸν χρυσόθρονος Ἄρτεμις ὦρσε,
χωσαμένη ὅ οἱ οὔ τι θαλύσια γουνῷ ἀλωῆς

Οἰνεὺς ἔρξ'· . . .
. . . .
ἡ δὲ χολωσαμένη δῖον γένος ἰοχέαιρα
ὦρσεν ἔπι, χλούνην σῦν ἄγριον ἀργιόδοντα
(*Il.* 9.533–35; 538–39)

Now golden throned Artemis had roused an evil among them, out of her anger, that Oineus had not at all given the first fruits in the garden's knoll. . . . And, she, because of *khólos*, the godborn archer-goddess, sent it forth, a shaggy boar, wild, sharp-tusked.

The wrath of Artemis presents a parallel to the wrath of the hero, which is held in abeyance until Phoenix says

ἀλλ' ὅτε δὴ Μελέαγρον ἔδυ χόλος, ὅς τε καὶ ἄλλων
οἰδάνει ἐν στήθεσσι νόον πύκα περ φρονεόντων,
ἤ τοι ὃ μητρὶ φίλῃ Ἀλθαίῃ χωόμενος κῆρ
κεῖτο παρὰ μνηστῇ ἀλόχῳ, καλῇ Κλεοπάτρῃ,
. . . .
τῇ ὅ γε παρκατέλεκτο χόλον θυμαλγέα πέσσων,
ἐξ ἀρέων μητρὸς κεχολωμένος. . . .
(*Il.* 9.553–56; 565–66)

But when *khólos* entered Meleager, since it causes to swell in their bodies the minds even of the very prudent, in as much as he was angry in his heart at his own dear mother, Althaea, he lay beside his wedded wife, fair Cleopatra. . . . Next to her he lay digesting his heartpaining *khólos*, with *khólos* over the curses of his mother.

The temporal mark of a proem's style (*hóte dḗ*) and the reintroduction of the term *khólos*, leads to a relative clause, in much the same way as *mênis* is succeeded by *hḗ murí' Akhaioîs álege' éthēke,* "which sent countless woes on the Achaeans," (*Il.* 1.2),[30] or *ándra* by *hós mála pollà . . . /plángkhthē* "who wandered much," *Od.* 1.1–2.[31]

The last example of *khólos* in Phoenix's exemplum shows again how words lead to wrath. Here the speech act that provokes *khólos* consists of the curses of Meleager's mother: *eks aréōn mētròs kekholōménos* (*Il.* 9.566) "in a state of anger because of the curses of his mother." This pulls the story of Meleager directly into line with the first part of the *Iliad*, where the great wrath has its inception in a verbal altercation with an older man.

In sum, Phoenix presents *khólos* in two lights, the first by which he shows the god stopping his own *khólos* before he killed his father, the second by which *khólos* appears to be part of the epic tales known as the *kléa andrôn*; in these cases the *khólos* arises from a *neîkos*, with the quarrel leading to an anger that causes the hero to withdraw. But at this point we might ask to examine that other kind of *khólos*, the one that responds to the death of a *phílos*.

The Speech of Ajax

In none of the speeches of *Iliad* 9 is *khólos* more directly considered than in the last speech, that of Ajax. In contrast to what Ajax will say, Phoenix presents a vision of catastrophe resulting from Achilles' loss of *tímē*, if Achilles' story turns out to be parallel to that of Meleager; and Odysseus's initial vision of catastrophe had centered on the disaster to Achaean interests, if Achilles refused to accept the gifts of Agamemnon. But now Ajax has something different to say on the subject of anger. Ajax, who will not speak to Odysseus in the *Odyssey's nekuia* (*Od.* 11.543–64), here addresses Odysseus but pointedly not Achilles. Instead he first meets Achilles with silence.[32] At the beginning of this speech (*Il.* 9.624–36), Ajax suggests to Odysseus that Achilles' intractability threatens the mission.[33] During this introductory blast at Achilles, Ajax refers to one context where a hero can have a potent reaction and yet restrain his desire to act: the death of a *phílos*:

> σχέτλιος, οὐδὲ μετατρέπεται φιλότητος ἑταίρων
> τῆς ᾗ μιν παρὰ νηυσὶν ἐτίομεν ἔξοχον ἄλλων,
> νηλής· καὶ μέν τίς τε κασιγνήτοιο φονοῖο
> ποινὴν ἢ οὗ παιδὸς ἐδέξατο τεθνηῶτος·
> καί ῥ' ὃ μὲν ἐν δήμῳ μένει αὐτοῦ πόλλ' ἀποτίσας,
> τοῦ δέ τ' ἐρητύεται κραδίη καὶ θυμὸς ἀγήνωρ
> ποινὴν δεξαμένῳ· σοὶ δ' ἄλληκτόν τε κακόν τε
> θυμὸν ἐνὶ στήθεσσι θεοὶ θέσαν εἵνεκα κούρης
> οἴης·
> (*Il.* 9.630–38)

> Wretch, he does not even turn to consider the *philótēs* ("friendship") of his companions, through which we honor him beyond all others, pitiless one: Yes anyone would receive recompense for the murder of a brother or even for his dead son; that man, on the one hand, continues on in his land, having paid a great deal, and his heart and manly spirit is restrained, with the receipt of the payment. But, for you, on the other hand, the gods have made the heart in your chest unassuageable and bad, for the sake of only a girl.

Ajax engages themes of *khólos* when he charges that even the murder of a *phílos* can be put into the perspective given by the institution of *poinḗ*, so that the heart can be restrained. Although he does not use the word *khólos*, we saw at the beginning of Part II that Helen's *phármakon ákholon* ("drug that stills anger") had as its case *a fortiori* the death of precisely these two members (among others) of one's *phíloi*:

> οὐδ' εἴ οἱ κατατεθναίη μήτηρ τε πατήρ τε,
> οὐδ' εἴ οἱ προπάροιθεν ἀδελφεὸν ἢ φίλον υἱὸν
> χαλκῷ δηιόῳεν, ὁ δ' ὀφθαλμοῖσιν ὁρῷτο.
> (*Od.* 4.224–26)

Not even if his mother should die or his father, nor if openly with bronze they slay his brother or beloved son, and he see it with his own eyes.

In this passage, the first line (*Od.* 4.224) is Odyssean and the second (*Od.* 4.225) is Iliadic, because the second presents a war situation and the first (at least potentially) a domestic one.[34] But Helen's drug is meant to still the *khólos* that arises from *all* such occasions. In Ajax's speech, the verbs of restraint are ones we have seen before apply to *khólos*-like situations: *erētúetai* (cf. *Il.* 1.192) and *allēkton*, the latter having a prominent place in *Iliad* 9 through the form *metallḗksanti* (*Il.* 9.260, 261). So that even though Ajax fails to mention *khólos*, we know that he must be indirectly referring to it. The other speakers have referred directly to it and Ajax, being careful not to speak at first directly to Achilles, is also careful to avoid mentioning the main problem, the *khólos* of Achilles. Perhaps as a warrior, second only to Achilles, the term for a warrior's wrath must or might as well go unsaid.

But Achilles sees what the speaker has avoided mentioning.[35]

Αἶαν διογενὲς Τελαμώνιε, κοίρανε λαῶν,
πάντα τί μοι κατὰ θυμὸν ἐείσαο μυθήσασθαι·
ἀλλά μοι οἰδάνεται κραδίη χόλῳ, ὁππότε κείνων
μνήσομαι, ὥς μ᾽ ἀσύφηλον ἐν᾽Αργείοισιν ἔρεξεν
᾽Ατρεΐδης, ὡς εἴ τιν᾽ ἀτίμητον μετανάστην.
(*Il.* 9.644–48)

Ajax god-descended son of Telamon, leader of men, you seem completely to have spoken something according to my spirit. But the heart swells on me with *khólos*, whenever I remember those things, how he harshly treated me among the Argives, Agamemnon did, as if I where someone without honor, an outcast.

Ajax's suppression of the word *khólos* is met by Achilles with a metaphor (*oidánetai*, *Il.* 9.646) that calls to mind this kind of anger's association with the body, such as we saw originally in Calchas's definition and exactly such as Achilles heard in Phoenix's exemplum.[36] At the beginning of Achilles' response to Ajax, he acknowledges his predisposition to accept his word (*Il.* 9.645). Achilles wishes to identify the *khólos* he has with his loss of *timḗ* "honor," (*Il.* 9.648 *atímēton* "without *timḗ*"), common enough ground for the two preeminent warriors of the Achaeans. In fact, this same kind of *khólos* over the loss of honor will consume Ajax, after that other ambassador, Odysseus, wins the arms of Achilles.[37] But beyond Achilles' range of view at this moment is that other kind of *khólos*, the kind derived from the death of a *phílos* that will impel Achilles toward the climax of the narrative. It turns out that "brave Achilles' stern reply," as Chapman formulated it, is deeply traditional, part of the epic of a *khólos* hero. I will argue in the next section that there are special features of this kind of anger that give it this exalted place in Homer's epic. There are strong indications in the *Iliad* that *khólos* is a genre term, one for the withdrawn hero's unhappy wrath.

The Genre of the *Iliad*: "Paris, You're No Achilles"

Thus far we have seen the prominent role played by *khólos* in a crucial moment of the *Iliad*'s narrative in *Iliad* 9. It seems to me that the use of *khólos* in the context of the *kléa andrôn* points to a term important for the literary history of early epic. This assertion can be supported from the evidence provided by an old crux in Homeric studies.

The role of *khólos* in the speeches of *Iliad* 9, sheds light on a passage that has been troublesome since antiquity. In *Il.* 6.326 Hector uses *khólos* in a way that seems distinctly inappropriate. Hector reproaches Paris on Hector's return to Troy in Book 6. The basis of the reproach is a certain *khólos*. Paris seems in fact to be angry at no one. What could motivate Hector to call Paris's emotional state *khólos*?

Since Aristarchus, this passage has been singled out as controversial, because there seems to be no reason for Hector to refer to any anger at all on Paris's part.[38] The scholarly debate hinges on the motive for Paris's *khólos*. Some feel comfortable with a putative *khólos* of Paris against Trojans.[39] Others find this problematic, since Hector has no basis on which to style Paris "angry" as he approaches him in the midst of dallying with Helen. Is the *khólos* of Paris explained by his denial that he experiences it and that he has *ákhos* instead?[40] Paris may be angry at the Trojans for their criticism of him after his rescue by Aphrodite in Book 3.

Why *does* Hector refer to Paris's *khólos*? Who died and made Paris angry? This passage has frustrated readers, inclined as those readers are to looking for a specific cause for Paris's anger. In light of a "wrath of Paris," parallels emerge: Hector and Paris, on the one hand, and Achilles and Meleager, on the other. From a neoanalytic point of view, this might indicate that another earlier epic has been refashioned to fit the *Iliad*'s narrative:

> Paris and Helen are of course presented as acting the parts of Meleager and Cleopatra, though only for a while. Just for this reason, too, Paris is to some extent surrounded by an aura of bravery. As happens with the heroes, Meleager and Achilles, an embassy seems to come to him too for appeasement, so to speak.
>
> (Kakridis 1949, 49)

Such a position can be set beside the analytic view that an older epic with Paris angered for some explicit reason is being mined by a redactor who has not bothered to give the *Iliad*'s audience an insight into what motivates Paris's *khólos*.

But the focus in the secondary literature on this passage is almost always on what *khólos* can mean to a reader of *this passage*, without a firm grasp of the use of the word from the point of view of the speaker in the narrative ensemble itself, that speaker being Paris's brother, Hector. Irene de Jong's application of the narratological concept of "focalization" provides the tool needed to show *khólos* not from the viewpoint of an objective narrator, but rather through Hector's perspective in this scene.[41] When Paris denies that he has *khólos*, he rejects Hector's interpretation of what he sees as he encounters him with Helen. Thus, what matters here is the view of Hector—that Paris seems to have *khólos*. Adopting the idea that *khólos* in this scene is focalized through Hector, I ask what function this has for *Iliad* 6. What leads the narrative to show Hector thinking that *khólos* is applicable to Paris?

In order to answer that question, I point to the use of the negative phrase *ou mèn kalá* (*Il.* 6.326). Indeed, in interpreting Paris's situation Hector bothers to style it as a remarkably *bad* instance of *khólos*. This question can be put into sharper focus by examining the hypothesis that *khólos* is the term for the genre of the *Iliad*, that *khólos* here refers specifically to the story of a withdrawn hero, the same narrative type as the story of Achilles or of Meleager. Hector is not referring to an event, wherein a particular warrior has withdrawn from a particular battle, but to a *story* about such an event.

In this manner, Hector is deploying a theme familiar to the tradition; what seems anomalous to an audience outside the Homeric context might not only be understandable, but it may also be conveying a meaning that we would be wise to understand. First, the hero withdraws over some dispute with a superior. Second, in his withdrawal, he is accompanied by his closest companion. Third, he is petitioned by his friends, in Kakridis's terms, in an ascending scale of affection, so that the last petitioner wins him over but too late for him to get the benefit of his return to his network of social relations.[42]

Now Phoenix's speech in the embassy depends on understanding that scenario. But in the scene between Paris and Hector, it is Hector's viewpoint and his alone that draws the analogy to Meleager and Achilles, a point of view that Paris strongly comes to deny in his response to Hector (*Il.* 6.333–41). So I suggest that Hector's use of *khólos* here is accurate and does not refer, as some scholars contend, to an anger of Paris outside the *Iliad*, nor to any putative remarks made by unnamed Trojans after the duel in Book 3. Furthermore, Hector uses *khólos* here as a criticism of Paris's behavior. Indeed, the term *khólos* pinpoints the inappropriateness of putting Paris in the same league with Achilles and Meleager.

Here is a list of the features of this scene and its narration that are relevant to *khólos*:

1. Hector finds Paris in this situation:
   a. He is in his quarters.
   b. He is a soldier not at war.
   c. He is with one near and dear.
   d. He is being approached by a close relation.
   e. He is being asked to return to the fight.[43]

2. These five items (1.a-e) point to the notion of *khólos* as it describes the situation of Meleager and Cleopatra, and Achilles and Patroclus.
3. What Hector says about Paris's situation is that it is *ou kalá* (*Il.* 6.326) "not good."
4. The word *kalós* can refer to the competent formation of an utterance or song.

Now both Kakridis and Willcock have argued that something of this nature is going on here.[44] But if *khólos* is the term for the genre to which the *Iliad* belongs, as does the story of Meleager, and if it is as such available for Hector's rebuke that Paris is a poor excuse for a *khólos* hero, something looms larger than the anger of Paris.

It is possible to add to our picture of early hexameter genre names beyond the term we are lucky enough to have cited in Homer, namely, *nóstos*. This term is available to us hanks to passages such as this:

> τοῖσι δ' ἀοιδὸς ἄειδε περικλυτός, οἱ δὲ σιωπῇ
> ἥατ' ἀκούοντες· ὁ δ' Ἀχαιῶν νόστον ἄειδε,
> λύγρον, ὃν ἐκ Τροίης ἐπετείλατο Παλλὰς Ἀθήνη.
> (*Od.* 1.325–27)

> And the renowned singer began to sing for them, and they sat in silence listening; and he sang the Achaeans' Return, the sad one out of Troy as enjoined by Pallas Athena.

Homeric narrative identifies for us a traditional genre by calling it *nóstos*, and the term survives into the later tradition to be identified by Proclus with a distinct part of the epic cycle. Thus, the traditional singers called one kind of poem a *nóstos*, of which we have one complete performance in the *Odyssey*.[45]

Now for ancient Greece, we have insufficient information about the rest of the "taxonomy of oral tradition"[46] to verify the likelihood of *khólos* as such a term. But a comparative literature of early cultures might suggest that a variety of terms in such taxonomies proves useful to the practitioners of verbal art. Consider, for example, the culture of medieval Ireland. As Proinsias MacCana has elucidated in *The Learned Tales of Medieval Ireland* (1980), the tale-types found in Ireland are "obviously the continuation of an ancient Celtic inheritance."[47] The rich Irish taxonomy includes terms derived from verbs (*táin*, verbal noun of *do-aig* "drives off, drives away"; *im(m)ram* "sea-voyage", verbal noun of *imm-rá* "rows around, navigates") as well as from nouns (*slógad*/ *slúagad* "a hosting, a military expedition" from *slóg* / *slúag* "host, army"). As a deverbative, *nóstos*, when used to signify a genre of literary production, is structurally parallel to the terms derived from verbs in Irish.[48] If *khólos* is another term for a kind of narrative, it resembles (in its application to a type of narrative) more the Irish denominative terms than the deverbative ones.

The term *khólos*, I suggest, is a likely candidate for a poetic technical term.[49] Proof that it is can only be had by the discovery of a list of such terms. But through the process of internal poetic reconstruction we can build the argument in a different way. Through comparative evidence it can be inferred that oral poets may indicate subgroupings of their repertoire through terms having something to do with the actions recounted in their narratives. There is one clear instance of such a term in the Greek tradition, the one that applies to the *Odyssey*. In this study of *khólos*, beginning with Calchas's definition, there emerges another term, the one that is used for the composition that explores the anger of three Homeric heroes: Achilles, Meleager, and, briefly, Paris. In *Il.* 6.326, *khólos* refers not to an emotion but to a narrative speech act, an element of discourse that Hector is evaluating as formally flawed (*ou kalá*).[50]

There are other indications in these lines that support the notion of Hector criticizing a narrative speech act and not an action when he critiques Paris's *khólos* as being *ou kalá* ("not good") (*Il.* 6.326). First, *kalá* used as part of a negative adverbial predicate shows sharp criticism.[51] Thus, when Zeus sends Iris to prevent Hera and Athena from entering the war to support the Greeks contrary to his *boulḗ*, he declares that for all these gods to fight would be bad: *ou gàr kalà sunoisómetha ptólemónde* (*Il.* 8.400), "For it will be unseemly for us to prosecute such a war." So too Antinoos predicts and evaluates the beggar Odysseus's ultimate withdrawal from Ithaca: *nûn dḗ s' oukéti kalà dièk megároió g' oíō / àps anakhōrḗsein* (*Od.* 17.460–61), "Surely now I no longer think that you will make a clean departure from the hall, in making your retreat." Just as Hector rebuked Paris, Ajax rouses the Achaeans to battle by means of a strong rebuke of their reluctance to enter the fray: *humeîs d' oukéti kalà methíete thoúridos alkês* (*Il.* 13.116), "But in no seemly fashion are you any longer holding back from brave valor." Thus the phrase *ou . . . kalá* is traditional in a context rebuking those who hold back from battle.

Moreover, in two significant passages discourse is evaluated as to whether it is *kalón* or not. In one, Eumaeus criticizes Antinoos' speech concerning the propriety of feeding beggars by saying that he speaks *ou kalá*: *Antíno', ou mèn kalà . . . agoreúeis* (*Od.* 17.381), "Antinoos . . . you make speech that is not fair." In another passage, in a manner quite close to Hector's rebuke, Priam praises the "death tale" of his son as told by Hermes (*Il.* 24.388) disguised as the *therápōn* of Achilles: *hōs moi kalà tòn oîton apótmou paidòs énispes* (*Il.* 24.388) "since you have spoken so well about the death of my ill-fated son." This line provides support for the argument that *kalós* and related forms can be used to evaluate speech acts as well- or ill-formed. Priam's speech also gives a parallel to Hector's use of *tónde* in *Iliad* 6. These two lines are especially revealing when set next to each other:

ὥς μοι <u>καλὰ τὸν οἶτον</u> ἀπότμου παιδὸς <u>ἔνισπες</u>.
(*Il.* 24.388)

How well you have told that violent death of my ill-destined son.

δαιμόνι', οὐ μὲν καλὰ χόλον τόνδ' ἔνθεο θυμῷ.
(*Il.* 6.326)

My, how ill-considered is this *khólos* of yours.

In each line, *kalá* is an adverbial term that evaluates an epic subgenre, in the one case identified as *oîton* and in the other as *khólon.* In the first passage, *oîton*, does not refer to Hector's death as a *fact*, but rather to the *account* (*énispes*, "you have told," *Il.* 24.388) of Hector's demise as presented just now by Hermes, in effect a performance of the death of Hector.[52] Thus, Priam uses *kalá* to evaluate a particular performance within the tradition of epic. "How well you have presented a version of my unlucky son's death" is a telling paraphrase of Priam's words to Hermes.[53]

What Paris has projected or performed in the second passage from *Iliad* 6, is a version of an epic tale narrated visually by the tableau which Hector sees before him as he enters the room. Hence, *khólon tónde* does not refer to any putative "anger" on Paris's part—there is no such anger in this scene. The reference, rather, is to the scene as a whole, as a kind of performance, told in this case from the point of view of Hector, a warrior returning from battle. One can imagine Hector with this *tónde* gesturing to Helen, the bed, the servants, even to Paris as he combs out his horse-hair helmet; then as Hector includes his own presence as a quasi-ambassador with a sweep of his hand, he says "A fine '*khólos*-epic' *you* have here, my friend."[54] In a sense, I conclude, Hector may be the earliest literary critic of early epic, since he points to the impropriety, given the circumstances of this performance, of a subgenre of the *kléa andrôn* ("songs of men"). Perhaps we can even see him as an early critic of ecphrases, taking the tableau before him and finding it wanting in verisimilitude.

In conclusion, *khólos* as used in *Il.* 6.326 and throughout Book 9 is the term that the tradition uses for its epic about Achilles. Just as performers and audiences had a traditional name for an epic genre that is the foundation for the narrative about Odysseus's return home, namely, *nóstos*, so there is a name for the genre forming the basis of the poem about Achilles. That name is *khólos*.[55]

Notes

1. The literature on *Iliad* 9 is immense, but my concern is to elucidate the aspect of this segment of the poem that helps with our understanding of Calchas's definition. Thus, for our purposes Muellner's work on *mênis* in *Iliad* 9 provides suitable background material. See also in the recent literature Nagy 1979, 49–58; Muellner 1996, 138–55; Nagler 1990; Scodel 1982; Rosner 1976.

2. *Il.* 9.426, *Il.* 9.517, the first instance in a speech by Achilles and the second in a speech by Phoenix.

3. There are 16 occurrences of *khólos* and related forms in Book 9, with 10 in Book 4, and 8 in Book 1; the *Odyssey* shows, as might be expected, the most examples in the gore-filled Book 22, but there are still only five examples, less than a third of that in *Iliad* 9.

4. The role of *khólos* in Book 9 as demonstrated in this chapter can be used as evidence to support the notion that book-length structures provided functional means for Homeric narrative artistry. That the book divisions of the *Iliad* respond to compositional practice remains a vital possibility. Cf. Nagy 1996, 161–62 n. 30, 181–84.

5. The examples are Agamemnon's anger at *Il.* 9.33, an instance of potential anger over a speech (here of Diomedes); Phoenix's anger at *Il.* 9.459 over his father's treatment of his behavior; Artemis's anger at being deprived of the first fruits at *Il.* 9.538; and there is one general allusion to the anger of heroes at *Il.* 9.523; all other references in *Iliad* 9 are either to Achilles or Meleager.

6. "But my heart continues to swell with *khólos*. . . ."

7. "Thus he spoke, but *khólos* still continues to hold his great hearted spirit."

8. "That one is unwilling to quench his *khólos*, but still the more is he filled with *ménos*."

9. Usually showing forms of *-paúō*, or the like.

10. As expressed in such formulations as *éti mâllon, líēn*, and so forth.

11. The "exception" is Agamemnon's direct reference to the relaxing of Achilles' anger at line 157, but since this line is, in an important way, quoted by Odysseus at 261, in can be considered as within the speeches of the ambassadors.

12. See Muellner 1996, 142–43, for a critique of Odysseus's presentation of the notion *philótēs*, since it is indeed *philophrosúnē* (256) that Odysseus opposes to the anger of Achilles.

13. On the association of *éris* and *khólos*, see Hogan 1981, 21 and 40–41 ("because success and fame are so highly valued, reason and propriety must vie with the *khólos* that accompanies *éris*"), the most telling example being *Il.* 18.107–8 (on which see the next chapter).

14. Mentioned in an important analysis by Whitman 1958, 192; see also Nagy 1979, 51–52, Muellner 1996, 143. I take this striking maneuver as part of the poetics of Homeric compositional practice. It is not obligatory for a messenger to deliver a message unmodified; see Iris's modification of Zeus's admonitions to Hera and Athena in *Il.* 8.423–24

15. Note the use of *kēróthi mâllon* here, an adonic clausula typically found with *(e)kholṓsato*). Is this a formulaic euphemism designed to move the rhetorical context away from *khólos*, as if matters were already settled?

16. Itself problematic; see Muellner 1996, 141–43.

17. The material extent of Agamemnon's offer cannot be modified, only its frame. Thus the problem remains, despite Odysseus's best effort, that Agamemnon is proffering an "emulous offer of gifts as an assertion of the *giver's* prestige" (Muellner 1996, 141).

18. Rosner's 12 instances (1976, 316, n. 10) need to be supplemented by the one instance of *mênis*, 517 (see above), 8 of these 13 being forms of *khólos*, with the other forms related to *khṓomai*. The relation of *khólos* to *khṓomai* will be explored in a separate study.

19. On *khólos* and *némesis*, see *Il.* 5.757–62, *Od.* 14.282–4, *Il.* 6.335, *Il.* 8.407 = 8.421; closely related to this passage are *Od.* 18.227 and *Od.* 22.59.

20. And Phoenix will then repeat *khólos* in successive lines at 565–66; each of these instances involve kinds of polyptoton, varying between nominal forms (at 260–61) or between verbal and nominal forms as here at at 565–66.

21. On which see Muellner 1996, 193; and especially note in this context Muellner's suggestion that Achilles' mention of his own *mênis* (through a verbal derivative) directly implicates the beginning of our *Iliad*.

22. On the directness of Phoenix's response see Rosner 1976, 315.

23. It should be remembered that Achilles in withdrawing threatens to give himself a *nóstos*.

24. See again Rosner 1976, 316 for the importance of *khólos* here, but I resist the notion that *khólos* and *mênis* are "synonyms," in that *mênis* occurs in precisely delineated contexts, while *khólos* can be used as an unmarked term for anger.

25. The term is from Scodel 1982; see also Rosner 1976.

26. See West 1982, Scodel 1982; to my knowledge, van Thiel's new edition is the first modern edition to promote 458–61 from the apparatus to the text proper.

27. Cf. Scodel 1982.

28. Cf. Schadewaldt on such issues at 1966, 139.

29. With Muellner (1976), I point out that Phoenix's bold statement at *Il.* 9.517–18 (*ouk àn égōgé se mênin aporrípsanta keloímēn / Argeíoisin amunémenai khatéousí per émpēs*, *Il.* 9.517–18, "I would not bid you to set aside your *mênis* to defend the Argives, though they be in dire need") presents a reference to *Iliad* 1.1. Thus the beginning of the Meleager tale is prepared for by a reference to the proem, the beginning of the *Iliad*; we can add here that the use of *epizaphelôs khalepaínoi* at Il. 9.516 in reference to Agamemnon's anger (mitigated in Phoenix's view by his offer of gifts) is in harmony with *epizáphelos khólos* at Il. 9.525. A function of the proem and its features is to call attention to thematic material through the use of keywords developed subsequently throughout the course of the overall composition. Cf. Kahane 1992 and Walsh 1995.

30. It is appropriate to see *epizáphelos* (*Il.* 9.525) as parallel to *ouloménēn* at *Iliad* 1.1, and to *polútropon*, at *Odyssey* 1.1, each being a 4-syllable word which is expanded by a relative clause as typically used in a proem. The separation between the first mention of *khólos* and the second in this regard may pose no problem whatsoever; alternatively, the separation between adjective and relative clause can be attributed to the non-professional style of this performance. In recounting the *kléa andrôn* to his friends (*en d' humîn eréō pántessi phíloisi*, *Il.* 9.528) Phoenix is bound by different expectations of style than would be, say, Demodocus in the court of Alkinoos. On distinctions between singers of different social status, cf. Segal 1994, 142–63. Professional singers before their audiences can be expected to have different performance styles than non-professionals. Segal notes the difference between Achilles' song in *Iliad* 9 and the songs of bards (Segal 1994, 153). These distinctions can be expanded: *khólos* as a theme can be used in mythic exempla as well as in full blown narratives, so that the theme emerges in differing modes, even while retaining its identity as theme.

31. Features typical of the traditional Homeric proem abound in this part of Phoenix's narrative; besides the ones already noted, see also the anaphora *póll' / pollà* at *Il.* 9.567 and *Il.* 9.568 corresponding to nearly identical (and often noted) anaphora, alliteration and polyptoton at the beginning of the *Odyssey* (*pollôn / pollà, Od.* 1.2, 3), and (apart from anaphora) the emphasis on quantity in the corresponding relative clause at the beginning of the *Iliad* (*Il.* 1.2–3, *murí' . . . / pollàs*). All of this is in preparation for the sudden noise of the battle *(Il.* 9.573) drawing the attention of those in Achilles tent to

the most important part of the narrative, namely, the besieged city seeking Meleager's return.

32. On this feature of his speech and the importance of silence as a signifying element of traditional speech, see Martin 1989, 142–43.

33. See again Muellner 1996, 143–68.

34. The second also shows exclusively male deaths.

35. As he did in Odysseus's speech, see Muellner 1996, 141–43.

36. Here the *khólos* that swells in his heart recalls Phoenix's imagery of *khólos* at *Il.* 9.553–554, *khólos hós . . . oidánei* ("*khólos* that swells . . ."). Achilles took Phoenix's exemplum to heart.

37. See above.

38. Heitsch 1967, 222; particularly insightful is L. Collins 1988, 27–39, with a thorough review of the literature to that time. And see Robert 1901, 196–98.

39. See for example Mawet 1979, 311, and for the relationship of *ákhos* to *khólos*, 308–313.

40. *Il.* 6.335–36; on *ákhos* and *khólos* see Mawet 1979, 308–13, Nagy 1979, 79–80.

41. de Jong 1987.

42. See Kakridis 1949, 18-24; cf. Nagy 1979, 104–5.

43. See again Kakridis 1949, 18–24, and cf. Willcock 1956–1957.

44. See Collins 1988.

45. On *nóstos* as genre see Nagy 1979, 97 n. 2, with Frame 1978 on the thematics of *nóstos*.

46. The phrase is MacCana's (1980, 21).

47. MacCana 1980, 73.

48. See Frame 1978, 6–33 for the derivational history of *nóstos*.

49. Note that we moderns have easily come to call the *Iliad* "the wrath" of Achilles. See my Introduction.

50. On distancing anger terms from "emotion," see Muellner 1996, 26, with reference to *mênis*. The complex relationship between emotion and cultural practice needs separate treatment. See my Introduction.

51. On *kalós* in Homer see Shipp 1978. Shipp's examples from *Iliad* 6 (1978, 206–7) are consistent with my interpretation of *kalós* as referring to the competence of an item of discourse.

52. What has impressed Priam so strongly is the delicately worded praise of Hector's value to the city of Troy (*Il.* 24.384–85).

53. In preparation is a study of *oîtos* as a potential generic term in early Greek poetry; an argument can be made for a connection with Old Irish *aided* ("death tale," a tale type recorded in the lists studied by MacCana [1980]).

54. This is not the last time that *khólos* is evaluated: In 16, Patroclus rebukes the *kind* of *khólos* that Achilles manifests (*Il.* 16.30: *mḕ emé g' hoûtos ge láboi khólos* "would that *this khólos* not take me"); later, imaginary Myrmidons similarly say, *hōde kakòs khólos émpese thumôi*, *Il.* 16.206, "This is an evil *khólos* that has fallen into your heart." Earlier Agamemnon imagines certain Trojans minimizing his threat to them: *aith' hoútōs epì pâsi khólon telése' Agamémnon*, *Il.* 4.178, "I wish Agamemnon always this kind of success for his *khólos*." Such self-consciousness about whether *khólos* is good or bad is reminiscent of the *Odyssey's* concern with whether a *nóstos* is good or bad. In passing, I note that evaluating *kótos* in this way is out of the question.

55. For a suggestive collocation of *khólos* with *nóstos* see *Od.* 1.78.

Chapter Eleven

The Culture and Poetics of *Χόλος* in the *Iliad*

The complexities of *khólos* also take us into the realm of poetics, especially in terms of the formulation with which this study began, Calchas's own statement: *eí per gár te khólon ge kaì autêmar katapépsēi* . . . (*Il.* 1.81), "For even if he should digest it completely in a day. . . ." And this is no chance phrasing, as we can see from the formula *khólon thumalgéa péss-* (*Il.* 4.513) "to digest heart-paining *khólos*," as used by Apollo to describe the state of Achilles in anger, or later from Phoenix's tale of Meleager, where he constructs the image of Meleager digesting his anger by the side of Cleopatra: *tē̂i hó ge parkatélekto khólon thumalgéa péssōn* (*Il.* 9.56), "by her did he lie, digesting his heart-paining *khólos*." Moreover, images based on Greek *péssō* are not restricted to notions of anger.[1]

Now, the text presents us with still other moments when *khólos* seems to ask for a theory of Homeric metaphor that would unpack its rich formulations: *khólos* seems to be curable;[2] enters one;[3] swells inside one;[4] can hold one's spirit;[5] is quenchable;[6] provides nourishment,[7] falls down from above.[8]

Having shown that Calchas's distinction between *khólos* and *kótos* depends for its demonstration on the differing contexts and the complexities presented to the reader by those contexts and having argued for widely different meanings for the kinds of anger represented by these two words, I still have left some crucial features of Calchas's original words. What does he mean by "digesting" anger when he tells Achilles that a king *khólon autêmar katapépsēi* (*Il. 1.81*) "digest his anger that day"?

When we immediately respond that it is a metaphor, this raises more questions than the one asked. Metaphor, assuredly, remains a vexed topic in Homeric studies,[9] so that we cannot merely refer a complex list, such as that which *khólos* presents to us, to some handy theoretical matrix. Instead, in this chapter I elucidate how *khólos* works in relation to its contexts in terms of one perspective on metaphor, to see if that makes clear some of what is going on in Homer. My reason for so doing is that the striking incidents of *khólos* in metaphorical settings compel us to pose *some* answers—even tentative ones—about how metaphors for anger are related to *khólos* in Homer.

The approach I use here to help understand *khólos* in the Homeric tradition can be studied in Lakoff and Johnson 1980, where we find techniques for the "systematic investigaton of expressions that are understood metaphorically."[10] The brief summary here is not meant to provide a full defense of the approach, which in the field of metaphor studies must be controversial.[11] Nonetheless, the success of this approach in dealing with *khólos* points out a direction to explore the further implications of a full-blown theory of Homeric metaphor based on these principles.

For Lakoff and Johnson, "most of our conceptual system is metaphorical in nature," with the result that to understand human cognition is to engage in the understanding of how metaphors "structure how we perceive, how we think, and what we do" (1980, 4). Such an approach has particular value, in my view, when an emotion is being examined, where "emotional concepts are . . . very clear examples of concepts that are abstract and yet have an obvious basis in bodily experience."[12] "Anger," Lakoff continues, "is a particularly rich example: it has a very elaborate conceptual structure" (1987, 377).

For our purposes, I accept, for the sake of argument, that the metaphors we examine can be *either* "creative" or ordinary. Now I am not going to provide a distinction between a "poetic" metaphor and one imbedded in the language, because on the view adopted here all such cases are metaphorical; what is important is to see how a concept such as "anger" or *khólos* is structured on the basis of a coherent cultural system of metaphor before we attempt a poetic analysis of the results of such processes. The notion of coherence is developed in Lakoff and Johnson (1980, 87–105), where numerous examples show that a group of statements can be inconsistent among themselves but coherent in terms of the metaphors being presented. In our case, we have a number of inconsistent metaphorical schemes, such as that *khólos* can be digested and that it can be quenched; on the surface these seem to be different ways of conceptualizing anger. The theory I adopt shows that these different conceptualizations of *khólos*, inconsistent though they be, come to form a coherent part of the metaphorical system that underlies *khólos*. This conjunction of difference and coherence fits Lakoff and Johnson's view that "in general, complete consistency across metaphors is rare; coherence, on the other hand, is typical" (1980, 96).

In sum, I suggest there is a coherent conceptual organization underlying anger in Homeric Greek, such as can be understood by looking at the metaphorical properties of the Homeric use of *khólos*.[13] A few basic principles are key to a project. The first is that "the words and expressions of a language can *code*, that is, be used to express aspects of a given conceptual metaphor to a greater or lesser extent."[14] Lakoff and Kövecses go on to point out that one can judge the productivity of such a code by noting the number of expressions related to it and, furthermore, that "the words and fixed expressions of a language can *elaborate* the conceptual metaphor."[15] In their examination of American English's metaphorical systems for anger, Lakoff and Kövecses (1987) identify *anger is heat* as the central metaphor, that is then coded by the words and fixed expressions in the language. Thus, to say "they were having a heated argument" is to code the central metaphor. The metaphor can be elaborated through expressions such as "Let him stew," where we see the indication that the anger is that which continues over a long period of time, at the same level of intensity.[16] For this discussion, I need one further concept from this method, in order to see how metaphors for anger come to be elaborated in Homer. Through metaphoric entailments, our knowledge about one part of experience is transferred to a second, namely, for example, from what we know about heat to what we are trying to express about anger. If it is clear that a protracted conversation is occurring and that the participants show that they are angry, it is possible from our knowledge that heat produces steam, to say that "they got all steamed up."[17]

Here are examples of metaphor used with *khólos* in Homeric diction (all from the *Iliad*):

> *Il.* 1.81 εἴ περ γάρ τε χόλον γε καὶ αὐτῆμαρ καταπέψῃ . . .
> For even if he digests completely his *khólos* even in a day . . .
>
> *Il.* 4.513 μάρναται, ἀλλ᾽ ἐπὶ νηυσὶ χόλον θυμαλγέα πέσσει.
> But he digests his heart-paining *khólos* by his ships.
>
> *Il.* 9.565 τῇ ὅ γε παρκατέλεκτο χόλον θυμαλγέα πέσσων,
> He slept with her, as he digested his heart-paining *khólos*.
>
> *Il.* 16.203 σχέτλιε Πηλέος υἱέ, χόλῳ ἄρα σ᾽ ἔτρεφε μήτηρ,
> Wretched son of Peleus, yes, your mother nursed you on *khólos*.

The first three examples use the verb *péssō*, to indicate the bodily process of digestion,[18] which indicates that, based on the terms of the metaphor, *khólos* is being taken as a kind of food. Using Lakoff and Johnson (1980, 25–32), I view this as the kind of metaphor, where "our experience of physical objects and substances provides a further basis for understanding" (25). In this case, the metaphor *anger is food* conceptualizes an emotion by referring to features of the entity or substance, food, continued as it is in the fourth example (*Il.* 16.203), where the food metaphor is even more explicit.[19]

But it is clear that by itself such a metaphor depends on correspondences between a source domain (food) and a target domain (anger). Here is one way that the metaphor *anger is food* is elaborated in the Homeric conceptual system:

Anger is food:

- it is consumed, *katapépsēi, Il.* 1.81, "completely digests it";
- it comes into the body (*thumalgéa, Il.* 5.513, *Il.* 9.565, "giving pains in the heart"; see also, *Il.* 18.110, *en stḗthessin*, "in the chest."
- it can be different types of food (in *Il.* 16.203, Patroclus refers to Thetis's mother's milk as *khólos*);[20] cf. *phármaka* ("drugs" at *Il.* 22.94).
- it has taste, *Il.* 18.109, *glukíōn mélitos*, "sweeter than honey"; cf. *drimús khólos*, *Il.* 18.322, "bitter *khólos*."
- it enters the body from outside, *Melégron édu khólos, Il.* 9.553, "*khólos* entered Meleager", cf. *Il.* 19.16; and note especially, *bebrōkòs kakà phármak', édu dé té min khólos ainòs, Il.* 22.94, "having eaten the evil poison, terrible *khólos* entered him" (where the participle *bebrōkṓs* guarantees this interpretation of the metaphor).

This group presents a coherent view of anger as being a kind of food that has certain attributes of culinary entities in early Greek culture, but not all of them. Thus, although anger can be seen as having taste, as being consumed in the body, which it enters from the outside, and as coming in different types and being either nutritive or poisonous, the system makes no attempt to elaborate the metaphor to include the concept of "meal" or "sacrifice," so important to the typical experience of consuming food in the Homeric poems.[21] Instead, only certain aspects of the category "food" are appropriated and elaborated to understand in directly experiential terms what otherwise would be a purely abstract notion, *khólos* or "anger."

But this is not the only metaphor involved in the understanding of *khólos* in the Homeric poems. The early Greek complex of ideas involved in health maintenance features *khólos* as a form of disease. In this case *khólos* is seen as something that is or causes a disease:

- *khólos* is a disease; one elaboration that emerges here is that anger can be treated:
- *khólos* can be cured, *Il.* 4.36, *khólon exakésaio,* "you would cure *khólos*"; *Od.* 3.145 *hōs tòn Athēnaíēs deinòn khólon exakésaito,* "Thus did he cure the terrible *khólos* of Athena."

This particular metaphor has a relationship to the metaphor *anger is food*, as can be seen from the context of *Il.* 4.36. Zeus, vexed as he is (*még' okhthḗsas, Il.* 4.30 "having come to be greatly vexed"), characterizes Hera's anger through the hyperbolic suggestion that she would cannibalize the Trojans if she were left to her own devices:

εἰ δὲ σύ γ' εἰσελθοῦσα πύλας καὶ τείχεα μακρὰ
ὠμὸν βεβρώθοις Πρίαμον Πριάμοιό τε παῖδας
ἄλλους τε Τρῶας, τότε κεν χόλον ἐξακέσαιο.
(*Il.* 4.34–36)

But if you were to approach the gates and great walls and you ate Priam raw and the sons of Priam and the other Trojans, then you would have thoroughly cured your *khólos*.

Here the digestive metaphor is picked up by *bebrṓthois,* and we have a pair of metaphors working together:

Anger is food:
Food is consumed.
Anger is a disease:
It can be cured by consuming a certain food.

In this way there is a correspondence between the seemingly inconsistent metaphors *anger is food* and *anger is a disease*, which is also present in the simile of the serpent that eats *kakà phármaka* and induces *khólos* (*Il.* 22.94); that is to say, besides the "evil drugs" there is the possibility of consuming "good drugs" that would produce the opposite (and hence curative) result. Here Zeus, in a hyperbole, suggests that cannibalism would be the only *cure* for Hera's *khólos*. Moreover, the metaphor *anger is a disease* can be further connected to eating through these elaborations:

Anger is food:
Food can be consumed thoroughly and finished (*katapépsēi*, *Il.* 1.81)
Anger is a disease:
Anger (*khólos*) can be cured

A disease can be cured thoroughly and finished (in both examples above, where we find the preverb *ex-* used to indicate completeness). Thus, although both metaphors are inconsistent with respect to their surface meaning (*disease* is a different category from the category *food*), the metaphorical system turns out to be coherent because *khólos*, in both instances, is seen as being able to be brought to a conclusion through the natural course of time, through physiological processes such as digestion or healing. In this way, Zeus's seeming mixed metaphor makes perfect sense as part of the extensive metaphorical system in Homer for *khólos*. The metaphorical system is coherent, though inconsistent.

The elaboration of the metaphor *khólos is food* also helps understand passages where *khólos* is seen to be inside the body.

Ἥρῃ δ' οὐκ ἔχαδε στῆθος χόλον.
(*Il.* 4.24)

But for Hera, her chest could not contain the *khólos*.

The body thus presents itself, in a manner consistent with the food metaphor (used explicitly a little later in this same passage), as a container for *khólos*.[22] Thus, *khólos* is conceptualized as part of a process whereby it enters the body and is consumed; alternatively, instead of being consumed and, hence, becoming less and less, it can increase, as in these examples:

ἀλλ᾽ ὅτε δὴ Μελέαγρον ἔδυ χόλος, ὅς τε καὶ ἄλλων
οἰδάνει ἐν στήθεσσι νόον
(*Il.* 9.553)

But when *khólos* entered Meleager, which swells the mind in others' bodies as well

ἀλλά μοι οἰδάνεται κραδίη χόλῳ
(*Il.* 9.646)

But my heart swells with *khólos*

In both cases, however we view the differences accounting for *kradíē, nóon,* and *stḗthea*, it is inside the body that *khólos* swells.[23] Since, through the digestive metaphor, *khólos* is inside the body, its increase will manifest itself as swelling.

In both the digestive and the healing metaphor, *khólos* is positioned inside the body, and when we adopt the notion that the metaphors can be described in a systematic fashion, certain other unique formulations can be interpreted in such a way as to fit the system. For example, in the same speech where Zeus accuses Hera of desiring to cannibalize the Trojans, he strikes a deal with her, that he be allowed to destroy a city where mortals loyal to her are found:

ὁππότε κεν καὶ ἐγὼ μεμαὼς πόλιν ἐξαλαπάξαι
τὴν ἐθέλω, ὅθι τοι φίλοι ἀνέρες ἐγγεγάασι,
μή τι διατρίβειν τὸν ἐμὸν χόλον, ἀλλά μ᾽ ἐᾶσαι·
(*Il.* 4.40–42)

Whenever I come to be eager to wipe out a city, the one I want, where the mortals are near and dear to you, don't grind down my *khólos*, but allow me.

"Grind down" is more appropriate as a translation for *diatríbein* than the usual "delay" for which there is no good parallel in the Homeric diction for *khólos*.[24] But keeping in mind the curative metaphor, consider the passages where we find highlighted the literal meaning of *tríbō* and related forms:

ἔνθα μιν ἐκτανύσας ἐκ μηροῦ τάμνε μαχαίρῃ
ὀξὺ βέλος περιπευκές, ἀπ᾽ αὐτοῦ δ᾽ αἷμα κελαινὸν
νίζ᾽ ὕδατι λιαρῷ, ἐπὶ δὲ ῥίζαν βάλε πικρὴν

χερσὶ διατρίψας, ὀδυνήφατον, ἥ οἱ ἁπάσας
ἔσχ' ὀδύνας· τὸ μὲν ἕλκος ἐτέρσετο, παύσατο δ' αἷμα.
(*Il.* 11.844–48)

Having stretched him out he cut the sharp-barbed arrow from his thigh with a knife, and he washed off the black blood from him with warm water, and he applied thereon a bitter root that kills pain (one which soothes every pain), after having ground it out with his hands. The wound began to dry, and the blood ceased to flow.

Here Patroclus, standing in for Machaon and Podaleirios, tends to the wounded Eurypylus by applying the standard techniques of Homeric health care that include surgery (*támne makhairēi*, "cut it out with a knife"), antisepsis (*níz' hudati liarôi* "he washed it with warm water"), and herbal medicine (*epì dè rhízan bále pikrễn*), "he applied thereon a bitter root") derived by "grinding" (*diatrípsas*) the herb, here with his hands.[25] For *tríbō*, the sense of grinding or wearing away is also present in a simile from *Iliad* 20:

ῥέε δ' αἵματι γαῖα μέλαινα.
ὡς δ' ὅτε τις ζεύξῃ βόας ἄρσενας εὐρυμετώπους
τριβέμεναι κρῖ λευκὸν ἐυκτιμένῃ ἐν ἀλωῇ,
ῥίμφά τε λέπτ' ἐγένοντο βοῶν ὑπὸ πόσσ' ἐριμύκων,
(*Il.* 20.494-97)

And the black earth was flowing with blood, as when someone yokes male broadfaced oxen to thresh the white barley on the well-built threshing floor, and easily did it turn to husks under the feet of the lowing oxen.

Here the notion of transformation by grinding is applied to grain, as it was to medicinal herbs, so that we can reliably see *-tríbō* as indicating an action that is used metaphorically by Zeus in his speech to Hera by way of its connections with different kinds of vegetable matter.

In the speech by Zeus, *khólos* depends on a correspondence between the medical meaning of *khólos* and the digestive meaning:

Anger is food:
Food is *prepared by grinding* natural material, such as grain.
Anger is disease:
Medicine used to treat the disease is *prepared by grinding*.

In this latter case, we can see that the connection between *khólos* and disease is elaborated metonymically, rather than metaphorically. That a plant used to treat an illness is ground up to make a medicine implies that the act of grinding up is part of the treatment of the disease. Thus, treating the disease "grinds it up," so that finally, to treat *khólos* is to "grind it up." So to "grind one's *khólos*" can mean to cure it. This notion then is coherent both with the medicinal and with the digestive part of the metaphorical system for *khólos*.

Related to this metaphorical system is the example with which we began our exploration of *khólos*, Helen's drug:

> ἔνθ' αὖτ' ἄλλ' ἐνόησ' Ἑλένη Διὸς ἐκγεγαυῖα·
> αὐτίκ' ἄρ' εἰς οἶνον βάλε φάρμακον, ἔνθεν ἔπινον,
> νηπενθές τ' ἄχολόν τε, κακῶν ἐπίληθον ἁπάντων.
> ὃς τὸ καταβρόξειεν, ἐπὴν κρητῆρι μιγείη,
> οὔ κεν ἐφημέριός γε βάλοι κατὰ δάκρυ παρειῶν,
> οὐδ' εἴ οἱ κατατεθναίη μήτηρ τε πατήρ τε,
> οὐδ' εἴ οἱ προπάροιθεν ἀδελφεὸν ἢ φίλον υἱὸν
> χαλκῷ δηιόῳεν, ὃ δ' ὀφθαλμοῖσιν ὁρῷτο.
> (*Od.* 4.219–26)

> There in turn godborn Helen took thought of other things; immediately she threw a drug into the wine that they were drinking, one that allays grief, and anger, and causes forgetfulnesss of all ills. The one who swallows it, whenever it is mixed in the mug, would not in the day cast down a tear from his cheeks, not even if his own mother died or his father, nor if before his very eyes they cut down a brother or beloved son.

Here, our approach to the conceptual system that houses *khólos* provides a motivation at the level of diction and meaning for the only occurrence of α-privative with *khólos*. Since *khólos* takes conceptual depth from the realms of nutrition and from medicine, *khólos* provides the link between Helen's *phármakon*, "drug," and the drink the company thinks it is enjoying.[26] That a drinking potion can have magical properties may well be cross-cultural, but the collocation of the two substances (medicinal herbs and comestibles) with the notion of *khólos* (the anger of the warrior) is bound to the intricate conceptual web displayed in Homeric poetry for *khólos*.[27]

Before seeking to motivate this group of metaphors diachronically, one more type of metaphor needs to be brought into the fold, namely, the metaphor involving fire. This type of image should come as no surprise to us, at least after Cedric Whitman's familiar demonstration of the importance of fire imagery in the *Iliad*. He stresses the ubiquity of fire in the cultural activities of the Homeric Greeks, in their funerals, sacrifices, watchfires, cooking, and the making and the use of their armor. For Whitman, the symbolism of fire is embodied in the fight with the river in *Iliad* 21: "But the really striking thing about Book XXI is the contest between fire and water" (1958, 140–41), itself made explicit when Hephaestus brings the contest to an end by quenching the fire:

> Ὣς ἔφαθ', Ἥφαιστος δὲ κατέσβεσε θεσπιδαὲς πῦρ,
> ἄψορρον δ' ἄρα κῦμα κατέσσυτο καλὰ ῥέεθρα.
> (*Il.* 21.381–82)

Thus he spoke; and Hephaestus quenched the fiercely blowing fire; and back with the current did the fair streams flow.

Since in the Homeric poems fire has a particular relationship to anger ("anger and fire are inseparably associated," Whitman 1958, 130),[28] *khólos* comes into play with the phraseology of fire, as we see in Odysseus's report to Agamemnon of the embassy's failure to get Achilles to quench his wrath:

Ἀτρεΐδη κύδιστε, ἄναξ ἀνδρῶν Ἀγάμεμνον,
κεῖνός γ' οὐκ ἐθέλει σβέσσαι χόλον, ἀλλ' ἔτι μᾶλλον
πιμπλάνεται μένεος, σὲ δ' ἀναίνεται ἠδὲ σὰ δῶρα.
(*Il.* 9.677–79)

O son of Atreus, most glorious, lord of men Agamemnon, that man is not willing to quench his *khólos*, but still more is he full of anger, and he denies you and his gifts.

That *khólos* takes the place of fire in Odysseus's metaphor is clear from passages like *katà d' ésbesen aithómenon pûr* (*Il.* 16.293), "and he put out the flaming fire," where Patroclus quenches the fire that is about to engulf the ships, and *Héphaistos dè katésbese thespidaès pûr* (*Il.* 21.381), "and Hephaestus quenched the fiercely blowing fire," where Hephaestus quenches the fire that threatens the river Scamander.

Furthermore, Whitman goes on to insist that *khólos* has a special relationship to fire, as when Achilles gazes at the arms that Thetis has delivered him in *Il.* 19.16–17 (*hōs eîd' hṓs min mâllon édu khólos, en dé hoi ósse / deinòn hupò blephárōn hōs ei sélas exepháanthen*, "And as he gazed the *khólos* entered into him the more, and there in his eyes shone terribly as if a flame").[29] Furthermore, the image of smoke at *Il.* 18.110 depends for its effect on the connection of fire and *khólos*.[30] Moreover, when Agamemnon asks Odysseus for the result of the embassy, he once again sets the image of the ships being set afire next to the *khólos* of Achilles:

εἴπ' ἄγε μ', ὦ πολύαιν' Ὀδυσεῦ, μέγα κῦδος Ἀχαιῶν,
ἤ ῥ' ἐθέλει νήεσσιν ἀλεξέμεναι δήιον πῦρ,
ἦ ἀπέειπε, χόλος δ' ἔτ' ἔχει μεγαλήτορα θυμόν;
(*Il.* 9.673–75)

But come, much praised Odysseus, great glory of the Achaeans, tell me whether he is willing to ward off the blazing fire from the ships or does he refuse, and does *khólos* continue to hold his great-hearted spirit?

Odysseus's response draws in the figure of "quenching fire" in a way that picks up the connection of *khólos* to fire (*Il.* 9.677–79, quoted above). Achilles' refusal to quench his anger is thus linked to his refusal to help the Achaeans, a refusal resulting in the literal setting of fires that threaten their *nóstos*.[31] Achilles, after all, specifically uses the image of the burning ships to mark a promised reentry into the war:

οὐ γὰρ πρὶν πολέμοιο μεδήσομαι αἱματόεντος,
πρίν γ' υἱὸν Πριάμοιο δαΐφρονος,"Εκτορα δῖον,
Μυρμιδόνων ἐπί τε κλισίας καὶ νῆας ἱκέσθαι
κτείνοντ' Ἀργείους, κατά τε σμῦξαι πυρὶ νῆας.
(*Il.* 9.650–53)

For I will not take thought of bloody warfare, until the son of Priam, godly Hector, reaches Myrmidon huts and ships as he kills off Argives, and burns down the ships with fire.

This explicit statement—essentially a compromise position between his and his *khólos*—is communicated to Agamemnon only metaphorically by Odysseus. What is important to remember is fire's relationship to the activity of the warrior, specifically Hector's attack on the ships and huts.[32]

The use of *smûxai* ("to burn down") in Achilles' response to Ajax points forward to the death of Hector where Homer will liken the turmoil in Troy at his death to the turmoil that would ensue—that will ensue—with the city ablaze:

ᾤμωξεν δ' ἐλεεινὰ πατὴρ φίλος, ἀμφὶ δὲ λαοὶ
κωκυτῷ τ' εἴχοντο καὶ οἰμωγῇ κατὰ ἄστυ.
τῷ δὲ μάλιστ' ἄρ' ἔην ἐναλίγκιον, ὡς εἰ ἅπασα
Ἴλιος ὀφρυόεσσα πυρὶ σμύχοιτο κατ' ἄκρης.
(*Il.* 22.408–11)

And his dear father pitiably lamented, and the people held firm with wailing and lament throughout the city. And it was truly just as if the whole of towering Ilium were burned down with fire utterly.

Given such stark examples of the importance of fire to the thematics of aggression in the *Iliad*, *khólos*, as the most frequent word for heroic wrath, often comes into play with notions of fire. For example, we can return to the beginning of Phoenix's speech, where he collates the fire that threatens the Achaean existence with Achilles' *khólos*:

εἰ μὲν δὴ νόστον γε μετὰ φρεσί, φαίδιμ' Ἀχιλλεῦ,
βάλλεαι, οὐδέ τι πάμπαν ἀμύνειν νηυσὶ θοῇσι
πῦρ ἐθέλεις ἀίδηλον, ἐπεὶ χόλος ἔμπεσε θυμῷ, . . .
(*Il.* 9.434–36)

If it is a return that you consider in your mind, glorious Achilles, and if you are unwilling at all to defend the swift ships against the ravaging fire, because *khólos* has fallen into your heart. . . .

Now this *khólos* phrase was found in position 11, in the formula *khólos émpese thumôi*. It occurs four times (once in a doublet):

Il. 9.436 πῦρ ἐθέλεις, ἀίδηλον, ἐπεὶ χόλος ἔμπεσε θυμῷ,
Il. 14.207 εὐνῆς καὶ φιλότητος, ἐπεὶ χόλος ἔμπεσε θυμῷ.
= 14.306
Il. 16.206 αὖτις, ἐπεί ῥά τοι ὧδε κακὸς χόλος ἔμπεσε θυμῷ.

The phrase *émpese thumôi* encompasses significant thematic concerns of the *Iliad*: twice it is used of a weapon that "fells" a victim.[33] The "weapon" that falls on the enemy in *Il.* 16.113 is fire. In the invocation of the Muses before Hector reaches the Achaean ships, we hear:

Ἔσπετε νῦν μοι, Μοῦσαι, Ὀλύμπια δώματ' ἔχουσαι,
ὅππως δὴ πρῶτον πῦρ ἔμπεσε νηυσὶν Ἀχαιῶν.
(*Il.* 16.112–13)

Tell me now, Muses, who have Olympian houses, how first fire fell on the Achaeans' ships.

Through this series of passages showing "falling upon" (or "attacking"), the narrative displays the results of the warrior's *khólos*. This grim metonymic process is made possible by the very visual quality of the epic. So too *émpese* is not merely "to fall upon" or "to fell"—it strongly suggests the image of the warrior hurling or shooting a missile or that missile striking the warrior.

Fire is a source domain for anger because of the destructive force of fire on the Trojan plain, where fire is indeed a weapon. Thus at *Il.* 21.342, Hephaistos poises to cast his fire against Scamander as if it were a spear: *Hēphaistos dè titúsketo thespidaès pûr* "and Hephaestus took aim with his divine fire." Moreover, fire metaphorically comes down from above like a missile, as can be seen from the Book 4 of the *Iliad*:

αὐτὰρ ἐπεὶ ἴδεν ἕλκος, ὅθ' ἔμπεσε πικρὸς ὀϊστός, . . .
(*Il.* 4.217)

But when he saw the wound where the bitter arrow had fallen. . . .

A similar effect can be seen in Book 15:

αὐχένι γάρ οἱ ὄπισθε πολύστονος ἔμπεσεν ἰός·
(*Il.* 15.451)

For at his neck did the arrow, the source of many pains, fall in from behind.

both of which are comparable to

Ἔσπετε νῦν μοι, Μοῦσαι Ὀλύμπια δώματ᾽ ἔχουσαι,
ὅππως δὴ πρῶτον πῦρ ἔμπεσε νηυσὶν Ἀχαιῶν.
(*Il.* 16.112–13)

Tell now to me Muses who have Olympian homes, how first fire fell on the ships of the Achaeans.

Now fire is in particular related—through the conceptualization that it falls *down* and *in* (*émpese*)—to weapons that pierce the body and remain in it until a surgeon can come to remove it as happens at *Il.* 4.217.

Thus, we can begin to see an emerging metaphoric system for *khólos* and fire in relationship to weaponry.

Fire is a weapon:
it goes from outside the body to inside the body
it falls down from above (as an arrow or spear)

which links with the digestive metaphoric complex

Anger is food:
It goes from outside the body to inside the body.
It moves downward (as if from mouth to stomach).

This situation leads to the metaphorical phrasing that implies that anger is a weapon, enters the body, and goes from outside to inside: thus, the formula *epeì khólos émpese thumôi*, "since *khólos* has fallen into his heart" (*Il.* 9.436, *Il.* 14.207, *Il.* 14.306, *Il.* 16.306), presents a metaphor based on the coherence of the system in which *khólos* operates. The phrase depends on the notion that *khólos* is something that has entered the body from the outside in the way an arrow or spear does; furthermore, the metaphor of fire acting in the fashion of such a weapon is linked to the notion that anger is like fire. Thus, Phoenix's formulation links both Achilles' anger and the fire that is to threaten the ships, where the relationship of fire as weapon and wrath as weapon is explicitly presented:

οὐδέ τι πάμπαν ἀμύνειν νηυσὶ θοῇσι
πῦρ ἐθέλεις ἀΐδηλον, ἐπεὶ χόλος ἔμπεσε θυμῷ,
(*Il.* 9.435–36)

You are unwilling at all to defend against the pernicious fire from the swift ships, since *khólos* has fallen in your heart.

And this particular phrasing is modified by Odysseus in his report to Agamemnon where, again, in harmony with the metaphorical system that links fire, anger, and weapons, we find that Achilles is as unwilling to quench his anger as he was unwilling to quench the fire that threatens Achaean ships: *Il.* 9.678 *keînós g' ouk ethélei sbéssai khólon*, "That one is not willing to quench his *khólos*."[34]

To summarize, the metaphorical uses of *khólos* are part of a coherent system involving three major metaphor types, (a) *khólos* is food; (b) *khólos* is disease; and (c) *khólos* is fire (as a weapon). Each of these types implies other predications which then can interact, so that *khólos* as something that enters the body from the outside is coherent across the three metaphors. Virtually all the metaphorical uses in Homeric poetry for *khólos* depend on the digestive, medicinal, or combustatory systems and the various ways in which they cohere.

Etymology and Metaphor

This poetic artistry linking *khólos* with other fundamental cultural elements is nowhere more delicately handled than in Achilles' words to Thetis, in response to her very short two-line lament emphasizing the shortness of Achilles' life and the link between the fate of Hector and her son's death:

ὠκύμορος δή μοι, τέκος, ἔσσεαι, οἷ' ἀγορεύεις·
αὐτίκα γάρ τοι ἔπειτα μεθ' Ἕκτορα πότμος ἑτοῖμος.
(*Il.* 18.95–96)

Oh child of mine, your life will be short, given what you say; for immediately following Hector, your fate is at hand.

And Achilles repeats the idea of immediacy, but hyperbolically curses himself:

αὐτίκα τεθναίην, ἐπεὶ οὐκ ἄρ' ἔμελλον ἑταίρῳ
κτεινομένῳ ἐπαμῦναι·
(*Il.* 18.98–99)

Would that I die, immediately, since I was not to be a defense for my friend, when he was getting killed.

Here, Achilles immediately (*autíka*) responds to Thetis's use of the word, as *hetaírōi* responds to Thetis's *hetoîmos* (*Il.* 18.96) with a severe comparison poised between Achilles' death and that of Patroclus (*tethnaíēn*, *kteinoménōi*, as reinforced by the enjambement). Achilles parses his mother's speech, extracting the notion of companionship and immediacy in order to throw an ironic spin on both. And thanks to Richard Martin's (1989) solution to the myriad problems presented by the language of Achilles we have a way of thinking about these linguistic feats by the hero of the *Iliad*:

> [Homer] fully reveals all the possibilities of his own poetic craft only in the extended speech of Achilles. The effect is to make Achilles sound like a poet. . . . The similarity arises because Homer, when he constructs Achilles by means of language, employs all his poetic resources and stretches the limits of his formulaic art to make the hero as large a figure as possible. In short, the monumental poem demands a monumental hero; the language of epic, pressed to provide speech for such a man, becomes the "language of Achilles."
> (Martin 1987, 223)

What Martin teaches us here is a potent lesson to learn, since I am about to suggest that the most extravagant use of the metaphorical possibilities available to *khólos* are performed by Achilles in this speech to his mother.

Here is part of Achilles' renunciation of his anger, at *Il.* 18.98–126, where he comes to curse wrath:

> ὡς ἔρις ἔκ τε θεῶν ἔκ τ᾽ ἀνθρώπων ἀπόλοιτο,
> καὶ χόλος, ὅς τ᾽ ἐφέηκε πολύφρονά περ χαλεπῆναι,
> ὅς τε πολὺ γλυκίων μέλιτος καταλειβομένοιο
> ἀνδρῶν ἐν στήθεσσιν ἀέξεται ἠύτε καπνός·
> ὡς ἐμὲ νῦν ἐχόλωσεν ἄναξ ἀνδρῶν Ἀγαμέμνων.
> (*Il.* 18.107–11)

> Thus let strife perish away from gods and mortals both, and *khólos*, which compels one to rage, thoughtful though he be, and sweeter by far than honey dripping down inside human bodies it increases, like smoke. Thus did the king of men Agamemnon now come to provoke *khólos* in me.

That Achilles should speak these words to Thetis presents us with a stark contrast to his account of the quarrel in Book 1. Although in Book 1 he could not admit to his *khólos*, instead saddling Agamemnon with the entire emotional weight of it, here he comes to admit that his *khólos* is the problem and that it is his, even though he still—and, to my mind, rightly—emphasizes the provocation of Agamemnon. Thus, Achilles is the *polúphrōn* ("a thoughtful one") who succumbs to a kind of temptation presented by *khólos*, which he seeks to motivate, we will see, by elaborating on the special sense provided to *khólos* by its systematic conceptual structure.

The placement of this curse on anger is dramatic precisely because it succeeds Achilles' curse on himself. The combination of these two is indeed a fatal parsing of *mênin Akhilêos*, with a focus not on *mênis* but on the more manageable forms of anger, *éris* and *khólos*.[35] Achilles moves then to fashion this anger in a resonant trope in which he takes his analysis further by styling his anger in elemental terms, as quoted above. There are two elements to the comparison that Achilles makes here. The first is that anger is like honey, because it is sweet—*khólos* surpasses the sweetness of honey; the second is that it is like smoke. Now we know, as mentioned, of the five comparisons in which anger is likened to fire, and of the other cases in which *khólos* is compared with a product of digestion, this is the only one that includes these elements together: smoke, honey, and the process of dripping down in the chest cavity.[36] Thus, Achilles joins his own suicidal wish to a wish for the death of the feature of the universe that has placed him in this painful place: he wishes death for the wrath of Achilles (*Il.* 18.107–8).

Etymology

An interpretation adequate to the complexity of this passage (*Il.* 18.107-111) can profit from a glance at the etymology of *khólos*. But since such a procedure has been doubted often in literary critical circles, it is worth establishing what is involved in using etymology as a tool for literary explanation.

Here is an expression of an understandable anxiety:

> [Etymologies] are far less reliable because they are abstractions which are not performed by language, but by linguistic science, which can never be wholly verified by language itself: that is by their actual usage. Hence when they are right, they are not proofs, but advance achievements of conceptual analysis, and only in this obtain a firm foundation.
>
> (Gadamer 1975, 92–93)[37]

Gadamer's statement articulates a common opinion regarding the validity of etymology for literary study. It is worth noting that Gadamer asserts this point through the concept of performance: etymology is not *performed*; in Gadamer's terms—and really since the rise of linguistic science—etymology is seen as the product of a certain kind of "work," the work of the linguist. One can begin to perceive here a rupture between work and play, science and art, a rupture whose applicability to the context of traditional cultures is subject to question, especially since performance in such contexts is opposed neither to work nor to science.

For now, it is sufficient to note that literary scholars often reject the value of historical linguistic method to interpret, elucidate, clarify, or even deal with literary material. With the polemic of this debate we need not concern ourselves at this moment. But the topic is important enough to merit our notice, because if one side of the polemic is accurate, then literary scholars need not consult those who discover new linguistic facts, synchronic or diachronic. Nor, under such conditions should historians of the language seek to inform those who see themselves as literary critics of any kind, including those of ancient Greek literature.[38]

On the contrary, a review of etymological research regarding *khólos* helps demonstrate that the historical background is indeed crucial for revealing the poetics of Achilles' comparison between *khólos* and honey. The wealth of data here gives depth to the primary assertion of this analysis: that historical linguistic method supplies acute tools for understanding the poetics of Homeric discourse.

Greek *khólos* comes from the root **ǵhel-*, for which Pokorny (429) gives a compendium of congeners indicating light or color, with an extensive legacy for this Proto-Indo-European root:

> **ǵhel-* (und **ghel-?*), auch als *i-*, *u-* oder *n*-Stamm; **ǵhel-e-*: *ǵhle-*, *ǵhlo-*: *ǵhle-* 'glänzen, schimmern'; als Farbadjektive: 'gelb, grun, grau oder blau'.

It is not necessary at this point to sort out the problems involved in identifying the particular color for the etymon nor in seeking a priority for one or another color word as opposed to a meaning referring to light intensity.[39]

Besides the numerous congeners of *khólos* in the Indo-European language family, in Greek itself we have not only *khólos* from this source but also *kholḗ*.[40] Now Greek *kholḗ* means "bile," where *khólos* in Homer is regularly glossed as "anger." Such a collocation of an original *ā*-stem with a thematic counterpart has been well-noted.[41] For now it is important to notice the semantic disparity between *khólos* and *kholḗ*. What have "anger" and "bile" to do with each other? Let us refer our question to the history of Indo-European **ǵhel-*. For neither "gall" nor "anger" is the base meaning of IE **ǵhel-*; rather we must turn to the color words that yield the most common meaning for the descendants of this root.

The etymology of Greek *khólos* is transparent and uncontroversial in contrast to *kótos*. Thus, besides *khólos* we have *kholḗ* "gall," "bile," and a panoply of derivatives.[42] Color words stand out among the derivatives in Greek from **ǵhel-*; see especially *khlōrós* "greenish-yellow," "pale green." We know the *r*-suffix is old from Latin *ruber* and related forms.[43] A clearly related form is *khloḗ*, "the first green shoot of plants," "greens."[44]

Now the root **ǵhel-* is widely distributed over the Indo-European world. Since the extensive distribution of the etymon is necessary to my argument, the forms may be recapitulated here with particular emphasis on their relation to *khólos*. Besides Greek, there are forms of **ǵhel-* in Indic, Iranian, Albanian, Italic, Celtic, Germanic, Baltic, and Slavic.

In the Indo-Iranian branch of Indo-European, Sanskrit shows the color word *hári-* "yellow," "golden," and the derivative *hárita-* "yellow," "green." Metonymic derivatives include, with the animatizing suffix *-ina*, *hariṇáḥ* "gazelle."

Avestan has *zari-* meaning "yellow," "yellowish," and *zairita-* with the same *-ita* suffix as in Skt. *hárita*, "yellow, green." The neuter noun for "gold," *zarani-*, occurs as the first element in a compound in more than a dozen Avestan words (Bartholomae 1904, 1678–1680), including *zaraniio.sruua-* "with golden horns." Compare also *zaraniia-*. Moreover, and significantly, Avestan has *zāra-*, "gall." This reflects a parallel situation where the early color term stands metonymically for a bodily product, as recognized by Bartholomae s.v. and Pokorny (429):

"*zāra-* m. 'Galle' (= gr. *kholḗ*), nach der Farbe benannt wie gr. *khólos*, lat. *fel*, anord. *gall* usw."[45] Similar metonymic patterning is to be seen in Old Persian *daraniyah-*, n. "gold."

Precisely the same kind of historical semantic sequence is seen in Italic, where we have Latin *fel*, *fellis*, a neuter noun meaning "gall" (with *f-* from a dialectical form). Latin elsewhere shows the expected form in the color term *helvus* "honey-yellow."[46]

The Celtic languages have many derivatives from Indo-European **ǵhel-* that also parallel the model of historical semantic change that I propose for *khólos*. Note that Old Irish, preserving as might be expected an extremely early semantic moment, continues the archaic meaning of **ǵhel-* in *gel-* "shining," "bright," "fair white," a thematic adjective that in turn forms the first term of many compounds, e.g. *gel-dét* "white tooth," *gel-cnes* "white skin" etc. The simplex adjective is used of complexion, limbs, metals and weapons, the sun, scenery, animals and inanimate objects.[47] A verb *gelaid* means "to make white or bleach," and intransitively "to shine," as in the proverb: *nī i n-aoin-fheacht ghealas an ghrian*, "It's not once that the sun shines."[48] Further, consider the noun *gelán*, an *o*-stem meaning "brightness," "a flash," "whiteness," from *gel-lán*, with simplification of the geminate,[49] and note the phrase *gelán na súl* "the white of the eyes."[50] In Old Irish, Thurneysen relates *glass* ("blue, green") to Gaulish *glastum* "woad";[51] and note the same *to-* suffix seen in Germanic, Sanskrit, and Lithuanian. Welsh has *gell*, for yellow; *glas-* "blue"; Breton has *gell* meaning "brown," and *glas* meaning "green"; as in the other branches of Indo-European, the color-etymon can be transferred to the object of that color: Welsh *glain* "jewel"; Breton *gal* "blueberry," Irish *gelbann* "sparrow." Especially evocative for its connection of this root to fire is Irish *gel-tine*, which as a compound consists of a color word and the word for fire so as to signify some kind of tinder. Even more evocative for the meaning of Greek *khólos* are the derivatives from the technical vocabulary of a warrior culture, e.g., *cathgal* "battle-valour"; *armgal* "armed conflict"; *bangal* "a woman's feat of arms"; *bruthgal* "ferocity, passion, fervour, ardour."[52]

The Germanic branch of the Indo-European family is also rich in derivatives from **ǵhel-* that witness the color meaning. Modern English "yellow" goes back to the Old English *geolu*, the equivalent of Old Saxon *gelo*, Old High German *gelo*. "Gold" shows a *to-* suffix, for which see again Sanskrit *hárita-*. In Old Norse, *gulr* means "yellow"; "golden," and, also from **ǵhel-* see *glāmr*, "moon." Compare here the animal name *golthorskr*, n. "yellow cod." Germanic also shares the predilection of Greek, Lithuanian, and Latin to identify bile with forms of **ǵhel-*: beside Modern English see Old Norse *gall* (neuter), Old English *gealla*, Old Saxon *galla*, etc., all based on an *n-* suffix as in Latin *fel*, *fellis* < **fel-nis*.

Slavic shows Russian *žolti-* "yellow," with Old Church Slavic preserving "gall" (Pokorny 430) in *zlъčъ*. Russian also has *želć* "bile." As for Baltic,

Lithuanian continues the color meaning from **ǵhel–* in *želvas* "green," *žalias* "green," with verbal derivative *žaliuoti* "grow with a green color," "display green foliage." Lithuanian shows the meaning of "gall" in *tulžìs* from metathesis of **žultìs* (Pokorny 430).

This impressive body of derivatives from Indo-European **ǵhel-* demonstrates that the situation in Greek, with this root originally designating a color coming to represent "bile," is paralleled within the historical semantics of Indo-European. Greek shares with Germanic, Baltic, Slavic, Iranian, Celtic, and Italic a relationship between this color and "bile." The same metonymic process is at work here as is at work in the naming of animals or plants after the color-term **ǵhel-*. That bile is so often represented in this group need not so much testify to an inherited lemma for these words (although that possibility should not be ruled out), as much as to a consistent tendency in the manner of naming this product of the human body.

We have seen that Indo-European **ǵhel-* in Greek yields two results of significance to this book. As in Lithuanian, Celtic, Italic, and Indo-Iranian, derivatives continuing the color-reference are numerous: *khlōrós, khlóos, khlóē, khloerós, melí-khlōros,* etc. And Greek has derivatives further attesting to the meaning "gall" or "bile": *kholṓdokhos* "gall bladder"; *kholṓdēs* "full of gall," "zornig"; and finally *kholikós* (Plutarch) and *kholaîos* "biliary" (Suda), and, of course, *kholḗ.*

It is reasonable to infer two things from the preceding data. First, Proto-Indo-European **ǵhel-*, through metonymy, often comes to refer to an object marked in some distinct way by the color to which **ǵhel-* refers. Second, Greek shows "gall" or "bile" where other Indo-European languages independently show the same result.

It is possible then to come to terms with the movement from Indo-European **ǵhel-* meaning a color to Greek *khólos*. This schema suggests a model for this evolution:

Stage 1: Color: **ǵhel-*.
Stage 2: Object: Bile, a liquid of the color identified in Stage 1.
Stage 3: Emotion: Anger, as associated with bile in Stage 2.

And at this point we can cite Sweetser's formulation that "there is, then, a general tendency to borrow concepts and vocabulary from the more accessible physical and social world to refer to the less accessible worlds of reasoning, emotion, and conversational structure."[53] It is this sort of mechanism that is at work in *Il.* 18.107–11.

For *khólos* and *kholḗ* we can observe the lemma "bile" comes to stand for a "physical action or sensation," the emotion of anger as represented in *khólos*. The exact details of the transformation are not yet important here; what matters is that a pathway is open for such a transformation to take place. There are only three survivals in the Homeric text from stage two of the model.[54]

The pair (*khólos* and *kholḗ*) thus represents two distinct stages in the historical semantics of Indo-European **ǵhel-* in Greek. But more important for Calchas's definition than these observations about the Greek lexicon is that the Greek poetic record in the epic displays this semantic history in a way that has literary consequence. This display, in fact, is crucial to the meaning of the simile where Achilles compares *khólos* to honey and smoke.

Yet, as we will shortly see, these distinct semantic stages coexist, even as different dialectical forms or different points in phonological, morphological, and syntactic linguistic history in the poetry of Homer. In other words, just as phonological and morphological linguistic features from distinct stages live side by side in Homeric poetry, so can semantic features created at different times exist simultaneously because of the traditional nature of the poetic art language.

Now consider again Achilles' language in *Il.* 18.107–11, where Achilles collocates different features of *khólos*: ashes, honey, the act of dripping down in the chest cavity. Of the five similes that relate to anger in the *Iliad*[55] this is one of two that uses *khólos* to signify anger.[56]

Cultural notions concerning *khólos* motivate Achilles' use of the word here. In Achilles' simile, an earlier stage of *khólos* survives than is represented by the usual gloss for *khólos* as "anger." This stage may be the recapitulation on Achilles' part of the real semantic history of *khólos*. In calling up the image of honey, *méli*, Achilles does the same thing he did in calling up the image of his mother's milk (in *Il.* 16.203)—honey is sweet, bile bitter. But honey can also be similar in color to bile.[57] We have Homer drawing on the earliest stage (the color stage) of Greek *khólos*. Put briefly, in this passage, Homeric poetry both preserves and displays the etymology of *khólos*.

As to the connection between *khólos* and fire (through *kapnós* by metonymy), it is worth pointing out the bold rhetorical use to which Achilles has put this image. Put simply, Achilles is using a binary opposition to highlight *khólos*. Thus *khólos* is opposed to *méli*, where *kataleiboménoio* is opposed to the implied word for the rising of the smoke.[58] The smoke (*kapnós*) as it rises complements the honey (*méli*) as it descends. And all of this is compatible with the elementary notion of the desirability and pleasure of honey being used to explain the complex psychology of anger.[59]

Here then we have a binary opposition of the kind studied by Levi-Strauss in *From Honey to Ashes*. To quote Levi-Strauss, there is "a correlative and antithetical term of liquid honey, corresponding to it point by point in the complementary scale of the dry, the burnt and the aromatic." Thus, in explicating *khólos*, Achilles does not so much first compare it to honey and then to smoke but he compares it to the opposition between honey and smoke (see Table 11.1).[60]

Table 11.1. Relationship between *Khólos*, honey, and smoke

This analysis only begins to unpack the complex nature of this figure. We know for example that Strabo refers to "unsmoked honey"[61]—the smoke being used "to induce passivity in bees when [the beekeepers] opened the hives." Are we to consider Achilles' (and Meleager's) passivity here? Certainly these technologies are ancient, as J. E. Jones demonstrates: "The ancients certainly knew how to use smoke to induce passivity in bees when they opened hives and knew also that heavy smoking contaminated the honey and spoiled its flavor" (Jones 1976, 86; cf. Jones, Graham, and Sackett 1973, 406). We know that smoke was used in the harvesting of honey from very early on.[62] The structural implications of all this are represented in Table 11.2.

Table 11.2. Oppositions between *Khólos* and honey

khólos ("anger")	*méli* ("honey")
bitter	sweet
waste	nourishment
the body	the culture
up	down

Within archaic Greek oral poetics the motivation for this comparison lies in the etymology of *khólos*. This etymology is preserved, I mean to say, in the poetics of this simile without ever being explicitly drawn out—it is not a *figura etymologica* in the traditional sense, where in fact a folk etymology will do as well as a true etymology.[63] Rather this figure preserves an earlier meaning of *khólos* than is called for by any purely synchronic demands of any particular oral performance. I add that what keeps the history of the term intact is the conservative nature of the early Greek oral medium combined with the stability of the conceptual metaphor underlying *khólos*.

It remains to be asked what kind of mechanism, within the oral medium, caused this figure to be preserved and to be available in the *Iliad*. For Gadamer's objection still has not been adequately addressed. If the evidence thus far indicates that the "real" etymology—established, verified, and demonstrated through the methods of historical linguistics—has literary value of an unmistakable kind, how can it be that an oral performer should be able to make use of what amounts to a knowledge belonging to his or her own linguistic past?

I respond to Gadamer's challenge in this way: the etymology of *khólos* in *Il.* 18.107–11 is an "essential idea" of the kind Parry suggested lies at the heart of oral formulaic discourse. But the term "formula," so often problematic, has usually referred to a synchronic mechanism, the kind of thing that would make *this* performance performable by an oral bard. For diachronic poetics one is in need of a diachronic notion of the formula, one that accounts for more than the production of phrases in a convenient and competent manner.

Calvert Watkins suggests a definition of the formula, along the lines required by the analysis above: "a formula is the verbal and grammatical device for encoding and transmitting a given theme or interaction of themes,"[64] where the theme is a cultural node—"something that matters in the culture."[65]

What I emphasize from this definition is the introduction of cultural value into our conception of the formula. It is, for example, significant that *kléos áphthiton* is a formula in Greek poetry: the notion itself is a "cultural node," a term crucial to the society available to be made, as a consequence, central to the poetics of that culture's epics. The methods of historical linguistics show that this cultural node is preserved from Indo-European.[66]

For Achilles' curse against anger, the verbal device is a Homeric simile that refers to a range of poetic features relevant to *khólos*, especially its connection with the human body through the production of bile. We have here the poetry preserving something that matters to it a great deal: its own understanding of the nature of anger. As the most frequent anger word, *khólos* is also the most important anger word with respect to the genre of the *Iliad*. I suggest that its relationship to traditional poetics gives *khólos* its conservative character as a cultural index. For within the *Iliad* what really matters is the anger of Achilles, be it *khólos* or *mênis*.[67]

The theoretical point here is worth restating: a traditional literature can indeed preserve inherited surface phraseology by means of formulaic phrases; and, as a consequence, there are likely to be similarly long lived, inherited semantic collocations available for poetic purposes. Thus, some semantic relationships which are present at one point in a word's history may survive diachronic semantic change through the conservative mechanism of an oral poetic tradition. In traditional literature, that is, in literature whose history can to a large extent be present in the form and content of the individual performance, etymology may provide clues to meanings hidden from view on the synchronic level—the synchronic "reading" of a traditional text implies diachronic reception of both form and content. Furthermore, the play of the singer's art can involve artistic manipulation of inherited linguistic features. It is no accident that an old etymology for *khólos* occurs in a scene where the narrative so clearly succeeds in evoking woe and wonder for the plight of Achilles.[68]

Notes

1. Cf. *Il.* 24.617, 639, (*kḗdea*, "woes"); and cf. *Il.* 8.513 (*bélos*, "missile") and at *Il.* 2.237 (*géra*, "gift"). See Kirk 1985, at *Il.* 8.512–13.

2. For example: *khólon eksakésaio Il.* 4.36,"you might heal (your) *khólos*; *hōs tòn Athēnaíēs deinòn khólon eksakésaito* (*Od.* 3.145), "Thus did he *cure* the terrible *khólos* of Athena."

3. As in the formula, *Meléagron édu khólos* (*Il.* 9.553), "*khólos* had entered Meleager" as comparable to *édu dé té min khólos ainós* (*Il.* 22.94), "and the dread *khólos* entered him"; see also *hōs min mâllon édu khólos* (*Il.* 19.16), "thus had khólos entered him the more."

4. *allá moi oidánetai kradíē khólōi, hoppóte keínōn (Il.* 9.646), "But my heart swells with *khólos* . . . ."

5. As in *ê apéeipe, khólos d' ét ékhei megalḗtora thumón* (*Il.* 9.675), "But *khólos* still holds his heart"; and see also *Il.* 18.322 *eí pothen ekseúroi; mála gàr drimùs khólos haireî*, "The more did *khólos* take him."

6. *keînós g' ouk ethélei sbéssai khólon, all' éti mâllon* (*Il.* 9.678), "That one is not willing to quench his *khólos*. . . ."

7. *skhétlie Pēléos huié, khólōi ára s' étrephe mḗter* (*Il.* 16.203), "Wretched son of Peleus, yes, your mother nursed you on *khólos*."

8. *aûtis, epeí rhá toi hôde kakòs khólos émpese thumōi*" (*Il.* 16.206), "Since an evil *khólos* has fallen in your heart."

9. On metaphor in Homer see Moulton 1979, 279–93, and the literature cited there. See also Parry 1971, 365–75. The usual observation is that Homeric verbal artistry is not rich in metaphor. But Muellner challenges that idea in his study of Homeric metaphor, where he argues that "there are expressive, artistic links between 'similes' and 'metaphors' in any given context" (1990, 60 and n. 2). Metaphor, thus, might be more a part of Homeric diction than has hitherto been thought, so that the relative scarcity of metaphor in Homer might be largely an illusion (cf. Petegorsky 1982). I suspect that early Homeric tradition understood the vitality of metaphor in a manner that is continued in systematic fashion by Aristotle (e.g., in *Rhetoric* 3.10, 1410b 35, *Poetics* 21, 1457b 7). The earlier status of these various controversies are reviewed in Moulton 1979, 279–80; see also for the earlier literature Keith 1914 and Stanford 1936.

10. Besides Lakoff and Johnson 1980, see the same authors 1989 and Lakoff 1987, where Lakoff presents a case study of anger in English (380–415); see also Lakoff and Kövecses 1987.

11. See, for example, Ortony 1979.

12. See also Hans Kurath 1921 for a review of such processes. I am grateful to Eve Sweetser for drawing my attention to this important study.

13. I rely heavily here on Lakoff and Kövecses 1987, 196, where the cognitive model of anger in American English is examined to show the "coherent conceptual organization underlying" the expressions for anger in contemporary speech.

14. Lakoff and Kövecses 1987, 198; updated in Lakoff 1987, 380–415.

15. Ibid.

16. These examples are from Lakoff and Kövecses 1987, 198.

17. There are other metaphors involved in this process. For examples and analysis, see Lakoff and Kövecses 1987, 199. The authors call the two entities in this process the

source domain (here "heat") of the metaphor and the *target domain* (here "anger") of the metaphor. Putting it in their terms, the metaphorical entailments are the carryovers of knowledge from the source to the target domains. Thus what a Homeric text knows about fire (a source domain) is also part of what it knows about anger (the target domain), in that the connection between the two is made effective by the carry over of knowledge from one domain to the other.

18. Though the scholia at *Il.* 4.513 further metaphorize the image to that of ripening. See also Kirk's note *ad loc.*

19. This metaphoric relationship is prominent in Shakespeare's *Coriolanus*; see Adelman 1978.

20. Recall here the relationship of *khólos* to *kholḗ*. Joan O'Brien's analysis of Hera's insatiable "demonic hatred" insists that "gall" is the "fundamental meaning" of *khólos* (1993, 80). O'Brien (1993) and Padel (1995, 53) both point to the complex nature of the relationship between *khólos* and body imagery.

21. Culinary practices and codes have been a major focus of structuralist analysis. See for example Detienne and Vernant 1989. But along with the demand for the elaboration of source domains for anger (such as culinary practice), a thorough review of the features of the target domain must be undertaken. The connection between source and target is at the same time both culture specific and coherent, in the sense discussed above, so that neither one "explains" the other; rather both participate in an interlocking system of meaning-formation.

22. There is more than a little affinity here between the body as a container for *khólos* and Lakoff's findings concerning the metaphor "The body is a container for the emotions" (Lakoff 1987, 383). In her discussion of the container metaphor, O'Brien (1993, 82 with n. 11) draws attention to *ménos aáskheton* (*Il.* 5.892) "uncontainable anger" in that it continues the metaphor of the "body-as-container."

23. Cf. Zeus's anger at *Il.* 15.136 characterized with *kudoimḗsōn*, "swelling," after that anger has been identified as *khólos kaì mênis*, at *Il.* 15.122. For this passage see also Muellner 1996, 114–16.

24. Cf. LSJ s.v. *diatríbō*, III.

25. The verb can also refer to threshing. The notion of delaying occurs in a number of Homeric passages (e.g., *Od.* 20.341), where the process involved is seen as taking time. Compare our "just standing around" as equivalent to "delaying." The special detail of grinding by hand indicates that a real physician would have had special tools, perhaps the equivalent of mortar and pestle, to do the grinding.

26. And compare *katabróxeien Od.* 4.222 with *bebrōkȭs kakà phármak'*, *Il.* 22.94 ("having consumed evil drugs"), where the *kakà phármaka* contrast with the "good drug" (Bergren 1981) of Helen. See Walsh 1999.

27. This passage is explored in a paper published as Walsh 1999, where I suggest that there is a parallel to this potion (with its effect on the drinker) in Nestor's cup, discussed by Watkins 1975, with literature. Homeric narrative elaborately structures the description of Helen's potion in a fashion parallel to that of Nestor's cup by means of an evaluative adjective (ευποτ[ον] in Nestor's cup), comparable to the three compound adjectives in the *Odyssey* passage, *nḗpenthes*, *ákholon*, *epílēthon*, in both examples followed by a generalizing relative clause explaining the effect of the drink on the drinker. The relative clause is characteristically more elaborate and descriptive in the Homeric text than is possible in the more epigrammatic and materially restricted medium of the inscription.

28. The other important work on fire in Homeric epic includes Graz 1965 and Nagy 1979, 331, who writes "The fact is that *pûr* 'fire' is a prime manifestation of *bíē*, on the cosmic level and on the heroic as well." On 321–2 Nagy goes on to say that "what strikes us in particular here is that the narrative is presenting the *bíē* of Achilles as parallel to the *biē* of fire itself." In these passages, Nagy focuses on the "elemental" aspects of *bíē*. My study meets his at just the place where *khólos* as a manifestation of *bíē* has an elemental relation to fire. Paragraphs 6 and 12 of Nagy's Chapter 20 are especially concerned with fire and the warrior. As to fire and anger, Muellner definitively establishes the relationship of *mênis* and fire (especially in its manifestation as Zeus's lightening bolt): "Massive devastation by celestial fire is the prime expression of *mênis*. . . ." (Muellner 1996, 167).

29. Whitman 1958, 132; Achilles' anger is again flame-like at *Il.* 19. 365–67.

30. See again Whitman (1958, 131-32).

31. Graz (1965, 260) on *Il.* 9.678 does not elaborate on the incendiary features of *khólos*; instead he focuses on *ménos*. Here *khólos* is a stronger candidate for being the central figure of this metaphor, though *sbénnumi* and its compound forms have a variety of objects (e.g., *ménos*, notably, at *Il.* 16.621).

32. For fire as an attribute of the hero, see again Nagy 1979, 330–47.

33. Cf. *Il.* 4.217, *Il.* 16.113. Once it is used of the victim *Il.* 4.108. Only three other abstract nouns function as subjects of *émpese*: *deós* in *Il.* 17.625, *kakón* in *Od.* 2.45, and *épos* in *Od.* 12.266. The *Iliad* presents a formulaic system that highlights the relation of fire, weaponry, and fear in addition *khólos*. The *Odyssey* gives no examples of either *khólos* or *pûr* ("fire") as the subject of *émpese*.

34. The last chapter of *The Best of the Achaeans* (Nagy 1979, 317–47) shows the thematics that bolster the fire imagery as expressing "the hero's cosmic affinity with fire and wind" (Nagy 1979, 351). As shown there, the phraseological robustness of the link between the hero and such imagery extends from the comparative evidence of Indo-European tradition to the particulars of Greek themes. The metaphoric processes discussed here fit nicely with this evidence. I also point to the important thinking of L. Muellner on Homeric metaphor in Muellner 1990, especially 96–99.

35. See Hogan's analysis of *éris* in this passage (1981, 21, 55), especially his contrast between *éris* and *khólos*. He notes that "Achilles condemns his own *khólos*, Agamemnon's provocation of it, and then the *khólos Hérēs* (*Il.* 18.119) associated with Heracles' *moira*," in a pattern that parallels Phoenix's own reference to his own *khólos* in combination with the exemplum of Meleager; in both cases biography precedes myth. See also Moulton 1979, 285 who emphasizes "the sense of clash which is in turn mitigated by the appropriateness of each separate image. As a whole, the complex description of anger is just what we might expect from a character so familiar with that emotion; the graphic images of honey and smoke, correlated by the antithesis of *kataleiboménoio* ('dripping down') and *aéxetai* ('increases,' 'grows up') are produced by a character of singular imagination." I only add that the character's imagination jibes with the cultural force of tradition.

36. There are five fire similes that directly involve the emotion of anger in the Homeric texts (*Il.* 1.104, *Il.* 18.110, *Il.* 19.17, *Il.* 19.366; *Od.* 4.662). See, conveniently, the schematization of Scott 1974, 66–68, 191, 199 and the discussion on 68. See also Fraenkel 1921, 56, in addition to his section *Gestirne, Blitz und Feuer* (47–52); he comments "Mit ihren Augen sieht der Sänger die Ereignisse unten auf der Welt; wie der Rauch einer brennenden Stadt steigt das flammende Wüten des Achilleus zu den

Schauenden empor," with the note "Zwischen Rauch und Feuer wird hier wie Σ 207 kein Unterschied gemacht. Weil beides untrennbar ist, genügt es eines zu nennen; gemeint ist die Gesamterscheinung" (52 with note).

On the association of gall and fire, see a remarkable example from a Sumerian incantation (Alster 1972). In his comment on this passage in the *Iliad*, Onians connects smoke with *thumós* but does not go further (1951, 50). See also on gall, Kurath 1921, 16–19. Neither Onians nor Kurath connect "gall" and "anger" through the notion of fire as do the Homeric and Sumerian texts.

37. Gadamer 1975, 92–93. See also MacCary 1982, 251 n. 1. For an excellent overview of the literary issues involved in etymological research see Francis 1983. For the major earlier assessment in Homeric studies, see Rank 1951. Despite modernism's suspicions of etymologizing as a literary trope, Bernard Peebles (1976) shows how etymology could be used as a cognitive and heuristic device in the medieval period.

38. See for example, work on the name of Achilles, Nagy 1976b, Holland 1993, with a reply by Nagy (1994). See too the work on the name Nestor by Frame 1978.

39. In Irwin 1974 one can find a thorough review of the literature to that date on color as it relates to Greek literature. In Chapter 1 ("The Problem") Irwin reviews studies in classical color terms from Newton forward. While I do not wish to establish the meaning of the color that was designated by any single derivative in ancient Greek, I insist that *khólos* is derived from a color term in a manner that is significant for the interpretation of *Il* 18.110–11. For *ǵhel- derivatives in Greek, see Irwin's Chapter 2 "χλωρός."

I cite these sources as a selective list of works to consider in exploring the semantic issues in reference to the color of *khólos*. Irwin 1974, 62–65; Ferrini 1978; Platnauer 1921; Wallace 1927; McNeill 1972; Rowe 1972. See also the classic study by Berlin and Kay 1969, with significant developments covered in Kay and MacDaniel (1978). Hilbert 1987 and Sahlins 1976 are important for the anthropology pertaining to these issues.

40. On *khólos* and *kholḗ*, see Padel 1995, 53–54; Kurath 1921, 16–19; Onians 1951, 52, 84–89.

41. These forms show noun derivatives from verb roots with the *-os, -ē* alteration:

phthóngos "sound," "speech"	*phthongḗ* "voice"
phóros "tribute"	*phorá* "payment," "crop"
phthóros "ruin," "destruction"	*phthorá* "decay"
plókos "wreath"	*plokḗ* "web"

The following forms, consisting of adjectives paired with nouns, unlike *khólos/kholḗ*, have different accentuation and root vocalism:

thermós "hot"	*thérmē* "heat"
leukós "bright"	*leúkē* "leprosy"

This pattern is not confined to Greek; see E. Hamp 1985 for a look at such forms. See also Chantraine 1979, 20–21; Watkins 1973, 88; Gagnepin 1959.

42. See Chantraine 1968–1980, s.v. *khólos*, where the duality of the derivative forms is made clear: "Très tôt la dualité des formes a donc permis une distinction entre la notion médicale de *bile* et la notion psychologique d' *humeur*. Cette distinction ne s'est pas étendue aux composés qui appartiennent presque tous au registre concret de la bile, mais peuvent comportes des acceptions morales." It is just that border between the body and the "acceptions morales" that is of interest here.

43. Chantraine 1979, 224 and compare *eruthrós*, "red."

44. Though Chantraine (1979), perhaps overcautiously, doubts the relation as felt.

45. Frisk (1960–1970) is cautious on the relationship to the Greek form: "nicht ganz sicher" (s.v. *khoöḗ*, 1110).

46. See Ernout-Meillet 1959–1960 s.v.

47. *Dictionary of the Irish Language*, s.v.

48. *Dioghluim Dána* 93 §22.

49. For final syllables in *-ā* see Thurneysen 1970, 31.

50. *Dictionary of the Irish Language*, s.v.

51. Thurneysen 1970, 96.

52. *Bruth-gal* calls to mind again the relationship between beverages, anger, and the body, by connecting an old root for a fermented wine (**bhru-to* found in Thracian βρυτος and Latin *dē-frutum*; we also have a derivative in Old Irish referring to the brewing of beer, *bruth*, cf. Vendryes 1959, B-106). Besides drawing from the *Dictionary of the Irish Language*, s.v., the list here comes from the robust collection of the compounds of *gal* in Irish (and other Celtic languages) in J. Lloyd-Jones 1947, with his succinct treatment of Greek *khólos* and derivatives on 89.

53. Sweetser 1990, 31; Kurath 1921, 10. Support for the type of model here presented can be found in Kurath's observations that "different stem-forms may be confined to different stages."

54. For the relation of *khólos* to a bodily fluid, see again the milk of Thetis at *Il.* 16.203 and at *Il.* 22.93–95, a serpent's venom. In the latter passage, a serpent (*drákōn*) imbibes "evil drugs" (*kakà phármaka*) following which *khólos* enters him, that is, becomes his venom (*édu dé té min khólos ainós)*. Here *khólos* is related to a kind of poison (as "evil drug"), which is mirrored by the fluid that is *khólos*. At stage 2 of the developmental model that I propose here, the color of honey by metonymy is transferred both to mother's milk and to poison, as it is to honey at *Il.* 18.108–9 (*khólos . . . hós te polù glukíōn mélitos* "*khólos* . . . which is far sweeter than honey"); on the structural relation of honey and poison in other traditions see Levi-Strauss 1973, 57–58. See also Moulton 1979, 285.

55. *Il.* 1.104, *Il.* 18.110, *Il.* 19.17, *Il.* 19.366; *Od.* 4.662.

56. The other is at *Il.* 19.17. At *Il.*1.104 the force that it serves as the medium of anger is *ménos*; at *Il.* 19.366 it is *ákhos*; *Od.* 4.662 recalls the *ménos* and *ákhos* of *Il.* 1.104.

57. Cf. Latin *helvus* above, and see Levi-Strauss 1973 on the color of honey.

58. Compare also *katasbénnumi* and *katasmúkhō*.

59. Cf. Nagler 1980, 89 for the compositional process here: "At any moment in the recitation one may hear something which resolves a tension the story had built up and which at the same time brings into play something recurrent in the epic-singing tradition or even in the cultural or archetypal inheritance of the community."

60. Thus Achilles' observation stands at the head of a long line of oppositions in the West: "There would seem to be no doubt that, in Western civilization, 'honey' and 'tobacco' phrases stand in opposition to each other" (Levi-Strauss 1973, 18).

61. See J. E. Jones 1976, 86: "The ancients certainly knew how to use smoke to induce passivity in bees when they opened hives and knew also that heavy smoking contaminated the honey and spoiled its flavor." Cf. Jones, Graham, and Sackett 1973, 406.

62. On the relationship moistness and dryness to life and death, see also Irwin 1974, 33–38. See also Plate 79b in Jones, Graham, and Sackett 1973 for the technology of beekeeping.

63. In a traditional society, the distinction between folk and real etymology is irrelevant. For a critique of such a distinction as a false dichotomy, see Nagy 1994.

64. Cf. Watkins 1981b. See Watkins 1995.

65. For this phrase and concept see Watkins 1995. I am indebted to his ongoing accomplishments in "Indo-European comparative literature" (his phrase).

66. The crucial study of this formula is Nagy 1974, which has elicited much vigorous discussion, as for example Finkelberg 1986. For this book, I set aside the controversy over the status of this important formula in order to emphasize that the significance of such a formula is its dynamic representation in synchronic verbal art of a coherent diachronic cultural inheritance. Albert Lord's work on the formula has rightly stressed the importance of theme in the development of formulaic systems.

67. See again Muellner 1996.

68. The means by which the narrative makes dynamic a formula and its history is the theme, a device well-elucidated in Lord 1960, 72–103.

Chapter Twelve

Conclusions and a Comparison

I began this study by reviewing the extensive literature on anger in Homer, with a view to finding a method that attends closely to Homeric poetic practice even as it looks to other disciplines including anthropology and linguistics. Such a project seems to be a comparative literature of early traditions and texts; but comparative literature also needs to compare literatures. So to conclude this work, I would like both to summarize what we have found about the distinctions made by Calchas and to compare material from a cognate and often-cited parallel to Achilles and his anger, the anger of Cú Chulainn, the hero of early Irish narrative.[1]

In Part I, I showed that Calchas's definition is given support by nearly every cited form of *kótos*, so that this long-lasting anger verges on the status of a social institution. Indeed, when we look to the anthropological literature on the feud, it becomes clear that *kótos* is close in meaning to the anger appropriate to the type of aggression known as the feud. Entirely different is *khólos* (Part II), with its focus on the body and the bodily experience of anger. Here the warrior's anger emerges in all its violent, aggressive and dangerous presence. Unlike *kótos*, it is bodied forth immediately, and for all its danger, Homeric culture thinks of it as controllable. Indeed this opposition between a controllable anger and one that is not susceptible to cultural manipulation may produce a necessary cultural strategy, a way of accommodating social actors to reality: once warriors are set loose to cultivate wrath as a kind of weapon, to bring that activity to a safe end poses a major problem for a culture. The better the warriors, the more severe the problem. For the early Greeks, to divide up the conceptual category so that there are at least two forms—one controllable so that it is limited and the second active and unstoppable until it reaches its *telos*—presents a strategy that seems protective of two things: the perceived need for the violence that satisfies some perceived social necessity (such as preserving *xenía* ["guest-friendship"] by seeking revenge on the Trojans) and the recognition that cultivating that violence is dangerous in the extreme.

This double-vision of anger may be central to the tradition from which the *Iliad* emerges. That tradition presents the warrior's anger, first as *mênis*, an anger that, according to Muellner, has cosmic implications.[2] Since *khólos*, as we have seen, is manageable, the operations of exchange *should* precipitate the return of Achilles from his state of *khólos*. That would make sense both for the culture's norms and the individual's needs. But, in this version of the traditional tale, Achilles sets out—to his ultimate dismay—to interrogate that anger and its double; not only a poet (see again Martin 1989) but also a theorist, Achilles lights on the cultural flaw that there is something suspect about the distinction drawn between a manageable and an unmanageable anger, so that his struggles come, by Book 9, to attempt major surgery on the body of the culture itself: what if his *khólos* became unmanageable? What if *khólos* became something more like *kótos* by taking on the characteristics of an obstinate feud? Might it not then also partake of vengeance's endless action? His threatened return to Phthia, his recruitment of Phoenix to stay the night in his tent—all such things point to a longed-for leap to feuding's obstinacy. When it comes down to it, Achilles has not accepted Calchas's definition: he mixes the outer forms of *khólos* and the cultural content of *kótos*, each of which belongs to a different sphere of activity altogether. He has made a chimera that carries him beyond the confines of *khólos* even to the threshold of *kótos*, only to find through Patroclus's death the heavy toll at culture's borders.

Achilles' *khólos* and Cú Chulainn's *ríastrad*

What are the comparative implications of the Greek cultural division of anger into these two forms of *khólos* and *kótos*? For comparative epic and the comparative literature of early poetry—from *Gilgamesh* to *Orlando Furioso*—are very clear that the anger of heroes is ubiquitous. The comparanda that elucidate how Homeric poetry differs from and enriches the comparative store of early poetry still need to be set out in a systematic manner. In that spirit, I will close this study with a brief look at the comparative perspective afforded us by early Irish saga. The conclusion will be that a formally parallel and diachronically related tradition displays not a *kótos*, not the style of feuding anger but more like *khólos* in its figuration of the warrior's anger. In both cases the *khólos*-style anger displays a central hero whose body is the focus of aggression, both passively and actively. We will see that the Greek concern with cosmic order, so prominent in both *kótos* and *mênis*, seems absent from early Irish epic, whose focus is the material impact of a hero's devastating wrath.

The Celtic branch of Indo-European as represented by Irish texts composed in the European middle ages preserves material of great antiquity; that is to say, in early Ireland we see antiquity present within a medieval European society.[3] As Myles Dillon has shown (1947, 1976) the Irish material is related to our Indic sources; in fact, in Ireland of the middle ages we have a conservative culture whose practice continues rite, verbal art, and other social material that is thousands of years old.[4]

Although Greek culture poses different problems for the comparatist than do the cultures of Ireland or India,[5] there are numerous points of comparison between the sagas and epics of medieval Ireland and Greece. In Ireland one monumental epic, the *Táin Bó Cúalnge*, takes pride of place over numerous shorter tales. In Greece, the monumental impulse yields two long epics, self-consciously standing for an entire tradition.[6] We also know that the *Iliad* and the *Odyssey* were exceptionally long in comparison with performances such as we see in *Odyssey* 8 or with what we know of the texts of the epic cycle. The Homeric Hymns might provide a better model for the length of a typical oral performance than do the *Iliad* or the *Odyssey*, whose very size puts them in a category of their own. So too the *Táin* far outstrips the other examples of Irish narrative.

Provocative parallels emerge from a comparison between Irish saga and Greek epic.[7] These comparisons are reinforced by particular moments in the *Iliad* and the *Táin* when the epics seem to body forth strikingly similar scenes of pathos. For example, at the height of the action of the *Táin*, Cú Chulainn arranges with Ailill to engage only in single combat. This seems to the advantage of both sides, as indeed do the duels of *Iliad* 3 and 7 seem advantageous to the warriors on the Trojan plain.

The first combatant Cú Chulainn meets in this way is Etarcomol, a foster son of Ailill and Medb. This familial relationship (fosterage) is exploited by the text to stress the youth or vulnerability of Cú Chulainn's first victim, as well as the emotional ties between Etarcomol, Ailill, and Medb. Moreover, Fergus, under whose protection the youth comes to Cú Chulainn, points out the danger involved. For convenience, I quote from the expressive translation of Thomas Kinsella:

> "I would rather you didn't come," Fergus said. "Not that I dislike you, but for fear of strife between Cú Chulainn and you. With your pride and insolence, and the other's ferocity and grimness, force, fury and violence, no good can come from your meeting."
>
> (Kinsella 1970, 117)

Etarcomol proves to be reckless indeed in facing Cú Chulainn. The two warriors verbally challenge each other, and after he agrees to meet Cú Chulainn in single combat the next day, Etarcomol turns to go. But he cannot wait. He turns back his chariot, approaches Cú Chulainn, and challenges him then and there:

> "It's you who wants this," Cú Chulainn said to Etarcomol. "It isn't my wish."
> "You have no choice," Etarcomol said.
> (Kinsella 1970, 119)

Cú Chulainn makes three passes at killing him, and on the third one Etarcomol pays the price for his boldness: "But the fool stubbornly persisted and Cú Chulainn struck down through the crown of his head and split him to the navel" (Kinsella 1970, 120).

This death arouses fury in Fergus, under whose protection Etarcomol has come forth, even as in the Greek tradition *khólos* is aroused in one whose *phílos* has been killed. When Fergus retrieves the body to bring back to Ailill, he does something that calls to mind one of the most dramatic moments of the *Iliad*:

> Fergus pierced Etarcomol's two heels with a spancel-ring and dragged him behind his chariot to the camp. . . . Medb saw this. "That is brutal treatment for the unfortunate dog," Medb said. "I say he was an ignorant whelp," Fergus said. . . . Then they dug a grave for him; his memorial stone was planted, his name written in ogam, and his lamentation made. Cú Chulainn murdered no more that night with his sling.
> (Kinsella 1969, 121)

Not only is tying Etarcomol to the back of the chariot parallel to Achilles' tying Hector to the back of his chariot, the brutal treatment of the human body in both epics being used to underscore the extent to which the violence of the hero has gone beyond even conventional warfare.[8]

I suggest that in this example we have a directly comparable element between Irish saga and Greek epic narrative. In both epics, an extraordinary moment shows single combat leading to the return of the loser, whose body is maltreated by dragging it behind a war chariot. This is true not only because of typological patterns assignable to the integrity of the epic genre in a world literary context, but also because Irish and Greek tradition have a shared cultural heritage. Such narrative elements can be multiplied, but I want now to turn to the *khólos* of Achilles, which I will argue may be a point of cultural heritage shared between these two cultures and their Indo-European congeners.

Just as Achilles has his wrath, so does Cú Chulainn have an anger that seems to define the hero and whose physical manifestation is one of the hallmarks of the *Táin*. It is worth quoting, at length, one of the most extensive descriptions of Cú Chulainn's anger, his *ríastrad* (often translated, in an attempt to account for the physical description, "warp-spasm"). I quote this passage at length to emphasize the detail that Irish saga devotes to description of the physical characteristics of *ríastrad*.

Is and sin cétríastarda im Choin Culaind, co nderna úathbásach n-ilrechtach n-ingantach n-anachnid de. . . . Imsloic indara súil dó ina chend, iss ed mod dánas tarsed fíadchorr tagraim do lár a grúade a iarthor a chlocaind. Sesceing a séitig co m-boí fora grúad sechtair. Ríastarda[9] a bél co urthrachda. Srengais in n-ól don fidba chnáma, comtar inéchnáig a inchróes. Táncatar a scoim ⁊ a thromma, co m-bátar ar eittelaig ina bél ⁊ ina bragit. . . . Airddithir remithir tailcithir tressithir sithithir séolchrand prímlungi móre in bunne díriuch dondfola atracht a fírchléithe a chendmullaig i certairddi, co n-derna dubchíaich n-druídechta de amail chíaich de rígbruidin, in tan tic rí dia tenecur hi fescur lathi gemreta.

Iarsin ríastrad sin ríastarda im Choin Culaind. . . .

(O'Rahilly 1967, 2262–63; 2273–81; 2291–95)

Then his first distortion came upon Cú Chulainn so that he became horrible, many-shaped, strange and unrecognizable. . . . He sucked one of his eyes into his head so that a wild crane could hardly have reached it to pluck it out from the back of his skull on to the middle of his cheek. The other eye sprang out on to his cheek. His mouth was twisted back fearsomely. He drew the cheek back from the jawbone until his inner gullet was seen. His lungs and his liver fluttered in his mouth and his throat. . . . As high, as thick, as strong, as powerful and as long as the mast of a great ship was the straight stream of dark blood which rose up from the very top of his head and became a dark magical mist like the smoke of a palace when a king comes to be attended to in the evening of a wintry day.

After Cú Chulainn had been thus distorted. . . .

(O'Rahilly 1967, 201–2)

This is not Homer, despite the graceful simile. Nonetheless, the luscious extravagance of this passage, the vivid description of Cú Chulainn's *ríastrad,* gives me the opportunity to contrast Cú Chulainn's wrath with Achilles' *khólos*. Now Greek *khólos* is a physical anger in contrast to the nonphysical *kótos*, as we have seen. In fact, the physicality of *khólos* is supported by its etymological relationship with English "gall." So too Cú Chulainn's *ríastrad* is directly linked to some kind of bodily process related to the emotion of anger.[10]

Tancatar a scoim ⁊ a thromma, co m-batar ar eittelaig ina bél ⁊ ina bragit.

His lungs and his liver fluttered in his mouth and his throat.

Both Greek and Irish exploit a link between the emotion of anger and the place of the human body in motivating emotion.[11]

Besides the physicality of *khólos*, there is one other analogy to *ríastrad* that suggests a more specific parallel. The most telling feature of Cú Chulainn's *ríastrad* is the distortion of the face, especially the rearrangement of his eyes (as quoted above). Homer's descriptions of Homeric *khólos* can also highlight a distortion of the face.

In this regard, consider the phrase *hupódra idṓn*, studied in detail by J. Holoka, who comes to the following conclusion:

> In both Homeric epics, to look darkly is to employ a nonverbal cue fraught with judgmental significance. The speaker, whatever his message, transmits by his facial demeanor that an infraction of propriety has occurred; he deplores the willful traducing of rules of conduct governing the relations between superordinates and inferiors. . . . In all instances, the facial gesture ὑπόδρα ἰδών charges the speech it introduces with a decidedly minatory fervency and excitement: a threshold has been reached and such inflammable materials as wounded pride, righteous indignation, frustration, same, and shock are nearing the combustion point.
>
> (Holoka 1983, 16)

Indeed, I suggest that this facial gesture has a special relationship with Greek *khólos*.

The strong emotion that a petitioner might expect to provoke in the party he has just found is to be registered in such a gesture. To discover the rhetorical situation in which a speaker finds himself is to read out the emotional state of the addressee from the look on his face. This gesture can be a smile, as when Odysseus decides to spare Medon:

> τὸν δ' <u>ἐπιμειδήσας</u> προσέφη πολύμητις Ὀδυσσεύς·
> "θάρσει, ἐπεὶ δή σ' οὗτος ἐρύσατο καὶ ἐσάωσεν,"
> (*Od.* 22.371–72)

> And <u>having smiled</u> many minded Odysseus spoke to him, "take heart since this one has preserved and saved you."

But things do not always go so well, so that the facial gesture can be the familiar glowering, as at the beginning of *Odyssey* 22, when, after the death of Antinoos the suitors try to rile Odysseus (*neíkeion*, 26) by expressing *khólos* (*kholōtoîsin epéessin*, 26, "with words of *khólos*"), only to have Odysseus revile them in very effective terms (cf. 42), when he speaks "glowering" (*hupódra idṓn*, *Od.* 22.34); the same line occurs when Eurymachus offers to make up for the goods that the suitors have taken (*Od.* 22.60), so that the phrase *hupódra idṓn* seems here to be a mark of Odysseus's *khólos*. Finally, the same gesture and the same phrasing marks the unfortunate Leodes' failed suppliancy to an enraged Odysseus on a rampage (*Od.* 22.320). Nor is it uncharacteristic of Odysseus to respond in this way. This look is the one that he gives to Thersites just before he insults him and hits him (*Il.* 2.245). And the phrase is not restricted to Odyssean contexts. So too Achilles comes to be *hupódra idṓn* prior to delivering his last speech in *Iliad* 1 to Agamemnon, just before Athene prevents him from letting his *khólos* go so far as to kill Agamemnon (*Il.* 1.148–49).

Holoka points out that Zeus is the only god to react with the gesture *hupódra idṓn*,[12] most prominently when Hera seduces Zeus in *Iliad* 14. If *hupódra idṓn* is connected to *khólos*, then Hera has not succeeded in avoiding Zeus's *khólos* after all (*mḗ pṓs moi metépeita kholṓseai, aí ke siōpêi / oíkhōmai pròs dôma bathurróou Ōkeanoîo* [*Il.* 14.310–11], "Lest you have *khólos* hereafter, if in silence I go to the house of deep-flowing Ocean.")

It can hardly surprise Hera that when Zeus sees the plight of Hector's Trojans before Poseidon's onslaught and he takes pity, his *khólos* (marked by *hupódra idṓn*) comes to the fore:

> Ἕκτορα δ᾽ ἐν πεδίῳ ἴδε κείμενον, ἀμφὶ δ᾽ ἑταῖροι
> ἥαθ᾽, ὁ δ᾽ ἀργαλέῳ ἔχετ᾽ ἄσθματι κῆρ ἀπινύσσων,
> αἷμ᾽ ἐμέων, ἐπεὶ οὔ μιν ἀφαυρότατος βάλ᾽ Ἀχαιῶν.
> τὸν δὲ ἰδὼν ἐλέησε πατὴρ ἀνδρῶν τε θεῶν τε,
> δεινὰ δ᾽ ὑπόδρα ἰδὼν Ἥρην πρὸς μῦθον ἔειπεν.
> (*Il.* 15.9–13)

And he saw Hector lying in the field, and around him his companions sat, and he was kept down by painful breathing, dazed in his heart, vomiting blood, since it wasn't the feeblest of the Achaeans who had struck him. And at the sight of him, the father of gods and men pitied him, and with a terribly glowering look he spoke a word to Hera.

In this case, the *idṓn* marks the subjective aspect of Zeus's experience, the effect of his seeing the object of pity (12). Objectively, he expresses that experience through his facial expression: *hupódra idṓn*.[13]

I have noted before that the verbs of seeing mark the onset of *khólos*. This collocation is important, since such an emphasis on vision is explicit in the phrase *hupódra idṓn*, which contains two roots meaning "see," or "look."

Pokorny (1959, 213) shows a root **derk-* meaning "to look or see," which gives Greek *dérkomai*. It is also the source of a mythic beast whose facial expression has a deadly effect: *drákōn*.[14] The importance of the notion of sight, and the "objective" or outwardly directed nature of **derk-* is clear from the description of Agamemnon's shield where the dragon is a prominent image:

> τῇ δ᾽ ἐπὶ μὲν Γοργὼ βλοσυρῶπις ἐστεφάνωτο
> δεινὸν δερκομένη, περὶ δὲ Δεῖμός τε Φόβος τε.
> τῆς δ᾽ ἐξ ἀργύρεος τελαμὼν ἦν· αὐτὰρ ἐπ᾽ αὐτοῦ
> κυάνεος ἐλέλικτο δράκων, κεφαλαὶ δέ οἱ ἦσαν
> τρεῖς ἀμφιστρεφέες, ἑνὸς αὐχένος ἐκπεφυυῖαι.
> (*Il.* 11.36–40)

And on it there was encircled Gorgo of the loathsome gaze, glowering terribly, and about [her] Rout and Fear; and on it was a belt of silver; and on that a steel-blue dragon curled, with the heads on it numbering three as they turned everywhere, though protruding from a single neck.

The fearsome aspect of Gorgo is the terror caused by her gaze.[15] It is significant that the adverb used here (*deinón*) is the only qualifier of the phrase *hupódra idṓn* in Homer. Furthermore, the *drákōn* of Agamemnon's shield continues the notion of the power of sight that can be used to attack another.[16]

The focus on seeing, sight, and the function of the eyes calls to mind the notion of the evil-eye, so extensively distributed throughout the Indo-European and Near Eastern cultural-symbolic systems (Dundes 1992, 257–318). Alan Dundes' in-depth review of the folkloric basis of such symbolic systems suggests that the connection between Greek anger and the symbolism of the gaze has to do with a deeply rooted folk-belief about the way that emotions work in the world. In particular, the metaphoric systems discussed in the previous chapter might be connected through a folk-based theory of the humors.[17]

The phrase *hupódra idṓn*, then, brings to the surface a powerful notion of "seeing" that involves aggression by an injured party. It emphasizes the strength of this action by using two forms from two different verbs meaning "to see." In this sense the phrase is "over-determined." We might ask what links seeing and the meaning of *khólos*.

In Homeric epic, one of the most powerful stimuli that may lead to *khólos* is the sight of an object or person. So, for example when Achilles receives the armor from Thetis in *Iliad* 19, as we have already noted, *khólos* is singled out as the wrath with which he is inspired. As a matter of fact, he sees his shield, so that *khólos* enters into him; and the outward manifestation of that is the horrifying glow of his eyes:

> οὐδέ τις ἔτλη
> ἄντην εἰσιδέειν, ἀλλ᾽ ἔτρεσαν. αὐτὰρ Ἀχιλλεὺς
> ὡς εἶδ᾽, ὥς μιν μᾶλλον ἔδυ χόλος, ἐν δέ οἱ ὄσσε
> δεινὸν ὑπὸ βλεφάρων ὡς εἰ σέλας ἐξεφάανθεν·
> τέρπετο δ᾽ ἐν χείρεσσιν ἔχων θεοῦ ἀγλαὰ δῶρα.
> αὐτὰρ ἐπεὶ φρεσὶν ᾗσι τετάρπετο δαίδαλα λεύσσων,
> αὐτίκα μητέρα ἣν ἔπεα πτερόεντα προσηύδα·
> (*Il.* 19.14–20)

> Nor did anyone dare to look at him straight on, but they trembled. But when Achilles looked, then the *khólos* entered him the more, and therein did his eyes terribly appear beneath his brow, like a flash. And he was delighted to hold the glorified gifts of the god in his hands. But when he delighted his mind in gazing at the finery, immediately he spoke winged words to his mother.

This passage resonates with the phrase *hupódra idṓn* in significant ways. In particular, it emphasizes a "look" that is in some sense *hupó-* ("beneath"); this usage helps clarify the sense of the *hupo-* in *hupódra idṓn*. The use of *deinón* here recalls *deiná* in *Il.* 15.13, *deinón* being, as we have just seen, the only adverbial form used in *hupódra idṓn* phrases.[18]

The precise moment at which one catches sight of a person or object is important. Thus Talthybius and Eurybates are understandably anxious (*Il.* 1.327) about making their trek to Achilles' tent to retrieve Briseis. When Achilles sees them, he reveals that his anger is not in fact directed at them:

> τὸν δ' εὗρον παρά τε κλισίῃ καὶ νηῒ μελαίνῃ
> ἥμενον· οὐδ ἄρα τώ γε ἰδὼν γήθησεν Ἀχιλλεύς.
> (*Il.* 1.329–30)

> They found him at the hut and the black ship, sitting; and at the sight of them Achilles did not take delight.

This passage is comparable to Zeus's reaction to seeing Iris and Apollo approach him in Book 15, after Athena has calmed down Ares, after Hera has yielded to Zeus's greater power:

> τὼ δ' ἀΐξαντε πετέσθην.
> Ἴδην δ' ἵκανον πολυπίδακα, μητέρα θηρῶν,
> εὗρον δ' εὐρύοπα Κρονίδην ἀνὰ Γαργάρῳ ἄκρῳ
> ἥμενον· ἀμφὶ δέ μιν θυόεν νέφος ἐστεφάνωτο.
> τὼ δὲ πάροιθ' ἐλθόντε Διὸς νεφεληγερέταο
> στήτην· οὐδέ σφωε ἰδὼν ἐχολώσατο θυμῷ,
> (*Il.* 15.150–55)

> The two darting forth flew on. And they both reached Ida rich in springs, mother of beasts, and they found the wide-faced son of Kronos on the peak of Gargaron as he sat. And around him encircled a fragrant cloud. And those two coming forth stood before cloud-gatherer Zeus; and at the sight of them he did not become angry in his heart.

This is clearly a typical scene of the kind that one sees in *Iliad* 9,[19] with common elements at the phraseological level including *heûron*, *hēmenon*, and *idṓn*. Clearly one of the repertoire of emotions available at a surprising sight is *khólos*. So it comes as no surprise that *tòn d' ar' hupódra idṓn* is metrically interchangeable with *tòn dè kholosaménē*.[20] Both phrases serve to mark the same emotional state of the speaker, except that one ends in a consonant and the other in a vowel.

Thus far we have observed that *khólos* is often marked by the sight of a disturbing person or situation and that the phrase *hupódra idṓn* doubly indicates through *-dra-* and *idṓn* the notion of seeing or looking. But there is one passage that clinches the relationship between sight and *khólos*. And that passage features prominently both *khólos* and *hupódra idṓn*.

To conclude a book on Achilles' anger, it is appropriate to gaze at the meeting between Priam and Achilles in *Iliad* 24; such an encounter could be organized around the notion of seeing. As Hermes and Priam approach Achilles' tent, Hermes declares the following:

> ἀλλ' ἤτοι μὲν ἐγὼ πάλιν εἴσομαι, οὐδ' Ἀχιλῆος
> ὀφθαλμοὺς εἴσειμι·
> (*Il.* 24.462–63)

> But indeed I will go back, nor will I go before the eyes of Achilles.

After Priam "finds" Achilles (*en dé min autòn / heûr', Il.* 24.472–73, "therein did he find him"), wonder seizes the onlookers:

> ὣς Ἀχιλεὺς θάμβησεν ἰδὼν Πρίαμον θεοειδέα·
> θάμβησαν δὲ καὶ ἄλλοι, ἐς ἀλλήλους δὲ ἴδοντο.
> (*Il.* 24.483–84[21])

> At that Achilles was awestruck as he caught sight of godly Priam; and the others too were in awe, and they gazed at one another.

What follows is one of the most famous scenes in literature, one of reconciliation and consolation that sheds light over the action of the entire poem.[22] But I wish to focus on one of the stress points of this passage, where the anger of Achilles threatens to return in full swing.

Priam has just asked to *see with his own eyes* the body of Hector; so he refuses Achilles' hospitality and demands the presentation of Hector's body:

> μή πώ μ' ἐς θρόνον ἵζε, διοτρεφές, ὄφρα κεν Ἕκτωρ
> κεῖται ἐνὶ κλισίῃσιν ἀκηδής, ἀλλὰ τάχιστα
> λῦσον, ἵν' ὀφθαλμοῖσιν ἴδω·
> (*Il.* 24.553–55)

> Don't set me on the throne, god born one, while Hector lies uncared for in the huts, but release him at once, so that I might see him with my eyes.

Achilles, now a wiser student of the emotions than he was in *Iliad* 1, refuses, but only with the ocular gesture that I now argue can convey the notion of *khólos.*

> Τὸν δ' ἄρ' ὑπόδρα ἰδὼν προσέφη πόδας ὠκὺς Ἀχιλλεύς·
> "μηκέτι νῦν μ' ἐρέθιζε, γέρον."
> (*Il.* 24.559–60[23])

> Then with a glowering look swift-footed Achilles spoke. "No longer anger me, old man."

That Achilles understands the implications of Priam's request is clear from Homer's description of the exchange of the ransom for Hector's body. Achilles orders the serving maids to wash and anoint the body, but only after hiding it:

νόσφιν ἀειράσας, ὡς μὴ Πρίαμος ἴδοι υἱόν,
μὴ ὁ μὲν ἀχνυμένῃ κραδίῃ χόλον οὐκ ἐρύσαιτο
παῖδα ἰδών,
(*Il.* 24.583–85)

And he set it aside, so that Priam not see his son, lest he not be able to restrain his *khólos*, after having gazed at the body.

Achilles even specifies when it would be appropriate to view the body:

ἅμα δ' ἠοῖ φαινομένηφιν[24]
ὄψεαι αὐτὸς ἄγων·
(*Il.* 24.600–601)

And together with the shining dawn, you yourself will look on him as you lead him back.

And all of these viewings are capped by our observation of the two men gazing in awe at one another:

ἤ τοι Δαρδανίδης Πρίαμος θαύμαζ' Ἀχιλῆα,
ὅσσος ἔην οἷός τε· θεοῖσι γὰρ ἄντα ἐῴκει·
αὐτὰρ ὁ Δαρδανίδην Πρίαμον θαύμαζεν Ἀχιλεύς,
εἰσορόων ὄψιν τ' ἀγαθὴν καὶ μῦθον ἀκούων.
(*Il.* 24.629–32)

Indeed Dardanian Priam was in awe of Achilles, his magnificence and his qualities; for he seemed just like the gods. And Achilles was in awe of Dardanian Priam, as he looked at his noble face and heard his speech.

To summarize: in *Iliad* 24, during the encounter between Achilles and Priam, the social interaction involves the semantics of the gaze, at one point used in a hostile sense by Achilles through the phrase *hupódra idṓn* in order to suppress the possible occasion of *khólos*. Achilles knows that to bring out the corpse of Hector would precipitate the *khólos* of Priam and compel him to respond in kind. Furthermore, his use of the facial gesture marked by the phrase *hupódra idṓn* is an act of aggression intended to make Priam back down. It is a preemptive display of *khólos*.

But are "seeing" and "looking" closely enough related to *khólos* to warrant a comparison with Cú Chulainn's facial distortion of *ríastrad*? What is the origin of Greek epic's nearly philosophical concern with the emotion of anger? When considering that question, we know now to keep in mind the intimate connection between the sense of sight and anger.[25] Watkins claims a "virtual semantic identity" for two phrases:

θεῶν ὄπις = θεῶν μῆνις

and he points out that both *mênis* and *ópis* are intimately connected to roots that have to do with sight. His note on this matter is worth quoting here:

> This equation ὄπις = μῆνις and the etymology of μῆνις (Doric μᾶνις) there proposed, a deformation of **mnānis*, are mutually supported by the discovery . . . that the root *mnā*- (**mneh*$_2$-) in Luvian means "to see," just like the root ὄπ- of ὄπις.
>
> (Watkins 1987, 298)

I would add that the basis of the connection between seeing and anger is twofold, one connection subjective: the stimulus that can give rise to anger may come in through the eyes; and the other objective: one way to express or to act on that anger is through the contortion of the eyes. The phrase *hupódra idṓn*, as linked with *khólos*, is, then, a precious artifact, for it shows that in Homeric poetry, a poetic medium that refrains from the kind of description we find in the *Táin's ríastrad*, the narrative sometimes marks Achilles' *khólos* with a phrase that recalls the most archaic layer of the semantics of anger in Indo-European.[26]

I conclude by citing Jan de Vries on another possible connection to Cú Chulainn's *ríastrad*:

> We have mentioned the strange distortion of the hero's face when he is attacked by furious rage in battle: the *ríastrad*. . . . What does this strange description mean, which shows us the unbridled and somewhat abstruse imaginative power of the Irish? It is a remarkable fact that we have what look like pictures of this on Armorican coins. . . . On many coins the face has a monstrously large eye situated below its normal position. Could not this allude to Cúchulainn's eye which came to rest on his cheek?
>
> . . . .
>
> The Viking Egill Skallagrimsson has similar berserk fits of rage. When he sat down he pulled one eyebrow up to the roots of his hair and the other down to his cheek. He had black eyes, and eyebrows which met above his nose.
>
> The effect of the facial distortion of Egill and Cú Chulainn is the same: one eye is hidden, whereas the other protrudes and seems extremely large.
>
> (De Vries 1963, 83–84)

After pointing out that the one-eyed connection may have sacral roots, De Vries goes on to make his boldest suggestion:

> We can no longer speak of a borrowing here. Evidently the Celts and the Germanic tribes each knew this mythical feature from their own tradition, and it is very possible that this tradition went back to Indo-European times.
>
> (De Vries 1963, 85)

I conclude my comparative observations on *khólos* with the suggestion that this old connection survives in a muted form in the Homeric epics. The use of the overdetermined phrase for "glowering" (*hupódra idṓn*) reveals an old connection between the enraged hero and the distortion of his eyes.[27]

It is a commonplace of Indo-European studies that one needs three independently motivated examples to make a secure reconstruction. Thus, I propose to add Achilles' *khólos* and its physical manifestation described in the phrase *hupódra idṓn* to the *ríastrad* of Cú Chulainn and the fit of Egil as the physical manifestation of the devastating wrath of the hero and the bequest of a long-lived poetic and cultural survival.

Notes

1. An early comparison between Greek and Irish heroic narrative is in Nutt's 1990 *Cuchulainn, the Irish Achilles*. See also O'Nolan 1969, Renehan 1989, and Harris 1989, especially Chapters 2 and 4.

2. Muellner 1996, 194.

3. See Dillon and Chadwick 1967, 239–69.

4. On the archaism of Irish traditions, see Dillon 1947 and Rees and Rees 1961. Important still is Arbois de Jubainville 1899. On the comparative method as used to uncover cultural survivals, see Littleton 1982. For points of comparison within the tales, see Melia 1979. For a recent comparison between Greece and Ireland, see Renehan 1987. See also Harris 1989; and the use made of Irish materials by Martin 1989, 85, 91, 232. For anger and warrior in Irish saga, see Henry 1982 and Lincoln 1975, 101–2. The importance of the Irish material has not been missed by medievalists working in early epic, see Armistead 1987 and Montgomery 1987, for example, and, with important insights into the relationship between Irish and other medieval literatures, Tymoczko 1982.

5. Littleton 1970, 229.

6. After Kirk's (1962) suggestion that the the monumentality is crucial to Homeric epic, we can turn to Martin's compelling notion that Homeric narrative is driven by an "expansion aesthetic" (1989, 218–20). Thus Martin makes the idea of monumentality a dynamic process. See also Thornton's important comparative data (1984, 15–16).

7. See Melia 1979.

8. Cf. Nagler 1974, 161 n. 42; Segal 1981.

9. Note the use of the verb, here reinforcing the notion that this particular kind of anger has its own characteristics; O'Rahilly's translation ("twisted") is literally correct, but the force of the figure is missed by not capturing the notion of "distortion." The distortion of the hero is a mythological motif found in early Irish literature (Cross 1952, 18, A526.6). See too Henry 1982.

10. Henry 1981; for the locus classicus on Achilles and Cú Chulainn, see Nutt 1900. The comparative features of *ríastrad* will be treated in a separate article; for now, note that it is one word among a dozen or so others for anger in the early Irish literature; this too provides a parallel to the Greek material.

11. Lakoff and Kövecses 1987; Lakoff 1987, 380–415.

12. Holoka 1983, 9–10.

13. Note that Zeus's smile at *Il.* 15.47 is the opposite of *hupódra idṓn*, as Odysseus's smile at Medon is the opposite of his reaction (*hupódra idṓn*) to Eurymachus and Leodes.

14. "Vom bannenden, lähmenden Blick" (Pokorny 1959).

15. See Vernant 1991a.

16. Another part of Agamemnon's armor also has dragons on display on his *thṓrax: kúneoi dè drákontes orōréxato Il.* 11.26 "and three dark-blue dragons were extended." This notion of the serpent or dragon as an early part of Indo-European mythos is explored in Watkins 1995 and see note 26 below.

17. The folkloric basis of the epic evidence will prove to be a fruitful area of research. For the humors in Greek philosophy, see Lloyd 1964. Dundes assertion that "it would appear that the formulations of humoral pathology simply formalized a folk theory already in existence" (Dundes 1992, 298) encourages me to see such a theory as underlying the connection of *khólos* to liquids and the eyes in the Homeric texts.

18. Holoka 1983, 3; on the alliteration here see Shewan 1925, 196.

19. Segal 1968; cf. Nagler 1974, 200–201; Nagy 1979, 49n. On the syntax of lines containing *heûron* see Chantraine 1963, 351.

20. Holoka 1983, 3.

21. Cf. *Il.* 24.482, and *Il.* 9.193–95 and note *íde* in 195.

22. See, e.g., Nagler 1974, 167–98.

23. On the close relationship of *mênis* and *éris*, see *Il.* 18.107–8 and *Il.* 3.415, *Il.* 23.490, *Il.* 19.58–59, *Il.* 20.253; and cf. Nagler 1988, 82, with Hogan 1981.

24. Dawn will accompany Priam back to Troy as Hermes accompanied him to Achilles' tent. Cf. Nagler 1974, 115.

25. See the discussion in Watkins 1987b, 298–99.

26. The phrase *hupódra idṓn* is used 14 times of Achilles and 12 times of others (Holoka 1983, 3–4). Cf. Watkins 1985, 12 for the connection with "dragon" (<the suffixed _*drk-on(t)-_ in *drákōn*) "monster with the evil eye"; now see Watkins 1995, 447, "the danger of the sight of the dragon is found in both traditions, Greek and Irish." The unconvinced should contemplate the simile at *Il.* 22.94–95.

27. Dumézil points out that "les grands guerriers de l' Europe du Nord—l'Irlandais Cûchulainn, les chefs vikings—pratiquaient une grimace héroïque qui était comme le certificat de leur puissance et la preuve de leur victoire" (1948, 172, with literature). For Beowulf see also Puhvel 1968. S. G. Armistead's consideration (1987) of the "furia guerrera" in two epic texts includes inspiring comparative work along these lines. See especially 267, where Armistead argues that the connection between Irish saga and Norse saga is more than typological, "cuando pensamos en los múltiples contactos culturales entre celtas y vikingos." I am encouraged by his conclusion: "Cabe preguntarse hasta dónde remonta el tópico de la furia guerrera en la tradicón épica indoeuropea." See also Montgomery 1987, for which reference I am grateful to S. G. Armistead. Generally, the school of thinking founded by Dumézil focuses on *lússa* as the Homeric term relevant to the anger of the berserkir (cf. Dumézil 1980, Lincoln 1975) I think *khólos* is a more likely candidate for the battle rage that comes to be associated with *lússa*. On Dumézil and early Greek studies, see Nagy 1981 and 1990b, 7–17. Cf. J. Nagy 1990.

Appendix One

Forms of *Κότος* Discussed in Part I

Group 1

Il. 8.449	ὀλλῦσαι Τρῶας, τοῖσιν κότον αἰνὸν ἔθεσθε
Il. 16.449	υἱέες ἀθανάτων, τοῖσιν κότον αἰνὸν ἐνήσεις
Od. 11.102	λήσειν ἐννοσίγαιον, ὅ τοι κότον ἔνθετο θυμῷ
Od. 13.342	πατροκασιγνήτῳ, ὅς τοι κότον ἔνθετο θυμῷ

Group 2

Il. 1.82	ἀλλά τε καὶ μετόπισθεν ἔχει κότον, ὄφρα τελέσσῃ
Il. 13.517	Δηίφοβος· δὴ γάρ οἱ ἔχεν κότον ἐμμενὲς αἰεί

Group 3

Il. 5.177	εἰ μή τις θεός ἐστι κοτεσσάμενος Τρώεσσιν
Il. 16.386	Ζεύς, ὅτε δὴῥ᾽ ἄνδρεσσι κοτεσσάμενος χαλεπήνῃ
Il. 18.367	οὐκ ὄφελον Τρώεσσι κοτεσσαμένη κακὰ ῥάψαι

Group 4

Od. 5.147	μή πώς τοι μετόπισθε κοτεσσάμενος χαλεπήνῃ
Od. 19.83	μή πώς τοι δέσποινα κοτεσσαμένη χαλεπήνῃ
Il. 14.191	ἠέ κεν ἀρνήσαιο κοτεσσαμένη τό γε θυμῷ

Group 5

Il. 5.747 ἡρώων, οἷσίν τε κοτέσσεται ὀβριμοπάτρη
(= *Il.* 8.391, *Od.* 1.101)
Il. 23.383 εἰ μὴ Τυδέος υἷι κοτέσσατο Φοῖβος Ἀπόλλων

Group 6

Il. 21.456 νῶι δέ τ' ἄψορροι κίομεν κεκοτηότι θυμῷ
Od. 9.501 ἀλλά μιν ἄψορρον προσέφην κεκοτηότι θυμῷ
Od. 19.71 δαιμονίη, τί μοι ὧδ' ἐπέχεις κεκοτηότι θυμῷ
Od. 22.477 χεῖράς τ' ἠδὲ πόδας κόπτον κεκοτηότι θυμῷ

Group 7

Il. 3.345 σείοντ' ἐγχείας ἀλλήλοισιν κοτέοντε
Il. 14.143 σοὶ δ' οὔ πω μάλα πάγχυ θεοὶ μάκαρες κοτέουσιν

Group 8

Il. 2.223 ἐκπάγλως κοτέοντο νεμέσσηθέν τ' ἐνὶ θυμῷ
Il. 1.181 οὐδ' ὄθομαι κοτέοντος. ἀπειλήσω δέ τοι ὧδε
Il. 4.168 τῆσδ' ἀπάτης κοτέων· τὰ μὲν ἔσσεται οὐκ ἀτέλεστα

Group 9

Il. 10.517 τῇ κοτέων Τρώων κατεδύσετο πουλὺν ὅμιλον
Il. 23.391 ἣ δὲ μετ' Ἀδμήτου υἱὸν κοτέουσα βεβήκει

Group 10 (Isolated forms)

Il. 5.191 ἔμπης δ' οὐκ ἐδάμασσα· θεός νύ τίς ἐστι κοτήεις
Il. 3.220 φαίης κε ζάκοτόν τέ τιν' ἔμμεναι ἄφρονά τ' αὔτως

Appendix Two

Forms of *Χόλος* Discussed in Part II

The Accusative Case (14 total)

Group 1 παύω + χόλον at the bucolic diaeresis

Il. 9.459 ἀλλά τις ἀθανάτων παύσεν χόλον ὅς ῥ' ἐνὶ θυμῷ
Il. 15.72 τὸ πρὶν δ' οὔτ' ἄρ ἐγὼ παύω χόλον, οὔτε τιν' ἄλλον
Od. 4.583 αὐτὰρ ἐπεὶ κατέπαυσα θεῶν χόλον αἰὲν ἐόντων
Il. 19.67 νῦν δ' ἤ τοι μὲν ἐγὼ παύω χόλον, οὐδέ τί με χρὴ

Group 2 παύω + χόλον in the first half of the line

Il. 9.260 παύε', ἔα δὲ χόλον θυμαλγέα· σοὶ δ' Ἀγαμέμνων
Il. 1.192 ἠὲ χόλον παύσειεν ἐρητύσειέ τε θυμόν

Group 3 χόλος with verbs other than παύω signifying the cessation or avoidance of anger

At the hephthemimeral caesura

Od. 1.433 εὐνῇ δ' οὔ ποτ' ἔμικτο, χόλον δ' ἀλέεινε γυναικός
Il. 4.178 αἴθ' οὕτως ἐπὶ πᾶσι χόλον τελέσει' Ἀγαμέμνων

At the bucolic diaeresis

Il. 1.283 λίσσομ' Ἀχιλλῆι μεθέμεν χόλον, ὅς μέγα πᾶσιν

Il. 15.138 τῶ σ' αὖ νῦν κέλομαι μεθέμεν χόλον υἷος ἑῆος
(Cf. *Il.* 2.241 ἀλλὰ μάλ' οὐκ Ἀχιλῆϊ χόλος φρεσίν, ἀλλὰ μεθήμων)

Elsewhere in the line

Od. 1.78 ὃν χόλον· οὐ μὲν γάρ τι δυνήσεται ἀντία πάντων
Il. 1.81 εἴ περ γάρ τε χόλον γε καὶ αὐτῆμαρ καταπέψῃ

Generally referring to avoidance of anger

Il. 15.223 οἴχεται εἰς ἅλα δῖαν, ἀλευάμενος χόλον αἰπὺν

Anomalous line (questioning of the propriety of χόλος)

Il. 6.326 δαιμόνι', οὐ μὲν καλὰ χόλον τόνδ' ἔνθεο θυμῷ

The Genitive Case (7 total)

Group 4

Il. 1.224 Ἀτρείδην προσέειπε, καὶ οὔ πω λῆγε χόλοιο
Il. 9.157 ταῦτά κέ οἱ τελέσαιμι μεταλλήξαντι χόλοιο
Il. 9.261 ἄξια δῶρα δίδωσι μεταλλήξαντι χόλοιο
Il. 9.299 ταῦτά κέ τοι τελέσειε μεταλλήξαντι χόλοιο

Od. 21.377 μνηστῆρες, καὶ δὴ μέθιεν χαλεποῖο χόλοιο

Il. 10.107 ἐκ χόλου ἀργαλέοιο μεταστρέψῃ φίλον ἦτορ
Od. 11.554 οὐδὲ θανὼν λήσεσθαι ἐμοὶ χόλου εἵνεκα τευχέων

The Accusative Case (4 total)

Group 5

Exceptions (χόλον in the accusative not referring to the cessation of anger, but to the continuation of anger)

Il. 14.50 ἐν θυμῷ βάλλονται ἐμοὶ χόλον ὥς περ Ἀχιλλεύς

Il. 4.513 μάρναται, ἀλλ' ἐπὶ νηυσὶ χόλον θυμαλγέα πέσσει
Il. 9.565 τῇ ὅ γε παρκατέλεκτο χόλον θυμαλγέα πέσσων
Il. 9.260 παύε', ἔα δὲ χόλον θυμαλγέα· σοὶ δ' Ἀγαμέμνων

The Nominative Case (23 total)

Group 6

Il. 1.387	᾿Ατρεΐωνα δ᾿ ἔπειτα χόλος λάβεν, αἶψα δ᾿ ἀναστὰς	
Il. 2.241	ἀλλὰ μάλ᾿, οὐκ ᾿Αχιλῆι χόλος φρεσίν, ἀλλὰ μεθήμων	
Il. 4.23	σκυζομένη Διὶ πατρί, χόλος δέ μιν ἄγριος ᾕρει	
Il. 6.166	ὣς φάτο, τὸν δὲ ἄνακτα χόλος λάβεν οἷον ἄκουσε	
Il. 8.460	σκυζομένη Διὶ πατρί, χόλος δέ μιν ἄγριος ᾕρει	(5)
Il. 9.436	πῦρ ἐθέλεις ἀίδηλον, ἐπεὶ χόλος ἔμπεσε θυμῷ	
Il. 9.525	ἡρώων, ὅτε κέν τιν᾿ ἐπιζάφελος χόλος ἵκοι	
Il. 9.553	ἀλλ᾿ ὅτε δὴ Μελέαγρον ἔδυ χόλος, ὅς τε καὶ ἄλλων	
Il. 9.675	ἢ ἀπέειπε, χόλος δ᾿ ἔτ᾿ ἔχει μεγαλήτορα θυμόν	
Il. 14.207	εὐνῆς καὶ φιλότητος, ἐπεὶ χόλος ἔμπεσε θυμῷ	(10)
Il. 14.306	εὐνῆς καὶ φιλότητος, ἐπεὶ χόλος ἔμπεσε θυμῷ	
Il. 15.122	πὰρ Διὸς ἀθανάτοισι χόλος καὶ μῆνις ἐτύχθη	
Il. 15.217	ἴστω τοῦθ᾿, ὅτι νῶιν ἀνήκεστος χόλος ἔσται	
Il. 16.30	μὴ ἐμέ γ᾿ οὖν οὗτός γε λάβοι χόλος, ὃν σὺ φυλάσσεις	
Il. 16.206	αὖτις, ἐπεί ῥά τοι ὧδε κακὸς χόλος ἔμπεσε θυμῷ	(15)
Il. 17.399	τόν γε ἰδοῦσ᾿ ὀνόσαιτ, οὐδ᾿ εἰ μάλα μιν χόλος ἵκοι	
Il. 18.108	καὶ χόλος, ὅς τ᾿ ἐφέηκε πολύφρονά περ χαλεπῆναι	
Il. 18.119	ἀλλά ἑ μοῖρ᾿ ἐδάμασσε καὶ ἀργαλέος χόλος῞Ηρης	
Il. 18.322	εἴ ποθεν ἐξεύροι· μάλα γὰρ δριμὺς χόλος αἱρεῖ	
Il. 19.16	ὡς εἶδ᾿, ὥς μιν μᾶλλον ἔδυ χόλος, ἐν δέ οἱ ὄσσε	(20)
Il. 20.255	πόλλ᾿ ἐτεά τε καὶ οὐκί· χόλος δέ τε καὶ τὰ κελεύει	
Il. 22.94	βεβρωκὼς κακὰ φάρμακ᾿, ἔδυ δέ τέ μιν χόλος αἰνός	
Od. 8.304	ἔστη δ᾿ ἐν προθύροισι, χόλος δέ μιν ἄγριος ᾕρει	(23)

Group 6a

Il. 9.553	ἀλλ᾿ ὅτε δὴ Μελέαγρον ἔδυ χόλος, ὅς τε καὶ ἄλλων
Il. 19.16	ὡς εἶδ᾿, ὥς μιν μᾶλλον ἔδυ χόλος, ἐν δέ οἱ ὄσσε
Il. 22.94	βεβρωκὼς κακὰ φάρμακ᾿, ἔδυ δέ τέ μιν χόλος αἰνός

Group 6b

Il. 1.387	᾿Ατρείωνα δ᾿ ἔπειτα χόλος λάβεν, αἶψα δ᾿ ἀναστὰς
Il. 6.166	ὣς φάτο, τὸν δὲ ἄνακτα χόλος λάβεν οἷον ἄκουσε
Il. 16.30	μὴ ἐμέ γ᾿ οὖν οὗτός γε λάβοι χόλος, ὃν σὺ φυλάσσεις

Group 6c

Il. 4.23	σκυζομένη Διὶ πατρί, χόλος δέ μιν ἄγριος ᾕρει

Il. 8.460 σκυζομένη Διὶ πατρί, χόλος δέ μιν ἄγριος ᾕρει
Od. 8.304 ἔστη δ' ἐν προθύροισι, χόλος δέ μιν ἄγριος ᾕρει

Group 6d

Il. 9.436 πῦρ ἐθέλεις ἀίδηλον, ἐπεὶ χόλος ἔμπεσε θυμῷ
Il. 14.207 εὐνῆς καὶ φιλότητος, ἐπεὶ χόλος ἔμπεσε θυμῷ
Il. 14.306 εὐνῆς καὶ φιλότητος, ἐπεὶ χόλος ἔμπεσε θυμῷ
Il. 16.206 αὖτις, ἐπεί ῥά τοι ὧδε κακὸς χόλος ἔμπεσε θυμῷ

Group 6e

Il. 9.525 ἡρώων, ὅτε κέν τιν' ἐπιζάφελος χόλος ἵκοι

Verbs

Group 7

Stems represented:
- Present
  - 2 examples
- Future Stem
  - 1 example
- Aorist Stem
  - 26 examples
    - 15 participles
- Perfect Stem
  - 27 examples
    - 15 participles
- Future Perfect Stem
  - 7 examples
- Aorist Passive Stem
  - 11 examples

Group 8

χόλος preceding a speech

Il. 3.413 τὴν δὲ χολωσαμένη προσεφώνεε δῖ' Ἀφροδίτη
Il. 24.55 τὸν δὲ χολωσαμένη προσέφη λευκώλενος Ἥρη
Od. 18.25 τὸν δὲ χολωσάμενος προσεφώνεεν Ἶρος ἀλήτης
Il. 23.482 τὸν δὲ χολωσάμενος Κρητῶν ἀγὸς ἀντίον ηὔδα
Il. 21.479 ἀλλὰ χολωσαμένη Διὸς αἰδοίη παράκοιτις

Group 8a

Il. 4.241	τοὺς μάλα νεικείεσκε <u>χολωτοῖσιν</u> ἐπέεσσιν
Od. 22.26	νείκειον δ' Ὀδυσῆα <u>χολωτοῖσιν</u> ἐπέεσσι
Od. 22.225	νείκεσσεν δ' Ὀδυσῆα <u>χολωτοῖσιν</u> ἐπέεσσιν
Il. 15.210	νεικείεν ἐθέλῃσι <u>χολωτοῖσιν</u> ἐπέεσσιν

Group 8a1

Il. 1.224	Ἀτρείδην προσέειπε, καὶ οὔ πω λῆγε <u>χόλοιο</u>

Group 8b

Il. 21.136	ὣς ἄρ' ἔφη, ποταμὸς δὲ <u>χολώσατο</u> κηρόθι μᾶλλον
Od. 9.480	ὣς ἐφάμην, ὃ δ' ἔπειτα <u>χολώσατο</u> κηρόθι μᾶλλον
Od. 17.458	ὣς ἔφατ', Ἀντίνοος δὲ <u>χολώσατο</u> κηρόθι μᾶλλον
Od. 18.387	ὣς ἔφατ', Εὐρύμαχος δὲ <u>χολώσατο</u> κηρόθι μᾶλλον
Od. 22.224	ὣς φάτ', Ἀθηναίη δὲ <u>χολώσατο</u> κηρόθι μᾶλλον

Group 9

χόλος preceding an action

Group 9a. Preceding murder

Il. 15.68	τοῦ δὲ <u>χολωσάμενος</u> κτενεῖ Ἕκτορα δῖος Ἀχιλλεύς
Il. 6.205	τὴν δὲ <u>χολωσαμένη</u> χρυσήνιος Ἄρτεμις ἔκτα
Od. 8.227	ἵκετ' ἐνὶ μεγάροισι· <u>χολωσάμενος</u> γὰρ Ἀπόλλων / ἔκτανεν . . .

Group 9b. Preceding other violence

Od. 12.348	εἰ δὲ <u>χολωσάμενός</u> τι βοῶν ὀρθοκραιράων
Il. 2.195	μή τι <u>χολωσάμενος</u> ῥέξῃ κακὸν υἷας Ἀχαιῶν
Il. 4.391	οἳ δὲ <u>χολωσάμενοι</u> Καδμεῖοι κέντορες ἵππων
Il. 9.538	ἣ δὲ <u>χολωσαμένη</u> δῖον γένος ἰοχέαιρα
Il. 2.599	αἳ δὲ <u>χολωσάμεναι</u> πηρὸν θέσαν, αὐτὰρ ἀοιδὴν

Group 10

Il. 1.9	Λητοῦς καὶ Διὸς υἱός· ὃ γὰρ βασιλῆι <u>χολωθεὶς</u>
Il. 2.629	ὅς ποτε Δουλίχιόνδ' ἀπενάσσατο πατρὶ <u>χολωθεὶς</u>
Il. 16.320	Ἀντιλόχῳ ἐπόρουσε κασιγνήτοιο <u>χολωθεὶς</u>

Il. 18.337 Τρώων ἀγλαὰ τέκνα, σέθεν κταμένοιο χολωθείς
Il. 23.23 Τρώων ἀγλαὰ τέκνα, σέθεν κταμένοιο χολωθείς
Il. 23.88 νήπιος, οὐκ ἐθέλων, ἀμφ' ἀστραγάλοισι χολωθείς
Od. 15.254 ὅς ῥ' Ὑπερησίηνδ' ἀπενάσσατο πατρὶ χολωθείς

Il. 13.206 καὶ τότε δὴ περὶ κῆρι Ποσειδάων ἐχολώθη
Il. 9.33 ἣ θέμις ἐστίν, ἄναξ, ἀγορῇ· σὺ δὲ μή τι χολωθῇς
Il. 13.660 τοῦ δὲ Πάρις μάλα θυμὸν ἀποκταμένοιο χολώθη

Od. 18.20 χερσὶ δὲ μή τι λίην προκαλίζεο, μή με χολώσῃς

Group 11

Il. 1.224 Ἀτρείδην προσέειπε, καὶ οὔ πω λῆγε χόλοιο
Il. 9.157 ταῦτά κέ οἱ τελέσαιμι μεταλλήξαντι χόλοιο
Il. 9.261 ἄξια δῶρα δίδωσι μεταλλήξαντι χόλοιο
Il. 9.299 ταῦτα κέ τοι τελέσειε μεταλλήξαντι χόλοιο
Od. 21.377 μνηστῆρες, καὶ δὴ μέθιεν χαλεποῖο χόλοιο

Il. 8.407 Ἥρῃ δ' οὔ τι τόσον νεμεσίζομαι οὐδὲ χολοῦμαι
Il. 8.421 Ἥρῃ δ' οὔ τι τόσον νεμεσίζεται οὐδὲ χολοῦται

Il. 9.523 μηδὲ πόδας· πρὶν δ' οὔ τι νεμεσσητὸν κεχολῶσθαι
Od. 18.227 μῆτερ ἐμή, τὸ μὲν οὔ σε νεμεσσῶμαι κεχολῶσθαι
Od. 22.59 ἰανθῇ· πρὶν δ' οὔ τι νεμεσσητὸν κεχολῶσθαι

Group 12: Complete list of *khólos* phrases from the *Iliad* and the *Odyssey*

Iliad

1.9 Λητοῦς καὶ Διὸς υἱός· ὁ γὰρ βασιλῆι χολωθείς
1.78 ἦ γὰρ ὀίομαι ἄνδρα χολωσέμεν, ὃς μέγα πάντων
1.81 εἴ περ γάρ τε χόλον γε καὶ αὐτῆμαρ καταπέψῃ
1.139 ἄξω ἑλών· ὁ δέ κεν κεχολώσεται ὅν κεν ἵκωμαι
1.192 ἦε χόλον παύσειεν ἐρητύσειέ τε θυμόν
1.217 καὶ μάλα περ θυμῷ κεχολωμένον· ὣς γὰρ ἄμεινον
1.224 Ἀτρεΐδην προσέειπε, καὶ οὔ πω λῆγε χόλοιο
1.283 λίσσομ' Ἀχιλλῆι μεθέμεν χόλον, ὃς μέγα πᾶσιν
1.387 Ἀτρεΐωνα δ' ἔπειτα χόλος λάβεν, αἶψα δ' ἀναστὰς
2.195 μή τι χολωσάμενος ῥέξῃ κακὸν υἷας Ἀχαιῶν
2.241 ἀλλὰ μάλ', οὐκ Ἀχιλῆι χόλος φρεσίν, ἀλλὰ μεθήμων
2.599 αἱ δὲ χολωσάμεναι πηρὸν θέσαν, αὐτὰρ ἀοιδὴν
2.629 ὅς ποτε Δουλίχιόνδ' ἀπενάσσατο πατρὶ χολωθείς
3.413 τὴν δὲ χολωσαμένη προσεφώνεε δῖ' Ἀφροδίτη

4.23	σκυζομένη Διῒ πάτρι, χόλος δέ μιν ἄγριος ᾕρει
4.24	Ἥρῃ δ' οὐκ ἔχαδε στῆθος χόλον, ἀλλὰ προσηύδα
4.36	ἄλλους τε Τρῶας, τότε κεν χόλον ἐξακέσαιο
4.42	μή τι διατρίβειν τὸν ἐμὸν χόλον, ἀλλά μ' ἐᾶσαι
4.178	αἴθ' οὕτως ἐπὶ πᾶσι χόλον τελέσει' Ἀγαμέμνων
4.241	τοὺς μάλα νεικείεσκε χολωτοῖσιν ἐπέεσσιν
4.391	οἱ δὲ χολωσάμενοι Καδμεῖοι, κέντορες ἵππων
4.494	τοὺς δ' Ὀδυσεὺς μάλα θυμὸν ἀποκταμένοιο χολώθη
4.501	τόν ῥ' Ὀδυσεὺς ἑτάροιο χολωσάμενος βάλε δουρὶ
4.513	μάρναται, ἀλλ' ἐπὶ νηυσὶ χόλον θυμαλγέα πέσσει
5.421	Ζεῦ πάτερ, ἦ ῥα τί μοι κεχολώσεαι, ὅττι κεν εἴπω
5.762	Ζεῦ πάτερ, ἦ ῥα τί μοι κεχολώσεαι, αἴ κεν Ἄρηα
6.166	ὣς φάτο, τὸν δὲ ἄνακτα χόλος λάβεν οἷον ἄκουσε
6.205	τὴν δὲ χολωσαμένη χρυσήνιος Ἄρτεμις ἔκτα
6.326	δαιμόνι', οὐ μὲν καλὰ χόλον τόνδ' ἔνθεο θυμῷ
6.335	οὔ τοι ἐγὼ Τρώων τόσσον χόλῳ οὐδὲ νεμέσσι
8.407	Ἥρῃ δ' οὔ τι τόσον νεμεσίζομαι οὐδὲ χολοῦμαι
8.421	Ἥρῃ δ' οὔ τι τόσον νεμεσίζεται οὐδὲ χολοῦται
8.460	σκυζομένη Διὶ πατρί, χόλος δέ μιν ἄγριος ᾕρει
8.461	Ἥρῃ δ' οὐκ ἔχαδε στῆθος χόλον, ἀλλὰ προσηύδα
9.33	ἣ θέμις ἐστίν, ἄναξ, ἀγορῇ· σὺ δὲ μή τι χολωθῇς
9.157	ταῦτά κέ οἱ τελέσαιμι μεταλλήξαντι χόλοιο
9.260	παύε' ἔα δὲ χόλον θυμαλγέα· σοὶ δ' Ἀγαμέμνων
9.261	ἄξια δῶρα δίδωσι μεταλλήξαντι χόλοιο
9.299	ταῦτά κέ τοι τελέσειε μεταλλήξαντι χόλοιο
9.436	πῦρ ἐθέλεις ἀίδηλον, ἐπεὶ χόλος ἔμπεσε θυμῷ
9.459	ἀλλά τις ἀθανάτων παῦσεν χόλον, ὅς ῥ' ἐνὶ θυμῷ
9.523	μηδὲ πόδας· πρὶν δ' οὔ τι νεμεσσητὸν κεχολῶσθαι
9.525	ἡρώων, ὅτε κέν τιν' ἐπιζάφελος χόλος ἵκοι
9.538	ἣ δὲ χολωσαμένη δῖον γένος ἰοχέαιρα
9.553	ἀλλ' ὅτε δὴ Μελέαγρον ἔδυ χόλος, ὅς τε καὶ ἄλλων
9.565	τῇ ὅ γε παρκατέλεκτο χόλον θυμαλγέα πέσσων
9.566	ἐξ ἀρέων μητρὸς κεχολωμένος, ἥ ῥα θεοῖσι
9.646	ἀλλά μοι οἰδάνεται κραδίη χόλῳ, ὁππότε κείνων
9.675	ἦ ἀπέειπε, χόλος δ' ἔτ' ἔχει μεγαλήτορα θυμόν
9.678	κεῖνός γ' οὐκ ἐθέλει σβέσσαι χόλον, ἀλλ' ἔτι μᾶλλον
10.107	ἐκ χόλου ἀργαλέοιο μεταστρέψῃ φίλον ἦτορ
11.703	τῶν ὁ γέρων ἐπέων κεχολωμένος ἠδὲ καὶ ἔργων
13.203	κόψεν Ὀιλιάδης, κεχολωμένος Ἀμφιμάχοιο
13.206	καὶ τότε δὴ περὶ κῆρι Ποσειδάων ἐχολώθη
13.660	τοῦ δὲ Πάρις μάλα θυμὸν ἀποκταμένοιο χολώθη
14.50	ἐν θυμῷ βάλλονται ἐμοὶ χόλον, ὥς περ Ἀχιλλεύς
14.207	εὐνῆς καὶ φιλότητος, ἐπεὶ χόλος ἔμπεσε θυμῷ
14.306	εὐνῆς καὶ φιλότητος, ἐπεὶ χόλος ἔμπεσε θυμῷ

14.310	μὴ πώς μοι μετέπειτα χολώσεαι, αἴ κε σιωπῇ
14.367	νηυσὶν ἔπι γλαφυρῇσι μένει κεχολωμένος ἦτορ
15.68	τοῦ δὲ χολωσάμενος κτενεῖ Ἕκτορα δῖος Ἀχιλλεύς
15.72	τὸ πρὶν δ' οὔτ' ἄρ' ἐγὼ παύω χόλον οὔτε τιν' ἄλλον
15.122	πὰρ Διὸς ἀθανάτοισι χόλος καὶ μῆνις ἐτύχθη
15.138	τώ σ' αὖ νῦν κέλομαι μεθέμεν χόλον υἷος ἑῆος
15.155	στήτην· οὐδέ σφωε ἰδὼν ἐχολώσατο θυμῷ
15.210	νεικείειν ἐθέλῃσι χολωτοῖσιν ἐπέεσσιν
15.217	ἴστω τοῦθ', ὅτι νῶιν ἀνήκεστος χόλος ἔσται
15.223	οἴχεται εἰς ἅλα δῖαν, ἀλευάμενος χόλον αἰπὺν
16.30	μὴ ἐμέ γ' οὖν οὗτός γε λάβοι χόλος, ὃν σὺ φυλάσσεις
16.61	ἀσπερχὲς κεχολῶσθαι ἐνὶ φρεσίν· ἤ τοι ἔφην γε
16.203	σχέτλιε Πηλέος υἱέ, χόλῳ ἄρα σ' ἔτρεφε μήτηρ
16.206	αὖτις, ἐπεί ῥά τοι ὧδε κακὸς χόλος ἔμπεσε θυμῷ
16.320	Ἀντιλόχῳ ἐπόρουσε κασιγνήτοιο χολωθείς
16.546	Μυρμιδόνες, Δαναῶν κεχολωμένοι ὅσσοι ὄλοντο
16.585	ἔσσυο καὶ Τρώων· κεχόλωσο δὲ κὴρ ἑτάροιο
17.399	τόν γε ἰδοῦσ' ὀνόσαιτ, οὐδ' εἰ μάλα μιν χόλος ἵκοι
17.710	νῦν ἰέναι, μάλα περ κεχολωμένον Ἕκτορι δίῳ
18.108	καὶ χόλος, ὅς τ' ἐφέηκε πολύφρονά περ χαλεπῆναι
18.111	ὡς ἐμὲ νῦν ἐχόλωσεν ἄναξ ἀνδρῶν Ἀγαμέμνων
18.119	ἀλλά ἑ μοῖρα δάμασσε καὶ ἀργαλέος χόλος Ἥρης
18.322	εἴ ποθεν ἐξεύροι· μάλα γὰρ δριμὺς χόλος αἱρεῖ
18.337	Τρώων ἀγλαὰ τέκνα, σέθεν κταμένοιο χολωθείς
19.16	ὡς εἶδ', ὥς μιν μᾶλλον ἔδυ χόλος, ἐν δέ οἱ ὄσσε
19.67	νῦν δ' ἦ τοι μὲν ἐγὼ παύω χόλον, οὐδέ τί με χρὴ
20.253	αἵ τε χολωσάμεναι ἔριδος πέρι θυμοβόροιο
20.255	πόλλ' ἐτεά τε καὶ οὐκί· χόλος δέ τε καὶ τὰ κελεύει
20.301	μή πως καὶ Κρονίδης κεχολώσεται, αἴ κεν Ἀχιλλεύς
21.136	ὣς ἄρ' ἔφη, ποταμὸς δὲ χολώσατο κηρόθι μᾶλλον
21.146	Ξάνθος, ἐπεὶ κεχόλωτο δαϊκταμένων αἰζηῶν
21.479	ἀλλὰ χολωσαμένη Διὸς αἰδοίη παράκοιτις
22.94	βεβρωκὼς κακὰ φάρμακ', ἔδυ δέ τέ μιν χόλος αἰνός
23.23	Τρώων ἀγλαὰ τέκνα, σέθεν κταμένοιο χολωθείς
23.88	νήπιος, οὐκ ἐθέλων, ἀμφ' ἀστραγάλοισι χολωθείς
23.482	τὸν δὲ χολωσάμενος Κρητῶν ἀγὸς ἀντίον ηὔδα
23.543	ὦ Ἀχιλεῦ, μάλα τοι κεχολώσομαι, αἴ κε τελέσσῃς
23.567	Ἀντιλόχῳ ἄμοτον κεχολωμένος· ἐν δ' ἄρα κῆρυξ
24.55	τὸν δὲ χολωσαμένη προσέφη λευκώλενος Ἥρη
24.114	ἀθανάτων κεχολῶσθαι ὅτι φρεσὶ μαινομένῃσιν
24.135	ἀθανάτων κεχολῶσθαι, ὅτι φρεσὶ μαινομένῃσιν
24.395	εἴα μάρνασθαι κεχολωμένος Ἀτρεΐωνι
24.584	μὴ ὁ μὲν ἀχνυμένῃ κραδίῃ χόλον οὐκ ἐρύσαιτο

Odyssey

1.69 Κύκλωπος κεχόλωται, ὃν ὀφθαλμοῦ ἀλάωσεν
1.78 ὃν χόλον· οὐ μὲν γάρ τι δυνήσεται ἀντία πάντων
1.433 εὐνῇ δ' οὔ ποτ' ἔμικτο, χόλον δ' ἀλέεινε γυναικός
2.185 οὐδέ κε Τηλέμαχον κεχολωμένον ὧδ' ἀνιείης
3.145 ὡς τὸν Ἀθηναίης δεινὸν χόλον ἐξακέσαιτο
4.221 νηπενθές τ' ἄχολόν τε, κακῶν ἐπίληθον ἁπάντων
4.583 αὐτὰρ ἐπεὶ κατέπαυσα θεῶν χόλον αἰὲν ἐόντων
6.147 μή οἱ γοῦνα λαβόντι χολώσαιτο φρένα κούρη
7.310 μαψιδίως κεχολῶσθαι· ἀμείνω δ' αἴσιμα πάντα
8.205 δεῦρ' ἄγε πειρηθήτω, ἐπεί μ' ἐχολώσατε λίην
8.227 ἵκετ' ἐνὶ μεγάροισι· χολωσάμενος γὰρ Ἀπόλλων
8.276 αὐτὰρ ἐπεὶ δὴ τεῦξε δόλον κεχολωμένος Ἄρει
8.304 ἔστη δ' ἐν προθύροισι, χόλος δέ μιν ἄγριος ᾕρει
9.480 ὣς ἐφάμην, ὁ δ' ἔπειτα χολώσατο κηρόθι μᾶλλον
11.544 νόσφιν ἀφεστήκει, κεχολωμένη εἵνεκα νίκης
11.554 οὐδὲ θανὼν λήσεσθαι ἐμοὶ χόλου εἵνεκα τευχέων
11.565 ἔνθα χ' ὁμῶς προσέφη κεχολωμένος, ἢ κεν ἐγὼ τόν
12.348 εἰ δὲ χολωσαμένος τι βοῶν ὀρθοκραιράων
14.282 ἱέμενοι κτεῖναι—δὴ γὰρ κεχολώατο λίην
15.214 ἂψ ἰέναι κενεόν· μάλα γὰρ κεχολώσεται ἔμπης
15.254 ὅς ῥ' Ὑπερησίηνδ' ἀπενάσσατο πατρὶ χολωθείς
16.425 δῆμον ὑποδείσας; δὴ γὰρ κεχολώατο λίην
17.458 ὣς ἔφατ', Ἀντίνοος δ' ἐχολώσατο κηρόθι μᾶλλον
18.20 χερσὶ δὲ μή τι λίην προκαλίζεο, μή με χολώσῃς
18.25 τὸν δὲ χολωσάμενος προσεφώνεεν Ἶρος ἀλήτης
18.227 μῆτερ ἐμή, τὸ μὲν οὔ σε νεμεσσῶμαι κεχολῶσθαι
18.387 ὣς ἔφατ', Εὐρύμαχος δ' ἐχολώσατο κηρόθι μᾶλλον
19.324 ἐνθάδ' ἔτι πρήξει, μάλα περ κεχολωμένος αἰνῶς
21.377 μνηστῆρες, καὶ δὴ μέθιεν χαλεποῖο χόλοιο
22.26 νείκειον δ' Ὀδυσῆα χολωτοῖσιν ἐπέεσσι
22.59 ἰανθῇ· πρὶν δ' οὔ τι νεμεσσητὸν κεχολῶσθαι
22.224 ὣς φάτ', Ἀθηναίη δὲ χολώσατο κηρόθι μᾶλλον
22.225 νείκεσσεν δ' Ὀδυσῆα χολωτοῖσιν ἐπέεσσιν
22.369 ἀνδρῶν μνηστήρων κεχολωμένος, οἵ οἱ ἔκειρον
24.248 ἄλλο δέ τοι ἐρέω, σὺ δὲ μὴ χόλον ἔνθεο θυμῷ
24.544 μή πώς τοι Κρονίδης κεχολώσεται εὐρύοπα Ζεύς

Bibliography

Abu-Lughod, L. 1986. *Veiled Sentiments: Honor and Poetry in a Bedouin Society*. Berkeley and Los Angeles: University of California Press.

Adelman, J. 1978. "'Anger's My Meat': Feeding Dependency and Aggression in *Coriolanus*." In D. Bevington and J. L. Halio 1978: 108–24.

Adkins, A. W. H. 1960. *Merit and Responsibility*. Oxford: The Clarendon Press.

———. 1969. "Threatening, Abusing, and Feeling Angry in the Homeric Poems." *JHS* 89: 7–21.

———. 1970. *From the Many to the One*. Ithaca: Cornell University Press.

———. 1972. *Moral Values and Political Behavior in Ancient Greece: From Homer to the End of the Fifth Century*. London: Chatto and Windus.

———. 1987. "Gagarin and the 'Morality' of Homer." *CP* 82: 311–22.

Aho, J. A. 1981. *Religious Mythology and the Art of War: Comparative Religious Symbolisms of Military Violence*. Contributions to the Study of Religion, 3. Westport, Conn.: Greenwood Press.

Allen, T. W., ed. 1906–11. *Homeri Opera*. 5 vols. Oxford: The Clarendon Press.

Allen, T. W., W. R. Halliday, and E. E. Sikes, eds. 1963. *The Homeric Hymns*. Oxford: The Clarendon Press.

Alster, B. 1972. "A Sumerian Incantation against Gall." *Orientalia*, n.s., 41: 349–58.

Ambrose, Z. P. 1963. "The Homeric and Early Epic ΤΕΛΟΣ." Ph.D. dissertation, Princeton University.

———. 1965. "Homeric τέλος." *Gl* 43: 38–62.

Ameis, K. F., and C. Hentze, eds. 1894. *Homers Ilias*. Leipzig: Teubner.

Anderson, W. S. 1964. "Anger in Juvenal and Seneca." *UCPCP* 19: 127–96.

d'Arbois de Jubainville, H. 1899. *Cours de littérature celtique*. Vol. 6 of *La civilisation des celtes et celle de l'épopée homérique*. Paris: A. Fontemoing.

Arend, W. 1933. *Die typischen Scenen bei Homer*. Berlin: Weidmann.

Armistead, S. G. 1987. "La 'furia guerrera' en dos textos épicos castellanos." In *Studia in Honorem Prof. M. de Riquer* 2: 255–69. Barcelona: Quaderna Crema.

Armstrong, J. I. 1958. "The Arming Motif in the *Iliad*." *AJP* 79: 337–54.

Atchity, K., ed. 1987. *Critical Essays on Homer*. Boston: G. K. Hall.

Atchity, K., and E. J. W. Barber. 1987. "Greek Princes and the Aegean Princesses: The Role of Women in the Homeric Poems." In K. Atchity 1987: 15–36.

Averill, J. R. 1982. *Anger and Aggression: An Essay on Emotion*. New York: Springer-Verlag.

———. 1983. "Studies on Anger and Aggression: Implications for Theories of Emotion." *American Psychologist* 38: 1145–60.

Bakker, E. J. 1991. "Peripheral and Nuclear Semantics in Homeric Diction: The Case of Dative Expressions for 'Spear'." *Mnemosyne* 44: 64–84.

Bakker, E. J., and N. van den Houten. 1992. "Aspects of Synonymy in Homeric Diction: An Investigation of Dative Expressions for 'Spear'." *CP* 87: 1–13.

Bartholomae, C. 1904. *Altiranisches Wörterbuch*. Strassburg: Karl J. Trübner.

Bassett, S. E. 1938. *The Poetry of Homer*. Berkeley and Los Angeles: University of California Press.

Beekes, R. S. P. 1972. "On the Structure of the Greek Hexameter: O'Neill Interpreted." *Gl* 50: 1–10.

Benveniste, E. 1973. *Indo-European Language and Society*. Translated by E. Palmer. London and Coral Gables, Fla.: University of Miami Press.

Bergren, A. L. 1975. *The Etymology and Usage of* ΠΕΙΡΑΡ *in Early Greek Poetry: A Study of the Interrelationships of Metrics, Linguistics, and Poetics*. American Classical Studies, 2. New York: American Philological Association.

———. 1981. "Helen's Good Drug." In S. Krésic 1981: 521–26.

Berlin, B., and P. Kay. 1969. *Basic Color Terms: Their Universality and Evolution*. Berkeley and Los Angeles: University of California Press. [See now the updated edition of 1991.]

Bethe, E. 1927. *Homer: Dichtung und Sage*. 3 vols. Leipzig: Teubner.

Betts, J. H., J. P. Hooker, and J. R. Green., eds. 1986. *Studies in Honour of T. B. L. Webster*. Bristol: Bristol Classical Press.

Bevington, D., and J. L. Halio, eds. 1978. *Shakespeare: Pattern of Excelling Nature*. Newark, Del.: University of Delaware Press.

Black-Michaud, J. 1975. *Feuding Societies*. Oxford: Blackwell.

Blanchard, R. J., and D. C. Blanchard, eds. 1986. *Advances in the Study of Aggression*. Orlando, Fla.: Academic Press, Inc.

Boedeker, D. D. 1974. *Aphrodite's Entry into Greek Epic*. Leiden: Brill.

———. 1984. *Descent from Heaven: Images of Dew in Greek Poetry and Religion*. American Classical Studies, 1. Chico, Calif.: Scholar's Press.

Böhme, J. 1929. *Die Seele und das Ich im homerischen Epos*. Leipzig: Teubner.

Bonner, R. J. 1912. "Administration of Justice in the Age of Hesiod." *CP* 7: 17–25.

Bouquiaux-Simon, O., and P. Mertens. 1981. "Papyrus homériques du Musée du Caire." *LAC* 81: 100–111.

Bremmer, J. 1983. *The Early Greek Concept of the Soul*. Princeton: Princeton University Press.

Broccia, G. 1967. *La forma poetica dell'Iliade e la genesi dell'epos omerico*. Messina: Università degli Studi.

Buck, C. D. 1949. *A Dictionary of Selected Synonyms in the Indo-European Languages*. Chicago: University of Chicago Press.

Burkert, W. 1985. *Greek Religion*. Translated by John Raffen. Cambridge, Mass.: Harvard University Press.

Byock, J. 1982. *Feud in Icelandic Saga*. Berkeley and Los Angeles: University of California Press.

———. 1993. "*Tháttr* and the Fundamental Oral Progression." *Oral Tradition* 10: 166–80.

Calhoun, C., and R. C. Solomon. 1984. *What Is an Emotion? Classic Readings in Philosophical Psychology*. New York: Oxford University Press.

Caswell, C. P. 1990. *A Study of* Thumos *in Early Greek Epic*. Leiden: Brill.

Chantraine, P. 1927. *Histoire du parfait grec*. Paris: Champion.

———. 1928. "Le role de l'élargissement *ē/ō* dans la conjug-aison grecque." *BSL* 28: 9–39.

———. 1963 [1953]. *Grammaire homérique*. Vol. 2, *Syntaxe*. Paris: Klincksieck.

———. 1968. *La formation des noms en grec ancien*. Paris: Klincksieck.

———. 1968–80. *Dictionnaire étymologique de la langue grecque*. 4 vols. Paris: Klincksieck.

———. 1973a [1958]. *Grammaire homérique*. Vol. 1, *Phonétique et morphologie*. 5th ed. Paris: Klincksieck.

———. 1973b. *Morphologie historique du grec*. 2d ed. Paris: Klincksieck.

———. 1975. "Sur quelques composés sigmatiques en -ής (νεαλής, composés en -πετής, ἐμμενές). In M. D. Moïnfar 1975: 75–85.

Clader, L. L. 1976. *Helen: The Evolution from Divine to Heroic in Greek Epic Tradition*. Leiden: Brill.

Clarke, M. 1999. *Flesh and Spirit in the Songs of Homer: A Study of Words and Myths*. Oxford: Oxford University Press.

Claus, D. B. 1981. *Toward the Soul: An Inquiry into the Meaning of "Psyche" before Plato*. Yale Classical Monographs, 2. New Haven: Yale University Press.

Clay, J. S. 1976. "The Beginning of the *Odyssey*." *AJP* 97: 313–26.

———. 1983. *The Wrath of Athena: Gods and Men in the Odyssey*. Princeton: Princeton University Press.

Clifford, J. 1988. *The Predicament of Culture: Twentieth-Century Ethnography, Literature, and Art*. Cambridge, Mass.: Harvard University Press.

Clifford, J., and G. Marcus, eds. 1986. *Writing Culture: The Poetics and Politics of Ethnography*. Berkeley and Los Angeles: University of California Press.

Cohen, D. 1991. *Law, Sexuality, and Society: The Enforcement of Morals in Classical Athens*. Cambridge: Cambridge University Press.

———. 1995. *Law, Violence, and Community in Classical Athens*. Cambridge: Cambridge University Press.

Collins, L. 1987. "The Wrath of Paris: Ethical Vocabulary and Ethical Type in the *Iliad*." *AJP* 108: 220–32.

———. 1988. *Studies in Characterization in the Iliad*. Beiträge zur Klassischen Philologie, 189. Frankfurt: Athenaeum.

Considine, P. 1966. "Some Homeric Terms for Anger." *AC* 9: 15–25.

———. 1969. "The Theme of Divine Wrath in Ancient East Mediterranean Literature." *Studi Micenei ed Egeo-Anatolici* 8: 85–159.

———. 1985. "The Indo-European Origin of Greek ΜΗΝΙΣ 'wrath'." *TPS* 85: 144–70.

———. 1986. "The Etymology of ΜΗΝΙΣ." In J. H. Betts et al. 1986: 53–64.

Cosset, E. 1990. "Les formules de Zeus au vocatif dans l'*Iliade*." *LAC* 59: 5–16.

Cross, T. P. 1952. *Motif-Index of Early Irish Literature*. Indiana University Publications, Folklore Series, 7. Bloomington: Indiana University Publications.

Cunliffe, R. J. 1963. *A Lexicon of the Homeric Dialect*. Norman, Okla.: University of Oklahoma Press.

Dale, A. M. 1954. *Euripides: Alcestis*. Oxford: The Clarendon Press.

Davies, A. M. 1986. "Fighting, Ploughing and the Karkamiš Kings." In A. Etter 1986: 129–45.

Davies, A. M., and W. Meid, eds. 1976. *Studies in Greek, Italic, and Indo-European Linguistics Offered to Leonard R. Palmer on the Occasion of His Seventieth Birthday*. Innsbruck: Innsbrucker Beiträge zur Sprachwissenschaft.

de Jong, I. J. F. 1987. *Narrators and Focalizers: The Presentation of the Story in the Iliad*. Amsterdam: B. R. Gruner.

Denniston, J. D. 1975. *The Greek Particles*. 2d ed. Oxford: The Clarendon Press.

Detienne, M. 1981. *The Creation of Mythology*. Translated by M. Cook. Chicago: University of Chicago Press.

Detienne, M., and J.-P. Vernant. 1974. *Les ruses de l'intelligence: La* mêtis *des grecs*. Paris: Flammarion.

———. 1989. *The Cuisine of Sacrifice among the Greeks*. Chicago: University of Chicago Press.

Devlin, K. J. 1989. "See Ourselves as Others See Us: Joyce's Look at the Eye of the Other." *PMLA* 104: 882–93.

de Vries, J. 1962. *Altnordisches etymologisches Wörterbuch*. 2d ed. Leiden: Brill.

———. 1963. *Heroic Song and Heroic Legend*. London: Oxford University Press.

Dickie, M. 1978. "Δίκη as a Moral Term in Homer and Hesiod." *CP* 73: 91–109.

Dillon, M. 1947. "The Archaism of the Irish Tradition." *PBA* 33: 253–78.

———. 1976. *Celts and Aryans*. Simla: Indian Institute of Advanced Study.

Dillon, M., and N. Chadwick. 1967. *The Celtic Realms*. New York: The New American Library.

Donlan, W. 1982. "Reciprocities in Homer." *CW* 75: 137–76.

Dougherty, C., and L. Kurke, eds. 1993. *Cultural Poetics in Archaic Greece: Cult, Performance, Politics*. Cambridge: Cambridge University Press.

Dumézil, G. 1948. *Mitra-Varuna: Essai sur deux représentations indo-européennes de la souveraineté*. Paris: Gallimard.

———. 1968–73. *Mythe et épopée*. 3 vols. Paris: Gallimard.

———. 1980. "Fury and Madness: μένος and λύσσα in the *Iliad*." *Yearbook of Comparative Criticism* 9: 132–40.

Dunbar, H., ed. 1880. *A Complete Concordance to the Odyssey of Homer*. Oxford: The Clarendon Press. [Revised edition by B. Marzullo (Hildesheim: G. Olms, 1962).]

Dundes, A., ed. 1992. *The Evil Eye: A Casebook*. Madison: University of Wisconsin Press.

Düntzer, H. 1872. "Der Zorn des Poseidon in der *Odyssee*." In *Homerische Abhandlungen*, 409–28. Leipzig: Teubner. [*Jahrbücher für classische Philologie*, 1861: 729–41.]

Durante, M. 1971. *Continuità della tradizione poetica dall'età micenea ai primi documenti*. Vol. 1 of *Sulla preistoria della tradizione poetica greca*. Incunabula Graeca, 50. Rome: Edizioni dell'Ateneo.

Ebeling, H., ed. 1880–85. *Lexicon Homericum*. 2 vols. Leipzig: Teubner.

Edwards, M. W. 1966. "Some Features of Homeric Craftsmanship." *TAPA* 97: 115–79.

———. 1968. "Homeric Speech Introductions." *HSCP* 74: 1–36.

———. 1991. *The Iliad: A Commentary*. Vol. 5, *Books 17–20*. Cambridge: Cambridge University Press.

Eisenberger, H. 1985. "Zur Erklärung von *Ilias* 1.282–84." *Gl* 63: 159–61.

Erbse, H., ed. 1969–77. *Scholia Graeca in Homeri Iliadem*. 7 vols. Berlin: de Gruyter.

Ernout, A., and A. Meillet. 1959–60. *Dictionnaire étymologique de la langue latine*. Paris: Klincksieck.

Etter, A., ed. 1986. *o-o-pe-ro-si: Festschrift für Ernst Risch*. Berlin: de Gruyter.

Eustathius. 1971–87. *Commentarii ad Homeri Iliadem pertinentes*. Edited by M. van der Valk. 4 vols. Leiden: Brill.

Fabb, N., A. Durant, and C. MacCabe, eds. 1987. *The Linguistics of Writing: Arguments between Language and Literature*. Manchester: Manchester University Press.

Fenik, B. 1968. *Typical Battle Scenes in the Iliad: Studies in the Narrative Techniques of Homeric Battle Descriptions*. Wiesbaden: F. Steiner.

———. 1974. *Studies in the Odyssey*. Wiesbaden: F. Steiner.

Ferrini, F. 1978. "Il problema dei termini di colore nella poesia omerica." *Annali della Facoltà di Lettere e Filosofia* (Università di Macerata) 11: 11–35.

Finkelberg, M. 1986. "Is ΚΛΕΟΣ ΑΦΘΙΤΟΝ a Homeric Formula?" *CQ* 36: 1–5.

Finley, M. I. 1977. *The World of Odysseus*. London: Chatto and Windus.

———. 1986. "Anthropology and the Classics." In *The Use and Abuse of History*, 102–19. London: Chatto and Windus.

Finnegan, R. 1977. *Oral Poetry: Its Nature, Significance, and Social Context*. Cambridge: Cambridge University Press.

Foley, J. M., ed. 1987. *Comparative Research on Oral Traditions: A Memorial for Milman Parry*. Columbus, Ohio: Slavica.

Fontenrose, J. E. 1960. *The Cult and Myth of Pyrrhos at Delphi*. Berkeley and Los Angeles: University of California Press.

Ford, A. 1992. *Homer: The Poetry of the Past*. Ithaca: Cornell University Press.

Fraenkel, E. 1909–10. *KZ* 43: 193.

Frame, D. 1971. "The Origins of Greek ΝΟΥΣ." Ph.D. dissertation, Harvard University.

———. 1978. *The Myth of Return in Early Greek Epic*. New Haven: Yale University Press.

Francis, E. D. 1983. "Virtue, Folly, and Greek Etymology." In C. Rubino and C. Schelmerdine 1983: 74–121.

Fränkel, H. 1921. *Die homerischen Gleichnisse*. Göttingen: Vandenhoeck & Ruprecht.

Freis, E., ed. 1967. *Festschrift für Joseph Klein*. Göttingen: Vandenhoeck & Ruprecht.

Friedrich, J. 1960. *Hethitisches Elementarbuch*. Heidelberg: Carl Winter.

———. 1991. *Kurzgefaßtes hethitisches Wörterbuch*. Heidelberg: Carl Winter.

Friedrich, W.-H. 1956. *Verwundung und Tod in der Iliad*. Göttingen: Vandenhoeck & Ruprecht.

Frisk, H. 1946. "ΜΗΝΙΣ: Zur Geschichte eines Begriffes." *Eranos* 44: 28–40.

———. 1960–70. *Griechisches etymologisches Wörterbuch*. 3 vols. Heidelberg: Carl Winter.

Gadamer, H. G. 1975. *Truth and Method*. New York: Seabury Press.

Gagarin, M. 1973. "ΔΙΚΗ in the *Works and Days*." *CP* 68: 289–301.

———. 1987. "Morality in Homer." *CP* 82: 285–306.

———. 1990. "The Ambiguity of *Eris* in the *Works and Days*." In M. Griffith and D. J. Mastronarde 1990: 173–83.

Gagnepin, J. 1959. *Les noms grecs en -ΟΣ et en -Ᾱ*. Paris: Klincksieck.

Galinsky, K. 1988. "The Anger of Aeneas." *AJP* 109: 321–48.

Garvin, P. 1964. *A Prague School Reader on Esthetics, Literary Structure and Style*. Washington, D.C.: Georgetown University Press.

Geen, R. G. 1990. *Human Aggression: Mapping Social Psychology*. Pacific Grove, Calif.: Brooks/Cole Pub. Co.

Gentili, B. 1988. *Poetry and Its Public in Ancient Greece: From Homer to the Fifth Century*. Translated by A. T. Cole. Baltimore: Johns Hopkins University Press.

Girard, R. 1979. *Violence and the Sacred*. Translated by P. Gregory. Baltimore: Johns Hopkins University Press.

———. 1987. "Generative Scapegoating." In R. G. Hammerton-Kelly 1987: 73–145.

Gonda, J. 1963. *The Vision of the Vedic Poets*. The Hague: Mouton.

Graz, L. 1965. *Le feu dans l'Iliade et l'Odyssée*. Paris: Klincksieck.

Griffin, J. 1978. "The Divine Audience and the Religion of the *Iliad*." *CQ* 28: 1–37.

———. 1986. "Homeric Words and Speakers." *JHS* 106: 36–57.

Griffith, M., and D. J. Mastronarde, eds. 1990. *Cabinet of the Muses: Essays on Classical and Comparative Literature in Honor of Thomas G. Rosenmeyer*. Atlanta: Scholar's Press.

Haft, A. J. 1989–90. "Odysseus' Wrath and Grief in the *Iliad*: Agamemnon, the Ithacan King, and the Sack of Troy in Books 2, 4, and 14." *CJ* 85: 97–114.

Hainsworth, B. 1993. *The Iliad: A Commentary*. Vol. 3, *Books 9–12*. Cambridge: Cambridge University Press.

Hainsworth, J. B. 1964. "Structure and Content in Epic Formulae: The Question of the Unique Expression." *CQ* 58: 155–64.

———. 1968. *The Flexibility of the Homeric Formula*. Oxford: The Clarendon Press.

———. 1969. *Homer*. Greece and Rome Monographs, 3. Oxford: The Clarendon Press.

Hammerton-Kelly, R. G., ed. 1987. *Violent Origins: Ritual Killing and Cultural Formation*. Stanford: Stanford University Press.

Hammond, N. G. L. 1985. "The Scene in *Iliad* 18.497–508 and the Albanian Blood-Feud." *Bulletin of the American Society of Papyrologists* 22: 79–86.

Hamp, E. 1985. "Thwaite." In U. Pieper and G. Stickel 1985: 161–67.

———. 1987. "Indo-Hittite *men-* 'see'." *JIES* 15: 391.

Harris, J. R. 1989. *Accidental Grandeur: A Defense of Narrative Vagueness in Ancient Epic Literature*. Lang Classical Studies, 1. New York: Peter Lang.

Harris, W. V. 2001. *Restraining Rage: The Ideology of Anger Control in Classical Antiquity*. Cambridge, Mass.: Harvard University Press.

Harrison, E. L. 1960. "Notes on Homeric Psychology." *Phoenix* 14: 63–80.

Hasluck, M. 1954. *The Unwritten Law in Albania*. Cambridge: Cambridge University Press.

Heider, K. G. 1991. *Landscapes of Emotion: Lexical Maps and Scenarios of Emotion Terms in Indonesia*. Cambridge: Cambridge University Press.

Heitsch, E. 1967. "Der Zorn des Paris: Zur Deutungsgeschichte eines homerischen Zetemas." In E. Freis 1967: 216–47.

Henry, P. L. 1982. "Furor Heroicus." *ZCP* 39: 235–42.

Heubeck, A. 1974. *Die homerische Frage*. Darmstadt: Wissenschaftliche Buchgesellschaft.

Heubeck, A., and A. Hoekstra. 1989. *A Commentary on Homer's Odyssey*. Vol. 2, *Books 9–16*. Oxford: The Clarendon Press.

Heubeck, A., S. West, and J. B. Hainsworth. 1988. *A Commentary on Homer's Odyssey*. Vol. 1, *Books 1–8*. Oxford: The Clarendon Press.

Hilbert, D. R. 1987. *Color and Color Perception: A Study in Anthropocentric Realism*. Stanford: Stanford University Press.

Hochschild, A. R. 1983. *The Managed Heart: The Commercialization of Human Feeling*. Berkeley and Los Angeles: University of California Press.

Hogan, J. C. 1981. "*Eris* in Homer." *GB* 10: 21–58.

Holland, D., and N. Quinn, eds. 1987. *Cultural Models in Language and Thought*. Cambridge: Cambridge University Press.

Holland, G. B. 1980. "A Definite Use of Early Greek *tis*. *BLS* 6: 1–6.

———. 1993. "The Name of Achilles: A Revised Etymology." *Gl* 71: 17–27.

Holoka, J. P. 1973. "Homer's Originality." *CW* 66: 257–93.

———. 1979. *Homer Studies 1971–77*. Classical World Special Survey, 73. Pittsburgh, Pa.: Classical Association of the Atlantic States.

———. 1983. "'Looking Darkly' (ὑπόδρα ἰδών): Reflections on Status and Decorum in Homer." *TAPA* 113: 1–16.

Holway, R. K. 1989. "Poetry and Political Thought in Archaic Greece: The *Iliad*, the *Theogony* and Political Life." Ph.D. dissertation, University of California, Berkeley.

Howald, E. 1924. "Meleager und Achill." *RhM* 73: 405–25.

———. 1946. *Der Dichter der Ilias*. Erlenbach and Zurich: Rentsch.

Humphreys, S. C. 1978. *Anthropology and the Greeks*. London: Routledge & Kegan Paul.

Huxley, G. L. 1969. *Greek Epic Poetry*. Cambridge, Mass.: Harvard University Press.

Ingalls, W. 1972. "Another Dimension of the Homeric Formula." *Phoenix* 26: 111–22.

———. 1976. "The Analogical Formula in Homer." *TAPA* 106: 211–26.

Irmscher, J. 1950. *Götterzorn bei Homer*. Leipzig: Harrassowitz.

Irwin, E. 1974. *Colour Terms in Greek Poetry*. Toronto: Hakkert.

Jackson, K. H. 1964. *The Oldest Irish Tradition: A Window on the Iron Age*. Cambridge: Cambridge University Press.

Jahn, T. 1987. *Zum Wortfeld "Seele-Geist" in der Sprache Homers*. Munich: Beck.

Jamison, S. W. 1977. "Function and Form in the *-aya* Formations of the Rig Veda and Atharva Veda." Ph.D. dissertation, Yale University.

———. 1981. "Voice Fluctuation in the Rig Veda: Medial *-anta* in Active Paradigms." In C. Watkins 1981a: 156–94. [Now see Jamison, *Function and Form in the* -aya *Formations of the Rig Veda and the Atharva Veda* (Göttingen: Vandenhoeck & Ruprecht, 1983).]

Janko, R. 1981. "Equivalent Formulae in the Greek Epos." *Mnemosyne* 34: 251–64.

———. 1984. *Homer, Hesiod and the Homeric Hymns*. Cambridge: Cambridge University Press.

———. 1992. *The Iliad: A Commentary*. Vol. 4, *Books 13–16*. Cambridge: Cambridge University Press.

Jones, J. E. 1976. "Hives and Honey of Hymettus: Beekeeping in Ancient Greece." *Archaeology* 29: 80–91.

Jones, J. E., A. J. Graham, and L. H. Sackett. 1973. *An Attic Country House below the Cave of Pan at Vari*. London: Thames and Hudson.

Kahane, A. 1992. "The First Word of the *Odyssey*." *TAPA* 122: 115–31.

———. 1994. *The Interpretation of Order: The Poetics of Homeric Repetition*. Oxford: The Clarendon Press.

Kakridis, J. T. 1949. *Homeric Researches*. Lund: C. W. K. Gleerup.

Kay, P., and C. K. MacDaniel. 1978. "The Linguistic Significance of the Meanings of Basic Color Terms." *Language* 54: 610–46.

Keith, A. L. 1914. *Simile and Metaphor in Greek Poetry*. Chicago: University of Chicago Press.

Kinkel, G., ed. 1877. *Epicorum Graecorum Fragmenta*. Leipzig: Teubner.

Kinsella, T. 1969. *The Táin*. Oxford: The Clarendon Press.

Kiparsky, P. 1987. "On Theory and Interpretation." In N. Fabb et al. 1987: 185–98.

Kirk, G. S. 1962. *The Songs of Homer*. Cambridge: Cambridge University Press.

———. 1968. "War and the Warrior in the Homeric Poems." In J.-P. Vernant 1968: 93–117.

———. 1985. *The Iliad: A Commentary*. Vol. 1, *Books 1–4*. Cambridge: Cambridge University Press.

———. 1990. *The Iliad: A Commentary*. Vol. 2, *Books 5–8*. Cambridge: Cambridge University Press.

Kirk, G. S., and A. Parry, eds. 1966. *Homeric Studies*. Yale Classical Studies, 20. New Haven: Yale University Press.

Krésic, S., ed. 1981. *Contemporary Literary Hermeneutics and Interpretation of Classical Texts*. Ottowa: Ottawa University Press.

Kurath, H. 1921. *The Semantic Sources of the Words for the Emotions in Sanskrit, Greek, Latin, and the Germanic Languages*. Menasha, Wisc.: George Banta Publishing Co.

Kurke, L. 1991. *The Traffic in Praise: Pindar and the Poetics of Social Economy*. Ithaca: Cornell University Press.

Lakoff, G. 1987. *Women, Fire, and Dangerous Things: What Categories Reveal about the Mind*. Chicago: University of Chicago Press.

Lakoff, G., and M. Johnson. 1980. *Metaphors We Live By*. Chicago: University of Chicago Press.

Lakoff, G., and Z. Kövecses. 1987. "The Cognitive Model of Anger Inherent in American English." In D. Holland and N. Quinn 1987: 195–221.

Lakoff, G., and M. Turner. 1989. *More than Cool Reason: A Field Guide to Metaphor*. Chicago: University of Chicago Press.

Laroche, E. 1965. "Études de linguistique anatolienne." *Revue Hittite et Asianique* 76: 33–54.

La Roche, J. 1866. *Die homerische Textkritik im Alterthum*. Leipzig: Teubner.

Latacz, J. 1966. *Zum Wortfeld "Freude" in der Sprache Homers*. Heidelberg: Carl Winter.

Laurenti, R., and G. Indelli. 1988. *Plutarco sul controllo dell'ira: Introduzione, testo critico, traduzione e commento*. Naples: D'Auria.

Leaf, W., ed. 1886. *The Iliad*. 2 vols. London: Macmillan.

Lebrun, R. 1980. *Hymnes et prières hittites*. Louvain-la-Neuve: Centre d'Histoire des Religions.

Lehrs, K. 1882. *De Aristarchi Studiis Homericis*. Leipzig: S. Hirzel.

Lemerise, E. A., and K. A. Dodge. 1993. "The Development of Anger and Hostile Interactions." In M. Lewis and J. M. Haviland 1993: 537–46.

Lesky, A. 1961. *Göttliche und menschliche Motivation im homerischen Epos*. Heidelberg: Carl Winter.

Leumann, M. 1950. *Homerische Wörter*. Basel: Friedrich Reinhardt.

Lévi-Strauss, C. 1973. *From Honey to Ashes*. Vol. 2 of *An Introduction to a Science of Mythology*. New York: Harper and Row.

Lewis, H., and H. Pedersen. 1961. *A Concise Comparative Celtic Grammar*. Göttingen: Vandenhoeck & Ruprecht.

Lewis, M., and J. M. Haviland, eds. 1993. *Handbook of Emotions*. New York: Guilford Press.

Lidov, J. B. 1977. "The Anger of Poseidon." *Arethusa* 10: 227–36.

Lincoln, B. 1975. "Homeric λύσσα 'wolfish rage'." *IF* 80: 98–105.

Littleton, C. S. 1970. "Some Possible Indo-European Themes in the *Iliad*." In J. Puhvel 1970: 229–46.

———. 1982. *The New Comparative Mythology*. 3d ed. Berkeley and Los Angeles: University of California Press.

Lloyd, G. E. R. 1964. "The Hot and the Cold, the Dry and the Wet in Greek Philosophy." *JHS* 84: 92–106.

———. 1971. *Polarity and Analogy: Two Types of Argumentation in Early Greek Thought*. Cambridge: Cambridge University Press.

Lloyd-Jones, H. 1983. *The Justice of Zeus*. Revised edition. Berkeley and Los Angeles: University of California Press.

———. 1987. "A Note on Homeric Morality." *CP* 82: 307–10.

Lloyd-Jones, J. 1947. "The Compounds of *Gal*." In *Essays and Studies Presented to Professor Tadhg Ua Donnchadha*, edited by S. Pender, 83–89. Cork: Cork University Press.

Lohmann, D. 1970. *Die Komposition der Reden in der Ilias*. Berlin: de Gruyter.

Long, A. A. 1970. "Morals and Values in Homer." *JHS* 90: 121–39.

Lonsdale, S. 1989. "If Looks Could Kill: παπταίνω and the Interpenetration of Imagery and Narrative in Homer." *CJ* 84: 325–33.

Lord, A. B. 1960. *The Singer of Tales*. Cambridge, Mass.: Harvard University Press.

Lord, M. L. 1967. "Withdrawal and Return: An Epic Story Pattern in the *Homeric Hymn to Demeter* and in the Homeric Poems." *CJ* 62: 241–48.

Louden, B. 1995. "Categories of Homeric Wordplay." *TAPA* 126: 27–46.

Lowenstam, S. 1981. *The Death of Patroklos: A Study in Typology*. Beiträge zur klassischen Philologie, 133. Königstein/Ts: Hain.

———. 1993. *The Scepter and the Spear: Studies on Forms of Repetition in the Homeric Poems*. Lanham, Md.: Rowman and Littlefield.

Lutz, C. A. 1988. *Unnatural Emotions: Everyday Sentiments on a Micronesian Atoll and Their Challenge to Western Theory*. Chicago: University of Chicago Press.

Lutz, C., and G. White. 1986. "The Anthropology of Emotions." *Annual Review of Anthropology* 15: 405–36.

Lynch, J. P., and G. B. Miles. 1980. "In Search of *thumos*: Toward an Understanding of a Greek Psychological Term." *Prudentia* 12: 3–9.

MacCana, P. 1980. *The Learned Tales of Medieval Ireland*. Dublin: Dublin Institute of Advanced Studies.

MacCary, W. T. 1982. *Childlike Achilles: Ontogeny and Phylogeny in the Iliad*. New York: Columbia University Press.

Manes, J. 1980. "Ways of Defining: Folk Definitions and the Study of Semantics." *Forum Linguisticum* 5: 122–39.

Martin, R. P. 1983. *Healing Sacrifice and Battle*: ΜΗΧΑΝΗ *and Related Concepts in Early Greek Poetry*. Innsbruck: Innsbrucker Beiträge zur Sprachwissenschaft.

———. 1989. *The Language of Heroes: Speech and Performance in the Iliad*. Ithaca: Cornell University Press.

———. 1993. "Telemachus and the Last Hero Song." *Colby Quarterly* 29: 222–40.

Mawet, F. 1979. *Recherches sur les oppositions fonctionelles dans le vocabulaire homérique de la douleur*. Brussels: Palais des Académies.

Mayrhofer, M. 1986–. *Etymologisches Wörterbuch des Altindoarischen*. Heidelberg: Carl Winter.

McNeill, N. B. 1972. "Colour and Colour Terminology." *Journal of Linguistics* 8: 21–33.

Meillet, A. 1925. *La méthode comparative en linguistique historique*. Paris: Champion.

Meister, K. 1921. *Die homerische Kunstsprache*. Leipzig: Teubner.

Melchert, H. C. 1979. "Three Hittite Etymologies." *KZ* 93: 262–71.

———. 1987. "PIE Velars in Luvian." In Watkins 1987a: 182–224.

———. 1994. *Anatolian Historical Phonology*. Amsterdam: Rodopi.

Melia, D. F. 1972. "Narrative Structure in Irish Saga." Ph.D. dissertation, Harvard University.

———. 1979. "Some Remarks on the Affinities of Medieval Irish Saga." *AAntH* 17: 255–61.

Meriggi, P. 1980. *Schizzo grammaticale dell'anatolico*. Rome: Accademia Nazionale dei Lincei.

Merry, W. W., ed. 1892. *Homer: Odyssey*. Oxford: The Clarendon Press.

Miller, W. I. 1983. "Choosing the Avenger: Some Aspects of the Bloodfeud in Medieval Iceland and England." *Law and History Review* 1: 159–204.

———. 1990. *Bloodtaking and Peacemaking: Feud, Law, and Society in Saga Iceland*. Chicago: University of Chicago Press.

Moïnfar, M. D., ed. 1975. *Mélanges linguistiques offerts à Émile Benveniste*. Louvain: Peeters.

Monro, D. B. 1891. *A Grammar of the Homeric Dialect*. 2d ed. Oxford: The Clarendon Press.

Montgomery, T. 1987. "Horatius, Cúchulainn, Rodrigo de Vivar." *Revista Canadiense de Estudios Hispánicos* 9: 541–57.

Moravcsik, R., and J. R. Wirth. 1986. "Markedness—An Overview." In F. R. Eckman, E. A. Moravcsik, and J. R. Wirth, eds., *Markedness*, 1–12. New York.: Plenum Press.

Morris, I. 1986. "The Use and Abuse of Homer." *CA* 5: 81–138.

———. 1993. "The Poetics of Power: The Interpretation of Ritual Action in Archaic Greece." In C. Dougherty and L. Kurke 1993: 15–45.

Moulton, C. 1979. "Homeric Metaphor." *CP* 74: 279–93.

Mueller, M. 1984. *The Iliad*. London: G. Allen & Unwin.

Muellner, L. 1976. *The Meaning of Homeric* EYXOMAI *through Its Formulas*. Innsbruck: Innsbrucker Beiträge zur Sprachwissenschaft.

———. 1990. "The Similes of the Cranes and Pygmies: A Study of Homeric Metaphor." *HSCP* 93: 59–101.

———. 1992. "Étymologie et sémantique de μῆνις." In F. Létoublon, ed., *La langue et les textes en grec ancien*, 121–35. Amsterdam: J. C. Gieben.

———. 1996. *The Anger of Achilles: Mênis in Greek Epic*. Ithaca: Cornell University Press.

Munding, R. 1961. "Die Bedeutung der Rechtsidee in der *Ilias*." *Philologus* 105: 161–77.

Murphy, G., ed. 1956. *Early Irish Lyrics: Eighth to Twelfth Century*. Oxford: The Clarendon Press.

———. 1961. *Early Irish Metrics*. Dublin: Royal Irish Academy.

Myers, F. R. 1988. "The Logic and Meaning of Anger among Pintupi Aborigines." *Man* 23: 589–610.

———. 1991. *Pintupi Country, Pintupi Self: Sentiment, Place, and Politics among Western Desert Aborigines*. Berkeley and Los Angeles: University of California Press.

Myers, J. L. 1932. "The Last Book of the *Iliad*." *JHS* 52: 264–96.

Nagler, M. N. 1967. "Towards a Generative View of the Oral Formula." *TAPA* 98: 269–311.

———. 1969. "Oral Poetry and the Question of Originality." In *Actes du Ve Congrès de l'Association Internationale de Littérature Comparée*, 451–59. Amsterdam: Swets & Zeitlinger.

———. 1974. *Spontaneity and Tradition: A Study in the Oral Art of Homer*. Berkeley and Los Angeles: University of California Press.

———. 1980. "Entretiens avec Tirésias." *CW* 74: 89–108.

———. 1987. "On Almost Killing Your Friends: Some Thoughts on Violence in Early Cultures." In J. M. Foley 1987: 425–63.

———. 1988. "Towards a Semantics of Ancient Conflict: *Eris* in the *Iliad*." *CW* 82: 81–90.

———. 1990. "Ethical Anxiety and Artistic Inconsistency: The Case of Oral Epic." In M. Griffith and D. J. Mastronarde 1990: 225–39.

———. 1992. "Discourse and Conflict in Hesiod: *Eris* and the *Erides*." *Ramus* 21: 79–96.

———. 1993. "Penelope's Male Hand: Gender and Violence in the *Odyssey*." *Colby Quarterly* 29: 241–57.

Nagy, G. 1974. *Comparative Studies in Greek and Indic Meter*. Cambridge, Mass.: Harvard University Press.

———. 1976a. "Formula and Meter." In B. A. Stolz and R. S. Shannon 1976: 239–60. [Rewritten as Chapter 2 of Nagy 1990b.]

———. 1976b. "The Name of Achilles: Etymology and Epic." In A. M. Davies and W. Meid 1976: 209–37.

———. 1979. *The Best of the Achaeans: Concepts of the Hero in Archaic Greek Poetry*. Baltimore: The Johns Hopkins University Press. [Revised edition 1999.]

———. 1981. "Essai sur Georges Dumézil et l'étude de l'épopée grecque." In *Pour un temps: Georges Dumézil*, edited by J. Bonnet et al., 137–45. Aix-en-Provence: Centre Georges Pompidou. [Rewritten as part of Chapter 1 of Nagy 1990b.]

———. 1990a. *Pindar's Homer: The Lyric Possession of an Epic Past*. Baltimore: The Johns Hopkins University Press.

———. 1990b. *Greek Mythology and Poetics*. Ithaca: Cornell University Press.

———. 1992. "Myth as Exemplum in Homer." In *Innovations in Antiquity*, edited by R. Hexter and D. Selden, 311–31. New York: Routledge.

———. 1994. "The Name of Achilles: Questions of Etymology and 'Folk Etymology.'" *Illinois Classical Studies* 19: 3–9.

———. 1996. *Poetry as Performance: Homer and Beyond*. Cambridge: Cambridge University Press.

Nagy, J. 1990. "Hierarchy, Heroes, and Heads: Indo-European Structures in Greek Myth." In *Approaches to Greek Myth*, edited by L. Edmunds, 199–238. Baltimore: The Johns Hopkins University Press.

Novaco, R. 1986. "Anger as a Clinical and Social Problem." In R. J. Blanchard and D. C. Blanchard 1986: 1–67.

Nutt, A. 1900. *Cuchulainn, the Irish Achilles*. Popular Studies in Mythology, Romance and Folklore, 8. London: D. Nutt.

O'Brien, J. 1993. *The Transformation of Hera: A Study of Ritual, Hero, and the Goddess of the Iliad*. Lanham, Md.: Rowman and Littlefield.

O'Neill, E. G., Jr. 1942. "The Localization of Metrical Word Types in the Greek Hexameter: Homer, Hesiod, and the Alexandrians." *YCS* 8: 103–78.

Onians, R. B. 1951. *The Origins of European Thought*. Cambridge: Cambridge University Press.

O'Nolan, K. 1969. "Homer and Irish Heroic Narrative." *CQ* 19: 1–19.

O'Rahilly, C. 1967. *Táin Bó Cúalnge from the Book of Leinster*. Dublin: Dublin Institute of Advanced Studies.

Ortony, A., ed. 1979. *Metaphor and Thought*. Cambridge: Cambridge University Press.

Otten, H. 1953. *Zur grammatikalischen und lexikalischen Bestimmung des Luvischen: Untersuchung der* Luvili-*Texte*. Deutsche Akademie der Wissenschaften zu Berlin, Institut für Orientforschung, Veröffentlichung 19. Berlin: Akademie-Verlag.

Otterbein, K. F. 1994. *Feuding and Warfare: Selected Works of Keith F. Otterbein*. War and Society 1. Langhorne, Pa.: Gordon and Breach.

Packard, D., and T. Meyers. 1974. *A Bibliography of Homeric Scholarship*. Malibu: Undena Publications.

Padel, R. 1995. *Whom the Gods Destroy: Elements of Greek and Tragic Madness*. Princeton: Princeton University Press.

Page, D. 1955. *The Homeric Odyssey*. Oxford: The Clarendon Press.

———. 1959. *History and the Homeric Iliad*. Berkeley and Los Angeles: University of California Press.

Pagliaro, A. 1956. *Nuovi saggi di critica semantica*. Messina: G. d'Anna.

———. 1961. *Altri saggi di critica semantica*. 2d ed. Messina: G. d'Anna.

Palmer, L. R. 1950. "The Indo-European Origins of Greek Justice." *TPS* 50: 149–68.

Paraskevaides, H. A. 1984. *The Use of Synonyms in Homeric Formulaic Diction*. Amsterdam: A. M. Hakkert.

Parry, A., ed. 1971. *The Making of Homeric Verse: The Collected Papers of Milman Parry*. Oxford: The Clarendon Press.

Pavese, C. 1972. *Tradizioni e generi poetici della Grecia arcaica*. Rome: Edizioni dell' Ateneo.

Peebles, B. M. 1976. "A Medieval Latin Development of the 'Etymology' of St. Martin's Name (Anecdota Martiniana III)." In *Paradosis: Studies in Memory of Edwin A. Quain*, 189–201. New York: Fordham University Press.

Peradotto, J. 1990. *Man in the Middle Voice: Name and Narration in the Odyssey*. Princeton: Princeton University Press.

Petegorsky, D. 1982. "Context and Evocation: Studies in Early Greek and Sanskrit Poetry." Ph.D. dissertation, University of California, Berkeley.

Peters, E. L. 1967. "Some Structural Aspects of the Feud among the Camel-herding Bedouin of Cyrenaica." *Africa* 37: 261–82.

Petersen, E. 1920. *Homers Zorn des Achilleus und der Homeriden Ilias*. Berlin: de Gruyter.

Pieper, U., and G. Stickel, eds. 1985. *Studia Linguistica Diachronica et Synchronica: Werner Winter, Sexagenario Anno 1983*. Berlin: de Gruyter.

Platnauer, M. 1921. "Greek Colour-Perception." *CQ* 15: 153–62.

Pokorny, J. 1959. *Indogermanisches etymologisches Wörterbuch*. Bern: Francke.

Porter, H. N. 1951. "The Early Greek Hexameter." *YCS* 12: 1–63.

Posner, R. A. 1979. "The Homeric Version of the Minimal State." *Ethos* 90: 27–46.

Prendergast, G. L., ed. 1962. *A Complete Concordance to the Iliad of Homer*. [Revised edition by B. Marzullo (Hildesheim: Olms, 1983).]

Pucci, P. 1987. *Odysseus Polutropos: Intertextual Readings in the Odyssey and the Iliad*. Ithaca: Cornell University Press.

Puhvel, J., ed. 1970. *Myth and Law among the Indo-Europeans*. Berkeley and Los Angeles: University of California Press.

Puhvel, M. 1968. "Beowulf and Irish Battle Rage." *Folklore* 79: 40–47.

Rank, L. P. 1951. *Etymologiseering en verwante verschijnselen bij Homerus*. Assen: Van Gorcum.

Redfield, J. 1975. *Nature and Culture in the Iliad: The Tragedy of Hector*. Chicago: University of Chicago Press.

———. 1991. "Classics and Anthropology." *Arion* 1: 5–23.

Rees, A., and B. Rees. 1961. *Celtic Heritage: Ancient Tradition in Ireland and Wales*. London: Thames and Hudson.

Reinhardt, K. 1938. *Das Parisurteil*. Frankfurt: Klostermann.

———. 1951. "Tradition und Geist im homerischen Epos." *Studium Generale* 4: 334–39.

———. 1960. *Tradition und Geist: Gesammelte Essays zur Dichtung*. Edited by C. Becker. Göttingen: Vandenhoeck & Ruprecht.

———. 1961. *Die Ilias und ihr Dichter*. Edited by U. Hölscher. Göttingen: Vandenhoeck & Ruprecht.

Renehan, R. 1984. Review of Claus 1981. *CP* 79: 327–34.

———. 1987. "The Heldentod in Homer: One Heroic Ideal." *CP* 82: 99–116.

Richardson, N. J., ed. 1974. *The Homeric Hymn to Demeter*. Oxford: The Clarendon Press.

———. 1993. *The Iliad: A Commentary*. Vol. 6, *Books 21–24*. Cambridge: Cambridge University Press.

Riedinger, J.-C. 1976. "Remarques sur la TIMH chez Homère." *REG* 89: 244–64.

Riggsby, A. M. 1992. "Homeric Speech Introductions and the Theory of Homeric Composition." *TAPA* 122: 99–114.

Rihll, T. 1986. "'Kings' and 'Commoners' in Homeric Society." *LCM* 11: 86–91.

Risch, E. 1974. *Wortbildung der homerischen Sprache*. 2d ed. Berlin: de Gruyter.

Robert, C. 1901. *Studien zur Ilias*. Berlin: Weidmann.

Rodgers, V. A. 1971. "Some Thoughts on δίκη." *CQ* 21: 289–301.

Rosaldo, M. Z. 1980. *Knowledge and Passion: Ilongot Notions of Self and Social Life*. Cambridge: Cambridge University Press.

Rosaldo, R. 1984. "Grief and a Headhunter's Rage: On the Cultural Force of Emotions." In *Text, Play, and Story: The Construction and Reconstruction of Self and Society*, edited by E. M. Bruner, 97–138. Chicago: University of Chicago Press.

Rosenkranz, B. 1952. *Beiträge zur Erforschung des Luvischen*. Wiesbaden: Harrassowitz.

Rosenwein, B. H., ed. 1998. *Anger's Past: The Social Use of an Emotion in the Middle Ages*. Ithaca: Cornell University Press.

Rosner, J. A. 1976. "The Speech of Phoenix: *Iliad* 9.434–605." *Phoenix* 30: 314–27.

Rowe, C. J. 1983. "The Nature of Homeric Morality." In C. Rubino and C. Schelmerdine 1983: 248–75.

Rowe, E. 1972. "Conceptions of Colour and Colour Symbolism in the Ancient World." In *The Realms of Colour*, edited by A. Portmann and R. Ritsema, 327–64. Eranos Yearbook, 41. Leiden: Brill.

Rubino, C. A., and C. W. Shelmerdine, eds. 1983. *Approaches to Homer*. Austin: University of Texas Press.

Ruijgh, C. J. 1967. *Études sur la grammaire et le vocabulaire du grec mycénien*. Amsterdam: A. M. Hakkert.

Russo, J. A. 1966. "The Structural Formula in Homeric Verse." In G. S. Kirk and A. Parry 1966: 217–40.

———. 1983. "The Poetics of the Ancient Greek Proverb." *Journal of Folklore Research* 20: 121–29.

Russo, J. A., M. Fernández-Galiano, and A. Heubeck. 1992. *A Commentary on Homer's Odyssey*. Vol. 3, *Books 17–24*. Oxford: The Clarendon Press.

Rüter, K. 1969. *Odysseeinterpretationen: Untersuchungen zum ersten Buch und zur Phaiakis*. Hypomnemata, 19. Göttingen: Vandenhoeck & Ruprecht.

Sacks, R. 1987. *The Traditional Phrase in Homer: Two Studies in Form, Meaning, and Interpretation*. Leiden: Brill.

Sahlins, M. 1976. "Colors and Cultures." *Semiotica* 16: 1–22.

———. 1981. *Historical Metaphors and Mythical Realities: Early History of the Sandwich Islands Kingdom*. Association for Sociology in Oceania, Publication 1. Ann Arbor: University of Michigan Press.

———. 1985. *Islands of History*. Chicago: University of Chicago Press.

Saxonhouse, A. W. 1988. "*Thymos*, Justice, and Moderation of Anger in the Story of Achilles." In *Understanding the Political Spirit: Philosophical Investigations from Socrates to Nietzsche*, edited by C. H. Zuckert, 30–47. New Haven: Yale University Press.

Schadewaldt, W. 1944. *Von Homers Welt und Werk: Aufsätze und Auslegungen zur homerischen Frage*. 2d ed. Stuttgart: Koehler.

———. 1958. "Der Prolog der *Odyssee*." *HSCP* 63: 15–32.

———. 1960. "Der Helios-Zorn in der *Odyssee*." In *Studi in onore di Luigi Castiglione*, 861–76. Florence: Sansoni.

———. 1987 [1966]. *Iliasstudien*. Darmstadt: Wissenschaftliche Buchgesellschaft.

Schein, S. 1984. *The Mortal Hero: An Introduction to Homer's Iliad*. Berkeley and Los Angeles: University of California Press.

Schmidt, C. E. 1885. *Parallel-Homer*. Göttingen: Vandenhoeck & Ruprecht.

Schmidt, J. H. H. 1876–86. *Synonymik der griechischen Sprache*. 3 vols. Leipzig: Teubner.

Schmitt, R. 1967. *Dichtung und Dichtersprache in indogermanischer Zeit*. Wiesbaden: Harrassowitz.

———. 1968. *Indogermanische Dichtersprache*. Darmstadt: Wissenschaftliche Buchgesellschaft.

Schulze, W. 1892. *Quaestiones Epicae*. Gütersloh: Bertelmann.

Schwartz, M. 1982. "The Indo-European Vocabulary of Exchange, Hospitality, and Intimacy (The Origins of Greek *ksénos, sún, phílos*; Avestan *xšnu-, xšąnman-*, etc.): Contributions to Etymological Methodology." *BLS* 8: 188–204.

———. 1985. "Scatology and Eschatology in Zoroaster: On the Paronomasia of *Yasna* 48.10 and on Indo-European H_2eg 'to make taboo' and the Reciprocity Verbs *K*ʷ*sen(w)* and *Megh*." *Acta Iranica* 25: 473–96.

———. 1986. "Coded Sound Patterns, Acrostics, Anagrams in Zoroaster's Oral Poetry." *MSS* 13: 327–92.

Schwyzer, E. 1931. "Drei griechische Wörter (3: μῆνις)." *RhM* 80: 213–17.

———. 1939. *Griechische Grammatik.* Munich: Beck.

Scodel, R. 1977. "Apollo's Perfidy: *Iliad* 24.59–63." *HSCP* 81: 55–57.

———. 1982. "The Autobiography of Phoenix." *AJP* 103: 128–36.

Scott, J. A. 1921. *The Unity of Homer.* Berkeley and Los Angeles: University of California Press.

Scott, W. C. 1974. *The Oral Nature of the Homeric Simile.* Leiden: Brill.

Scully, S. 1984. "The Language of Achilles: The ΟΧΘΗΣΑΣ Formulas." *TAPA* 114: 11–29.

Seaford, R. 1994. *Reciprocity and Ritual: Homer and Tragedy in the Development of the City-State.* Oxford: The Clarendon Press.

Segal, C. 1968. "The Embassy and the Duels of *Iliad* 9.182–190." *GRBS* 9: 101–14.

———. 1971. *The Theme of the Mutilation of the Corpse in the* Iliad. Leiden: Brill.

———. 1994. *Singers, Heroes, and Gods in the Odyssey.* Ithaca: Cornell University Press.

Shannon, R. S. 1975. *The Arms of Achilles and Homeric Compositional Technique.* Leiden: Brill.

Shewan, A. 1925. "Alliteration and Assonance in Homer." *CP* 20: 193–209.

Shipp, G. P. 1978. "ΚΑΛΟΣ in Homer." *Museum Philologum Londiniense* 3: 203–11.

Sinos, D. S. 1980. *Achilles, Patroklos, and the Meaning of Philos.* Innsbruck: Innsbrucker Beiträge zur Sprachwissenschaft.

Sjoestedt, M.-L. 1982. *Gods and Heroes of the Celts.* Translated by Myles Dillon. Berkeley and Los Angeles: University of California Press.

Skeat, W. W. 1963. *An Etymological Dictionary of the English Language.* Oxford: The Clarendon Press.

Slatkin, L. M. 1986. "The Wrath of Thetis." *TAPA* 116: 1–24.

———. 1991. *The Power of Thetis: Allusion and Interpretation in the Iliad.* Berkeley and Los Angeles: University of California Press.

Sommer, F. 1948. *Zur Geschichte der griechischen Nominalkomposita.* Munich: Beck.

Sommer, F., and A. Falkenstein. 1938. *Die hethitisch-akkadische Bilingue des Hattusili I (Labarna 2).* Munich: Beck.

Stanford, W. B. 1936. *Greek Metaphor.* Oxford: Blackwell.

———, ed. 1947–48. *The Odyssey of Homer.* 2 vols. London: Macmillan.

———. 1983. *Greek Tragedy and the Emotions: An Introductory Study.* London: Routledge.

Starke, F. 1985. *Die keilschrift-luwischen Texte in Umschrift.* Studien zu den Boğazköy-Texten, 30. Wiesbaden: Harrassowitz.

Stinton, T. 1990. *Collected Papers on Greek Tragedy.* Oxford: The Clarendon Press

Stolz, B. A., and R. S. Shannon, eds. 1976. *Oral Literature and the Formula.* Ann Arbor: University of Michigan Press.

Sullivan, S. D. 1980. "How a Person Relates to θυμός in Homer." *IF* 85: 138–50.

———. 1988. *Psychological Activity in Homer: A Study of* phrên. Ottawa: Carleton University Press.

Sweetser, E. 1984. "Semantic Structure and Semantic Change: A Cognitive Linguistic Study of Modality, Perception, Speech Acts, and Logical Relations." Ph.D. dissertation, University of California, Berkeley.

———. 1990. *From Etymology to Pragmatics: Metaphorical and Cultural Aspects of Semantic Structure*. Cambridge: Cambridge University Press.

Szemerényi, O. 1954. "Greek ταφών-θάμβος-θεάομαι." *Gl* 33: 238–66.

———. 1992. *Scripta Minora: Selected Essays in Indo-European, Greek and Latin*. Vol. 3. Edited by P. Considine and J. T. Hooker. Innsbruck: Innsbrucker Beiträge zur Sprachwissenschaft.

Taplin, O. 1986. *Homeric Soundings: The Shaping of the Iliad*. Oxford: Oxford University Press.

Tavris, C. 1982. *Anger: The Misunderstood Emotion*. New York: Simon and Schuster.

———. 1989. *Anger: The Misunderstood Emotion*. Revised edition. New York: Simon and Schuster.

Thalmann, W. G. 1984. *Conventions of Form and Thought in Early Greek Epic Poets*. Baltimore: The Johns Hopkins University Press.

———. 1986. "Aeschylus's Physiology of the Emotions." *AJP* 107: 489–511.

———. 1988. "Thersites: Comedy, Scapegoats, and Heroic Ideology in the *Iliad*." *TAPA* 118: 1–28.

Thornton, A. 1984. *Homer's Iliad: Its Composition and the Motif of Supplication*. Göttingen: Vandenhoeck & Ruprecht.

Thurneysen, R. 1921. *Die irische Helden- und Königsagen bis zum siebzehnten Jahrhundert*. Halle (Saale): M. Niemeyer.

———. 1970. *A Grammar of Old Irish*. Dublin: Dublin Institute of Advanced Studies.

Treston, H. J. 1923. *Poine: A Study in Ancient Greek Blood-Vengeance*. London: Longmans, Green, and Co.

Tucker, E. F. 1990. *The Creation of Morphological Regularity: Early Greek Verbs in -éō, -áō, -óō, -íō*. Göttingen: Vandenhoeck & Ruprecht.

Turpin, J.-C. 1988. "Un prétendu tabou linguistique de la langue épique: ΜΗΝΙΣ." In ΗΔΙΣΤΟΝ ΛΟΓΟΔΕΙΠΝΟΝ. *Logopédies: Mélanges de philologie et de linguistique grecques offerts à Jean Taillardat*, 247–60. Louvain: Peeters.

Tymoczko, M. 1982. "Strategies for Integrating Irish Epics into European Literature." *Dispositio* 7: 123–40.

Usener, H. 1948. *Götternamen: Versuch einer Lehre von der religiösen Begriffsbildung*. Frankfurt: Shulte-Bulmke.

van Bennekom, R. 1984. "Hom. *Il*. A 282–84." *Gl* 62: 149–50.

van Groningen, B. A. 1946. "The Proems of the *Iliad* and the *Odyssey*." *Mededeelingen der Koninklijke Nederlandsche Akademie van Wetenschappen, Afd. Letterkunde* 9, 8: 279–94.

———. 1958. *La composition littéraire archaïque grecque*. Amsterdam: Noord-Hollandsche Uitgevers Maatschappij.

van Leeuwen, J. F. 1894. *Enchiridium Dictionis Epicae*. Leiden: Sijthoff.

van Otterlo, W. A. A. 1948. *De ringcompositie als opbouwprincipe in de epische gedichten van Homerus*. Amsterdam: Noord-Hollandse Uitgevers Maatschappij.

van Thiel, H., ed. 1991. *Homeri Odyssea*. Hildesheim: Olms.

———. 1996. *Homeri Ilias*. Hildesheim: Olms.

Vendryes, J., ed. 1959–. *Lexique étymologique de l'irlandais ancien*. Dublin: Dublin Institute of Advanced Studies.

Vernant, J.-P. 1959. "Aspects mythiques de la mémoire en Grèce." *Journal de Psychologie* 56: 1–29.

———, ed. 1968. *Problèmes de la guerre en Grèce ancienne*. Paris: L'École des Hautes Études.

———. 1991a. "Death in the Eyes: The Figure of the Other." In J.-P. Vernant 1991b: 111–38.

———. 1991b. *Mortals and Immortals: Collected Essays*. Edited by F. I. Zeitlin. Princeton: Princeton University Press.

Vian, F. 1968. "La fonction guerrière dans la mythologie grecque." In J.-P.Vernant 1968: 53–68.

Vidal-Naquet, P. 1981. *Le chasseur noir: Formes de pensée et formes de société dans le monde grec*. Paris: F. Maspero.

Visser, E. 1987. *Homerische Versifikationstechnik: Versuch einer Rekonstruktion*. Frankfurt: Peter Lang.

———. 1988. "Formulae or Single Words?" *WJA* 14: 21–37.

Vleminck, S. 1983. "Τῖμος." *LEC* 51: 13–16.

Voegelin, E. 1956. *The World of the Polis*. Vol. 2 of *Order and History*. Baton Rouge: Louisiana State University Press.

Waanders, F. M. J. 1983. *The History of* ΤΕΛΟΣ *and* ΤΕΛΕΩ *in Ancient Greek*. Amsterdam: Gruner.

Wackernagel, J. 1892. *IF* 1: 1–104.

———. 1955–79. *Kleine Schriften*. 3 vols. Göttingen: Vandenhoeck & Ruprecht.

Wallace, F. E. 1927. *Color in Homer and in Ancient Art*. Northampton, Mass.: Smith.

Walsh, T. R. 1995. "*Odyssey* 1.6–9: A Little More than Kine." *Mnemosyne* 48: 385–410.

———. 1999. "Towards the Poetics of Potions: Helen's Cup and Indo-European Comparanda." In *Proceedings of the Tenth Annual Indo-European Conference*, 147–63. Washington, D.C.: Institute for the Study of Man.

Watkins, C. 1967. "Language of Gods and Men: Remarks on Some Indo-European Metalinguistic Traditions." In J. Puhvel 1970: 1–17.

———. 1973. "'River' in Celtic and Indo-European." *Eriu* 24: 80–89.

———. 1975. "Observations on the 'Nestor's Cup' Inscription." *HSCP* 80: 25–40.

———. 1977a. "À propos de μῆνις." *BSL* 72: 187–209.

———, ed. 1977b. *Indo-European Studies, III*. Cambridge, Mass.: Department of Linguistics, Harvard University.

———, ed. 1981a. *Indo-European Studies, IV*. Cambridge, Mass.: Department of Linguistics, Harvard University.

———. 1981b. "Aspects of Indo-European Poetics." In C. Watkins 1981a: 764–99.

———. 1983. "Roman Jakobson and Slavic Mythology." In *A Tribute to Roman Jakobson, 1896–1982*, 39–46. Berlin: Mouton.

———, ed. 1985. *The American Heritage Dictionary of Indo-European Roots*. Boston: Houghton Mifflin.

———, ed. 1987a. *Studies in Memory of Warren Cowgill (1929–1985): Papers from the Fourth East Coast Indo-European Conference*, Studies in Indo-European Language and Culture, 3. Berlin: de Gruyter.

———. 1987b. "How to Kill a Dragon in Indo-European." In C. Watkins 1987a: 270–79.

———. 1994. *Selected Writings: I, Language and Linguistics; II, Culture and Poetics*. Innsbruck: Innsbrucker Beiträge zur Sprachwissenschaft.

———. 1995. *How to Kill a Dragon in Indo-European: Aspects of Indo-European Poetics*. Oxford: The Clarendon Press.

Webster, T. B. L. 1957. "Some Physiological Terms in Greek Tragedy." *JHS* 77: 149–54.

———. 1958. *From Mycenae to Homer*. New York: Norton.

Weitenberg, J. S. S. 1984. *Die hethitischen* u-*Stämme.* Amsterdam: Rodopi.

West, M. L., ed. 2000. *Homeri Ilias*. Leipzig: Teubner.

West, S. 1982. "Crime Prevention and Ancient Editors (*Iliad* 9.458–61)." *LCM* 7: 84–86.

Whitman, C. 1958. *Homer and the Heroic Tradition*. Cambridge, Mass.: Harvard University Press.

Willcock, M. M. 1956–57. "B 356, Z 326, and A 404." *PCPhS*, n.s., 4: 23–26.

Windisch, E. 1905. *Die altirische Heldensage Táin Bó Cúalnge nach dem Buch von Leinster*. Leipzig: Hirzel.

Woodhouse, W. J. 1930. *The Composition of Homer's Odyssey*. Oxford: The Clarendon Press.

General Index

Citation Index

About the Author

Thomas R. Walsh, who has a doctorate in Comparative Literature from the University of California, Berkeley, taught at Occidental College in Los Angeles from 1987 to 2003, first in the Department of Comparative Literature, and then in the Department of English and Comparative Literary Studies. After having become a member of the Senior Faculty, Walsh took early retirement. He now continues to teach at the university level and to pursue research on topics of significance to the comparative literature of early and pre-modern cultures.

www.ingramcontent.com/pod-product-compliance
Lightning Source LLC
Chambersburg PA
CBHW030625110726
47901CB00002B/317

* 9 7 8 0 7 3 9 1 1 2 6 4 9 *